# Professional .NET 2.0 Generics

Tod Golding

WILEY

Wiley Publishing, Inc.

Published by Wiley Publishing, Inc., Indianapolis, Indiana

Published simultaneously in Canada

Library of Congress Cataloging-in-Publication Data

ISBN-13: 978-0-7645-5988-4

ISBN-10: 0-7645-5988-5

Printed in the United States of America

10  9  8  7  6  5  4  3  2  1

# About the Author

**Tod Golding** has 20 years of experience as a software developer, lead architect, and development manager for organizations engaged in the delivery of large-scale commercial and internal solutions. He has an extensive background leveraging .NET, J2EE, and Windows DNA technologies, which has allowed him to become equally skilled with C#, Java, and C++. Tod has worked and consulted at a variety of companies, including stints with Microsoft and Borland.

Tod has a B.S. in Computer Science from California State University, Sacramento. He started his writing career as a journalist for the *Sacramento Bee* daily newspaper. Prior to this book, he was also a contributing author for the *XML Programming Bible*, another Wiley publication. Tod currently resides in Sacramento, California, where he owns and operates Blue Puma Software.

# Credits

**Vice President and Executive Group Publisher:**
Richard Swadley

**Vice President and Publisher:**
Joseph B. Wikert

**Acquisitions Editor:**
Jim Minatel

**Editorial Manager:**
Mary Beth Wakefield

**Senior Production Editor:**
Tim Tate

**Development Editor:**
Sharon Nash

**Production Editor:**
Felicia Robinson

**Technical Editor:**
Mark A. Strawmyer

**Text Design & Composition:**
Wiley Composition Services

# Acknowledgments

Even though my name stands alone on the cover of this book, it certainly couldn't have come to life without the support, encouragement, hard work, and creative input of many others.

My family has to be at the top of the list of those that deserve thanks. The sacrifices made by my wife, Janine, during the past year were nothing short of heroic. Her support never waned, and I could not have finished this project without her. Thanks, too, to my children, Chelsea and Ryan, who always showed interest in my progress. Their smiling faces were always a great source of inspiration.

I'd also like to thank everyone at Wiley Publishing. Without Jim Minatel's insight and guidance, this book could not have gotten off the ground. His flexibility and willingness to work with a moving target provided me with the freedom this topic needed. I also can't go without mentioning Wiley's Sharon Nash and Felicia Robinson, who managed all the logistics associated with editing this book. Thanks, too, to Mark A. Strawmyer for all of his contributions on the technical editing front.

There are also all those who helped push me along during the genesis of this book. My long-time friend, Bill Clark, provided perspective and creative influence that helped shape my approach to generics.

Finally, special thanks go to Mike Cohn, who has always pushed me to take on new challenges. His early prodding and mastery of the 100-hour workweek clearly had the single greatest impact on getting me moving on this project.

# Contents

# Contents

# Contents

# Contents

# Contents

Contents

# Contents

# Introduction

Although generics are new to .NET platform, the concepts that motivated their introduction have been around for years. However, while their value was often acknowledged, they were frequently stereotyped as being highly complex, unwieldy, and unapproachable. This reputation always seemed to obscure their value and limit their ability to capture the mindshare of the broader population of developers. The real truth here, though, is that generics simply couldn't become truly mainstream without first having more languages and environments add support for generics. And, prior to version 2.0 of the .NET Framework, Visual Basic, C# and J#, developers were unable to use any generic constructs. As a result, many of these developers remained unaware of the power and value of generics. You can't miss something if you've never had it.

Now, with .NET Framework adding full support for generics, this dynamic will certainly change. And, as generics begin to move out of the shadows and into the limelight, you're going to want to be in a position to maximize their value in your own solutions. To get to that point, though, you'll need to understand all the nuances associated with creating and consuming generics, how they reach their way into and influence the fabric of the .NET Framework.

The overriding goal of this book, then, is to provide a soup-to-nuts blend of basic syntax, key concepts, and examples of generic libraries that will provide you with a foundation that will help you determine how and when you might want to start leveraging generics. And, as you get more familiar with generics and you start understanding some of their obvious—and not so obvious—implications, it's likely you'll also find yourself leveraging generics much more heavily than you may have ever expected.

## Not Just Syntax Candy

Developers often look at new language features with a bit of skepticism. Every time some new twist is added to a language, there are those who seem to want to minimize its impact. You can look at nearly any language feature and pick it apart. Do you really need overloaded methods, for example? You certainly could create separate method names for each signature and achieve the same result. That's not the point, though. To reduce the argument to that level is to miss the underlying relevance of the feature. The presence of overloaded methods impacts the way clients interact with your class and has a direct impact on the readability, usability, and maintainability of your code.

This same logic should be applied when considering generics. Do you really *have* to use generic containers? No. All the old `System.Collections` types, with all their glaring type-safety and efficiency flaws, are still right there for you to use. The question is: why would you continue to use them in the presence of generics? Perhaps there are compatibility issues or other forces that may require you to use non-generic types. Those conditions aside, though, there's no real valid argument for using a non-generic container in place of its generic equivalent.

My point here is that generics are more than just some new, optional way to parameterize your types. If you drink the Kool-Aid (and you should), you'll find generics influencing your entire approach to how you create and consume types. At a minimum, you'll find yourself raising your type-safety expectations.

# Overcoming Stereotypes

C++ templates, perhaps the most widely used generic implementation, have a reputation among many developers for adding complexity and reducing readability. This reputation, justified or not, seems to lead some to conclude that supporting generics in *any* language somehow compromises the syntactic elegance of that language. There's this notion that generics makes your code appear as though it has been run through an encryption algorithm.

So, as generics were coming onto the scene, there were many who seemed to be of this mindset. They mapped C++ templates onto generics and immediately assumed that the addition of parameterized types somehow has undermined the quality of some of the .NET languages. This, from my perspective, seems to be an unfair mapping.

The .NET implementation of generics certainly shares some syntactic elements with C++ templates. As you look at generics in more detail, you should find that generics—by their very nature—do not promote the same level of obfuscation that is sometimes found within C++ templates. This limits their power, but it also limits their impact on readability and maintainability.

# Approaching Generics

A number of different approaches can be taken when tackling a topic of this nature. Some books will take a more specification-oriented angle where topics are tackled from an almost lexical perspective. Others books will take a more conceptual view and focus more on providing examples of what's valid without trying to recite, precisely, which syntax patterns are valid.

For this book, I definitely lean more toward the conceptual model. My goal here is to expose you to all the elements of generics without necessarily exploring every permutation of syntax that is possible. My goal here is to get developers to see the broader implications of generics, and that will be most successfully achieved through a detailed examination of the key conceptual aspects associated with creating and consuming generic types.

# What Does This Book Cover?

*Professional .NET 2.0 Generics* represents a soup-to-nuts, detailed look at all the facets of generics, providing developers with a comprehensive view of what can be achieved through the application of generics.

The contents of the book fall into some logical categories. The book starts out with a series of chapters that are focused primarily on the conceptual aspects of generics. Although these chapters use .NET generics to convey these concepts, they're really more broadly applicable to anyone who might be interested in understanding the overall value of using generics.

Beyond the conceptual, the book then moves on to a series of chapters that are dedicated to exploring the specific syntactic mechanics of using .NET generics. These chapters look at all the ways generics are applied to classes, methods, delegates, and so on and explore all the rules that govern their declaration and consumption.

Once coverage of the mechanics are completed, the book then turns its attention to those libraries that will provide you with some of the fundamental, out-of-the-box types that typically come with any environment that supports generics. The book addresses this with two chapters that explore the BCL generic types that are included with the .NET Framework and a third-party library that provides even more standard generic types that you're likely to find yourself leveraging in your own code.

To round things out, the book also examines some of the broader generic issues, including generic guidelines, a comparison with C++ templates, and a peek under the hood of the .NET generics implementation.

# Who Is This Book For?

This book is targeted at a fairly wide spectrum of developers. Certainly, its broadest appeal will be those developers who are first-time generic programmers. That population of developers will extract the most benefit from the full range of topics I'm targeting here, spanning everything from the basic introduction to syntax and concepts to the libraries and discussion of the underlying mechanics of generics.

The next tier of likely readers are those developers who might be transitioning from C++ templates or even Java generics. If you fall into this category, you might find yourself more interested in diving directly into the syntax and reference materials.

Overall, this book should be of value to anyone who wants a more comprehensive understanding of the features and characteristics of the .NET implementation of generics. Even if you're not a .NET developer, you may find generic topics here that are of value to you.

While this book is targeted at a fairly broad audience, it is not likely to be appropriate for anyone that is relatively new to the field of computer science. Generics will simply be too difficult to tackle if you don't have a firm handle on basic object-oriented programming concepts and techniques.

# Language Considerations

As a CLS-compliant feature, generics are supported under C#, Visual Basic, C++, and J#. And, as is the case for many .NET authors, there is always the issue of how to address a technology that spans all these languages without diving deeply into the syntactic nuances of each one. This is especially true with something like generics, where the generic syntax between, say, VB and C#, varies quite a bit.

These realities, coupled with my strong belief that you need to see examples in *your* language of preference, led me down the path of showing examples in both Visual Basic and C#. My logic was based on the fact that these two languages appear to be two of the more popular among .NET developers and are also likely to be the languages where there will be the largest population of first-time generics programmers.

Throughout this book, then, you will notice that I have provided side-by-side examples in both Visual Basic and C#. And, to round things out, I've also included separate chapters on C++ and J#, pointing out the specifics of each of these two languages. C++ is especially interesting, because it allows you to leverage a combination of both templates and generics.

# Synopsis

The sections that follow give you an overview of each of the chapters of the book, providing a snapshot of the fundamental role each chapter plays in the overall landscape of the book. This breakdown should provide you with a clear view of what the book covers and what materials are best targeted at your specific needs.

## Chapter 1: Generics 101

This chapter is a basic generics primer. It lays out all the fundamental building blocks of generic concepts, allowing first-time generics developers to establish a solid generics foundation that serves as the basis for much of what appears in the ensuing chapters. The focus of this chapter is more on the underlying concepts that make generics necessary and less on the detailed mechanics of working with generic types. If generics are completely new to you, you need to start here.

## Chapter 2: Valuing Type Safety

This book is littered with references to the value and importance of type safety. To appreciate generics is to appreciate type safety. This chapter builds on the concepts that are established in Chapter 1, exploring the basic elements of type safety that we've all been forced to live with outside the world of generics. The goal here is to provide a clear illustration of how and why developers should value type safety and explain how generics can improve the overall type safety profile of their code.

## Chapter 3: Generics ≠ Templates

Generics are often confused with C++ templates and, although they share some common heritage and goals, they are most certainly different. And, before digging into the syntax of generics, it is important to clarify how generics differ from templates. Naturally, if you've never dealt with templates before (and never plan to) this distinction will be of little value. However, if you've come from a C++ background, you'll want to be very clear about how these differences might affect your overall approach to the .NET generics implementation.

## Chapter 4: Generic Classes

A big part of the value of generics is having the ability to introduce your own generic types (or extend existing generic types). As such, it's vital that you have a good grasp of what is involved in the definition of generic classes. This chapter's look at generic classes should help to crystallize the true power of what can be achieved with generics. It explores all the facets of how generics influence the signature and implementation of a type. Overall, this chapter should cover all the traditional topics that are associated with non-generic classes, including a look at how inheritance and polymorphism are implemented using generic types.

## Chapter 5: Generic Methods

With generic classes out of the way, the book then turns its attention to the more subtle, less complex area of generic methods. This chapter is focused on highlighting the overall utility and power that can be achieved through making a method generic. In fact, some of the most immediate and useful applications of generics will likely be made through the use of generic methods. So, even though they're relatively straightforward, it's important to see what, conceptually, they enable.

## Chapter 6: Generic Delegates

Delegates are one of the more heavily used features of the .NET platform, and they are also one of the most obvious areas where generics allow you to simplify your code. This chapter looks at how the concept of delegates is naturally extended through generics, allowing single delegates to replace all the various permutations of delegates you might have previously required. Once you've been exposed to the simplicity and type safety of generic delegates, you may never use a non-generic delegate again.

## Chapter 7: Generic Constraints

At this stage in the book, you already will have been exposed to many common applications of generics. You will now be at a point where you'll need to consider how to add more specificity to the parameters that are supplied to your generic classes, methods, delegates, and so on. This chapter provides a detailed view of how constraints are applied to your type parameters to achieve this goal. Constraints are a core concept to .NET generics, and they have significant influence on how you will approach the design and interface of your type hierarchies.

## Chapter 8: BCL Generics

This chapter provides a comprehensive view of all the generic types that are included as part of the .NET Framework's Base Class Library (BCL). Although this chapter largely serves as a reference, it also provides a conceptual view of the namespace. This conceptual view will give you a much better understanding of how and when each of these generic types can be employed in your own solutions. As part of this, the chapter also discusses how you might extend these classes and introduce your own, derivative types. The chapter is filled with examples that exercise many of the key features of each type. Because you're likely to be using many of these classes in place of the old, non-generic versions, it's important to familiarize yourself with the basics of this library.

## Chapter 9: Reflection, Serialization, and Remoting

Generics also reach into other areas of the .NET platform. This chapter looks at three key areas of the platform that were modified or improved via generics. Specifically, the chapter examines how .NET's reflection, remoting, and serialization are influenced by generics. The generic elements of each of these areas are explored with examples that highlight the key areas that deserve special, generic attention.

## Chapter 10: Generics Guidelines

With the introduction of any new language feature also comes the need for guidelines that provide some rules and conventions for how that feature should be applied. Generics are no different. They, too, come with an ever-growing list of guidelines that shape their usage. This chapter looks at this evolving area, providing developers with a compilation of those guidelines that are emerging in the area of generics. The chapter provides a point-by-point breakdown of each guideline and explains the rationale that motivated its creation.

## Chapter 11: Under The Hood

Understanding the syntax and concepts of generics isn't really enough. If you're really going to understand their efficiencies and behavior, you'll need to dig deeper. That deeper, "under the hood view" of generics is the focus of this chapter. The chapter looks at how the CLR manages all aspects of generic types and explains how .NET is able to represent generic types at run-time. This discussion also includes a look at some basic benchmarks that highlight the run-time efficiencies that can be achieved with generic types.

## Chapter 12: Using Generics with C++

The examples throughout the other chapters in this book are focused entirely on using generics with Visual Basic and C#. However, the concepts in these chapters apply to any of the .NET languages that can create or consume generic types. And, each of these other languages includes its own set of generic nuances. This chapter looks, specifically, at how the C++ language can be used with generic types. This chapter also discusses how generic types can be mixed with C++ templates in a way that offers C++ developers the best of both worlds.

## Chapter 13: Using Generics with J#

Just as Chapter 12 looked at the nuances of C++ with generic types, this chapter looks at how developers can employ generics as part of the J# code. It looks at how all the fundamental types are used with J#, explaining the syntax variations and exploring some of the generic limitations imposed within J#.

## Chapter 14: Power Collections

Since the introduction of generics, developers have been scrambling to create new, third-party libraries, many with overlapping goals. Among these, the Power Collections library appears to have the most momentum and support and, as such, is likely to continue to be a key player in the generic library space. Given this reality, it made sense to include a complete chapter that provides conceptual and reference information for this library. Much like Chapter 8, this library includes comprehensive coverage of all the types in the library along with examples that exercise its more interesting interfaces.

# Conventions

Throughout this book, you will find that the text conforms to a common set of conventions. This following represent some of the examples of conventions that I have followed accompanied by an explanation of their meaning:

> **Boxes like this one hold important, not-to-be forgotten information that is directly relevant to the surrounding text.**

```
All code examples are highlighted with a gray background with a heading that
designates the language being employed in the example.
```

As for styles in the text:

- ❑ Any code that appears within text or any reference to a namespace is shown as follows: `MyClass<T>` or `System.Collections.Generic`.

- ❑ Emphasized words are shown in *italics*.

- ❑ All generic types appearing within the text use the C# representation. So, a generic class would appear as: `MyClass<T>`.

# Source Code

All of the source code for this book is available at the Wrox Press Web site, which is located at `http://www.wrox.com`. This site should provide you with a clear path to source code for all the Wrox books. Just locate the title of this book and you should be all set.

Generally speaking, the examples should match precisely what you see in the book. You'll also come across some scenarios where the example directories have a superset of what's in the book. These examples typically just represent additional scenarios that were outside the scope of what ended up being included in the text.

# Errata

I'd like to think this book is 100% bug free. However, as a developer, I know just how unlikely that is. There are certainly going to be mistakes that find there way into any book. And, while I hope the list of issues is short, there still needs to be a centralized location for capturing these errors so they can be shared with the rest of the development community.

For Wrox books, this information is all captured through the `www.wrox.com` Web site. Simply look up this book and, once you locate it, select the "errata" link. This will allow you to both report and view the errata for this book.

# p2p.wrox.com

In the true spirit of the programmer-to-programmer motto, Wrox maintains a series of forums at `p2p.wrox.com` where members of the development community share ideas and opinions. You'll discover everyone from authors to editors contributing content and generally interacting in these forums. They provide a great avenue for exchanging ideas.

# 1

# Generics 101

For many programmers, generics will be an entirely new language feature. As such, it is important to establish a foundation of concepts that will clarify the role and significance of generics in the overall scheme of the .NET platform. This chapter provides this fundamental, conceptual view of generics that should provide you with a solid base of ideas that can be built upon in the chapters that follow. Along the way, you'll get the opportunity build your first generic types and get some exposure to the basic mechanics of generic types. This chapter also introduces a set of new terms that are used when referring to common generic concepts. You'll need to have a clear understanding of these terms because they are used throughout the book. Naturally, if you're already comfortable with the basics of generics, you may want to skip over this chapter.

## Why Generics?

Most programmers can point to that one moment in their career where the light of abstraction or generalization went off in their head. If you have a background in structured programming, this might have been uncovered during a foray into the world of function pointers. Or, maybe it just occurred to you one day when you discovered you could extend the functionality of one of your methods by parameterizing some aspect of its behavior. If you're from the OO crowd, this probably happened one day when you stumbled upon your first real good use for polymorphism. At that moment, whenever it was, you realized that goal of generality, extensibility, and reusability that everyone had been evangelizing.

Now, with generics, you have an opportunity to wrap your brain around another form of generalization. This new brand of generalization will provide you with a host of new concepts to toss into your proverbial bag of coding and design techniques. And, once you've mastered generics, you may find yourself wondering how you lived without them for so long.

To understand the fundamental value of generics, you really need to see a compelling example. Let's start with a sample of some code that you might write without generics. Suppose you've decided to write your own Pyramid Manager product that will allow you to track the relationships between each of the salespeople in a pyramid scheme. You need to start with a basic domain object that will hold the common attributes of each of salesperson. The object is as follows:

```vb
[VB code]
Public Class SalesPerson
    Private _id As Integer
    Private _name As String

    Public Sub New(ByVal id As Integer, ByVal name As String)
        Me._id = id
        Me._name = name
    End Sub

    Public ReadOnly Property Id() As Integer
        Get
            Return Me._id
        End Get
    End Property


    Public ReadOnly Property Name() As String
        Get
            Return Me._name
        End Get
    End Property

    Public Overrides Function ToString() As String
        Return Me._name
    End Function
End Class
```

```csharp
[C# code]
public class SalesPerson {
    private int _id;
    private string _name;

    public SalesPerson(int id, string name) {
        this._id = id;
        this._name = name;
    }

    public int Id {
        get { return this._id; }
    }

    public string Name {
        get { return this._name; }
    }

    public override string ToString() {
        return this._name;
    }
}
```

Now that you have an object to hold each salesperson, you'll want to place these salespeople into some form of hierarchical data structure where each `SalesPerson` can be associated with one or more "child" `SalesPerson` objects. Fortunately, you already have a tree structure that will let you represent just such a structure (this is an extremely simplified variant of the existing BCL `TreeNode`):

```
[VB code]
Imports System.Collections

Public Class TreeNode
    Private _nodeData As Object
    Private _childNodes As ArrayList

    Public Sub New(ByVal nodeData As Object)
        Me._nodeData = nodeData
        Me._childNodes = New ArrayList
    End Sub

    Public ReadOnly Property Data() As Object
        Get
            Return Me._nodeData
        End Get
    End Property

    Public ReadOnly Property Children() As TreeNode()
        Get
            Return Me._childNodes.ToArray()
        End Get
    End Property

    Default Public ReadOnly Property Item(ByVal index As Int32) As TreeNode
        Get
            Return Me._childNodes(index)
        End Get
    End Property

    Public Function AddChild(ByVal nodeData As Object) As TreeNode
        Dim newNode As New TreeNode(nodeData)
        Me._childNodes.Add(newNode)
        Return newNode
    End Function

    Overrides Function ToString() As String
        Return Me._nodeData.ToString()
    End Function
End Class
```

```
[C# code]
using System.Collections;

public class TreeNode {
    private object _nodeData;
    private ArrayList _childNodes;

    public TreeNode(object nodeData) {
```

```
        this._nodeData = nodeData;
        this._childNodes = new ArrayList();
    }

    public object Data {
        get { return this._nodeData; }
    }

    public TreeNode[] Children {
        get { return (TreeNode[])this._childNodes.ToArray(typeof(TreeNode)); }
    }

    public TreeNode this[int index] {
        get { return (TreeNode)this._childNodes[index]; }
    }

    public TreeNode AddChild(object nodeData) {
        TreeNode newNode = new TreeNode(nodeData);
        this._childNodes.Add(newNode);
        return newNode;
    }

    public override string ToString() {
        return this._nodeData.ToString();
    }
}
```

As you can see, your tree uses the least common denominator type of object to represent each of the items it manages. The result could certainly be considered a *generic* data container in that it can be populated with any data type. In this case, you're going to want to populate this structure with instances of your SalesPerson class. Here's some simple code that demonstrates how you would go about building a simple instance of your pyramid structure:

```
[VB code]
Dim rootNode, child1 As TreeNode
rootNode = New TreeNode(New SalesPerson(111, "Head Honcho"))
child1 = rootNode.addChild(New SalesPerson(222, "Big Cheese"))
rootNode.addChild(New SalesPerson(333, "Top Dog"))
child1.addChild(New SalesPerson(444, "Big Enchilada"))
child1.AddChild(New SalesPerson(555, "Mr. Big"))
```

```
[C# code]
TreeNode rootNode = new TreeNode(new SalesPerson(111, "Head Honcho"));
TreeNode child1 = rootNode.AddChild(new SalesPerson(222, "Big Cheese"));
rootNode.AddChild(new SalesPerson(333, "Top Dog"));
child1.AddChild(new SalesPerson(444, "Big Enchilada"));
child1.AddChild(new SalesPerson(555, "Mr. Big"));
```

So, your pyramid is set now and you're ready to start rolling in the dough. But wait, as you might expect with any pyramid scheme, there's a catch. As you begin to work more intimately with your tree, you're going to discover that it has a significant flaw. Imagine a scenario where you've navigated to a specific node in the tree and you want to access the information about the SalesPerson associated with that node in the tree. The code to retrieve the instance of the SalesPerson would appear as follows:

```
[VB code]
Dim aSalesPerson As SalesPerson
aSalesPerson = DirectCast(child1(0).Data, SalesPerson)
```

```
[C# code]
SalesPerson aSalesPerson = (SalesPerson)child[0].Data;
```

As you can see, in order to get your SalesPerson object out of the TreeNode, you are forced to cast the object type to the correct type. What's the big deal with that, you say? Well, if you value type safety in your code at all — and you should — you will find this cast a necessary evil that you'd much rather avoid. Later, in Chapter 2, "Valuing Type Safety," you see just how problematic this really is. If you're not already repulsed by this, you will be by the time you're more acclimated to generics.

The other downside you need to consider here, which may be even more significant, is the efficiency of this structure. Each time you put an item into your tree, it must be represented as an object. In this example, the SalesPerson was already an object, so no extra overhead was needed to make it conform to the requirements of your tree. However, to protect the innocent, let's assume you're going to eliminate the use of the SalesPerson type and simply populate the tree with sales totals for each person. So, your code to populate would be modified as follows:

```
[VB code]
Dim rootNode, child1 As TreeNode
rootNode = New TreeNode(3000.23)
child1 = rootNode.AddChild(1403.43)
rootNode.AddChild(943.94)
child1.AddChild(5123.94)
child1.AddChild(94994.0)
```

```
[C# code]
TreeNode rootNode = new TreeNode(3000.23);
TreeNode child1 = rootNode.AddChild(1403.43);
rootNode.AddChild(943.94);
child1.AddChild(5123.94);
child1.AddChild(94994.00);
```

In order to represent these numbers in your tree structure, each number will end up being boxed so it can be represented as an object. And, as you are probably aware, this process of boxing is going to introduce more overhead. This may seem negligible. However, you need to remember that containers of this nature can be populated with relatively large numbers of objects, which means any extra overhead associated with processing each item will impact performance exponentially.

At this stage, you'd probably agree that you'd like to overcome some of these shortcomings. What options are available to you? The typical solution to this dilemma is to create a type-safe version of the container that will support direct references to the type you want contained. For the Pyramid Manager example, creating a tree that accepts and returns SalesPerson objects would achieve this. Here's what the revised, type-safe version looks like:

[VB code]

```vb
Imports System.Collections

Public Class SalesPersonNode
    Private _nodeData As SalesPerson
    Private _childNodes As ArrayList

    Public Sub New(ByVal nodeData As SalesPerson)
        Me._nodeData = nodeData
        Me._childNodes = New ArrayList
    End Sub

    Public ReadOnly Property Data() As SalesPerson
        Get
            Return Me._nodeData
        End Get
    End Property

    Public ReadOnly Property Children() As Array
        Get
            Return Me._childNodes.ToArray()
        End Get
    End Property

    Default Public ReadOnly Property Item(ByVal index As Long) As SalesPersonNode
        Get
            Return Me._childNodes(index)
        End Get
    End Property

    Public Function AddChild(ByVal nodeData As SalesPerson) As SalesPersonNode
        Dim newNode As SalesPersonNode = New SalesPersonNode(nodeData)
        Me._childNodes.Add(newNode)
        Return newNode
    End Function

    Overrides Function ToString() As String
        Return Me._nodeData.ToString()
    End Function
End Class
```

[C# code]

```csharp
using System.Collections;

public class SalesPersonNode {
    private SalesPerson _nodeData;
    private ArrayList _childNodes;

    public SalesPersonNode(SalesPerson nodeData) {
        this._nodeData = nodeData;
        this._childNodes = new ArrayList();
    }

    public SalesPerson Data {
```

```
        get { return this._nodeData; }
    }

    public SalesPerson[] Children {
        get {
            return (SalesPerson[])this._childNodes.ToArray(typeof(SalesPerson));
        }
    }

    public SalesPerson this[int index] {
        get { return (SalesPerson)this._childNodes[index]; }
    }

    public SalesPersonNode AddChild(SalesPerson nodeData) {
        SalesPersonNode newNode = new SalesPersonNode(nodeData);
        this._childNodes.Add(newNode);
        return newNode;
    }

    public override string ToString() {
        return this._nodeData.ToString();
    }
}
```

This new `SalesPersonNode` gives you a very type-safe approach to building your pyramid. It also allows you to introduce more domain-specific operations to the collection without fear of breaking its generality. The biggest problem with this, though, is that it forces you to create a separate class for every data type you want to contain. For example, if you want to go back to the previous example where the tree held only numbers, you'd need to make a `DoubleTreeNode`. And, for the most part, that's what developers have often done. They essentially end up bloating their overall code size to support each of these type-specific structures. Or, they've ended up living with some of the downside of the less type-safe solutions (blech). Neither approach is all that appealing.

## Enter Generics

As you can imagine by now, the problems pointed out in these examples are at the very core of the rationale for introducing generics. With generics, you can finally strike a balance between type safety and generality while, at the same time, eliminating the need to overpopulate your libraries with a gaggle of unnecessary classes. Let's look at how generics would be applied to the Pyramid Manager example. Making this change will mostly involve rewriting the `TreeNode` class. The `SalesPerson` object will remain unscathed as part of this conversion.

```
[VB code]
Imports System.Collections

Public Class TreeNode(Of T)
    Private _nodeData As T
    Private _childNodes As ArrayList

    Public Sub New(ByVal nodeData As T)
        Me._nodeData = nodeData
        Me._childNodes = New ArrayList
```

```
        End Sub

    Public ReadOnly Property Data() As T
        Get
            Return Me._nodeData
        End Get
    End Property

    Public ReadOnly Property Children() As TreeNode(Of T)()
        Get
            Return Me._childNodes.ToArray()
        End Get
    End Property

    Default Public ReadOnly Property Item(ByVal index As Long) As TreeNode(Of T)
        Get
            Return Me._childNodes(index)
        End Get
    End Property

    Public Function AddChild(ByVal nodeData As T) As TreeNode(Of T)
        Dim newNode As TreeNode(Of T) = New TreeNode(Of T)(nodeData)
        Me._childNodes.Add(newNode)
        Return newNode
    End Function

    Overrides Function ToString() As String
        Return Me._nodeData.ToString()
    End Function
End Class
```

[C# code]
```
using System.Collections;

public class TreeNode<T> {
    private T _nodeData;
    private ArrayList _childNodes;

    public TreeNode(T nodeData) {
        this._nodeData = nodeData;
        this._childNodes = new ArrayList();
    }

    public T Data {
        get { return this._nodeData; }
    }

    public TreeNode<T>[] Children {
        get { return (TreeNode<T>[])this._childNodes.ToArray(typeof(TreeNode<T>));}
    }

    public TreeNode<T> this[int index] {
        get { return (TreeNode<T>)this._childNodes[index]; }
```

```
    }

    public TreeNode<T> AddChild(T nodeData) {
        TreeNode<T> newNode = new TreeNode<T>(nodeData);
        this._childNodes.Add(newNode);
        return newNode;
    }

    public override string ToString() {
        return this._nodeData.ToString();
    }
}
```

The first thing you should notice here is how the declaration of `TreeNode` changed. The class name now has some additional information appended to it, which indicates that it is a generic type. As such, your `TreeNode` will now accept a type as a parameter. This means that you can officially abandon your need to cling to the `object` data type as the means of genericizing your `TreeNode`. Instead, you can use this incoming parameter `T` to represent the specific type of object that will be contained by your tree node.

The other change you'll notice is that all the references to the `object` data type have been replaced with a type parameter, `T`. In reality, as you look at this class now, it doesn't seem all that different from the non-generic version. You've essentially just modified it to accept a parameter that is used as a place-holder for the data type that will end up being substituted at run-time.

Now that you have a new generic type, you need to figure out how to populate it with data. As a consumer of a generic type, you should find that working with a generic type doesn't introduce any significant new concepts. Mostly, you just need to provide the additional type parameter to the class when you declare each new instance of the `TreeNode`. This will provide the compiler and the CLR all the information they need to successfully construct the run-time representation of your generic class. Here's the generic version of the code that is used to populate the tree:

```
[VB code]
Dim rootNode, child1 As TreeNode(Of SalesPerson)
rootNode = New TreeNode(Of SalesPerson)(New SalesPerson(111, "Head Honcho"))
child1 = rootNode.AddChild(New SalesPerson(222, "Big Cheese"))
rootNode.AddChild(New SalesPerson(333, "Top Dog"))
child1.AddChild(New SalesPerson(444, "Big Enchilada"))
child1.AddChild(New SalesPerson(555, "Mr. Big"))
```

```
[C# code]
TreeNode<SalesPerson> rootNode =
        new TreeNode<SalesPerson>(new SalesPerson(111, "Head Honcho"));
TreeNode<SalesPerson> child1 =
        rootNode.AddChild(new SalesPerson(222, "Big Cheese"));
rootNode.AddChild(new SalesPerson(333, "Top Dog"));
child1.AddChild(new SalesPerson(444, "Big Enchilada"));
child1.AddChild(new SalesPerson(555, "Mr. Big"));
```

Notice that, as each `TreeNode` is constructed, it must be provided with a data type. In this example, a `SalesPerson` data type is provided, which then forces all references to the type parameter `T` to be replaced, at run-time, with the type `SalesPerson`. And, as you access the contents of your tree, it's able to return you these `SalesPerson` instances without requiring those unappealing casts that you were forced to employ in the previous example.

Although this example only provides a small glimpse into the functionality of a generic type, it should make it apparent that generics are going to find their way into your code. With generics, I cannot imagine any scenario where you'd ever want to compromise and use any kind of data container that wasn't type safe.

## Hello Generics

Every programming book known to man seems to include the obligatory "Hello World" example. It's the de facto standard that is used to provide a quick, minimal glimpse of a functioning program. And, with the generics rationale out of the way, it only seems fair to offer up my own "Hello Generics" example that takes the classic version and spruces it up with a slight generics twist. This example will also give you another opportunity to see generics in action.

```vb
[VB code]
Public Class HelloGenerics(Of T)
    Private _thisTalker As T

    Public Property Talker() As T
        Get
            Return Talker
        End Get
        Set(ByVal value As T)
            Me._thisTalker = value
        End Set
    End Property

    Public Sub SayHello()
        Dim helloWorld As String
        helloWorld = _thisTalker.ToString()
        Console.WriteLine(helloWorld)
    End Sub
End Class
```

```csharp
[C# code]
public class HelloGenerics<T> {
    private T _thisTalker;

    public T Talker {
        get { return this._thisTalker; }
        set { this._thisTalker = value; }
    }

    public void SayHello() {
        string helloWorld = _thisTalker.ToString();
        Console.WriteLine(helloWorld);
    }
}
```

The first step is to create a new generic type, `HelloGenerics`, that accepts a single type parameter. The idea here is to build a generic type can accept any object type and ask it to say "Hello World". So, instead of having the limitation of saying hello in a single language, the generic type is going to be used to provide a more dynamic, more worldly solution that says hello in a variety of tongues. After all, if it's going to say hello to the world, it should not expect that everyone is going to understand English.

The next step is to create a pool of objects that can be passed as parameters to the `HelloGenerics` type, each with its own language-specific variation on how to say hello. You should notice that these can be objects of any type and they are not required to share any common base class that provides a virtual interface for saying hello. Although valid, that would be the pure OO way to do this and would not demonstrate the generic approach to this problem. The lineup of international objects is as follows:

```
[VB code]
Public Class GermanSpeaker
    Public Overrides Function ToString() As String
        Return "Hallo Welt!"
    End Function
End Class


Public Class SpanishSpeaker
    Public Overrides Function ToString() As String
        Return "Hola Mundo!"
    End Function
End Class

Public Class EnglishSpeaker
    Public Overrides Function ToString() As String
        Return "Hello World!"
    End Function
End Class


Public Class APLSpeaker
    Public Overrides Function ToString() As String
        Return "!dlroW olleH"
    End Function
End Class
```

```
[C# code]
public class GermanSpeaker {
    public override string ToString() {
        return "Hallo Welt!";
    }
}

public class SpanishSpeaker {
    public override string ToString() {
        return "Hola Mundo!";
    }
}

public class EnglishSpeaker {
    public override string ToString() {
        return "Hello World!";
```

```
        }
    }

public class APLSpeaker {
    public override string ToString() {
        return "!dlroW olleH";
    }
}
```

Two random observations stood out after I put these classes together. First, I fully expected the German version of this to be much longer. Every international translation of software I ever worked on for Germany seemed to double the length of every string. Also, I tossed APL in here because, as a programming language, it always seemed foreign to me.

The next step in this process is to get this generic type actually speaking. This is accomplished by constructing a few instances of HelloGenerics. The following code will take care of this last bit of work:

```
[VB code]
Dim talker1 As New HelloGenerics(Of GermanSpeaker)()
talker1.Talker = New GermanSpeaker()
talker1.SayHello()

Dim talker2 As New HelloGenerics(Of SpanishSpeaker)()
talker2.Talker = New SpanishSpeaker()
talker2.SayHello()
```

```
[C# code]
HelloGenerics<GermanSpeaker> talker1 = new HelloGenerics<GermanSpeaker>();
talker1.Talker = new GermanSpeaker();
talker1.SayHello();

HelloGenerics<SpanishSpeaker> talker2 = new HelloGenerics<SpanishSpeaker>();
talker2.Talker = new SpanishSpeaker();
talker2.SayHello();
```

All that's left now is to run this code and you'll see the multilingual "Hello World" break through all new international barriers. Although not all that practical (what "hello world" app is?), this example does help to clarify the basic steps that are involved in building and consuming a simple generic type.

## A More Conceptual View

At this stage, it's my hope that you have a much better feeling for why the term *generics* was coined to describe this language feature. Generics bring a new level of generality to your types, which allows you to separate the behavior of a class from the data types that it operates on. This is, in essence, precisely what makes the type generic. Through generics, you are able to add parameters to your types much like you would add parameters to your methods to extend their generality. And, just as parameters for your methods allow you to alter the nature of your method, so too do generic type parameters allow you to alter the representation of your classes, methods, and so on.

The beauty of generics, as you see in more detail in the ensuing chapters, is that this mechanism allows you to build more adaptable, more general versions of your code. Your classes, methods, and interfaces are able to take on this new dimension of generality while still allowing you to write more robust, more type-safe code. The truth is, the type-safety benefits — on their own — make generics worth the cost of admission.

So, as you begin to work with generics, you should try to be more than a consumer of the standard generic types. You should look for opportunities to construct your own generic types, introduce generic methods, or leverage any number of the generic mechanisms that are covered in the scope of this book. Once you get comfortable with the concepts, you're likely to find yourself infusing generics into your approach to a much wider spectrum of solutions than you may have initially envisioned.

## Parametric Polymorphism

While I'm being conceptual, it's important to introduce the idea of *parametric polymorphism*. The term is often used to describe the flavor of polymorphism that can be achieved with generic types. To understand the concept, let's turn back the time machine and look at the classic example that is used to convey the root concept of polymorphism. The diagram in Figure 1-1 shows a basic object hierarchy with a Shape base class and a series of specialized shape types.

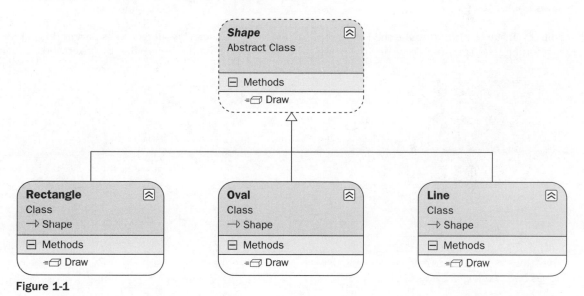

Figure 1-1

This example demonstrates how behavior can be generalized to a base class (Shape) and, through polymorphism, provides a specific implementation of a Draw method for each type of Shape. The beauty of polymorphism is that you can introduce new, specialized behaviors for a Shape without altering anything about the client's fundamental view of a Shape. If you decide you want to add a Square, you can add it and it will immediately be on equal footing with any other Shape in the system.

This little trip down polymorphic memory lane illustrates the fundamental idea behind polymorphism. So, what is parametric polymorphism? Well, instead of achieving polymorphism through inheritance, generics allow you to achieve the functional equivalent by allowing you to parameterize your types. Where regular polymorphism might use a virtual method table to override the methods of a parent object, parametric polymorphism achieves a similar result by allowing a single class to dynamically substitute the types referenced in its internal implementation. This ability to alter a class's behavior via a type parameter is seen simply as an alternative form of polymorphism, thus the name parametric polymorphism.

While I think it would be incomplete to discuss generics without including parametric polymorphism, it's also fair to say that the .NET implementation of generics imposes some constraints that limit the amount of polymorphic behavior it can achieve. C++ and other compile-time approaches to generics, as discussed in Chapter 3, "Generics ≠ Templates," provide developers with a richer set of polymorphic possibilities.

# Terminology

In addition to nailing down generic concepts, it's important to establish a clear set of terms that are used to describe the different facets of generics. It's also important for you to have some precision in your generic vocabulary, because many of these terms are referenced heavily throughout the remainder of this book.

First, I'll start by building the shell of a simple generic type that can be referenced as part of this exploration of generic terminology. The following generic Stack type should serve that purpose well:

```
[VB.NET Example]
Public Class Stack(Of T)
    Private items() as T
    Private count As Integer

    Public Sub Push(item as T)
        ...
    End Sub

    Public Function Pop() as T
        ...
    End Function
End Class
```

```
[C# Example]
public class Stack<T> {
    private T[] items;
    private int count;

    public void Push(T item) {...}
    public T Pop() {...}
}
```

## *Type Parameters*

A type parameter refers to the parameter that is used in the definition of your generic type. In the Stack example, the class accepts one type parameter, T. Each generic type can accept one or more type parameters, and this list of parameters will define the signature of your type. The names used for these parameters are then referenced throughout the implementation of your new type. For the Stack, you can see where multiple references have been added to the Stack's type parameter, T.

Although type parameters can be applied to classes, structs, and interfaces, they cannot be directly applied to indexers, properties, or events. So, when you invoke a property of an object, for example, you cannot supply any type arguments. This is not to say that these constructs have no awareness of type parameters. Indexers, properties, and events can all reference type parameters in their signatures; they simply can't explicitly accept their own type arguments. Instead, those types must be defined as part of the surrounding class.

## Open Types

Although `Stack` shares many of the characteristics of any class you might declare, its ability to accept a type parameter as part of its declaration means you need to further qualify the existing naming convention to accurately describe this new construct. Instead of referring to this as a class, generics consider the `Stack<T>` an "open type." My assumption here is that the term "open" is meant to convey the idea that the type is not fully defined and is "open" to taking on multiple concrete representations. If you have some exposure to C++ templates, you may be more comfortable referring to this as a parameterized type. For the sake of this discussion, though, we will stick with the accepted .NET generics terminology.

## Constructed Types

Open types and type parameters are all about defining the structure of your generic type. A constructed type, on the other hand, represents a concrete instance of one of your open types. To create a constructed type from your open `Stack` type, you'd execute the following code:

```
[VB code]
Dim myStringStack As New Stack(Of String)
```

```
[C# code]
Stack<sting> myStringStack;
```

This constructed type shares many of the attributes of traditional .NET types. They do, however, have some distinguishing syntactic characteristics worth exploring.

## Type Arguments

Type arguments are likely the simplest concept to explain. Whenever you instantiate a constructed type, you must provide specific types for each of the type parameters required by the given open type you are constructing. So, when you declared the constructed type `Stack<string>` in the preceding section, the `string` type passed in would be considered a type argument.

## Open and Closed Constructed Types

When creating a constructed type, you are not always required to provide a type argument. Take a look at the following snippet of a generic type declaration, which illustrates a scenario where this would be valid:

```
[VB.NET Example]
Public Class MyType(Of T)
    Private constructedType1 As MyOtherType1(Of Integer)
    Private constructedType2 As MyOtherType(Of T)
    ...
End Class
```

```
[C# Example]
public class MyType<T> {
    private constructedType1<Integer> member1;
    private constructedType2<T> member2;
    ...
}
```

This example creates an open type MyType, which has two data members that are constructed types. The first data member, constructedType1, is considered a *closed* constructed type because its type argument is fixed or "closed" to further definition. Its type argument will always be an Integer. The other data member, constructedType2, throws in a new twist. Instead of passing a concrete type as its type argument, it passes a type argument of T, which is the type parameter defined for the generic type. Despite this variation, the type is still considered a constructed type. However, because its parameter is still open to run-time definition, it is referred to as an open constructed type.

## Generic Methods

So far, the examples of generic types have been limited to generic classes. However, generics can also be applied to individual methods. The following is a very simple example of a generic method:

```
[VB.NET Example]
Public Function CalculateValue(Of T)(myParam1 as T, myParam2 as Integer) As T
    Dim var1 As T
    ...
End  Function
```

```
[C# Example]
public T CalculateValue<T>(T myParam1, int myParam2) {
    T var1;
    ...
}
```

Like open types, generic methods also accept a type parameter. And, like open types, generic methods can reference this parameter as part of their signature or implementation. In fact, this example loads up the references to the type parameter to illustrate this point. The return type, one of its parameters, and a local variable all reference the type parameter T. Chapter 5, "Generic Methods," looks more closely at the details of generic methods.

## Type Instantiation

The first time the Just-In-Time (JIT) compiler comes across a constructed type in your code, it must transform that type into the appropriate IL representation. During this process, it will examine each of the incoming type arguments and substitute each of the open type's parameters with the data types of these arguments. The result will be the accurate run-time representation of your constructed type. This transformation process is considered "type instantiation" because it yields an actual instance of the constructed type.

## Arity

*Arity* simply refers to the number of type parameters that are used by a generic type. So, if your type has three type parameters, it is said to have an arity of 3. And, just to be complete, a type that has no type parameters has an arity of zero. You'll often find this term used in scenarios where you are using reflection to examine the characteristics of generic types.

## Generic Types

*Generic types* is probably the most heavily used term referenced throughout this book. It is the all-encompassing term that is intended to describe any class, struct, event, or delegate that accepts one or more type parameters. This term is not really part of any formally accepted generics terminology and is somewhat synonymous with the idea of an open type. However, it's often a more useful term to invoke when attempting to describe the broadest definition of any type that supports generic behavior.

## Bringing It All Together

So, now that you're equipped with generics terminology, let's take it out for a spin. When you declare a generic type, that type is referred to as an open type (`MyType<T>`). And, when you declare an instance of that type by passing type arguments into the type parameters (`MyType<int>`), you form a constructed type. Whew. That was a mouthful. Still, it's just that kind of phrasing that's sure to make you a hit at the next Christmas party.

# Summary

The goal of this chapter was to introduce the basic concepts associated with constructing and consuming generic types. It started out by examining a simple non-generic solution. As part of that example, you looked at some of the pitfalls that are typically associated with using these non-generic types. With that as a backdrop, you then went on to explore how generics can be applied to overcome the issues that are highlighted in these examples. The chapter also touched, briefly, on some of the higher-level conceptual aspects of generics, which should give you a better idea of how generics concepts can be applied when constructing your own types. To round things out, the chapter also included a "Hello Generics" example that provides a generic version of the traditional "Hello World" application. Finally, the chapter wrapped up with a look at generic terminology. Understanding this terminology is fundamental to concepts that appear throughout this book. Collectively, these topics should give you a reasonable starting point for learning more about generics.

# 2

# Valuing Type Safety

This book is filled with references to the importance of type safety. The term gets thrown around very loosely inside and outside the world of generics. So much so, that it seems like its meaning is often lost in the shuffle as a core value for many developers. Now, with generics, it's worth reexamining the value of type safety because it's one of the motivating factors that influenced the introduction of this new language feature. This chapter revisits the origins of type safety and discusses some of the unsafe trends that have become a common occurrence. Certainly, this is an area where there may be some disagreement. However, it's an area that needs to be discussed as part of sharpening your awareness and understanding the impact generics will have on your everyday approach to designing and building solutions.

## Motivation

Types have to matter. With every class you write, you need to be focused on how that class represents itself to clients. Each time clients touch the interfaces of your class, they are binding to the specific types exposed in the signature of that interface. As such, you need to be concerned about the type-safety implications that accompany each of these interactions. Does your interface provide a clear set of types that make every attempt to eliminate ambiguity, or does your interface favor generality at the expense of type safety?

From my perspective, a great deal of what generics has to offer is focused squarely on allowing you to achieve a much greater level of type safety without having to compromise on generality (or bloat your code with more specialized classes). Generics should, in some respects, force you to apply a higher standard to the classes you write and consume. They should put you in a position where you look at the type safety of each interface with a significantly higher level of scrutiny than you might have in the pre-generics era.

As best I can tell, this fundamental mindset is sometimes lost in the discussions surrounding generics. Whenever developers look at a new language feature, they often ask, "What new functionality can I build with this feature that I couldn't build before?" Though generics do enable *new* capabilities, that's not the point. Generics aren't just about doing something new — they're about doing something *better*. Through generics, you should be able to bring a new dimension of type safety and expressiveness to your code that will undoubtedly improve its quality, usability, and maintainability.

The goal, then, as you move through this chapter, is to bring some light to how generics can influence the type safety of your code. There are simply too many permutations of type-safety scenarios to address them all. That's not my approach. I just want to provide enough insight to establish a theme that I hope influences how you look at applying generics to your new and existing solutions.

The truth is, though, if you don't see code and value its ability to adequately convey and constrain its types, you are likely to miss out on one of the key benefits of generics.

# Least Common Denominator Programming

In the early days of Java, I remember discussing templates with a few of the C++ converts. Whenever the conversation turned to templates (the C++ variation of generics), they usually said: "I don't need templates because everything in Java descends from an object." And, I'm assuming this same train of thought has actually carried forward into some segment of the .NET community, where every class is also rooted in a common object type.

This general mindset has always puzzled me. I understand that having everything rooted in a single object hierarchy enables some generality. It even makes sense to me that a number of classes would leverage this reality. At the same time, I don't think it would be accurate to view this feature as somehow replacing or offsetting the need for generics.

The `Object` data type, in fact, can end up being quite a crutch. Developers will leverage it in a number of situations where they want to provide a highly generalized interface that accepts any number of different data types. `ArrayList` is the great example of a class that takes this approach. As a data container, it needs to be able to hold any type of object. So, it's forced to use the `Object` data type to represent the types it holds. You'll also see situations where developers will accept or return `Object` parameters in an interface that needs to handle a wide variety of unrelated objects.

This use of the `Object` type is natural and expected. If `ArrayList` and other classes didn't leverage this mechanism, they would be forced to introduce class after class of specialized types to support each unique type they needed to manage. I wouldn't want to see `DoubleArrayList`, `StringArrayList`, and so on. That would often be too high of a price to pay for type safety.

So, as you code, you constantly face this question of deciding when it might be appropriate to leverage the `Object` data type and, each time you make the compromise, you also compromise the type safety of your code. With generics, the idea is to break this pattern of least common denominator coding. For example, the BCL now replaces those non-generic, type-safety-hating classes from the `System.Collections` namespace with new, type-safe versions in the `System.Collections.Generic` namespace.

In many respects, I see a generic type, `T`, as the direct replacement for an `Object` data type. By using `T`, you are still indicating that any type (value or reference) can be accepted, which allows you to retain the generality you needed. At the same time, unlike the `Object`, `T` will represent a binding to a very specific data type. So, you get the best of both worlds.

# A Basic Example

Type safety is likely a term you happened upon quite frequently in your travels as an object-oriented programmer. And, for you, the concept may already be crystallized. That said, I want to be sure we're on equal footing before examining some of the broader issues surrounding type safety and generics. So, to establish some common ground, let's look at a simple scenario that provides a very basic example of the importance of type safety.

The example you'll construct here consists of an object hierarchy with a Person class at the root and two descendant classes, Customer and Employee. The Person class provides an abstraction of those attributes that are common to every person. In this example, these shared attributes are represented by the Id, Name, and Status properties of the Person class.

The Customer and Employee classes also add their own specializations and behavior. Specifically, each of these classes also has a one-to-many relationship with another class. A Customer is associated with one or more Orders and an Employee contains references to one or more "child" Employee objects that represent those employees that are managed by a specific person.

Now, in working with these Customer and Employee objects, assume you've identified several places in your code that are providing general-purpose handling of Person objects. To further promote this generality, you've decided you also would like to allow clients of your Person class to access the items associated with a Person. To accommodate this, you've moved one more property, Items, up into your Person class.

Unfortunately, because the classes associated with each Person don't necessarily share a common base class, you are forced to represent this new property as an Object type. The beauty of this approach is that your Person class now exposes a generalized approach to exposing an interface all clients can use to retrieve the items associated with any type of Person.

Here's how this Person object might be represented:

```
[VB Code]
Public Class Person
    Public Const ACTIVE_STATUS As Int32 = 1
    Public Const INACTIVE_STATUS As Int32 = 2
    Public Const NEW_STATUS As Int32 = 3

    Private _name As String
    Private _id As String
    Private _status As Int32
    Private _items As ArrayList

    Public Sub New(ByVal Id As String, ByVal Name As String, ByVal Status As Int32)
        Me._id - Id
        Me._name = Name
        Me._status = Status
        Me._items = New ArrayList()
    End Sub

    Public ReadOnly Property Id() As String
        Get
```

```
                Return Me._id
            End Get
        End Property

        Public ReadOnly Property Name() As String
            Get
                Return Me._name
            End Get
        End Property

        Public ReadOnly Property Status() As Int32
            Get
                Return Me._status
            End Get
        End Property

        Public ReadOnly Property Items() As Object()
            Get
                Return Me._items.ToArray()
            End Get
        End Property

        Public Sub AddItem(ByVal newItem As Object)
            Me._items.Add(newItem)
        End Sub
    End Class
```

```
[C# code]
public class Person {
    public const int ACTIVE_STATUS = 1;
    public const int INACTIVE_STATUS = 2;
    public const int NEW_STATUS = 3;

    private string _id;
    private string _name;
    private int _status;
    private ArrayList _items;

    public Person(String Id, String Name, int Status) {
        this._id = Id;
        this._name = Name;
        this._status = Status;
        this._items = new ArrayList();
    }

    public string Id {
        get { return this._id; }
    }

    public string Name {
        get { return this._name; }
    }
```

```
    public int Status {
        get { return this._status; }
    }

    public Object[] Items {
        get { return this._items.ToArray(); }
    }

    public void AddItem(Object newItem) {
        this._items.Add(newItem);
    }
}
```

On the surface, there's nothing glaringly wrong with this class. Its interface is intuitive enough. It does have some type-safety issues, though. Some are obvious and some not.

The Status property represents the simplest form of type-safety violation and likely falls into the "obvious" bucket. Even though constants are used to define the valid range of values that can be assigned to this property, you cannot prevent clients from setting it to *any* valid integer value. By making this property an integer, you've really limited your ability to enforce any kind of compile- or run-time type checking of this value. I guess you could actually validate it against the known range at run-time, but that's awkward at best. The real type-safe solution here would be to make your property an Enum.

So, the Status provides a simple, clean example of why type safety is important. However, that scenario didn't require generics to be resolved. To see where generics would be applied, you must first assemble some sample code that exercises the Person object. Let's start with some simple code that creates a Customer object and populates it with some orders (the code for the Customer object is not shown here, but it is available as part of the complete examples that can be downloaded from the Wrox Web site).

```
[VB code]
Public Function PopulateCustomerCollection() As ArrayList
    Dim custColl As New ArrayList()
    Dim cust As New Customer("1", "Ron Livingston", 1)
    cust.AddItem(New Order(DateTime.Parse("10/1/2004"), "SL", "Swingline Stapler"))
    cust.AddItem(New Order(DateTime.Parse("10/03/2004"), "XR", "Xerox Copier"))
    cust.AddItem(New Order(DateTime.Parse("10/07/2004"), "FX", "Fax Paper"))
    custColl.Add(cust)

    cust = New Customer("2", "Milton Waddams", 2)
    cust.AddItem(New Order(DateTime.Parse("11/04/2004"), "PR-061", "Printer"))
    cust.AddItem(New Order(DateTime.Parse("11/07/2004"), "3H-24", "3-hole punch"))
    cust.AddItem(New Order(DateTime.Parse("12/12/2004"), "DSK-36", "CDRW Disks"))
    custColl.Add(cust)

    cust = New Customer("3", "Bill Lumberg", 3)
    cust.AddItem(New Order(DateTime.Parse("10/01/2004"), "WST4", "Waste basket"))
    custColl.Add(cust)

    Return custColl
End Function
```

```
[C# code]
public ArrayList PopulateCustomerCollection() {
    ArrayList custColl = new ArrayList();
    Customer cust = new Customer("1", "Ron Livingston", 1);
    cust.AddItem(new Order(DateTime.Parse("10/1/2004"),"SL", "Swingline Stapler"));
    cust.AddItem(new Order(DateTime.Parse("10/03/2004"), "XR", "Xerox Copier"));
    cust.AddItem(new Order(DateTime.Parse("10/07/2004"), "FX", "Fax Paper"));
    custColl.Add(cust);

    cust = new Customer("2", "Milton Waddams", 2);
    cust.AddItem(new Order(DateTime.Parse("11/04/2004"), "PR-061", "Printer"));
    cust.AddItem(new Order(DateTime.Parse("11/07/2004"), "3H-24", "3-hole punch"));
    cust.AddItem(new Order(DateTime.Parse("12/12/2004"), "DSK-36", "CD-RW Disks"));
    custColl.Add(cust);

    cust = new Customer("3", "Bill Lumberg", 3);
    cust.AddItem(new Order(DateTime.Parse("10/01/2004"), "WST4", "Waste basket" ));
    custColl.Add(cust);

    return custColl;
}
```

Now, you're thinking, what's wrong with this? The answer is: nothing. This code is perfectly fine as it is. However, think about what the interface of the Person object enables here. Imagine if you were to change this same code to the following:

```
[VB code]
Dim cust As New Customer("1", "Ron Livingston", 1)
cust.AddItem(New Dog("Sparky", "Mutt"))
```

```
[C# code]
Customer cust = new Customer("1", "Ron Livingston", 1);
cust.AddItem(new Dog("Sparky", "Mutt"));
```

Instead of associating orders with your Customer, you've now associated a set of Dog objects with your Customer. Because the interface of your class must accept Objects as its incoming type, there's nothing that prevents you from adding *any* flavor of object to your Customer — even if the implied rules of your Customer indicate this is invalid. It's not until someone starts to consume your Customer object that they will catch the error that this introduces.

In fact, let's look at some of the type-safety issues that this class represents from the consumer's perspective. The following example creates a method that iterates over a list of customers, dumping out the information for each customer and their associated orders:

```
[VB code]
Public Sub DisplayCustomers(ByVal customers As ArrayList)
    For custIdx As Int32 = 0 To (customers.Count - 1)
        Dim cust As Customer = customers(custIdx)
        Console.Out.WriteLine("Customer-> ID: {0}, Name: {1}", cust.Id, cust.Name)
        Dim orders() As Object = DirectCast(cust.Items, Object())

        For orderIdx As Int32 = 0 To (orders.Length - 1)
            Dim ord As Order = DirectCast(orders(orderIdx), Order)
```

```
            Console.Out.WriteLine("  Order-> Date: {0}, Item: {1}, Desc: {2}", _
                                    ord.OrderDate, ord.ItemId, ord.Description)
        Next
    Next
End Sub
```

```
[C# code]
public void DisplayCustomers(ArrayList customers) {
    for (int custIdx = 0; custIdx < customers.Count; custIdx++) {
        Customer cust = (Customer)customers[custIdx];
        Console.Out.WriteLine("Customer-> ID: {0}, Name: {1}", cust.Id, cust.Name);

        Object[] orders = (Object[])cust.Items;
        for (int orderIdx = 0; orderIdx < orders.Length; orderIdx++) {
            Order ord = (Order)orders[orderIdx];
            Console.Out.WriteLine("  Order-> Date: {0}, Item: {1}, Desc: {2}",
                                    ord.OrderDate, ord.ItemId, ord.Description);
        }
    }
}
```

Now, in looking at these methods, you can see where moving your items collection up into the `Person` class is causing some real type-safety concerns. Its declaration starts everything off on the wrong foot. It uses an `ArrayList` to hold the incoming list of customers and, because `ArrayLists` can only represent their contents as objects, you're required to cast each object to a `Customer` as it comes out of the list. So, if a client happens to pass in an `ArrayList` of employees, your method will accept it and then toss an exception when you attempt to cast one of its items to a `Customer`. Strike one.

The other area of concern is centered on the processing of the orders associated with each `Customer`. You'll notice here that, as you get the array of orders from the `Items` property of the `Customer`, you are required to cast the returned array to an array of `Objects`. That's right—because the `Items` property returns an array of `Objects`, you cannot directly cast this to an array of orders, which is what you really want. Strike two.

Finally, because you're dealing with an array of `Objects` here, you're forced to cast each object to an `Order` as it is extracted from this array. Strike three.

As you look at this line of thought, I imagine you might have a few reactions. First, you might take the position that this is just the cost of generality and that, as long as you're careful, a few casts here and there aren't exactly dangerous. Still, it seems to defeat the purpose of representing your `customers` and `orders` with these fairly expressive interfaces, only to push the value and safety that comes with this aside to achieve some higher level of generality. The introduction of these casts also creates yet one more area for producing errors and maintenance overhead.

The other angle here might be to suggest that you could avoid a great deal of this casting by adding specific interfaces in your `Customer` and `Employee` classes that returned the appropriate types. This would allow you to keep the generality in your base class and would simply cast the items to their specific types on the way out to a client. This is a reasonable compromise and is likely how many people have historically addressed a problem of this nature. It certainly limits each client's exposure to the `Object` representation of the `Items` property. Still, using `Objects` to represent these items is troubling from a pure type-safety perspective.

# Applying Generics

The question that remains is, how can generics be applied to overcome some of the type-safety problems illustrated in this example? You still want your Person class to expose an interface for retrieving each of its items, but you want the types of those items to be safe. Because generics give you a way to parameterize your types, you can use them, in this scenario, to parameterize your Person class, allowing it to accept a type parameter that will specify the type of the elements collected by the Items property. The resulting, generically improved Person class now appears as follows:

```
[VB code]
Public Class Person(Of T)
    Public Enum StatusType
        Active = 1
        Inactive = 2
        IsNew = 3
    End Enum

    Private _name As String
    Private _id As String
    Private _status As StatusType
    Private _items As List(Of T)

    Public Sub New(ByVal Id As String, ByVal Name As String, _
                                        ByVal Status As StatusType)
        Me._id = Id
        Me._name = Name
        Me._status = Status
        Me._items = New List(Of T)
    End Sub

    Public ReadOnly Property Id() As String
        Get
            Return Me._id
        End Get
    End Property

    Public ReadOnly Property Name() As String
        Get
            Return Me._name
        End Get
    End Property

    Public ReadOnly Property Status() As StatusType
        Get
            Return Me._status
        End Get
    End Property

    Public ReadOnly Property Items() As T()
        Get
            Return Me._items.ToArray()
        End Get
    End Property
```

```
        Public Sub AddItem(ByVal newItem As T)
            Me._items.Add(newItem)
        End Sub
    End Class
```

```
[C# code]
public class Person<T> {
    public enum StatusType {
        Active = 1,
        Inactive = 2,
        IsNew = 3
    };

    private string _id;
    private string _name;
    private StatusType _status;
    private List<T> _items;

    public Person(String Id, String Name, StatusType Status) {
        this._id = Id;
        this._name = Name;
        this._status = Status;
        this._items = new List<T>();
    }

    public string Id {
        get { return this._id; }
    }

    public string Name {
        get { return this._name; }
    }

    public StatusType Status {
        get { return this._status; }
    }

    public T[] Items {
        get { return this._items.ToArray(); }
    }

    public void AddItem(T newItem) {
        this._items.Add(newItem);
    }
}
```

That's only step one in the purification of this class. You also need to change the internal representation of the items data member. Instead of clinging to that old, type-ignorant ArrayList, you can use one of the new generic List collections (from the System.Collections.Generic namespace described in Chapter 8, "BCL Generics") to bring a greater level of type safety to this data member. To be complete, the Status property is also changed from an integer to an enum type.

Finally, to round out this transformation, you'll notice that the parameterization of the Person class allows you to change the AddItem() method to enforce type checking. Now, each object type that gets added must match the type of the type parameter, T, to be considered valid. No more adding dogs to customers.

An added bonus associated with this approach is that clients are still not required to have any awareness of the fact that you've applied generics to solve this problem. The Customer and Employee classes, which descend from Person, simply specify the type of their related items as part of their inheritance declarations. Here's a snippet of these class declarations to clarify this point:

```
[VB code]
Public Class Customer
    Inherits Person(Of Order)
    ...
End Class

Public Class Employee
    Inherits Person(Of Employee)
    ...
End Class
```

```
[C# code]
public class Customer : Person<Order> {
    ...
}

public class Employee : Person<Employee> {
    ...
}
```

As you can see, even though you've leveraged generics to add type safety to your Person class, these two classes retain the same interface they supported under the non-generic version. In fact, the client code used to populate the Customer and Employee structures would not require any modifications (with the exception of the change that was introduced to make Status an enum).

Although the code to populate the Customer and Employee classes was unscathed as a result of making Person generic, the code that was used earlier to dump information about customers does require changes (all of them for the better). Here's how the new version of the DisplayCustomers() method has been influenced as a result:

```
[VB code]
Public Sub DisplayCustomers(ByVal customers As List(Of Customer))
    For custIdx As Int32 = 0 To (customers.Count - 1)
        Dim cust As Customer = customers(custIdx)
        Console.Out.WriteLine("Customer-) ID: {0}, Name: {1}", cust.Id, cust.Name)

        Dim orders() As Order = cust.Items
        For orderIdx As Int32 = 0 To (orders.Length - 1)
            Dim ord As Order = orders(orderIdx)
            Console.Out.WriteLine("  Order-> Date: {0}, Item: {1}, Desc: {2}", _
                                  ord.OrderDate, ord.ItemId, ord.Description)
        Next
    Next
End Sub
```

```
[C# code]
public void DisplayCustomers(List<Customer> customers) {
    for (int custIdx = 0; custIdx < customers.Count; custIdx++) {
        Customer cust = customers[custIdx];
        Console.Out.WriteLine("Customer-> ID: {0}, Name: {1}", cust.Id, cust.Name);

        Order[] orders = cust.Items;
        for (int orderIdx = 0; orderIdx < orders.Length; orderIdx++) {
            Order ord = orders[orderIdx];
            Console.Out.WriteLine("  Order-> Date: {0}, Item: {1}, Desc: {2}",
                                   ord.OrderDate, ord.ItemId, ord.Description);
        }
    }
}
```

This type safety work, as you can see, has yielded some nice benefits. Though the code isn't smaller (that wasn't the goal anyway), it is certainly much safer. Gone are the plethora of casts that muddied the prior version of this class.

## Casting Consequences

In the previous example, you saw how using the Object data type forced the client code to use a series of casts to convert the Object to the appropriate data type. This need to cast has a number of implications in terms of the general type safety of your code. Consider the following example:

```
[VB code]
Dim custList As ArrayList = CustomerFinder.GetCustomers()
For idx As Int32 = 0 To (custList.Count - 1)
    Dim cust As Customer = DirectCast(custList(idx), Customer)
Next
```

```
[C# code]
ArrayList custList = CustomerFinder.GetCustomers();
for (int idx = 0; idx < custList.Count; idx++) {
    Customer cust = (Customer)custList[idx];
}
```

Certainly, as discussed earlier, the casts that you see in this example are anything but type-safe. However, there's more wrong here than just the absence of type safety. First, the cast that is applied here will have an impact on performance. Although the added overhead is not large, it could still be significant in scenarios where you might need a tight, high-performing loop.

The larger issue, though, is centered more around the fact that casts may not always succeed. And a failed cast can mean unexpected failures in your application. In this example, this code simply presumes that the collection contains Customer objects and that each of these casts never throws an exception. This approach just assumes that, as the code evolves, it will never alter the representation of the objects returned by this GetCustomers() call. Creating this blind-faith, implied contract between a client and method is dangerous and prone to generating unexpected errors.

You can attempt to manage this through exception handling. This would be achieved by adding the following exception handling block:

```
[VB code]
Try
    Dim custList As ArrayList = CustomerFinder.GetCustomers()
    For idx As Int32 = 0 To (custList.Count - 1)
        Dim cust As Customer = DirectCast(custList(idx), Customer)
    Next
Catch ex As InvalidCastException
    Console.Out.WriteLine(ex.Message)
End Try
```

```
[C# code]
try {
    ArrayList custList = CustomerFinder.GetCustomers();
    for (int idx = 0; idx < custList.Count; idx++) {
        Customer cust = (Customer)custList[idx];
    }
} catch (InvalidCastException ex) {
    Console.Out.WriteLine(ex.Message);
}
```

This modification ensures that you'll catch the casting errors. This is certainly the appropriate action to take and will, at minimum, allow you to easily detect when the errors occur. Because there's likely no appropriate action to take in response to this error, it will likely result, in most cases, in some form of hard error. It's really the only option you have.

You might think you could use the `for each` construct to make this problem go away. Suppose you were to change the loop to the following:

```
[VB codes]
For each cust As Customer in custCollection
    . . .
Next
```

```
[C# code]
foreach (Customer cust in custCollection) {
    . . .
}
```

This seems, on the surface, like safer code. After all, it does eliminate the need for a cast. While it would seem as though this solves the problem, it's probably obvious why it really doesn't. Even though you don't explicitly do a cast in this situation, the resulting code still does. So, if your `custCollection` doesn't contain `Customer` objects, it too will yield an `InvalidCastException`. In many respects, this loop actually causes more problems than the prior example. If you happen to capture an exception here, and you want to continue processing additional items, you cannot use the `continue` construct.

This whole idea of trying to adopt a strategy for dealing with the occurrence of `InvalidCastExceptions` seems like it's focusing on the wrong dimension of the problem. If you weren't forced to use unsafe types, you wouldn't be in a position of having to coerce them to another type with the hope that the conversion is successful. Although I'm not saying casting should be eliminated, I am saying it's something you should attempt to avoid.

Fortunately, with generics, this entire discussion is moot. There wouldn't be any casting in these examples if they leveraged generics and, therefore, there won't be any need to worry about strategies for dealing with failed casts (at least in this scenario).

## Interface Type Safety

An interface lets you define a signature for a type entirely separate from any implementation of that type. And, because a number of classes might be implementing your interfaces, you should be especially diligent about ensuring their type safety. To clarify this point, let's start by looking at the ICloneable interface you may have already been using:

```
[VB code]
Public Interface ICloneable
    Function Clone() As Object
End Interface
```

```
[C# code]
Interace ICloneable {
    Public object Clone();
}
```

By now, it should be clear that there's absolutely nothing type-safe about this interface. Any class that implements this interface is free to return any object type in its implementation of the Clone() method. Once again, each client is left to their own devices to figure out how to handle the possible fallout of an invalid type being returned from this method.

So, as you can imagine, interfaces are one of the most natural places to leverage the benefits of generics. With one minor modification, this once type-unfriendly interface can become fully type-safe. The generic version would appear as follows:

```
[VB code]
Public Interface ICloneable(Of T)
    Function Clone() As T
End Interface
```

```
[C# code]
Interace ICloneable<T> {
    Public T Clone();
}
```

Each class that implements this interface will be required to return a type T from its Clone() method. If any code attempts to return any other type, the compiler will now capture this condition and throw an error—a much better alternative than entrusting your safety to run-time detection of type collisions.

## *Scratching the Surface*

The preceding examples represent just a few of the countless permutations of how the type safety of your solutions can be improved through the application of generics. The goal here isn't to point out every way generics can be leveraged to improve the type safety of your code. Instead, the idea here is to simply scratch the generic surface enough to expose the impact generics can have on the general type safety of your code.

Once you get in this mindset, you'll find yourself looking at your interfaces in a new light. As you do, you'll find that generics actually provide solutions for a broad spectrum of issues, including interfaces, methods, delegates, classes, and so on. Ultimately, you should find yourself wondering why generics weren't part of the language sooner. If you're in that camp, you're going to have a greater appreciation for the value of generics and are likely to see the more global implications of applying generics to your existing solutions.

# Safety vs. Clarity

There's a lot of debate in the .NET development community about the influence of generics on the readability of code. Some view the introduction of generics as an abomination that muddies the syntactic qualities of each language they touch. I find this perspective puzzling. I don't know if this is rooted in the complexity of C++ templates or if the objection is made on some more general basis. Whatever the reason, I still have trouble understanding the fundamental logic behind this mindset.

Although generics add some verbosity to your code, that very verbosity is what enables generics to bring clarity to your code. Consider these two contrasting examples:

```
[VB code]
Public Function FindCustomers(searchParams As HashTable) As ArrayList

Public Function FindCustomers(searchParams As Dictionary(Of string, Int32)) _
                                                  As List(Of Customer)
```

```
[C# code]
public ArrayList FindCustomers(ArrayList searchParams);

public List<Customer> FindCustomers(Dictionary<string, int> searchParams);
```

This example includes non-generic and generic versions of a `FindCustomers()` method. Although the non-generic version is certainly shorter than its generic counterpart, it tells you nothing about the types required for the incoming parameters or the type of objects being returned. If you put aside the obvious type-safety problems here and focus solely on the expressive qualities of these two declarations, you'd have to favor the generic version. Its signature tells you precisely what data types are used for your incoming key/value parameter pairs. It also is very explicit about the type of objects that will be held in the returned list.

So, when I look at these two examples, I see the added syntax introduced by generics as a blessing. I don't see it as muddying the profile of my method. Instead, I see it as adding a much-needed means of qualifying, in detail, the nature of my types.

The truth is, generics should allow you to demand much more from the APIs you consume and expose. When an API hands you back an `ArrayList`, what is it really telling you? It's as if it's saying: "Here's a collection of objects; now you go figure out what it contains." It then becomes your job to track down, sometimes through multiple levels of indirection, the code that created and populated the `ArrayList` to determine what it contains. You are then forced to couple, through casting or some other mechanism, your code to the types contained in the collection with the expectation that the provider of the collection won't change its underlying representation. This whole mechanism of passing out untyped parameters and then binding to their representations creates a level of indirect coupling that can end up being both error-prone and a maintenance headache.

When I look at an interface, I don't want there to be any ambiguity about what it accepts or what it returns. There shouldn't be room for interpretation. Through generics, you are provided with new tools that can make your interfaces much more expressive. And, although this expressiveness makes the syntax more verbose and may rarely make your code run faster, it should still represent a significant factor in measuring the quality of your code.

As developers get more comfortable with generics, any objections to the syntactic impact of this new language feature are likely to subside. The benefits they bring to your code are simply too significant to be brushed aside simply because they tend to increase the verbosity of your declarations.

# Summary

Type safety is one of the key value propositions of generics. As such, it is vital for you to have a good grasp on how generics can be applied in ways that will enhance the overall type safety of your solutions. The goal of this chapter was to try and expose some of the type-safety compromises developers have been traditionally forced to make and discuss how generics can be employed to remedy these problems. The chapter looked at how types have been required to use least common denominator object types to achieve some level of generality and, in doing so, accept the overhead and safety issues that accompany that approach. As part of exploring these type-safety issues, the chapter also looked at how generics could be applied to eliminate a great deal of these type-safety problems. You also learned how generics bring a new level of expressiveness to your code and how generics can improve the quality and maintainability of your solutions. Overall, the chapter should give you a real flavor for how generics will influence the expectations you place on the signatures of the types you create and consume.

# 3

# Generics ≠ Templates

In the early stages of introducing generics, there was a fair amount of confusion surrounding the scope and capabilities of this new language feature. Many developers jumped to the conclusion that generics would be the functional equivalent of C++ templates. And, while these two constructs share common heritage, they definitely cannot be viewed — in any respect — as being one in the same. It's important, especially for those with a template orientation, to understand how generics and templates differ. This information may also be helpful, in a more conceptual sense, to anyone transitioning to generics. Overall, after reading this chapter, you should come away with a much clearer picture of the fundamental differences that exist between generics and templates implementations.

## Shared Concepts

There's no doubt that generics and templates are trying to solve similar problems. Certainly, as the architects sidled up to the whiteboard in Redmond to create the generics specification, they knew they would be borrowing heavily from the concepts that had long existed in the world of templates. You will discover that generics actually have a great deal of conceptual overlap with templates, offering the familiar generic classes, methods, and so on that many have already been exposed to in the world of C++ templates.

Syntactically, if you are already familiar with C++ templates, you're likely to find the transition to generics fairly painless. The use of type parameters and their application throughout the classes and methods mirrors the patterns employed by templates.

As you move through this chapter and focus on the differences between generics and templates, it's important that you don't lose sight of that emphasis. The goal here is to simply point out key differences that can help those familiar templates better understand the fundamental differences — for better or worse — that come with the .NET implementation of generics.

# Run-Time vs. Compile-Time

Generics and C++ templates take very different approaches to how and when objects are instantiated. Generics are instantiated at run-time by the CLR, and templates are instantiated at compile-time. This fundamental difference is at the root of almost every point of variation between generics and templates. And, as you will see, these variations end up creating a fairly significant ideological divide between these two technologies.

In the sections that follow you'll be exposed to the specific implications of run-time and compile-time instantiation. Understanding the mechanics of these two varying approaches will provide a good foundation for the rest of this discussion.

## Compile-Time Instantiation (Templates)

The term "templates" does an excellent job of conveying how a compiler processes templates. When you declare a template in C++, the code you write is providing a series of type placeholders that will be replaced with actual types at compile time. Let's look at a simple declaration of a C++ template class to see how the compiler will process it:

```
template <class T>
class Stack {
    public:
        Stack(int = 10) ;
        ~Stack() { delete [] stackPtr; }
        int push(const T&);
        int pop(T&);
        int isEmpty() const { return top == -1; }
        int isFull() const { return top == size - 1; }
    private:
        int size;
        int top;
        T* stackPtr;
};
```

This class defines a `Stack` template that can be used to perform all the basic operations to maintain the state of a stack container. As a template, this stack can be used to contain a variety of different data types. The code that would be used to create instances of this `Stack` might appear as follows:

```
Stack<char> charStack;
Stack<long> longStack;
Stack<double> doubleStack;
Stack<int> intStack;
```

Each of these instances of the stack template is being used to store a different data type. When you compile this code, the compiler will actually generate separate code for each instance you see here. During this process, it will replace every occurrence of the type parameter `T` with the supplied type. The result, from the preceding example, ends up yielding four different instances of `Stack`. In the end, it's as if you decided to write four separate stack classes, one for each data type. The template syntax ends up being more like custom tags that tell the compiler to generate the code you would've had to write yourself. That's the basic, compile-time mentality associated with writing templates.

The key idea here is that all the classes that are generated from your template are processed and generated by the compiler in *advance* of executing any code. And, as long as the type substitution yields valid code, the compiler will deem your new type as being valid. It also means the run-time environment is not required to supply any new functionality to support templates. The code generated through this process is no different than code you might write yourself.

## Run-Time Instantiation (Generics)

The run-time instantiation model that is employed by generics takes a very different approach to supporting generics. In fact, version 2.0 of the .NET Framework has introduced a series of extensions to the CLR to add run-time support for generics.

In the .NET implementation, generic specializations are created on demand. Each instance of these generated specializations will share their underlying code wherever possible. To understand this better, consider a sample `Stack` class and the underlying IL that is generated by the compiler. For a non-generic implementation of the `Stack`, the IL is devoid, as you would expect, of any generic mechanisms. The generated IL for its `Pop()` method would appear as follows:

```
.method public hidebysig instance object Pop() cil managed
{
    // Code Size: 29 byte(s)
    .maxstack 4
    .locals (
            object obj1,
            int32 num1)
    L_0000: ldarg.0
    L_0001: ldfld object[] NonGenericStack::_data
    L_0006: ldarg.0
    L_0007: dup
    L_0008: ldfld int32 NonGenericStack::_posIdx
    L_000d: ldc.i4.1
    L_000e: sub
    L_000f: dup
    L_0010: stloc.1
    L_0011: stfld int32 NonGenericStack::_posIdx
    L_0016: ldloc.1
    L_0017: ldelem.ref
    L_0018: stloc.0
    L_0019: br.s L_001b
    L_001b: ldloc.0
    L_001c: ret
}
```

There aren't any real surprises here. Because the non-generic `Stack` is forced to use objects to represent each item in the `Stack`, its IL looks like any other IL you might have seen before. Now, consider what this method would look like as a generic implementation that was required to support generics at run-time. The `Pop()` method for your generic version must be able to represent the same generic model your class does, where types are represented by type parameters that serve as placeholders for the type arguments that will be used as you instantiate each variation of the class. Here's a look at how the IL achieves this:

```
.method public hidebysig instance !0 Pop() cil managed
{
    // Code Size: 33 byte(s)
    .maxstack 4
    .locals (
        !0 local1,
        int32 num1)
    L_0000: ldarg.0
    L_0001: ldfld !0[] Stack`1<!0>::_data
    L_0006: ldarg.0
    L_0007: dup
    L_0008: ldfld int32 Stack`1<!0>::_posIdx
    L_000d: ldc.i4.1
    L_000e: sub
    L_000f: dup
    L_0010: stloc.1
    L_0011: stfld int32 Stack`1<!0>::_posIdx
    L_0016: ldloc.1
    L_0017: ldelem.any !0
    L_001c: stloc.0
    L_001d: br.s L_001f
    L_001f: ldloc.0
    L_0020: ret
}
```

Notice that the generics concepts are carried forward into the generated IL. There are now the equivalent of type parameters, each of which is identified with a pre-pended "!", angle brackets for the class declaration, and a new IL opcode (`ldelem.any`), all here to support the CLR's ability to instantiate generic types at run-time. The key point here is that a generic type will be compiled and placed in an assembly *before* any instances of that generic type are created. The generic type exists at run-time completely separate from any instances of that type.

Personally, I think this is one of the most interesting achievements of the .NET generics implementation. It introduces the opportunity for a series of optimizations and reduces your code bloat significantly. That, and it's just plain cool seeing generics represented in IL.

> **If you're interested in examining the IL of your own code, you can access the same information shown here with the ILDASM tool that comes with Visual Studio 2005.**

## Lost in Translation

So, the question is: How does this difference in compile-time and run-time instantiation end up influencing what can be achieved with templates and generics? To understand this, you have to step back and consider what requirements these two approaches impose on the compiler as it translates your generic code into executable instructions. The following scenario will serve as the basis for considering how compile-time and run-time solutions process code differently:

```
[VB code]
Public Class Gun
    Public Sub Fire()
        Console.Out.WriteLine("Gun->Fire")
    End Sub
End Class

Public Class Rocket
    Public Sub Fire()
        Console.Out.WriteLine("Rocket->Fire")
    End Sub
End Class

Public Class Shooter(Of T)
    Dim _shooterItem As T

    Public Sub New(ByVal shooterItem As T)
        Me._shooterItem = shooterItem
    End Sub

    Public Sub ShootIt()
        Me._shooterItem.Fire()
    End Sub
End Class

Public Sub TestShooter()
    Dim aRocket As New Shooter(Of Rocket)(New Rocket())
    Dim aGun As New Shooter(Of Gun)(New Gun())
    aRocket.ShootIt()
    aGun.ShootIt()
End Sub
```

```
[C# code]
public class Gun {
    public void Fire() {
        Console.Out.WriteLine("Gun->Fired");
    }
}

public class Rocket {
    public void Fire() {
        Console.Out.WriteLine("Rocket->Fired");
    }
}

public class Shooter<T> {
    private T _shooterItem;

    public Shooter(T shooterItem) {
        this._shooterItem = shooterItem;
    }

    public void ShootIt() {
        this._shooterItem.Fire();
    }
```

```
    }

public void TestShooter() {
    Shooter<Rocket> aRocket = new Shooter<Rocket>(new Rocket());
    Shooter<Gun> aGun = new Shooter<Gun>(new Gun());
    aRocket.ShootIt();
    aGun.ShootIt();
}
```

This example creates two simple classes: Gun and Rocket. Both of these classes happen to include a Fire() method, but they aren't specializations of any particular shared base class. They are, for the purposes of this discussion, two standalone, unrelated classes that just happen to share a common method name.

Now, with the Gun and Rocket classes in place, the example introduces a Shooter class that will accept these types as parameters. You should pay special attention to its ShootIt() method, which invokes the Fire() method on the supplied types. Given the idea that type parameters are simply substituted with type arguments and that Gun and Rocket objects both have a Fire() method, you'd think the compiler would be able to resolve this and everything would be fine. And, in a compile-time, template-based environment this concept works (with C++ syntax, of course).

Because the compiler will preprocess every instance of a template *before* it is executed, it can determine if the Fire() method can be resolved for every instance and throw a compile-time error if the method cannot be resolved. Basically, templates perform pure substitution without concern for the nature or heritage of their type parameters. If the signature compiles, templates are happy. This approach is sometimes referred to as "lazy structural constraints," implying that the compiler is supporting a more relaxed model for constraining these types.

With a run-time environment, the story is quite different. Remember, in run-time generic environments, each generic type is not instantiated until run-time. And, with this run-time model, all of your run-time instances of a given type will attempt to share their code at run-time. Given this delay, the run-time environment cannot be as free-wheeling as the template environment. It must have assurances — ahead of time — that all of the invocations on the type parameter can be resolved without any awareness of what generic instances might end up being declared within your application. In essence, this means that the compiler must verify that every operation that is performed on your type parameters is valid for every possible type argument that could be supplied to your class.

To resolve this issue, the .NET languages have added the concept of "constraints" to the declaration of your generic types. These constraints allow you to qualify the type of your type parameters. This allows you to limit the scope of type parameters to a set of types that conform to a specific interface. It also solves the CLR's run-time instantiation problem because it can now be assured, by the compiler, that all operations performed on your type parameters are valid.

So, given this perspective, let's turn your attention back to the genetics portion of the previous example. When the compiler attempts to process this code, it's going to complain about the call to Fire() in the Shooter class. That's because, as you now know, the type parameter supplied to the class is not constrained by an interface that guarantees that these type parameters will support a Fire() method. To add this constraint, you must force your Gun and Rocket classes to implement a common interface and use this interface as a constraint on your type parameter declaration in the Shooter class. The result is as follows:

```
[VB code]
Public Interface IShooter
    Sub Fire()
End Interface

Public Class Gun
    Implements IShooter

    Public Sub Fire() Implements IShooter.Fire
        Console.Out.WriteLine("Gun->Fire")
    End Sub
End Class

Public Class Rocket
    Implements IShooter

    Public Sub Fire1() Implements IShooter.Fire
        Console.Out.WriteLine("Rocket->Fire")
    End Sub
End Class

Public Class Shooter(Of T As IShooter)
    Dim _shooterItem As T

    Public Sub New(ByVal shooterItem As T)
        Me._shooterItem = shooterItem
    End Sub

    Public Sub ShootIt()
        Me._shooterItem.Fire()
    End Sub
End Class
```

```
[C# code]
public interface IShooter {
    void Fire();
}

public class Gun : IShooter {
    public void Fire() {
        Console.Out.WriteLine("Gun->Fired");
    }
}

public class Rocket : IShooter {
    public void Fire() {
        Console.Out.WriteLine("Rocket->Fired");
    }
}

public class Shooter<T> where T : IShooter {
    private T _shooterItem;

    public Shooter(T shooterItem) {
```

```
        this._shooterItem = shooterItem;
    }

    public void ShootIt() {
        this._shooterItem.Fire();
    }
}
```

You can now see how the compiler can process this code and still allow run-time instantiation of the Shooter class. By the time you're instantiating types at run-time, the compiler will have already verified that every type argument that could be supplied to Shooter implements the IShooter interface.

## The Brouhaha

The run-time nature of generics and the presence of constraints don't sit well with some members of the development community. This is especially prominent among the C++ template diehards, who view constraints as too limiting. I believe that, for that segment of the population that leverages the meta-programming capabilities of templates, generics will often fall short of their expectations. Generics simply aren't trying to fill that void — at least not yet. And, based on their run-time nature, it seems unlikely they ever will. Still, this should not detract from their overall value.

## Code Bloat

Although the compile-time nature of templates allows for a greater degree of flexibility, this flexibility also comes at a cost. Because every template instance must be preprocessed by the compiler, the code for every type must also be generated in advance. Now, there are certainly optimizations that attempt to limit the general bloat that accompanies this approach, but they still fall well short of the size and efficiency of the run-time model employed by generics.

Although code bloat is worth mentioning, it's also fair to say that most C++ programmers do not view this bloat as a pressing concern. Still, in some scenarios, the ability of generics to represent a generic type at run-time and share this type among many instances does have its benefits. And, if you're trying to conserve every last byte of memory and you can accept some of the constraints associated with generics, this issue may carry more weight with you.

## Assemblies and Type Equivalence

Whenever you compile a .NET class, it is placed in an assembly. Now, given that simple reality, consider what happens in this model where the compiler must instantiate all templates at compile-time. Suppose you have a Stack template and you have declared an instance of Stack<char> in assembly A1 and you have also declared an instance of Stack<char> in assembly A2.

When the compiler preprocesses these instances, it must qualify each type with the name of the assembly that "owns" that type. If you drill into the underlying IL, in fact, you'll see that these assembly qualifiers have been pre-pended to your types. For this scenario, then, you'll end up with two types being generated for your templates: [A1]Stack<char> and [A2]Stack<char>. Here you can see that, even though these stacks are really the same type, the compiler will end up generating separate types for each assembly.

This may seem harmless on the surface. However, consider a scenario where there is some interaction between these two assemblies centered on your Stack<char> type. Perhaps assembly A2 calls into a method of class in assembly A1 that returns a Stack<char>. It would seem like this wouldn't cause any problems. But, if you consider the fact that the Stack<char> type in A2 is actually seen as a completely different type than the Stack<char> found in A1, it might be clear why this is going to cause a problem. You might as well have called a method that returns a double and tried to shove it into a string.

This problem is a byproduct of the compile-time nature of templates. When you compile Stack<char>, the compiler is going to generate a new type that is the conceptual equivalent of your having created your own StackChar class. By the time the compiler is done with your template, the idea that it started out as a template is completely abandoned and a new, generated type exists in its place. This compiled class is then placed in an assembly. And, this type will not be treated as being equivalent to any instance of Stack<char> that might get compiled into another assembly.

In contrast, the run-time nature of generics allow them to bypass this problem entirely. Because each generic type is compiled separately from the specializations of that type, the generic type is allowed to exist in an assembly as a type that can then be specialized and referenced from a variety of different assemblies.

# Templates Extras

A handful of features that are part of templates are not part of generics. The following sections provide a brief overview of each of these areas. If you are part of the generics-only crowd, this will help you understand what additional features are available to you in the world of templates. If you are template-aware, this section will further qualify those features that are not currently supported by generics.

## *Template Specialization*

With templates, developers are allowed to create specializations of a template that provide alternative implementations based on a type argument. Consider the following example of a Stream template class that includes a specialization for the long type argument:

```
template <class T>
class stream {
    public:
        void foo() { cout << "Called stream<T>::foo()" << endl; }
};

template <>
class stream<long> {
    public:
        void foo() { cout << "Called stream<long>::foo()" << endl; }
};

int main() {
 stream<char> charStream;
 stream<long> longStream;
 return 0;
}
```

You'll notice in this example that two stream templates are declared, each with its own implementation of the foo() method. The first of these two templates will be used for the majority of type arguments. The second template will only be invoked if you supply a long type argument. The idea here is that you can provide specializations for any number of data types. Generics have no equivalent to this concept.

## Non-Type Parameters

Templates support the ability to accept what are labeled "non-type" parameters. A non-type is considered a type that is neither a reference nor a value parameter. It's essentially a numeric constant or a literal string and is sometimes used in numeric-focused template libraries. They are also used in combination with other features as part of the overall "meta-programming" model that is employed by some template programmers.

## Type Parameter Inheritance

Templates allow you to define a class that descends directly from a type parameter. This is a very powerful feature that C++ developers have used to build what are called "mix-ins." This pattern occurs when you mix-in the implementation of another type through inheritance. Inheriting implementation isn't all unique. What's unique here is that what's being "mixed in" is determined at compile-time based on the type argument you supply when specializing a template. This, I believe, is viewed as a fairly powerful aspect of templates that can only be achieved in the compile-time model employed by templates. Some attempts have been made to emulate this pattern with generics, but the results appear to have been, well, mixed.

# Cross-Language Support

Generics are part of the CLS specification. This reality means that developers can build multilanguage solutions that make heavy use of generics. This is one of the distinguishing characteristics of the generics implementation and represents an important advantage over templates, which are limited to use within the C++ language.

# Debugging

If you've ever worked with templates, you know that debugging templates is almost impossible. This is true of any environment where there's preprocessing of the code. This is one area where generics offer a significant productivity advantage over templates. Generics are essentially treated like first-class citizens within the IDE's debugging environment.

# Mix and Match Nirvana

C++ programmers really aren't limited to an all or nothing decision. Generics are available to C++ programmers as part of the .NET Framework and, as such, you really have the opportunity to leverage any mix of templates and generics that you deem appropriate. In fact, Chapter 12, "Using Generics with C++," discusses how you can use generics with C++. To me, this makes most of the discussions of pros and cons moot.

## Summary

The chapter had a two-fold purpose. One goal was to provide a clear delineation between templates and generics, explaining the main areas where these two technologies diverge. Along these lines, time was devoted to explaining the side effects of the compile-time and run-time models employed by templates and generics, respectively. The other goal here was to expose those unfamiliar with templates to some of the features that are supported exclusively by templates. This background should round out your overall generics perspective and allow you to see some of what's available to you should you decide to step into the world of templates. Ultimately, the overriding theme here should be that templates and generics share a common heritage with diverging approaches, each with its own strengths and weaknesses.

# 4

# Generic Classes

Many developers will view themselves primarily as consumers of generics. However, as you get more comfortable with generics, you're likely to find yourself introducing your own generic classes and frameworks. Before you can make that leap, though, you'll need to get comfortable with all the syntactic mutations that come along with creating your own generic classes. The goal of this chapter, then, is to dig into all of the details associated with building generic classes, explaining how generics extend the existing rules for defining and consuming classes. Fortunately, as you move through this chapter, you'll notice that the syntax rules for defining generic classes follow many of the same patterns you've already grown accustomed to with non-generic types. So, although there are certainly plenty of new generic concepts you'll need to absorb, you're likely to find it quite easy to make the transition to writing your own generic types.

## Parameterizing Types

In a very general sense, a generic class is really just a class that accepts parameters. As such, a generic class really ends up representing more of an abstract blueprint for a type that will, ultimately, be used in the construction of one or more specific types at run-time. This is one area where, I believe, the C++ term *templates* actually provides developers with a better conceptual model. This term conjures up a clearer metaphor for how the type parameters of a generic class serve as placeholders that get replaced by actual data types when a generic class is constructed. Of course, as you might expect, this same term also brings with it some conceptual inaccuracies that don't precisely match generics.

The idea of parameterizing your classes shouldn't seem all that foreign. In reality, the mindset behind parameterizing a class is not all that different than the rationale you would use for parameterizing a method in one of your existing classes. The goals in both scenarios are conceptually very similar. For example, suppose you had the following method in one of your classes that was used to locate all retired employees that had an age that was greater than or equal to the passed-in parameter (minAge):

[VB code]

```
Public Function LookupRetiredEmployees(ByVal minAge As Integer) As IList
    Dim retVal As New ArrayList
    For Each emp As Employee In masterEmployeeCollection
        If ((emp.Age >= minAge) And (emp.Status = EmpStatus.Retired)) Then
            retVal.Add(emp)
        End If
    Next
    Return retVal
End Function
```

[C# code]

```
public IList LookupRetiredEmployees(int minAge) {
    IList retVal = new ArrayList();
    foreach (Employee emp in masterEmployeeCollection) {
        if ((emp.Age >= minAge) && (emp.Status == EmpStatus.Retired))
            retVal.Add(emp);
    }
    return retVal;
    }
}
```

Now, at some point, you happen to identify a handful of additional methods that are providing similar functionality. Each of these methods only varies based on the status (Retired, Active, and so on) of the employees being processed. This represents an obvious opportunity to refactor through parameterization. By adding status as a parameter to this method, you can make it much more versatile and eliminate the need for all the separate implementations. This is something you've likely done. It's a simple, common flavor of refactoring that happens every day.

So, with this example in mind, you can imagine applying this same mentality to your classes. Classes, like methods, can now be viewed as being further generalized through the use of type parameters. To better grasp this concept, let's go ahead and build a non-generic class that will be your candidate for further generalization:

[VB code]

```
Public Class CustomerStack
    Private _items() As Customer
    Private _count As Integer

    Public Sub Push(item as Customer)
        ...
    End Sub

    Public Function Pop() As Customer
        ...
    End Function
End Class
```

[C# code]

```
public class CustomerStack {
    private Customer[] _items;
    private int _count;

    public void Push(Customer item) {...}
    public Customer Pop() {...}
}
```

This is the classic implementation of a type-safe stack that has been created to contain collections of `Customers`. There's nothing spectacular about it. But, as should be apparent by now, this class is the perfect candidate to be refactored with generics. To make your stack generic, you simply need to add a type parameter (`T` in this example) to your type and replace all of your references to the `Customer` with the name of your generic type parameter. The result would appear as follows:

```
[VB code]
Public Class Stack(Of T)
    Private _items() As T
    Private _count As Integer

    Public Sub Push(item As T)
        ...
    End Sub

    Public Function Pop() As T
        ...
    End Function
End Class
```

```
[C# code]
public class Stack<T> {
    private T[] _items;
    private int _count;

    public void Push(T item) {...}
    public T Pop() {...}
}
```

Pretty simple. It's really not all that different than adding a parameter to a method. It's as if generics have just allowed you to widen the scope of what your classes can parameterize.

## Type Parameters

By now, you should be comfortable with the idea of type parameters and how they serve as a type place-holder for the type arguments that will be supplied when your generic class is constructed. Now let's look at what, precisely, can appear in a type parameter list for a generic class.

First, let's start with the names that can be assigned to type parameters. The rules for naming a type parameter are similar to the rules used when defining any identifier. That said, there are guidelines that you should follow in the naming of your type parameters to improve the readability and maintainability of your generic class. These guidelines, and others, are discussed in Chapter 10, "Generics Guidelines."

A generic class may also accept multiple type parameters. These parameters are provided as a delimited list of identifiers:

```
[VB code]
Public Class Stack(Of T, U, V)
```

```
[C# code]
public class Stack<T, U, V>
```

As you might suspect, each type parameter name must be unique within the parameter list as well as within the scope of the class. You cannot, for example, have a type parameter T along with a field that is also named T. You are also prevented from having a type parameter and the class that accepts that parameter share the same name. Fortunately, the names you're likely to use for type parameters and classes will rarely cause collisions.

In terms of scope, a type parameter can only be referenced within the scope of the generic class that declared it. So, if you have a child generic class B that descends from generic class A, class B will not be able to reference any type parameters that were declared as part of class A.

The list of type parameters may also contain constraints that are used to further qualify what type arguments can be supplied of a given type parameter. Chapter 7, "Generic Constraints," will look into the relevance and application of constraints in more detail.

## Overloaded Types

The .NET implementation of generics allows programmers to create overloaded types. This means that types, like methods, can be overloaded based on their type parameter signature. Consider the declarations of the following types:

```
[VB code]
Public Class MyType
    ...
End Class

Public Class MyType(Of T)
    ...
End Class

Public Class MyType(Of T, U)
    ...
End Class
```

```
[C# Code]
public class MyType {
}

public class MyType<T> {
    ...
}

public class MyType<T, U> {
    ...
}
```

Three types are declared here and they all have the same name and different type parameter lists. At first glance, this may seem invalid. However, if you look at it from an overloading perspective, you can see how the compiler would treat each of these three types as being unique. This can introduce some level of confusion for clients, and this is certainly something you'll want to factor in as you consider building your own generic types. That said, this is still a very powerful concept that, when leveraged correctly, can enrich the power of your generic types.

Notice here that you have `MyBaseClass`, which accepts a single type parameter. Then, you subclass `MyBaseClass` with `MySubClass`, which accepts two type parameters. The key bit of syntax to notice here is that one of the type parameters used in the declaration of `MySubClass` was also referenced in the declaration of the parent class, `MyBaseClass`.

Although this example simply passed the type parameters from the subclass to the base class, you can also use type arguments when inheriting from another class or implementing a generic interface. In this case, your generic class declarations could appear as follows:

```
[VB code]
Public Class MyBaseClass(Of U)
    ...
End Class

Public Class MySubClass(Of T)
    Inherits MyBaseClass(Of Integer)
    ...
End Class
```

```
[C# code]
public class MyBaseClass<U> {
}

public class MySubClass<T> : MyBaseClass<int> {
}
```

The subclass has been altered here and now only accepts a single type parameter. And, in place of the type parameter U that was being passed to `MyBaseClass`, you now pass the type argument `Integer`. After looking at these two examples, it should be clear that your classes can subclass another class using both open and constructed types (and some variations in between). It's probably obvious at this stage, but I should point out that your generic classes can also subclass non-generic, closed base classes as well.

Now that you know what works, let's take a quick look at some of the combinations of inheritance patterns that will not work. Suppose you have a closed type that inherits from a generic class:

```
[VB code]
Public Class MyBaseClass(Of T, U)
End Class

Public Class MySubClass1
    Inherits MyBaseClass(Of T, U)
End Class

Public Class MySubClass2
    Inherits MyBaseClass(Of Int32, String)
End Class
```

```
[C# code]
public class MyBaseClass<T, U> { }

public class MySubClass1 : MyBaseClass<T, U> { }

public class MySubClass2 : MyBaseClass<int, string> { }
```

In this example, you have two closed types that inherit from a generic class. MySubClass1 attempts to inherit using an open type and MySubClass2 inherits as a constructed type. When you attempt to compile this code, you're going to notice that MySubClass1 will generate an error. The compiler has no point of reference that allows it to resolve the types of T and U. As a constructed type, MySubClass1 doesn't accept any type parameters and, therefore, has no parameters that can be used because it inherits from MyBaseClass<T, U>. MySubClass2 doesn't accept type parameters either, but it still compiles because it uses type arguments and forms a constructed type as part of its inheritance declaration.

There's one more inheritance scenario that's worth discussing here. Let's look at an example where you use a constructed type as a type argument in the declaration of your inherited class:

```
[VB code]
Imports System.Collections.Generic

Public Class MyBaseClass(Of T, U)
End Class

Public Class MySubClass1(Of T)
    Inherits MyBaseClass(Of List(Of T), T)
End Class

Public Class MySubClass2(Of T)
    Inherits MyBaseClass(Of List(Of T), Stack(Of T))
End Class
```

```
[C# code]
using System.Collections.Generic;

public class MyBaseClass<T, U> { }

public class MySubClass1<T> : MyBaseClass<List<T>, T> { }

public class MySubClass2<T> : MyBaseClass<List<T>, Stack<T>> { }
```

If you look at this example closely, you'll discover that it's really just a variation on one of the earlier examples of inheritance. The key difference here is that a mixture of constructed types and type parameters are used where the constructed types end up leveraging the type parameter from the subclass. The goal here is just to get you comfortable with the possibilities and to get you to view a constructed type like any other type argument you might pass when inheriting from a generic class.

Finally, it's worth noting that a generic class cannot use one of its type parameters as its inherited type. It must descend from an existing closed or open type. For example, the following would not be legal:

```
[VB code]
Public Class MyType(Of T)
    Inherits Of T
    ...
End Class
```

```
[C# code]
public class MyType<T> : T {
    ...
}
```

At this stage, after looking at all these examples, you should have a much better idea for how the mechanics of generic inheritance work. The rules that govern inheritance are fairly logical and don't really fall outside what you might expect. The main idea to take away here is that you can use both type parameters and type arguments as parameters when subclassing a generic class.

## Protected Members

Any discussion of inheritance would be incomplete without also examining the accessibility of protected members. First, I should make it clear that all the rules that govern access to protected members are unchanged for closed types. Things get a bit more interesting when you look at protected members that appear within a generic class. These members are accessible too. In fact, they are accessible in some ways you might not expect.

Here's an example that declares a base class with a protected, generic field that will then be referenced in a descendant class:

```
[VB code]
Public Class MyBaseClass(Of T)
    Protected _var1 As T

    Public Sub New(ByVal var1 As T)
        Me._var1 = var1
    End Sub
End Class

Public Class MySubClass(Of T, U)
    Inherits MyBaseClass(Of T)
    Private _var2 As U

    Public Sub New(ByVal var1 As T, ByVal var2 As U)
        MyBase.New(var1)
        Me._var2 = var2
    End Sub

    Private Sub Foo1()
        Dim localVar as T = Me._var1
    End Sub

    Private Sub Foo2()
        Dim sub1 As New MySubClass(Of Integer, String)(1, "12")
        Dim val1 As Integer = sub1._var1
        Dim sub2 As New MySubClass(Of Double, Double)(1.0, 5.8)
        Dim val2 As Double = sub2._var1
    End Sub
End Class

[C# code]
using System;

public class MyBaseClass<T> {
    protected T _var1;

    public MyBaseClass(T var1) {
```

```
            this._var1 = _var1;
        }
    }

public class MySubClass<T, U> : MyBaseClass<T> {
    private U _var2;

    public MySubClass(T var1, U var2) : base(var1) {
        this._var2 = var2;
    }

    private void Foo1() {
        T localVar = this._var1;
    }

    private void Foo2() {
        MySubClass<int, String> sub1 = new MySubClass<int, String>(1, "12");
        int val1 = sub1._var1;
        MySubClass<Double, Double> sub2 = new MySubClass<Double, Double>(1.0, 5.8);
        Double val2 = sub2._var1;
    }
}
```

This example actually ends up illustrating two key points. It includes a protected field in the base class, var1, that is then accessed by the subclass. The method Foo1() accesses var1 successfully, much like it would any other inherited, protected data member. The method Foo2() is the more interesting example. It constructs two separate instances of MySubClass and, because it's in the scope of the descendant class, it is able to access the protected member var1 via these constructed types.

# Fields

The fields of a generic class follow all the same syntax rules that are applied to non-generic fields. The primary incremental change here is the ability to reference type parameters in the declaration of your class's fields. Here's an example where this is applied:

```
[VB code]
Public Class MyType(Of T, U)
    Private _myFirstDataMember As T
    Private _mySecondDataMember As U
    Public Sub New(ByVal val1 As T, ByVal val2 As U)
        Me._myFirstDataMember = val1
        Me._mySecondDataMember = val2
    End Sub

    Public Function GetFirstDataMember() As T
        Return Me._myFirstDataMember
    End Function

    Public Function GetSecondDataMember() As U
        Return Me._mySecondDataMember
```

```
            End Function
    End Class

    Public Class MyApp
        Shared Sub Main()
            Dim testType As New MyType(Of String, String)("val1", "Val2")
            Console.WriteLine(testType.GetFirstDataMember())
            Console.WriteLine(testType.GetSecondDataMember())
        End Sub
    End Class
```

```
    [C# code]
    using System;

    class MyType<T, U> {
        private T _myFirstDataMember;
        private U _mySecondDataMember;

        public MyType(T val1, U val2) {
            this._myFirstDataMember = val1;
            this._mySecondDataMember = val2;
        }

        public T GetFirstDataMember() {
            return this._myFirstDataMember;
        }

        public U GetSecondDataMember() {
            return this._mySecondDataMember;
        }
    }

    class MyApp {
        static void main(String[] args) {
            MyType<string, string> testType =
                        new MyType<string, string>("Val1", "Val2");
            Console.WriteLine(testType.GetFirstDataMember());
            Console.WriteLine(testType.GetSecondDataMember());
        }
    }
```

As you can see, the generic class is able to create a pair of fields that reference the type parameters that are part of the class declaration. In fact, the type of any field declared in your generic class can reference any type parameter that is passed into your class. You'll also notice that the constructor initializes these fields using the same syntax you would use for any non-generic field.

## Static Fields

Although type parameters can be used in the place of most types in a class, they cannot be applied to any static field. In fact, the behavior of static fields does not change within a generic class. Consider the following implementation of an object cache:

[VB code]

```vb
Imports System.Collections.Generic

Public Class MyCache(Of K, V)
    Private Shared _objectCache As New Dictionary(Of K, V)

    Public Sub New()
    End Sub

    Public Function FindValueInDB(ByVal key As K) As V
        'findValue (not shown) would lookup the key in
        'a repository, add it to our cache, and return the value
    End Function

    Public Function LookupValue(ByVal key As K) As V
        Dim retVal As V
        If (_objectCache.ContainsKey(key) = True) Then
            _objectCache.TryGetValue(key, retVal)
        Else
            retVal = FindValueInDB(key)
        End If
        Return retVal
    End Function
End Class

Public Class MyApp
    Public Shared Sub Main()
        Dim cache1 As New MyCache(Of String, String)()
        Dim val1 As String = cache1.LookupValue("key1")

        Dim cache2 As New MyCache(Of String, String)()
        Dim val2 As Integer = cache2.LookupValue("key1")
    End Sub
End Class
```

[C# code]

```csharp
using System.Collections.Generic;

class MyCache<K, V> {
    private static Dictionary<K, V> _objectCache;

    public MyCache() {
        MyCache<K, V>._objectCache = new Dictionary<K, V>();
    }

    private V findValueInDB(K key) {
        // findValue (not shown) would lookup the key in
        // a repository, add it to our cache, and return the value
        return default(V);
    }

    public V lookupValue(K key) {
        V retVal;
        if (_objectCache.ContainsKey(key) == true) {
            _objectCache.TryGetValue(key, out retVal);
        } else {
```

```
            // findValue (not shown) would lookup the key in
            // a repository, add it to our cache, and return the value
            retVal = findValueInDB(key);
        }
        return retVal;
    }
}

class MyApp {
    public static void main(String[] args) {
        MyCache<string, string> cache1 = new MyCache<string, string>();
        string val1 = cache1.lookupValue("key1");

        MyCache<string, int> cache2 = new MyCache<string, int>();
        int val2 = cache2.lookupValue("key1");
    }
}
```

This example defines a generic class, MyCache, that employs a static field to hold a set of keys and their corresponding values. It represents a simple wrapper for the generic Dictionary class, adding a single lookupValue method. Each time this method is called, it will determine if the provided key already exists in the cache. If the key is found, the corresponding value will be returned. If the key is not found, the code class will look it up in a database, place it in the cache, and return it to the client.

The goal here was to construct a simple cache that could make this added lookup capability available to a wide variety for data types. You could, for example, leverage this class to hold a cache strings and turn around and reuse it, as I did here, to manage a *separate* cache of integers. And, in that regard, it delivers what I had intended. The problem comes in when two constructed types use the same type arguments.

In these instances, your constructed types actually end up sharing more than their implementation — they also share their static fields. So, although it seemed as though your two constructed types represented unique instances, they did not. They both shared a single instance from the static objectCache field.

You can only imagine what this does to your cache. If you declare two constructed types with matching type arguments and you want them treated entirely separately, it won't be possible. The static cache being maintained by the class will end up being shared by these two instances.

In general, this aspect of static fields shouldn't be viewed as a limitation. It's mostly significant and worth discussing because the behavior may not match what you're expecting. It could also be the source of a few difficult-to-locate bugs. If nothing else, this is at least something you'll want to keep in mind whenever you opt to include static data in one of your generic classes.

## Constructed Fields

It should go without saying that constructed generic types can also be used throughout the implementation of your generic classes. Specifically, you are allowed to have fields that are open or closed constructed types. Here's a quick look at a simple example:

```
[VB code]
Imports System.Collections.Generic

Public Class MyType(Of T)
```

```
        Private _myList As New List(Of T)
        Private _myStrings As New List(Of String)

        Public Function GetItem(ByVal param1 As List(Of Integer)) As T
            Dim localVar As New List(Of T)
            Return _myList(0)
        End Function
End Class
```

```
[C# code]
using System.Collections.Generic;

class MyType<T> {
    private List<T> _myList;
    private List<string> _myStrings;

    public T getItem(List<int> param1) {
        List<T> localVar;
        return _myList[0];
    }
}
```

You'll notice the class is littered with open and closed constructed types. After you're familiar with generics, these constructed types will start to look like any other data type you might reference in your class. The syntax variations for generics seem to just fade into the background.

# Methods

Methods represent your primary point of contact with clients. As such, their flexibility, expressiveness, and general type safety should be of a great deal of importance to you. You want to make your client's life as simple as possible and, because you may likely be both the producer and the consumer of these methods, you're also likely to be especially motivated to build a good interface.

With generics, you actually have the opportunity to build a set of interfaces that are likely to last more than a few days. If you think about it, generics allow you to be 100% vague about types that are supported by your interfaces. It's as if every parameter and every return type is of the type object. All that, and you still get a type-safe interface.

Okay, that may be a bit extreme. But, if you consider that your type parameters can essentially appear anywhere within the signature of a method, it doesn't seem like that big of a stretch. At the same time, while you feel this extra degree of freedom in defining your interface, the consumers of your interface get to work with specific types without dealing with casting or conversion.

> For this chapter, my focus is exclusively on generic classes. And, for that reason, the discussion of methods is intentionally constrained to how type parameters influence the methods of your class. Chapter 5, "Generic Methods," looks at generic methods that can exist entirely outside the scope of a generic class and have their own set of dynamics.

Let's take a quick look at a sample class that illustrates a few variations on how you might go about using type parameters in the interface of your generic class:

```vb
[VB code]
Class MyType(Of V)
End Class

MustInherit Class MyShape(Of T, U)
    Public Sub New()
    End Sub

    MustOverride Sub Draw()
    MustOverride Function GetIndexes() As T()

    Overridable Function
            AddValue(ByVal index As T, ByVal value As MyType(Of U)) As Boolean
        ...
    End Function

    Overridable Function GetValue(ByVal index As T) As MyType(Of U)
        ...
    End Function
End Class
```

```csharp
[C# code]
class MyType<V> {}

abstract class MyShape<T, U> {
    public MyShape() {}

    public abstract void draw();
    public abstract T[] GetIndexes();

    public virtual bool AddValue(T index, MyType<U> value) {

        ...
    }

    public virtual MyType<U> GetValue(T index) {
        ...
    }
}
```

In this class you define a set of methods, both abstract and virtual, that leverage the type parameters used in the declaration of your generic class. For both the abstract and virtual methods, you are free to include type parameters and open types wherever you would place traditional types. As you can see, very few limitations are imposed on the methods of your class. And, fortunately, most of the concepts you've become accustomed to with non-generic methods will still apply to your methods.

## Overloading Methods

Whenever you define a method — especially an overloaded method — you need to understand how the compiler will evaluate the signature of that method. Specifically, you need to have a firm grasp on how the compiler evaluates the uniqueness of a given generic method. For example, consider how the compiler will evaluate the following two methods:

```
[VB code]
Class MyType(Of T)
    Public Function Foo() As Boolean
    End Function

    Public Function Foo() As T
    End Function
End Class
```

```
[C# code]
class MyType<T> {
    public bool Foo() { ... }
    public T Foo() { ... }
}
```

While these two methods would seem to have different signatures, the compiler has no means by which it can uniquely identify these two methods because they only differ by their return types — one of which is a type parameter. This is not especially surprising because non-generic methods also fail when they only differ by their return types. Here's a less obvious example:

```
[VB code]
Class MyType(Of T)
    Public Function Foo(ByVal myString As String) As Boolean
    End Function

    Public Function Foo(ByVal myValue As T) As Boolean
    End Function
End Class
```

```
[C# code]
class MyType<T> {
    public bool Foo(String myString) {  }
    public bool Foo(T myValue) {  }
}
```

On the surface, it would seem as though the compiler would not be able to distinguish between these two methods. However, this is one where C# and VB vary in their implementations. The C# generics specification only requires a method's signature to be unique prior to the class's instantiation. So, given these constraints, the C# compiler is able to view these two methods as being unique. VB, on the other hand, isn't so kind. It continues to throw an error and complain about the uniqueness of the method's signature.

Although the C# language may support this syntax, it still creates a situation that could cause some level of confusion for clients of your method. As such, relying on this mechanism may not be a good idea — especially given the overriding generic theme of providing clear, expressive interfaces for your types.

The name you assign to your type parameters can also create some confusion when you are trying to evaluate the signature of a method. Typically, you look at the name of a type to determine if two types match. For example, in the next snippet of code you have two `Integer` parameters in the signature of two separate methods:

```vb
[VB code]
Class MyType(Of T)
    Public Sub Foo(val1 As Integer, val2 As Integer)
    End Sub

    Public Sub Foo(val1 As Integer, val2 As Integer)
    End Sub
End Class
```

```csharp
[C# code]
class MyType<T> {
    public void Foo(int val1, int val2) { ... };
    public void Foo(int val1, int val2) { ... };
}
```

To most developers going to be, it's clear that these two methods are going to collide and throw a compile-time error. Now, let's take that same concept and use type parameters instead of native types:

```vb
[VB code]
Class MyType(Of T, U, V)
    Public Sub Foo(ByVal val1 As T, ByVal val2 As V)
    End Sub

    Public Sub Foo(ByVal val1 As U, ByVal val2 As V)
    End Sub
End Class
```

```csharp
[C# code]
class MyType<T, U, V> {
    public void Foo(T val1, V val2) { ... }
    public void Foo(U val1, V val2) { ... }
}
```

These two methods, based on type parameter names alone, would appear to have unique signatures. There are certainly scenarios where, with different permutations of type arguments, these signatures would be deemed unique. At the same time, it's also true that there could be combinations of type arguments that could create collisions.

It turns out the VB and C# take different approaches to verifying the uniqueness of these signatures. VB says if there can be at least one combination of type arguments that *could* cause these methods to be duplicates, then the compiler will throw an error. This will be true even if there are no constructed types in your code that create a collision. C#, on the other hand, takes the more optimistic approach. It allows this class to compile because there are combinations of type arguments that could be valid.

## *Overriding Methods*

Now that you have a better idea of how type parameters influence the signature of methods, you need to consider how type parameters are applied when you override methods in a generic class. First, it's important to point out that, if your generic class descends from a closed type, you can still override the parent methods just as you would in any non-generic class.

Where this gets more interesting is when your base class is generic class (open or constructed type). For this scenario, you can still override methods from your generic base class. However, there are some nuances you must keep in mind. Let's start by looking at the common, simple case:

```vb
[VB code]
Public Class MyBaseClass(Of T)
        Overridable Sub Foo(ByVal val As T)
            Console.WriteLine("In BaseClass")
        End Sub
    End Class

    Public Class MySubClass1(Of T, U)
        Inherits MyBaseClass(Of T)

        Overrides Sub Foo(ByVal val As T)
            Console.WriteLine("In SubClass")
        End Sub
    End Class

    Public Class MySubClass2(Of T, U)
        Inherits MyBaseClass(Of Integer)

        Overrides Sub Foo(ByVal val As T)
            Console.WriteLine("In SubClass")
        End Sub
End Class
```

```csharp
[C# code]
public class MyBaseClass<T> {
    public virtual void Foo(T val) { }
}

public class MySubClass1<T, U> : MyBaseClass<T> {
    public override void Foo(T val) { }
}

public class MySubClass2<T, U> : MyBaseClass<int> {
    public override void Foo(T val) { }
}
```

This example declares a generic base class (MyBaseClass) that includes one overridable method, Foo. It then implements two generic subclasses that both override the Foo method. On the surface, there doesn't appear to be any issues. Both of these classes provide identical signatures for the method. So, why does MySubClass2 fail to compile? Well, if you look more closely, you'll notice that MySubClass2 uses a constructed type in its inheritance declaration. Meanwhile, MySubClass1 uses an open type for its declaration. This one point of difference is crucial. With MySubClass1, the type parameter T used inheritance declaration and the overridden method can be guaranteed to match. That doesn't hold true for MySubClass2. The type of T can, and likely will, differ from the integer type, which is what is provided to the parent's T type parameter. As you might expect, the compiler is going to detect this and throw an error during the compilation of MySubClass2.

The theme here is that the type parameters and type arguments supplied to an inherited generic class play a significant role in defining what's legal when overriding a method. As type parameters are referenced in overridable methods of the parent class, those type parameters must be resolvable to the same type of the overriding base class. Here's one more example to solidify this point:

```
[VB code]
Public Class MyBaseClass(Of T, U)
    Overridable Sub Foo(ByVal val1 As T, ByVal val2 As U)
        Console.WriteLine("In BaseClass")
    End Sub
End Class

Public Class MySubClass1(Of T, U, V)
    Inherits MyBaseClass(Of T, V)

    Overrides Sub Foo(ByVal val1 As T, ByVal val2 As U)
        Console.WriteLine("In SubClass")
    End Sub
End Class
```

```
[C# code]
public class MyBaseClass<T, U> {
    public virtual void Foo(T val1, U val2) { }
}

public class MySubClass1<T, U, V> : MyBaseClass<T, V> {
    public override void Foo(T val2, U val2) { }
}
```

Once again, the signatures of the methods seem to match. And, once again, the compiler isn't happy. The mismatch here is that the subclass supplies T and V as type arguments to the parent's corresponding T and U type parameters. This means that the U type parameter in the base class actually maps to the V type parameter in the subclass. So, when you reference the T and U parameters in the overriding method, the U parameter actually represents V and causes a compile error.

The rules for overriding in generic classes aren't much more involved than that. You won't find yourself getting tripped up by this too often. And, when you do, the compiler does a reasonable job detecting and reporting errors in this scenario.

## Arrays of Type Parameters

The methods within your generic class may also include arrays of type parameters. This gives you the ability to pass type-safe arrays to your methods. This syntax is as follows:

```
[VB code]
Class MyType(Of T)
    Shared Sub Foo(ByVal params As T())
    End Sub
End Class

Public Class MyTest
    Public Shared Sub Test()
```

```
            MyType(Of Integer).Foo(New Integer() {123, 321})
            MyType(Of String).Foo(New String() {"TEST1", "TEST2", "TEST3"})
      End Sub
End Class
```

```
[C# code]
public class MyType<T> {
    public static void Foo(T[] parms) { }
}
public class MyTest {
    public static void Test() {
        MyType<int>.Foo(new int[] { 123, 321 });
        MyType<string>.Foo(new string[] { "TEST1", "TEST2", "TEST3" });
    }
}
```

This works exactly as you might expect. In fact, the syntax matches that of any other array you may pass to a method.

# Operator Overloading

For some reason, operator overloading seems particularly interesting when it comes to generics. Here you have this new generic class and now you're allowed to define operations on that class without any awareness of the types it will be managing. Not sure why, but that's just plain cool to me. It's as if you can define all these semantics of your generic types at an all new level of abstraction.

The other thing to be excited about here is the enhanced operator overloading support in Visual Studio 2005. Specifically, Visual Basic finally has *real* support for operator overloading that allows Visual Basic to define operators that are more in line with the traditional model that has been historically provided as part of other languages.

All that said, the important part here is to understand the syntax rules that govern the definition and invocation of overloaded operators within generic classes.

```
[VB code]
Public Class MyType(Of T)
    Public Shared Operator +(ByVal op As MyType(Of T)) As MyType(Of T)
        Console.WriteLine("In unary ++ operator")
        Return New MyType(Of T)()
    End Sub
End Class
```

```
[C# code]
using System;

public class MyType<T> {
    public static MyType<T> operator ++(MyType<T> op) {
        Console.WriteLine("In ++ operator");
        return new MyType<T>();
    }
}
```

This example implements the + unary operator. You can see here that this example simply substitutes the generic open type, MyType, in the appropriate locations in the signature of the operator method. This is a requirement for your overloaded generic operators. In fact, all unary operations must take one parameter of the instance type.

Any time there's a discussion of operator overloading, it must also be accompanied by discussion of type conversion. It makes sense. After all, operator overloading is what enables you to provide specific conversion operators that determine how one type can be converted to another. For example, if you cast MyType1 to MyType2, an overloaded operator could be used to define the behavior of this conversion (assuming you want this to be a valid conversion).

In the world of generics, you can't really define conversion from one concrete type to another. There's nothing concrete about your types at all. That's the whole point. The syntax of generics, however, does provide you with the mechanisms you'll need to express these conversions in a generic fashion. Here's a quick example of an overloaded operator that provides type conversion:

```
[VB code]
Public Class MyType(Of T)
    Public Shared Widening Operator CType(ByVal source As MyType(Of T)) _
        As MyType(Of String)

        Console.WriteLine("In unary string conversion operator")
        Return New MyType(Of T)()
    End Sub
End Class
```

```
[C# code]
public class MyType<T> {
    public static implicit operator MyType<String>(MyType<T> source) {
        Console.WriteLine("In unary string conversion operator");
        return new MyType<String>();
    }
}
```

This example provides an operator that will convert instances of MyType to constructed type of MyType(Of String). This can be fairly handy and provides an excellent alternative to providing operator overloads for every possible source type.

There are a few gotchas you'll want to plant in your memory when providing conversion operators. First, you cannot perform conversions if your source and target conversion types are in the same object hierarchy. Also, it's important to note that your conversion operators may end up overloading a conversion operator that is already defined. If this turns out to be the case, your overloaded conversion operator will never end up getting called.

# Nested Classes

Generic classes do not fundamentally change the nature of nested classes. Of course, by definition, any class that's nested inside a generic class is also deemed "generic" in that the overall constructed type cannot be created without someone providing type parameters.

That said, generics also extend the functionality of existing nested classes, allowing them to have full access to the type parameters of their *outer* class. In addition, you also have the option of making your nested classes be generic. Following is an example where a nested class references the type parameters of its outer class:

```
[VB code]
Imports System.Collections.Generic

Public Class OuterClass(Of T, U)
    Public var1 As New Dictionary(Of T, U)

    Public Class InnerClass
        Private var1 As T
        Private var2 As New List(Of U)
    End Class
End Class
```

```
[C# code]
using System.Collections.Generic;

public class OuterClass<T, U> {
    public Dictionary<T, U> var1;

    public class InnerClass {
        private T var1;
        private List<U> var2;
    }
}
```

As you can see, the declaration of your inner class matches that of any other nested class. However, within your inner class, you'll notice that the example declares a few data members that use the type parameters from your outer class. In fact, the example declares a number of different constructed types from the pool of type parameters that were supplied to your generic class.

This gets a little more interesting when you make your inner class accept its own type parameters. Here's an example that does just that:

```
[VB code]
Imports System.Collections.Generic

Public Class OuterClass(Of T, U, V)

    Public Class InnerClass(Of T, V)
        Private var1 As New Dictionary(Of T, V)
        Private var2 As U
    End Class
End Class
```

```
[C# code]
using System.Collections.Generic;

public class OuterClass<T, U, V> {
    public class InnerClass<T, V> {
        private Dictionary<T, V> var1;
```

```
        private U var2;
    }
}
```

The outer class for this example accepts three type parameters: T, U, and V. Your inner class also accepts type parameters named T and V. So, the question is, what will happen with the var1 data member that you've declared in your inner class? Will it share the same types that are supplied to the outer class for the T and V type parameters? Nope. Once you used these type parameter names for your inner class, you effectively lost all ability to reference the type parameters from your outer class. They are inaccessible. Meanwhile, the other data member in your inner class, var2, is able to successfully reference the U type parameter from the outer class. This is possible because U was not included in the type parameter list of the inner class.

This problem would mostly be chalked up to bad habits. As a rule of thumb, the creator of an inner class should never reuse the type parameter names of its outer class as part of its declaration. Otherwise, you will be forever and unnecessarily prevented from accessing the type parameters of your outer class. You don't want to live with that kind of guilt.

# Consuming Generic Classes

Okay, you've had a good long look at what goes into defining a generic class. Now, it's time to explore those rules that govern constructed types. First, it should be clear by now that a constructed type shares all the freedoms as any other type and can be placed in any syntactical context that would be used for non-generic types. Once you marry a type argument to the open type, they are conceptually "merged" to form a specific concrete type. The sooner you're comfortable with that notion, the sooner you'll begin to view constructed types on equal ground with Strings and Integers (actually, given my bias, I would tend to view them as generally superior to these types on the sheer merit of their constitution).

A number of variations exist on how you might declare a constructed type. The simplest variety is what is considered a closed constructed type. It's simple because the type arguments supplied are of simple, concrete types. Open constructed types use the type parameters from their surrounding generic class as part of their declaration. These two types are likely familiar by now. However, Chapter 1, "Generics 101," provides examples if you want a more detailed explanation.

In addition to accepting all the primitive types as type arguments, a constructed type can also be created using other constructed types as type arguments. For example:

```
[VB code]
Dim myGenericType1 As New MyType(Of List(Of Integer))
Dim myGenericType2 As New MyType2(Of Dictionary(Of Integer, String), String)
```

```
[C# code]
MyType1<List<int>> myGenericType1;
MyType2<Dictionary<int, string>, string> myGenericType2;
```

This fits with the theme that a constructed type is just like any other type and, as such, can behave like any other type argument. You also have the option of using type parameters in these declarations, which would simply make your declaration an open constructed type (because its type will be determined at run-time). It's also worth noting that these types can also be passed as arrays by applying the array modifier to these arguments.

# *Accessibility*

Whenever you look at introducing new syntax for types, you must also look at the rules that govern accessibility for these new types. Each time you declare a constructed type, the accessibility of that type's parameters must be taken into consideration. Here's a basic example that highlights how accessibility can influence a constructed type:

```
[VB code]
Public Class MyType(Of T)

End Class

Public Class AccessTest
    Private Class PrivateClass
    End Class

    Public Function GetMyType() As MyType(Of PrivateClass)
    End Function
End Class
```

```
[C# code]
public class MyType<T> {}

public class AccessTest {
    private class PrivateClass {}
    public MyType<PrivateClass> getMyType() { }
}
```

This example creates a closed class, `AccessTest`, which contains a nested class (`PrivateClass`) as well as a public method. You'll notice that this method actually returns a constructed type, `MyType`, which was constructed using `PrivateClass` as a type argument.

The problem with this implementation is that `PrivateClass`, which has private accessibility, is being used in the construction of the publicly accessible return type of the method `getMyType()`. As you might suspect, the compiler catches and throws an error when you attempt to compile this example. This same brand of error would also apply in situations where you attempt to use a protected type as a parameter to a publicly accessible constructed type.

The rule of thumb here is that the accessibility of any class's constructed types is constrained by the accessibility of the type arguments passed to that constructed type. Let's look at another example:

```
[VB code]
Public Class MyType(Of T)
End Class

Public Class AccessTest
    Public class PublicClass
    End Class
    Protected class ProtectedClass
    End Class
    Private class PrivateClass
    End Class

    Public Function Foo1() As MyType(Of ProtectedClass)
```

```
        End Function

        Protected Function Foo2 As MyType(Of ProtectedClass)
        End Function

        Protected Function Foo3 As MyType(Of PublicClass)
        End Function

        Private Function Foo4 As MyType(Of PrivateClass)
        End Function
End Class
```

```
  [C# code]
class MyType<T> {}
class AccessTest {
    public class PublicClass {}
    protected class ProtectedClass {}
    private class PrivateClass {}
    public MyType<ProtectedClass> Foo1() { }
    protected MyType<ProtectedClass> Foo2() { }
    protected MyType<PublicClass> Foo3() { }
    private MyType<PrivateClass> Foo4() { }
}
```

In this example, three classes are declared — PublicClass, ProtectedClass, and PrivateClass —
and they are passed as type arguments to construct return value types for four different methods. The
first method, Foo1(), passes a ProtectedClass to a constructed type with public accessibility, which,
as you might expect, yields a compile error. This publicly accessible method cannot return a constructed
type that has been constructed with a protected type. The remaining methods will all successfully compile because the accessibility of their type arguments do not "exceed" the accessibility of each method.

These scenarios seem pretty straightforward. However, there's one more variation that's worth exploring.
What happens in the instances where you have multiple type arguments being passed to your constructed
type, each with varying levels of accessibility? Consider the following example:

```
  [VB code]
Public Class AType(Of T, U)
End Class

Public Class MyType
    Public Class PublicClass
    End Class
    Protected Class ProtectedClass
    End Class
    Protected Friend Class ProtectedFriendClass
    End Class
    Private Class PrivateClass
    End Class

    Public Function Foo1() As AType(Of PublicClass, PublicClass)
    End Function
    Protected Function Foo2() As AType(Of ProtectedClass, ProtectedFriendClass)
    End Function
    Protected Friend Function Foo3() As AType(Of PublicClass, ProtectedFriendClass)
```

```vb
        End Function
        Friend Function Foo4() As AType(Of PublicClass, PublicClass)
        End Function
        Private Function Foo5() As AType(Of PublicClass, PrivateClass)
        End Function

        Public Function Foo6() As AType(Of ProtectedClass, PublicClass)
        End Function
        Protected Function Foo7() As AType(Of ProtectedClass, PrivateClass)
        End Function
        Protected Friend Function Foo8() As AType(Of ProtectedClass, PublicClass)
        End Function
    End Class
```

```csharp
[C# code]
class AType<T, U> {}
class MyType {
    public class PublicClass {}
    protected class ProtectedClass {}
    protected internal class ProtectedInternalClass {}
    private class PrivateClass {}

    public AType<PublicClass, PublicClass> Foo1() {}
    protected AType<ProtectedClass, ProtectedInternalClass> Foo2() {}
    protected internal AType<PublicClass, ProtectedInternalClass> Foo3() {}
    internal AType<PublicClass, PublicClass> Foo4() {}
    private AType<PublicClass, PrivateClass> Foo5() {}

    public AType<ProtectedClass, PublicClass> Foo6() {}
    protected AType<ProtectedClass, PrivateClass> Foo7() {}
    protected internal AType<ProtectedClass, PublicClass> Foo8() {}
}
```

For the most, there are no major surprises here. As you might expect, the "least" accessible type argument will determine the accessibility of each constructed type. Following this logic, you will find that the first five methods will all successfully compile. Method `Foo3()`, for example, is valid because both `protected` and `protected internal` type arguments conform to the accessibility of the method (which is `protected` in this case). The final three methods will all generate errors at compile time because each one violates these same accessibility rules. In reality, because private methods have no outside accessibility, they can be constructed with arguments that support every flavor of accessibility.

The following table provides a more complete breakdown of the accessibility rules that cover all the permutations of accessibility.

| VB Accessibly | C# Accessibility | Valid Type Arguments |
|---|---|---|
| Public | public | public |
| Protected | protected | protected, protected friend/internal, public |
| protected friend | protected internal | protected internal, public |

| VB Accessibly | C# Accessibility | Valid Type Arguments |
|---|---|---|
| Friend | internal | internal, protected friend/internal, public |
| Private | private | public, protected, protected friend/internal, friend/internal, private |

This list covers all the cases for methods declared within a class. However, these rules change somewhat if you declare your methods within the scope of an internal class. The following table calls out accessibility rules for an internal class.

| VB Accessibly | C# Accessibility | Valid Type Arguments |
|---|---|---|
| Public | public | public, protected friend/internal, friend/internal |
| Protected | protected | protected, protected friend/internal, friend/internal, public |
| protected friend | protected internal | public, protected, protected internal, internal |
| Friend | internal | friend/ internal, protected friend/internal, public |
| Private | private | public, protected, protected friend/internal, friend/internal, private |

# The Default Keyword

When you're dealing with the implementation of a generic class, you may come across situations where you'd like to assign or access default values for your type parameters. However, because the actual type of your type parameter is unknown at the point of implementation, you have no way of knowing what's a valid default value for any given type parameter. To address this need, the generics specification introduced a new "default" keyword. This keyword was needed to allow you to determine the default value for generic types.

The language specification identifies a set of rules for the default values that will be returned for specific types of type parameters. These rules are as follows:

1. If a type parameter is s reference type, it will always return a default value of `null`.

2. If a type parameter is one of the built-in types, the default value will be assigned to whatever default is already defined for that type.

3. If a type parameter is a struct type, the default value will be the predefined default value for each of the fields defined in that struct.

This mechanism is essential in the implementation of some class types. Here's a simple example that demonstrates one application of the default keyword:

```
[C# code]
using System.Collections.Generic;

public class MyCache<K, V> {
```

```
    private Dictionary<K, V> _cache;
    public V LookupItem(K key) {
        V retVal;
        if (_cache.ContainsKey(key) == true)
            _cache.TryGetValue(key, out retVal);
        else
            retVal = default(V);
        return retVal;
    }
}
```

This example provides the shell of the implementation of a cache. It includes a `LookupItem()` method that looks for a specific key in the cache and returns a default value if it's not found. This is a basic application of the default mechanism. You could also use this feature to initialize the values of type parameters in advance of using them.

> **You'll notice that I did not provide an example of how to use the default keyword with Visual Basic. That's because Visual Basic does not currently support the default keyword in this context. In VB, the closet equivalent to this concept would be to set an instance of a type parameter equal to `nothing`.**

# System.Nullable<T>

With the introduction of version 2.0 of the .NET Framework, developers are finally provided with a solution to the age-old problem of dealing with nullable types. The basic issue here is that not all data types provide a mechanism for determining if they have a "null" value. Clearly, with objects, there's a well-defined means of making this determination. However, with an `int` data type, there's no predefined value that could be used to determine if that int has been assigned a value. To resolve this, Visual Studio 2005 is introducing a new `Nullable` type that provides a uniform way of determining if a value is null.

Although nullable types are not exactly a generics concept, they are implemented using generics. A type is made nullable using the built-in `Nullable` generic class (which is in the `System` namespace). This generic class will be used to keep track of when its underlying type is assigned a value. Consider this example:

```
[VB code]
Public Class MyTest
    Public Shared Sub NullableTest(ByVal intVal1 As Nullable(Of Int32), _
                                   ByVal intVal2 As Int32)
        If (intVal1.HasValue() = True) Then
            Console.WriteLine(intVal1)
        Else
            Console.WriteLine("Value1 is NULL")
        End If

        If (intVal2 > 0) Then
            Console.WriteLine(intVal2)
        Else
```

```
                Console.WriteLine("Value2 is Null?")
            End If
    End Sub
End Class
```

```
[C# code]
using System;

public class MyTest {
    public static void NullableTest(Nullable<int> intVal1, int intVal2) {
        if (intVal1.HasValue == true)
            Console.WriteLine(intVal1);
        else
            Console.WriteLine("Value1 is NULL");

        if (intVal2 > 0)
            Console.WriteLine(intVal2);
        else
            Console.WriteLine("Value2 is Null?");
    }
}
```

This example declares a method that accepts two integer variables, one of which is nullable and one which is not. The body of this method then attempts to write out the value of each of these parameters to the console. Of course, you want your method to detect if either parameter has been actually assigned a value and only write that value out to the console. If it hasn't been assigned a value, you just dump a message indicating that no value exists. Simple enough.

Because the `intVal1` parameter was declared as a nullable type, you can easily detect if it is null by checking the `HasValue` property. Meanwhile, the `intVal2` parameter is never assigned a value, leaving you with no definitive means of determining if it's null. As a compromise, you could artificially decide that if it's greater than 0 it will be treated as non-null. However, that's an arbitrary rule you've defined in your code. Using the `Nullable` class gives you a universal, absolute definition for null that you can use throughout your code. It should be noted that the `Nullable` class only holds value types (int, double, and so on).

While the `Nullable<T>` type might look and behave like any other generic data container you'll find in the .NET framework, it is actually afforded special treatment by the CLR. As developers were initially trying out the `Nullable<T>` type, they discovered a few scenarios that yielded unexpected results. Consider the following example:

```
[VB code]
Dim intVal As New Nullable(Of Int32)
intVal = Nothing
Dim refVal As Object

refVal = intVal
If refVal Is Nothing Then
    Console.Out.WriteLine("Value is null")
End If
```

```
[C# code]
Nullable<int> intVal = null;
object refVal;

refVal = intVal;
if (refVal == null)
    Console.Out.WriteLine("Value is null");
```

This example declares a `Nullable<int>` instance before assigning that instance to `refVal`, which is an `object` data type. By making this assignment, you end up forcing your nullable `integer` type to be boxed. Now, if `Nullable<T>` were just another generic type, this boxing would have caused the null state of the value type to be lost during the boxing process. As you can imagine, this was not exactly the intended behavior.

To overcome this problem, the CLR was forced to make the nullable type a true runtime intrinsic. It was only at this level that runtime could provide behavior that would be more in line with what developers were expecting. So, as the CLR processes the un-boxing of the nullable types, it provides special handling to ensure that the null state of the value is not lost in translation.

By adding this capability, the CLR also added support for explicitly un-boxing a reference directly into a `Nullable<T>` type. The end result is a nullable type that is more directly supported by the CLR, which ultimately translates into a type that behaves much more intuitively.

> **C# provides an alternative syntax for declaring nullable types. By simply appending a ? to your type (`int?`) you will have the equivalent of `Nullable<int>`. This mechanism provides developers with a shorthand way of declaring nullable types. While the declaration is certainly shorter, this syntax could be seen as impacting the readability of your code. In the end, it's more a matter of preference.**

# Accessing Type Info

Now that you're actively building and consuming generic types, you might have an occasion when you'll want to access the specific type information for your generic types. Here's a simple example that dumps type information for a few generic classes:

```
[VB code]
Public Class OneParamType(Of T)
End Class

Public Class TwoParamType(Of T, U)
End Class

Public Class TypeDumper(Of T, U, V)
    Shared Sub DumpTypeInfo()
        Console.WriteLine(GetType(T))
        Console.WriteLine(GetType(U))
       Console.WriteLine(GetType(V))
        Console.WriteLine(GetType(OneParamType(Of String)))
        Console.WriteLine(GetType(OneParamType(Of T)))
        Console.WriteLine(GetType(TwoParamType(Of U, Integer)))
```

```
                Console.WriteLine(GetType(TwoParamType(Of T, V)))
        End Sub

        Public Sub ShowTypeInfo()
                TypeDumper(Of String, Integer, Double).DumpTypeInfo()
        End Sub
End Class
```

```
[C# code]
using System;

public class OneParamType<T> {}

public class TwoParamType<T, U> {}

public class TypeDumper<T, U, V> {
    public static void DumpTypeInfo() {
        Console.WriteLine(typeof(T));
        Console.WriteLine(typeof(U));
        Console.WriteLine(typeof(V));
        Console.WriteLine(typeof(OneParamType<String>));
        Console.WriteLine(typeof(OneParamType<T>));
        Console.WriteLine(typeof(TwoParamType<U, int>));
        Console.WriteLine(typeof(TwoParamType<T, V>));
    }

    public static void ShowTypeInfo() {
        TypeDumper<String, int, Double>.DumpTypeInfo();
    }
}
```

This example creates a `TypeDumper` class that accepts three type arguments and includes a
`DumpTypeInfo()` method that displays type information about each of these parameters in different contexts. Then, to see this method in action, the example includes a `ShowTypeInfo()` method that supplies
`string`, `int`, and `double` type arguments. The output of calling this method will appear as follows:

```
System.String
System.Int32
System.Double
OneParamType`1[System.String]
OneParamType`1[System.String]
TwoParamType`2[System.Int32, System.Int32]
TwoParamType`2[System.String, System.Double]
```

It's mostly what you'd expect. The one piece of information you might not have expected here is the
number that appears after `OneParamType` and `TwoParamType`. That number represents the "arity" of
the type, which corresponds to the number of type parameters that were used to construct the type.

# Indexers, Properties, and Events

For the most part, generics represent a graceful extension to the languages of the .NET platform. That
said, there are some areas of classes where generics cannot be applied. Specifically, generics cannot be
applied to the indexers, properties, or events that appear in your classes. Each of these members can

reference type parameters in their signature. However, they are not allowed to directly accept type parameters. That distinction may not be clear. Following is a quick example that will help clarify this point. Let's start with an example that would be considered valid:

```
[VB code]
Imports System.Collections.Generic

Public Delegate Sub PersonEvent(Of T)(ByVal sender As Object, ByVal args As T)

Public Class Person(Of T)
    Private _children As List(Of T)

    Public Sub New()
        Me._children = new List(Of String)()
    End Sub

    Public Property Children() As List(Of T)
        Get
            Return Me._children
        End Get
        Set(ByVal value As List(Of T))
            Me._children = value
        End Set
    End Property

    Default Property Item(ByVal index As Long) As T
        Get
            Return Me._children(index)
        End Get
        Set(ByVal value As T)
            Me._children(index) = value
        End Set
    End Property


    Event itemEvent As PersonEvent(Of T)
End Class
```

```
[C# code]
using System.Collections.Generic;

public delegate void PersonEvent<T>(object sender, T args);

public class Person<T> {
    private List<T> _children;

    public Person() {
        this._children = new List<String>();
    }

    public List<T> Children {
        get { return this._children; }
        set { this._children = value; }
```

```
        }

    public T this[int index] {
        get { return this._children[index]; }
        set { this._children[index] = value; }
    }

    event PersonEvent<T> itemEvent;
}
```

You'll notice that this example includes references to its type parameter T in the declaration of a property, an indexer, and an event. In all of these cases, however, these members are referencing a type parameter that was supplied to the class. The difference is that none of these members can directly accept their own type parameters. So, the following would *not* be considered legal:

```
[VB code]
Public Class MySampleClass

    Public Sub New()
    End Sub

    Public ReadOnly Property Children(Of T)() As String
        Get
            ...
        End Get
    End Property

    Default Property Item(Of T)(ByVal index As Long) As String
        Get
            ...
        End Get
        Set(ByVal value As String)
            ...
        End Set
    End Property

    Event(Of T) itemEvent As SampleEvent
End Class
```

```
[C# code]
using System.Collections.Generic;

public class MySampleClass {

    public MySampleClass() {}

    public String Children<T> {
        get { ... }
        set { ... }
    }

    public String this<T>[int index] {
        get { ... }
```

```
            set { ... }
    }

    Event<T> SampleEvent itemEvent;
}
```

This is an example where the property, indexer, and event all accept their own type arguments. None of these forms of declarations will be deemed acceptable. Fortunately, this same constraint is not applied to methods.

# Generic Structs

Classes and structs, for the most part, are synonymous. Essentially, whatever you can do with a class you can also do with a struct. Knowing this, you would be correct in assuming that all the same generic concepts you've seen applied to generic classes are also applicable to structs. Just to round things out, let's look at a simple example of a generic struct:

```
[VB code]
Imports System.Collections.Generic

Public Structure SampleStruct(Of T)
    Private _items As List(Of T)

    Public Function GetValue(ByVal index As Int32) As T
        Return Me._items(index)
    End Function

    Public Sub AddItem(ByVal value As T)
        Me._items.Add(value)
    End Sub

    Public Function ValidateItem(Of T)(ByVal value As Object) As Boolean
        Dim retVal As Boolean = False
        If (GetType(T).ToString.Equals(value)) Then
            retVal = True
        End If
        Return retVal
    End Function
End Structure
```

```
[C# code]
using System.Collections.Generic;

public struct SampleStruct<T> {
    private List<T> _items;

    public T GetValue(int index) {
        return this._items[index];
    }

    public void AddItem(T value) {
```

```
        this._items.Add(value);
    }

    public bool ValidateItem<T>(object value) {
        bool retVal = false;
        if (typeof(T).ToString() == value.ToString())
            retVal = true;
        return retVal;
    }
}
```

The generic syntax you see here conforms, precisely, to the patterns that you've seen applied to generic classes. So, everything you've seen in this chapter regarding generic classes should be applied, universally, to generic structs.

# Generic Interfaces

As part of looking at generic classes, it also makes sense to look at how generics can also be applied to the interfaces that are implemented by generic (or non-generic) classes. In many respects, generic interfaces actually conform to the same set of rules that govern the definition and usage of their non-generic counterparts. Here's a simple generic interface just to demonstrate the fundamentals of the syntax:

```
[VB code]
Public Interface SimpleInterface(Of T)
    Function IsValid(ByVal val As T) As Boolean
    Function GetValue() As T
    Function GetAllValues() As List(Of T)
End Interface

Public Interface ExtendedInterface(Of T)
    Inherits SimpleInterface(Of T)
    Sub Refresh()
End Interface

Public Class TestClass(Of T)
    Implements ExtendedInterface(Of T)
    . . .
    . . .
End Class
```

```
[C# code]
public interface SimpleInterface<T> {
    bool IsValid(T val);
    T GetValue();
    List<T> GetAllValues();
}
public interface ExtendedInterface<T> : SimpleInterface<T> {
```

```
    void Refresh();
}

public class TestClass<T> : ExtendedInterface<T> {
    . . .
       . . .
}
```

If you're already familiar with working with interfaces, this should be fairly trivial. You can see here that the interface accepts a type parameter that is then littered, in different forms, through the methods supplied by the interface. This also includes an example of generic interface inheritance so you can see type parameters used in that context. Finally, to make this complete, the example adds a class that implements that interface. There should be nothing particularly surprising here.

You should keep a few simple things in mind when working with generic interfaces. First, you should understand that each class that implements a generic interface can implement one and only one instance of generic interface. In the preceding example, suppose TestClass actually accepted two type parameters. In that scenario, it could not implement ExtendedInterface<T> and ExtendedInterface<U>. In this case, there would be instances where the compiler would not be able to resolve which method to call.

In some instances where you've implemented multiple interfaces, it may be necessary to qualify your method calls to be able to explicitly call out a method that's associated with a given interface. This can be achieved by simply pre-pending the interface declaration to a method.

# Summary

All in all, you should come away from this chapter feeling like generic classes are not all that different their non-generic counterparts. Throughout this chapter, you have been exposed to each of the elements of a class and learned how generics are used to extend this model and make your classes more versatile, type-safe, and efficient. This included looking at constructors, inheritance, fields, methods, overloading, and all the constructs that are influenced by the introduction of generics. The chapter also looked at some of the rules that govern accessibility of generic classes. Finally, the chapter examined a series of other aspects of working with generic classes, including generic interfaces, generic structs, nullable generic types, and the default keyword. Equipped with this knowledge, you're likely to find plenty of new opportunities to leverage generic classes as part of your own solutions.

# 5

# Generic Methods

As developers get acclimated to generics, they tend to focus their attention squarely on generic classes. And, although generic classes may represent a big part of what generics bring to the table, they only represent one facet of what can be achieved with generics. As an example, the .NET generics implementation also allows you to create individual generic methods. These methods employ the same concepts that are associated with generic classes. And, as you will see in this chapter, this ability to leverage generics at this finer level of granularity can come in quite handy. As part of looking at generic methods, this chapter covers all the basic mechanics associated with declaring and consuming a generic method. Along the way, you'll also see a few examples that illustrate different patterns for introducing generic methods into your existing solutions.

## The Basics

To illustrate the fundamental value of generic methods, let's start with the simplest of examples. Suppose you have a `Max()` function that accepts two `double` values, compares them, and returns the greater of the two values. This function might appear as follows:

```
[VB code]
Public Function Max(ByVal val1 As Double, ByVal val2 As Double) As Double
    Return IIf(val2 < val1, val1, val2)
End Function
```

```
[C# code]
public double Max(double val1, double val2) {
    return (val2 < val1) ? val1 : val2;
}
```

This method is handy for number-crunching applications. However, once you decide you want to apply this same `Max()` function to additional data types, you have a problem. This method can only be applied to `double` data types. You only have a few real, type-safe options that you can use to resolve this problem. One approach would be to create specific versions of this method to support each data type. However, doing that would force you to bloat your namespace with `MaxString`, `MaxInt`, and `MaxLong` methods. Not good. To get around the bloat issue, you might consider going back to using an `object`-based interface and tossing all type safety to the wind. Your last option here would be to provide several overloaded versions of `Max()` that accepted different types. That might represent some measure of improvement, but it's still not ideal.

This discussion of taking on bloat or compromising type safety is probably starting to sound like a broken record at this point. You see the same patterns over and over again in your code. You start out with a nice, general-purpose class or method only to find that, as you attempt to broaden its applicability, you find that you actually have few good options to extrapolate that generality to additional data types. The dilemma is right in the sweet spot of generics.

So, let's look at how generics can be applied to the `Max()` method. The following code represents the generic version of the `Max()` method:

```
[VB code]
Public Function Max(Of T As IComparable)(ByVal val1 As T, ByVal val2 As T) As T
    Dim retVal As T = val2
    If (val2.CompareTo(val1) < 0) Then
        retVal = val1
    End If
    Return retVal
End Function
```

```
[C# code]
public T Max<T>(T val1, T val2) where T : IComparable {
    T retVal = val2;
    if (val2.CompareTo(val1) < 0)
        retVal = val1;
    return retVal;
}
```

The syntax and concepts here are right in line with what you've already seen with generic classes. The `Max()` method, like a parameterized type, now accepts one or more type parameters as part of its signature. Once you've outfitted your method with a type parameter, you can then proceed to reference that type parameter throughout the scope of your function. Method parameters, return types, and types appearing in the body of your methods may all reference the type parameters that are supplied to your generic methods.

> **For this example to work properly, I was required to apply a constraint to my type parameter, indicating that each `T` must implement `IComparable`. Constraints are addressed in detail in Chapter 7, "Generic Constraints."**

All that remains at this stage is to start making some calls to this new, generic `Max()` method. Let's take a quick look at how clients would invoke the `Max()` method with a few different type arguments:

```
[VB code]
Dim doubleMax As Double = Max(Of Double)(3939.99, 39999.99)
Dim intMax As Int32 = Max(Of Double)(339, 23)
Dim stringMax As String = Max(Of String)("AAAA", "BBBBBB")
```

```
[C# code]
double doubleMax = Max<double>(3939.99, 39999.99);
int intMax = Max<int>(339, 23);
string stringMax = Max<string>("AAAA", "BBBBBB");
```

Calling a generic method, as you can see, is not all that different than calling a non-generic method. The only new wrinkle here is the introduction of a type argument immediately following the name of your method.

# A Deeper Look

With that syntactical introduction behind us, let's now consider some more detailed examples of generic methods. The following class defines a class, SimpleClass, which declares a series of generic methods that illustrate some of the variations that are available to you when creating your own generic methods. To make things more interesting, all of these generic methods in this example are placed within a generic class. The code for the class is as follows:

```
[VB code]
Public Class SimpleClass(Of T, U)
    Private _outerVal1 As T
    Private _outerVal2 As U

    Public Sub New(ByVal val1 As T, ByVal val2 As U)
        Me._outerVal1 = val1
        Me._outerVal2 = val2
    End Sub

    Public Sub Foo1(Of I)(ByVal innerVal As I)
        Console.Out.WriteLine("Method Param Type   : {0}", innerVal.GetType())
        Console.Out.WriteLine("Class Param Type(T): {0}", _outerVal1.CctType())
    End Sub

    Public Function Foo2(Of I)(ByVal innerVal As I) As U
        Console.Out.WriteLine("Method Param Type     : {0}", innerVal.GetType())
        Console.Out.WriteLine("Method Return Type(U): {0}", _outerVal1.GetType())
        Return _outerVal2
    End Function

    Public Sub Foo3(Of T)(ByVal innerVal As T)
        Console.Out.WriteLine("Method Param Type  : {0}", innerVal.GetType())
    End Sub

    Public Shared Function Foo4(Of I, J)(ByVal val1 As I, ByVal val2 As J, _
                                  ByVal outer As U) As Nullable(Of T)
        Dim retVal As New Nullable(Of T)
        Console.Out.WriteLine("Static Method Param1 Type : {0}", val1.GetType())
```

```
            Console.Out.WriteLine("Static Method Param2 Type : {0}", val2.GetType())
            Console.Out.WriteLine("Static Method Param3 Type : {0}", outer.GetType())
            Console.Out.WriteLine("Static Method Return Type : {0}", retVal.GetType())
            Return retVal
        End Function
    End Class
```

```csharp
[C# code]
public class SimpleClass<T, U> {
    private T _outerVal1;
    private U _outerVal2;

    public SimpleClass(T val1, U val2) {
        this._outerVal1 = val1;
        this._outerVal2 = val2;
    }

    public void Foo1<I>(I innerVal) {
        Console.Out.WriteLine("Method Param Type  : {0}", innerVal.GetType());
        Console.Out.WriteLine("Class Param Type(T): {0}", _outerVal1.GetType());
    }

    public U Foo2<I>(I innerVal) {
        Console.Out.WriteLine("Method Param Type   : {0}", innerVal.GetType());
        Console.Out.WriteLine("Method Return Type(U): {0}", _outerVal1.GetType());
        return _outerVal2;
    }

    public void Foo3<T>(T innerVal) {
        Console.Out.WriteLine("Method Param Type  : {0}", innerVal.GetType());
    }

    public static Nullable<T> Foo4<I, J>(I val1, J val2, U outer) {
        Nullable<T> retVal = default(T);
        Console.Out.WriteLine("Static Method Param1 Type : {0}", val1.GetType());
        Console.Out.WriteLine("Static Method Param2 Type : {0}", val2.GetType());
        Console.Out.WriteLine("Static Method Param3 Type : {0}", outer.GetType());
        Console.Out.WriteLine("Static Method Return Type : {0}", retVal.GetType());
        return retVal;
    }
}
```

This generic class accepts two type parameters, T and U, and implements four different generic methods. Let's start by looking at the Foo1() method, which accepts a single type parameter I. What's slightly different here is that this method also accesses the T type parameter that belongs to the surrounding class. The goal here is simply to illustrate the accessibility of the surrounding class's type parameters. Every generic method declared in this class may, within any part of its implementation, reference the type parameters that are associated with that class. To keep things simple, this particular example just includes a line of code that writes out the type of the class's T type parameter.

From the perspective of a generic method, type parameters should be treated like any other type that would traditionally be declared within the scope of your class. The rules that govern your method's ability to reference type parameters conform to the same rules that govern the use of non-generic type parameters. The Foo2() method demonstrates one more variation on this theme, referencing the type parameter U as its return type. The idea here is that you shouldn't limit your view of type parameters to just those supplied in the declaration of your method. Leveraging the type parameters of your class and your method in tandem broadens the scope of what can be achieved within a generic method.

The Foo3() method exposes another issue you need to consider when using generic methods within a generic class. The type parameter it accepts shares the same name, T, as a type parameter used by the surrounding class. At a minimum, this creates some confusion. It's not clear what type T will ultimately be assigned. As it turns out, the T you've used for Foo3() will actually take precedent over the T that's available from your generic class. This, in effect, ends up preventing this method from making any use of the T type parameter that is part of SimpleClass. Clearly, this practice limits the versatility of your generic methods and should be discouraged. Even if your class doesn't need to leverage the type parameters from the class, it would still create some degree of confusion to have these type parameters share the same name. Fortunately, the compiler will generate a warning in this scenario. So, if you happen to do this unintentionally, you'll be notified.

Generic methods may also be static, as demonstrated by the Foo4() method of this example. This method actually illustrates a few separate points. First, it's static and, as such, can be invoked without requiring clients to create an instance of SimpleClass. Even though it's static, it can still reference the type parameters from the class. At first glance, that may seem wrong. However, remember that the type parameters do not reference instance data, they simply define types. This means they can be littered freely throughout your static methods. For this method, U is used as the type of the third parameter and T as part of the return type. Finally, for one last bit of variety, this method also illustrates the use of multiple type parameters.

Calling this static method follows the same conventions as you've seen with calling static methods on generic classes. The only exception is the addition of the new type arguments that accompany the method. Let's look at a small snippet of code that calls the static Foo4() method to see what this might look like:

```
[VB code]
SimpleClass(Of DateTime, String).Foo4(Of Int32, Double)(42, 323.3234, "A Param")
```

```
[C# code]
SimpleClass<DateTime, String>.Foo4<int, double>(42, 323.3234, "A Param");
```

You'll notice that this combination of a static generic method within a generic class, both of which accept two type parameters, gets a little unwieldy. Still, it can't be accused of lacking expressiveness or type safety.

# Apply Constraints

Anywhere you're allowed to create a generic type, you are also allowed to qualify that type with constraints. For a generic method, the application of constraints to the incoming type parameters is relatively simple. Chapter 7 looks at constraints in detail, but here's a quick peek at the mechanics of how constraints are applied to the type parameters of your generic methods:

```
[VB code]
Public Sub Foo(Of I As IComparable)(ByVal val1 As I)
End Sub
```

```
[C# code]
public void Foo<I>(I val1) where I : IComparable {}
```

As you can see, the syntax here leverages the same approach that you may have seen applied to generic classes. You simply add the interface qualifier for a given type parameter and that will allow you to treat any reference to that the type parameter as conforming to the supplied interface.

# Type Parameter Names

The introduction of generic methods can create a problem in terms of naming your type parameters. As a rule of thumb, you should typically use a common naming scheme for your type parameters. For example, a key/value pair of type parameters would typically be assigned TKey and TValue as parameter names. As discussed earlier, this approach brings consistency to your naming and, in turn, improves the general readability and maintainability of your classes.

This general approach can complicate the naming of your type parameters for generic methods. Consider a situation in which you have a generic class that accepts key/value type parameters and, within that class, you also have a method that accepts its own key/value pair of type parameters. If you're trying to use consistent naming, you'd want to use the TKey and TValue parameter names for your class *and* your method. However, following this naming scheme also causes your class and method parameter names to collide. The type for TKey and TValue essentially become ambiguous. In fact, as you saw in the previous example, using the same type parameter names for a method and class ends up hiding your class's type parameters from your method.

For these scenarios, you may want to consider adopting an alternative naming scheme for your generic method's type parameters that can achieve uniformity while minimizing its potential to collide with the type parameter names being used by your generic classes. Naturally, this is only an issue for generic methods that are part of a generic class. Still, you're likely to want your generic methods in non-generic classes to comply with the same standard. This is more a matter of style but is something you should keep in mind as you begin to introduce more generic methods into your solutions.

# Overloading Generic Methods

When working with generic methods, it's important to understand how the introduction of type parameters impacts the uniqueness of your method's signature. This is especially significant if you're creating overloaded versions of your method. Fortunately, for the most part, generic methods conform to the same rules as non-generic methods. The addition of type parameters, however, does create a few new wrinkles that are worth considering.

The following examples of generic method declarations illustrate how the compiler will go about evaluating your methods. This first set of declarations looks at uniqueness for a mix of generic and non-generic methods:

```
[VB code]
Public Sub Foo(ByVal myStrParam As String)
End Sub

Public Sub Foo(Of I)(ByVal myStrParam As String)
End Sub
```

```
[C# code]
public void Foo(string myStrParam) {}

public void Foo<I>(string myStrParam) {}
```

The two methods declared here share much in common. They both have the same name, Foo, and they have identical parameter signatures. Well, kind of. The second declaration is a generic method that introduces an additional parameter, a type parameter. This additional parameter, as you might suspect, becomes part of the method's overall signature and creates a point of distinction that allows the compiler to treat each of these method declarations as being unique.

It's worth noting that the return type of a method can never be used as a distinguishing characteristic of your method's interface. This rule, which applies to non-generic methods, also applies to their generic counterparts. The following example illustrates this rule applied in a generic setting:

```
[VB code]
Public Foo(Of I, J)(ByVal val1 As I, ByVal val2 As List(Of J)) As List(Of I)
End Function

Public Sub Foo(Of K, L)(ByVal val1 As K, ByVal val2 As List(Of L))
End Sub
```

```
[C# code]
public List<I> Foo<I, J>(I val1, List<J> val2) {}

public void Foo<K, L>(K val1, List<L> val1) {}
```

Now, when you initially look at this pair of methods, it's natural to think they're unique. They have different type parameter names and different return types. However, as it turns out, this is not enough to make these methods different in a way that can be distinguished by calling clients. The fact that the type parameter names are different means little, because these parameters will simply be replaced by actual types at run-time. If you consider this and you know return types don't influence the uniqueness of a method's signature, then you'll understand why this example will report a collision at compile-time. If you think about it, it makes sense.

Although type parameter names, on their own, do not directly influence the uniqueness of your generic method's signature, the application of those type parameters to form new types definitely plays a role in shaping the signature of your methods. Consider the signatures of the following methods:

```
[VB code]
Public Sub Foo(Of I)(ByVal val2 As Collection(Of I), ByVal val2 As I)
End Sub

Public Sub Foo(Of I)(ByVal val2 As Collection(Of I), ByVal val2 As List(Of I))
End Sub
```

```
[C# code]
public void Foo<I>(Collection<I> val1, I val2) {}

public void Foo<I>(Collection<I> val1, List<I> val2) {}
```

This example has two methods with the same name and the same type parameter name. Still, this does not cause a collision because the types of the incoming parameters are different. In this case, the type parameter I was used to shape a new open type, which is what the compiler ultimately uses in evaluating the signature of the method. Once you're comfortable with viewing a type parameter as a type placeholder for *any* incoming type, the logic behind evaluating method signatures becomes very straightforward.

## Uniqueness with Generic Classes

The type parameters used by a generic *class* can also influence uniqueness of its generic methods. The preceding section touched on one aspect of this, but let's dig a little deeper and look at some permutations of method signatures that leverage the type parameters of their surrounding class:

```
[VB code]
Public Class TestClass(Of T, U)
    Public Sub Foo(Of K, L)(ByVal val1 As K, ByVal val2 As L)
    End Sub

    Public Sub Foo(Of U, T)(ByVal val1 As T, ByVal val2 As U)
    End Sub

    Public Sub Foo(Of A, B)(ByVal val1 As T, ByVal val2 As U)
    End Sub
End Class
```

```
[C# code]
public class TestClass<T, U> {
    public void Foo<K, L>(K val1, L val2) {}

    public void Foo<U, T>(T val1, U val2) {}

    public void Foo<A, B>(T val1, U val2) {}
}
```

This example offers up a few things for you to consider. First, you should notice that all three methods declared here accept two type parameters, each with its own variation on how it declares the signature of its incoming parameters. And, although it may not initially look like it, all three of these methods are deemed unique by the compiler. The first two are different simply because of the ordering of their parameters. The second method just inverts the order of the parameters in the signature of the method and that's enough to make it different from the first method. The third method is unique because it does not reference its type parameters (A and B) in its signature. Instead, it references the T and U type parameters from the class. So, although methods two and three look the same, their type parameters are different and account for the difference that enables the compiler to succeed.

It's important to note that the T and U parameters referenced in the second method do not have any relation to the T and U that were supplied in the class declaration. As discussed earlier, if you use a name for a method type parameter that is already employed by the class, this just hides the method's awareness of the type parameters provided by the class. In this scenario, T and U are completely disconnected from the T and U of the class. Thus, they do not collide with the T and U references in the last method, because those types are referencing the type parameters of the surrounding class.

As part of thinking about the uniqueness of your methods, you must keep in mind the fact that the compiler, in evaluating your methods, must be able to verify that every permutation of the signature is valid. So, in some subtle cases where you think you may have a unique signature, you may run into a few compiler errors. For example:

```
[VB code]
Public Class TestClass(Of T, U)
    Public Sub Foo(Of I)(ByVal val1 T, ByVal val2 As I, ByVal val3 as U)
    End Sub

    Public Sub Foo(Of I)(ByVal val1 U, ByVal val2 As T, ByVal val3 as I)
    End Sub
End Class
```

```
[C# code]
public class TestClass<T, U> {
    public void Foo<I>(T val1, I val2, U val3) {}

    public void Foo<I>(U val1, T val2, I val3) {}
}
```

Although these signatures are certainly unique as declared here, they are not truly unique if you consider the permutations of the type parameters that can be supplied to these type parameters. If you pass your method and class all the same type argument, say a String, there will be no means of differentiating between the signatures of these two methods. The result would be a compile-time error.

## Constraints and Uniqueness

Constraints qualify the interface of your type parameters. Given this reality, it would seem logical that constraints would have some influence over the uniqueness of your generic methods. For example, consider the following two generic method declarations:

```
[VB code]
Public Sub Foo(Of I As IMyInterface1)(ByVal val1 As I)
End Sub

Public Sub Foo(Of I As IMyInterface2)(ByVal val1 As I)
End Sub
```

```
[C# code]
public void Foo<I>(I val1) where I : IMyInterface1 {}

public void Foo<I>(I val1) where I : IMyInterface2 {}
```

In looking at these two methods, you will notice that they both have identical signatures with the exception of the constraints that are applied to their type parameters. The first method constrains its type parameter to the IMyInterface1 type and the second constrains its type parameter to the IMyInterface2 type. And, while you might expect that to allow these two methods to be considered unique, it doesn't. The compiler ignores constraints when it is evaluating the uniqueness of a generic method's signature. The result is a compile-time error when processing these two methods.

# Overriding Generic Methods

Generic methods may also be overridden by descendant classes. In fact, generic methods introduce surprisingly few new facets when it comes when overriding methods. The syntax for overriding generic methods follows the same pattern as non-generic methods where the overriding method must match, precisely, the parameters of the parent method. With a generic method, the only difference is that the parameters can be expressed as type parameters. Here's a simple example:

```vb
[VB code]
Public Class Person(Of T, U)
    Public Overridable Sub Foo1(Of I)(ByVal val1 As T)
    End Sub

    Public Overridable Sub Foo1(Of I)(ByVal val1 As Int32)
    End Sub

    Public Overridable Sub Foo2(Of I, J)(ByVal val1 As U)
    End Sub

    Public Overridable Sub Foo3(Of I, U)(ByVal val1 As I, ByVal val2 As U)
    End Sub

    Public Overridable Sub Foo4(Of D, E, F)(ByVal val1 As D, ByVal val2 As E)
    End Sub

    Public Overridable Function Foo5(Of I As IComparable)(ByVal val1 As I) As I
    End Function

End Class

Public Class Employee(Of T, U)
    Inherits Person(Of String, U)

    'Error: can't verify this is unique for all permutations
    Public Overrides Sub Foo1(Of I)(ByVal val1 As Int32)
    End Sub

    Public Overrides Sub Foo2(Of I, J)(ByVal val1 As U)
    End Sub

    Public Overrides Sub Foo3(Of I, U)(ByVal val1 As I, ByVal val2 As U)
    End Sub

    Public Overrides Sub Foo4(Of A, B, C)(ByVal val1 As A, ByVal val2 As B)
    End Sub
End Class
```

```csharp
[C# code]
public class Person<T, U> {
    public virtual void Foo1<I>(T val1) {}
    public virtual void Foo1<I>(int val1) {}
    public virtual void Foo2<I, J>(U val1) {}
    public virtual void Foo3<I, U>(I val1, U val2) {}
```

```
        public virtual void Foo4<D, E, F>(D val1, E val2) {}
        public virtual I Foo5<I>(I val1) where I : IComparable {
            return default(I);
        }
}

public class Employee<T, U> : Person<string, U> {
    public override void Foo1<I>(int val1) {}
    public override void Foo2<I, J>(U val1) {}
    public override void Foo3<I, U>(I val1, U val2) {}
    public override void Foo4<A, B, C>(A val1, B val2) {}
}
```

A series of examples are shown in this section, each of which attempts to override a generic method. The goal here is to provide a sampling of permutations so you can have a better feel for what's possible. This example sets things up by declaring a generic class, Person, and creating a descendant generic Employee class that overrides a handful of its parent's virtual, generic methods.

Most of the overrides, at this stage, are just as you would expect. The overriding method simply matches the signature of its parent. You should pay particular attention the role type parameters play in this example. In some instances, the type parameters of the surrounding class are referenced and, in others, the generic methods reference their own type parameters. The Foo2() method, for example, accepts type parameters of I and J and references the U type parameter that is part of the class declaration.

The other method here that offers a slight twist is Foo4(). This method matches the parent's signature but uses entirely different type parameter names. This is only meant to demonstrate that — even in an overriding scenario — the names of the type parameters are still just placeholders. The fact that these names are different in the base class does not prevent you from successfully overriding it with alternate type parameter names.

This first example (and those that follow) demonstrates a few areas where VB and C# diverge in their approach to overriding generic methods. In this first set of examples, C# compiles both of these classes successfully. However, VB throws an error on the Foo1() here. It preemptively determines that there are instances where the type for the T parameter can make overloaded versions of Foo1() that collide.

The next example takes this a little further and adds another class that changes the inheritance scheme. The following generic Customer class also extends the Person class and overrides two of its generic methods:

```
[VB code]
Public Class Customer(Of T, U)
    Inherits Person(Of T, U)

    'Error: can't verify this is unique for all permutations
    Public Overrides Sub Foo1(Of I)(ByVal val1 As T)
    End Sub

    Public Overrides Function Foo5(Of I As IComparable)(ByVal val1 As I) As I
    End Function
End Class
```

```
[C# code]
public class Customer<T, U> : Person<T, U> {
    public override void Foo1<I>(T val1) {}

    public override I Foo5<I>(I val1) {
        return default(I);
    }
}
```

In contrast with the previous example, this class uses the T and U type parameters in its inheritance declaration. By referencing the same type parameter for T in both the base and descendant class, you are able to override the Foo1() method that references the T parameter in the base class. This is only possible because the T in both classes is guaranteed to reference the same type. Of course, Foo1() fails in the VB example again for the same reasons discovered in the previous example.

The other override here, the Foo5() method, demonstrates how constraints factor into the signature of a generic method that's being overridden. Here, you might think that Foo5() would not successfully override the declaration in its parent, because the Person class included a constraint as part of its declaration. For C#, the inclusion of the matching constraint would actually generate a compile-time error here. When constraints are part of the base class in C#, the overriding method always inherits the constraints and cannot alter them. The opposite is true in VB, where the overriding method is required to include the constraint as part of the method's signature. The rationale behind this inconsistency is not clear.

There's one final scenario worth exploring. You'll notice that the Person class actually includes an overloaded method, Foo1(). This method has one version that accepts a T type parameter and the other accepts an integer. Now, consider this example where the T type argument supplied to the parent is an integer:

```
[VB code]
Public Class Vendor(Of T, U)
    Inherits Person(Of Int32, U)

    Public Overrides Sub Foo1(Of I)(ByVal val1 As Int32)
    End Sub
End Class
```

```
[C# code]
public class Vendor<T, U> : Person<int, U> {
    public override void Foo1<I>(int val1) {}
}
```

This class would seem to be valid. Its declaration of the Foo1() method certainly matches that of the parent class. The problem here isn't that the method doesn't match — it's that two methods from the Person class both match this signature. This issue is caused by the use of an integer in its inheritance from the Person class. That integer causes that the Foo1(T val1) method to collide with the other Foo1() declaration.

As noted earlier, this is one area where VB and C# vary in their handling of the Foo1() method. VB identifies this error at the point of declaration, whereas C# won't throw the error until a type argument is supplied that creates a situation where the signatures of the overloaded methods collide.

# Type Inference

One really handy aspect of generic methods is their ability to examine the types of incoming arguments and infer which method should be invoked. This eliminates the need to explicitly specify type arguments when calling a generic method. Consider the following method declaration and corresponding calls:

```
[VB code]
Public Sub InferParams(Of I, J)(ByVal val1 As I, ByVal val2 As J)
    Console.Out.WriteLine("I: {0}, J: {1}", val1.GetType(), val2.GetType())
End Sub

InferParams(Of Int32, String)(14, "Test")
InferParams("Param1", 3939.39)
InferParams(93, "Param2")
```

```
[C# code]
public void InferParams<I, J>(I val1, J val2) {
    Console.Out.WriteLine("I: {0}, J: {1}", val1.GetType(), val2.GetType());
}

InferParams<int, string>(14, "Test");
InferParams("Param1", 3939.39);
InferParams(93, "Param2");
```

This example declares a generic method that accepts two type parameters and provides three examples of calls to that method. The first call provides explicit type arguments. In this case, the types of the supplied parameter must match the types specified in the type parameter list. The next two examples both successfully call the InferParams() method without supplying any type arguments. They both use type inference, where the type is inferred from the types of the supplied arguments.

Leveraging this mechanism makes sense in most situations. However, in instances where you've overloaded a method, you may encounter some degree of ambiguity. Suppose you were to add the following overloaded method to the preceding example:

```
[VB code]
Public Sub InferParams(Of I, J)(ByVal val1 As Int32, ByVal val2 As String)
    Console.Out.WriteLine("I: {0}, J: {1}", val1.GetType(), val2.GetType())
End Sub
```

```
[C# code]
public void InferParams<I, J>(int val1, string val2) {
    Console.Out.WriteLine("I: {0}, J: {1}", val1.GetType(), val2.GetType());
}
```

This method overloads the previous InferParams() method, adding a version that includes specific integer and string types in its parameter list. Now, when you execute the sample calls to this method, it's not clear, from looking at the code, which method will get called. As it turns out, the example that supplied explicit type parameters would get you into this new method, and the version that infers the parameter types will get you into the other version of this method. Still, if you're overloading like this, it's probably not wise to rely on inference for your type parameters.

# Generic Methods and Delegates

Delegates leverage references to methods. And, generic methods are no exception to that rule. They can participate in the definition of a delegate like any other non-generic method. However, given their ability to accept type parameters, you have a few additional factors to keep in mind when using a generic method for a delegate. This next set of examples demonstrate how generic methods can be used as part of a delegate. To get started, you'll need to create the following delegate and generic methods:

```vb
[VB code]
Public Delegate Sub MyDelegate(ByVal val1 As Int32, ByVal val2 As Double, _
                        ByVal z As String)

Public Sub DelegateMethod1(Of I, J, K)(ByVal val1 As I, ByVal val2 As J, _
                        ByVal val3 As K)
End Sub

Public Sub DelegateMethod2(Of I, J, K)(ByVal val1 As Int32, ByVal val2 As Double, _
                        ByVal val3 As String)
End Sub

Public Sub DelegateMethod3(Of I, J, K)()
End Sub
```

```csharp
[C# code]
public delegate void MyDelegate(int val1, double val2, string val3);

public void DelegateMethod1<I, J, K>(I val1, J val2, K val3) {}
public void DelegateMethod2<I, J, K>(int val1, double val2, string val3) { }
public void DelegateMethod3<I, J, K>() { }
```

This example declares a single delegate that has a signature of integer, double, and string, respectively. It also has three variations of generic methods that it attempts to this delegate. The following declarations declare four separate instances of MyDelegate, each of which uses a flavor of the generic methods declared above:

```vb
[VB code]
Dim d1 As New MyDelegate(AddressOf DelegateMethod1)
Dim d2 As New MyDelegate(AddressOf DelegateMethod1(Of Int32, Double, String))
Dim d3 As New MyDelegate(AddressOf DelegateMethod2(long, DateTime, Int32))
Dim d4 As New MyDelegate(AddressOf DelegateMethod3(Of Int32, Double, String))
```

```csharp
[C# code]
MyDelegate d1 = new MyDelegate(DelegateMethod1);
MyDelegate d2 = new MyDelegate(DelegateMethod1<int, double, string>);
MyDelegate d3 = new MyDelegate(DelegateMethod2<long, DateTime, int>);
MyDelegate d4 = new MyDelegate(DelegateMethod3<int, double, string>);
```

For the first delegate here, d1, the example supplies DelegateMethod1 as its method. The declaration of DelegateMethod1 indicates that it requires three type parameters. However, even though you've supplied no type arguments here, this delegate still compiles. By leaving off the arguments, you've simply indicated that this method will rely upon type inference to resolve its type parameters. In contrast, the next two delegate declarations, d2 and d3, supply specific type parameters. For these methods to be valid, their signatures must match that of the delegate precisely. In the case of d2, you achieve this match by providing matching type arguments (integer, double, and string). The d3 delegate, on the other hand, would appear to be a mismatch. However, if you look at the declaration of DelegateMethod2 more closely, you'll discover that — even though it accepts three type parameters — none of those parameters are referenced in the signature of the method. So, in reality, this method will accept three parameters of *any* type.

The last delegate here actually causes a compile error. Its signature appears to match that of the delegate. However, MyDelegateMethod3 that is used here does not include any parameters. Thus, even though three matching types are supplied as type parameters, those type parameters are not referenced in the method's signature.

# Type-Safe Database Access Example

With generic methods, you can bring an additional dimension to the implementation of type safety and abstraction to your methods. Specifically, through type parameters, you can express information about the types operated on within your method and the types returned by your methods. You can imagine that, through the application of type parameters, you'll also identify opportunities where a generic method might be used in the place of multiple non-generic methods.

Consider a simple scenario where a generic method could be used to satisfy some of these objectives. In this example, the goal is to create a general GetItems() method that could retrieve a collection of objects from a database. This method might return Person, Customer, Employee, or Order objects. And, with generics, you expect the list returned to be a type-safe collection. The following generic method achieves these goals:

```
[VB code]
Imports System.Data.OleDb
Imports System.Collections.Generic
Imports System.Collections.ObjectModel

Public Class GetDatabaseItems
    Dim dbConn As New OleDbConnection("")

    Public Function GetItems(Of T)(ByVal sql As String) As Collection(Of T)
        Dim selectCmd As New OleDbCommand(sql, dbConn)
        Dim retVal As New Collection(Of T)
        Dim dataReader As OleDbDataReader = selectCmd.ExecuteReader()
        While (dataReader.Read() = True)
            retVal.Add(DirectCast(dataReader(0), T))
        End While

        Return retVal
    End Function
End Class
```

```
[C# code]
using System;
using System.Collections.Generic;
using System.Collections.ObjectModel
using System.Data.OleDb;

public class GetDatabaseItems {
    OleDbConnection dbConn = new OleDbConnection("");

    public Collection<T> GetItems<T>(String sql) {
        OleDbCommand selectCmd = new OleDbCommand(sql, dbConn);
        Collection<T> retVal = new Collection<T>();
        OleDbDataReader dataReader = selectCmd.ExecuteReader();
        while (dataReader.Read() == true)
            retVal.Add((T)dataReader[0]);

        return retVal;
    }
}
```

Here, within the implementation of this method, you execute a SQL statement and place each item returned from the query into a generic collection. So, clients of this method will get back a collection that matches their expectations. This allows you to eliminate the need to pollute your code with a series of specialized methods that return the appropriate collection type.

There's nothing earth-shattering about what this method achieves. However, it does provide one simple example of what can be accomplished with generic methods.

# Summary

The goal of this chapter was to explore all the syntactic variations associated with defining and consuming generic methods. As part of this effort, you looked at the rules that govern overloading and overriding generic methods. The injection of type parameters into method signatures required a closer look at how those type parameters influenced the overall signature and uniqueness of methods spanning a number of scenarios. You also saw how generic methods could be used as part of delegates. Ultimately, in the bigger picture, this chapter should have provided you good insight into the value and general applicability of generic methods.

# 6

# Generic Delegates

Delegates represent one of those subtle, helper mechanisms that can easily get overshadowed by some of the bigger concepts found in the .NET Framework. However, they play an important role in the grand scheme of the framework and, given their nature, they were a natural fit to be extended and enhanced via generics. This chapter looks at all the facets of generic delegates as well as the advantages generic delegates have to offer over their non-generic counterparts. The chapter also explores how generics can be leveraged as part of other classes that are included in the framework. Overall, you should come away from this with a better grasp of the fundamental tools you need to consume and build your own generic delegates.

## Delegate Basics

You may already be familiar with the non-generic delegates. However, for the sake of cohesiveness and to better understand the value generics bring to delegates, it may be useful to first establish a clear view of the general role of delegates in the .NET platform. By first examining the basics of delegates, you'll have a better foundation for understanding how generics have been applied to enhance their overall functionality.

Fundamentally, a delegate is meant to serve as a type-safe reference to a method. When you declare a delegate, you are only declaring the signature of a method without any corresponding implementation. That delegate is given a name and can then be referenced like any other type. Now, whenever you declare a method with a signature that matches the signature of your delegate, that method (and its implementation) can be passed as a parameter to any method that references your delegate type. So, you could have three different methods that all match your delegate signature and, at runtime, pass any one of these methods as a parameter to another method that includes your delegate in its signature. This essentially gives you an alternative form of polymorphism.

That may still be a bit abstract. Here's a more concrete example to solidify this concept. Suppose you introduce the following delegate declaration, which serves as a delegate that is used to update `Employee` objects:

```
[VB code]
Public Delegate Sub UpdateEmployee(ByVal val As Employee)
```

```
[C# code]
public delegate void UpdateEmployee(Employee val);
```

This declaration now provides you with a delegate type, `UpdateEmployee`, which can be referenced throughout your application and can be used to call alternative implementations of this method. For example, the following two methods could be created and referenced as implementations of your delegate type:

```
[VB code]
Public Sub UpdateSickStatus(ByVal emp As Employee)
    If (emp.LastSickDate.CompareTo(DateTime.Parse("12/31/2003")) <= 0) Then
        emp.Status = "Refund"
    Else
        emp.Status = "No Action"
    End If
End Sub

Public Sub UpdateVacationDays(ByVal emp As Employee)
    If (emp.HireDate.CompareTo(DateTime.Parse("1/1/2000")) <= 0) Then
        emp.VacationDays = emp.VacationDays + 5
    End If
End Sub
```

```
[C# code]
public static void UpdateSickStatus(Employee emp) {
    if (emp.LastSickDate.CompareTo(DateTime.Parse("12/31/2003")) <= 0)
        emp.Status = "Refund";
    else
        emp.Status = "No Action";
}

public static void UpdateVacationDays(Employee emp) {
    if (emp.HireDate.CompareTo(DateTime.Parse("1/1/2000")) <= 0)
        emp.VacationDays = emp.VacationDays + 5;
}
```

These two methods are meant to operate on an `Employee` object. The first method, `UpdateSickStatus()`, will set the status of each employee based on their last sick date. If they haven't been sick since 12/31/2003, they get a status of "Refund." The second method, `UpdateVacationDays()`, gives five extra vacation days to any employee that was hired by the company on or before 1/1/2000.

Although these two methods serve distinctly different purposes, they both serve as valid implementations of your delegate because they both match its signature. That's really the only requirement that's applied when determining if a method meets the requirements of a delegate. With these two implementations in place, you can now pass references around to either of these two methods via your delegate type. For example, the following method will accept either implementation of these two methods:

```
[VB code]
Public Sub TestNonGenericDelegates(ByVal updater As UpdateEmployee)
    Dim empList As New ArrayList()

    empList.Add(New Employee("John Cleese", DateTime.Parse("12/1/2003"),
                                    DateTime.Parse("1/1/2001")))
    empList.Add(New Employee("Eric Idle", DateTime.Parse("2/6/2004"),
                                    DateTime.Parse("3/2/1999")))
    empList.Add(New Employee("Michael Palin", DateTime.Parse("9/8/2003"),
                                    DateTime.Parse("4/7/1992")))

    For Each emp As Employee In empList
        updater(emp)
    Next
End Sub
```

```
[C# code]
public void TestNonGenericDelegates(UpdateEmployee updater) {
    ArrayList empList = new ArrayList();

    empList.Add(new Employee("John Cleese", DateTime.Parse("12/1/2003"),
                                    DateTime.Parse("1/1/2001")));
    empList.Add(new Employee("Eric Idle", DateTime.Parse("2/6/2004"),
                                    DateTime.Parse("3/2/1999")));
    empList.Add(new Employee("Michael Palin", DateTime.Parse("9/8/2003"),
                                    DateTime.Parse("4/7/1992")));

    foreach (Employee emp in empList)
        updater(emp);
}
```

You'll notice that this method accepts the delegate you declared as a parameter, iterating over a list of employee objects and invoking this delegate on each employee in the list. The advantage here is that you can now call this method with any number of different delegate implementations, each of which will perform its own, custom operation on each Employee.

The last step in this process is to create some calls to this method so you can see it in action. Here's some sample code that calls this method, passing each of the two delegates declared earlier:

```
[VB code]
Sub Main()
    TestNonGenericDelegates(AddressOf UpdateSickStatus)
    TestNonGenericDelegates(AddressOf UpdateVacationDays)
End Sub
```

```
[C# code]
static void Main(string[] args) {
    Program testProg = new Program();
    testProg.TestNonGenericDelegates(UpdateSickStatus);
    testProg.TestNonGenericDelegates(UpdateVacationDays);
}
```

After looking at this example, you should have a better understanding of how delegates provide you with a mechanism for expressing the signature of a method as a type and how different methods can be represented as being of that "delegate type."

This concept certainly wasn't new to the world of programming when it was introduced as part of the .NET framework. Developers have been tossing around pointers to methods for years. However, previous approaches tended to pass method pointers around without any verification of the method signature, which, as you can imagine, was anything but type-safe. Delegates eased this pain by checking the signature of each method at compile-time, eliminating any chance of an invalid method being supplied to a caller.

# Adding Generics to the Equation

As the previous example demonstrates, the types that appear in the signature of each delegate are fundamental to their usage. With the declaration of each delegate you create, you are conveying a signature that dictates the types that must be used by each method that chooses to implement that delegate. That binding to specific types in these delegate interface declarations comes with some baggage. At a minimum, it requires you to create a separate delegate for each combination of types you want to appear in the signature of a given delegate.

Suppose that somewhere within your domain objects, you also have an Order class that has no relation to the Employee that was part of the previous example. In working with this Order class, you have determined that you have a similar delegate requirement. That is, you need to be able to have a delegate that can be used to update information about an Order. To achieve this, you're required to introduce yet another delegate:

```
[VB code]
Public Delegate Sub UpdateOrder(ByVal val As Order)
```

```
[C# code]
public delegate void UpdateOrder(Byval val As Order);
```

This seems silly, though. In reality, this delegate is only required because its signature has introduced a new type. However, conceptually, it's no different than the UpdateEmployee() delegate you saw earlier. In seeing this reality, many programmers will opt to eliminate this redundancy, sacrifice type safety, and use an Object data type here. The resulting delegate signature would get altered as follows:

```
[VB code]
Public Delegate Sub Update(ByVal val As Object)
```

```
[C# code]
public delegate void Update(Byval val As Object);
```

Although this may seem like a logical choice, it does come at a cost. Consider, for a moment, what this new delegate signature imposes upon each delegate implementation. Within the implementation of each of these methods, you would be required to cast the incoming parameter to the appropriate type and then reference that type throughout the remainder of the delegate.

This approach creates a situation in which developers — instead of the compiler — must assume responsibility for ensuring that the methods consuming the delegate will always supply the appropriate object type for each invocation of the delegate. Once you've placed an `Object` type in your signature, you've basically decided to take on this added burden.

This problem with delegates is consistent with the themes you've seen with classes, methods, and so on. You continually face this dilemma of trading generality for type safety. And, as with other areas, generics end up providing the solution that doesn't require you to compromise on either front. Through generic delegates, you have the opportunity to use type parameters to define the signature of your delegates. So, instead of defining separate delegates for each data type, you can use a delegate template to identify the type placeholders for your delegate's signature.

This means you can now introduce a single delegate that can be applied to any number of data types that accept a single type parameter. The declaration of this new delegate could appear as follows:

```
[VB code]
Public Delegate Sub UpdateItem(Of T)(ByVal val As T)
```

```
[C# code]
public delegate void UpdateItem<T>(T val);
```

As you can see, your delegate has now taken on a type parameter. This type parameter is then referenced within your parameter list, allowing each implementation to supply its own type argument without requiring a separate delegate declaration for each type being processed by that delegate. Lets' take a quick look at how this generic type ends up influencing the implementation of the two delegate methods that were used in the previous example:

```
[VB code]
Public Sub TestGenericDelegate(updater As UpdateItem(Of Employee))
    Dim empList As New MyList(Of Employee)()

    empList.Add(New Employee("John Cleese", DateTime.Parse("12/1/2003"),
                                      DateTime.Parse("1/1/2001")))
    empList.Add(New Employee("Eric Idle", DateTime.Parse("2/6/2004"),
                                      DateTime.Parse("3/2/1999")))
    empList.Add(New Employee("Michael Palin", DateTime.Parse("9/8/2003"),
                                      DateTime.Parse("4/7/1992")))

    empList.UpdateItems(updater)
End Sub
```

```
[C# code]
public void TestGenericDelegate(UpdateItem<Employee> updater) {
    MyList<Employee> empList = new MyList<Employee>();

    empList.Add(new Employee("John Cleese", DateTime.Parse("12/1/2003"),
                                      DateTime.Parse("1/1/2001")));
    empList.Add(new Employee("Eric Idle", DateTime.Parse("2/6/2004"),
                                      DateTime.Parse("3/2/1999")));
    empList.Add(new Employee("Michael Palin", DateTime.Parse("9/8/2003"),
                                      DateTime.Parse("4/7/1992")));

    empList.UpdateItems(updater);
}
```

On the surface, this doesn't look all that different than the non-generic version of this method. You'll notice that it now takes advantage of the new `UpdateItem` generic delegate as the incoming parameter. What's more significant here is not in what was added but, rather, what was removed. You'll notice that this example now updates the entire list contents by simply invoking the `UpdateItems()` method on the list, passing the delegate as a parameter to this method. To support this behavior, you must introduce a new generic class, `MyList`, that descends from the framework's supplied `List` class and adds this one method. The implementation of this new list is as follows:

```
[VB code]
Public Class MyList(Of T)
    Inherits List(Of T)

    Public Sub UpdateItems(ByVal updater As UpdateItem(Of T))
        Dim items As List(Of T).Enumerator = Me.GetEnumerator()
        While (items.MoveNext() = True)
            updater(items.Current)
        End While

    End Sub
End Class
```

```
[C# code]
public class MyList<T> : List<T> {
    public void UpdateItems(UpdateItem<T> updater) {
        List<T>.Enumerator items = this.GetEnumerator();
        while (items.MoveNext() == true)
            updater(items.Current);
    }
}
```

The `UpdateItems()` method included in this new list takes the `UpdateItem` generic delegate as its only parameter. It iterates over the contents of the list, invoking the supplied delegate on each member of the list.

In looking at this, you might easily overlook the value being added here. You might conclude that all you've done here is move the processing of individual items out of your client and into the list. You could have done the equivalent with the non-generic version by creating a new `ArrayList` class that includes an operation to update the contents of the list using a delegate. Assume you decided to take that path. The resulting method, within the array list, might look similar to the following:

```
[VB code]
Public Delegate Sub UpdateItem(ByVal val As Object)

Public Class MyArrayList
    Inherits ArrayList

    Public Sub UpdateItems(ByVal updater As UpdateItem)
        Dim items As IEnumerator = Me.GetEnumerator()
        While (items.MoveNext() = True)
            updater(items.Current)
        End While
    End Sub
End Class
```

```
[C# code]
public delegate void UpdateItem(Object val);

public class MyArrayList : ArrayList {
    public void UpdateItems(UpdateItem updater) {
        IEnumerator items = this.GetEnumerator();
        while (items.MoveNext() == true)
            updater(items.Current);
    }
}
```

This certainly compiles. However, because you don't want to create a separate list class for every type that will be using this delegate, you're also forced to change your UpdateItem() delegate's interface, removing the Employee type and replacing it with an Object. Still, if this works, what's the big deal? Well, this change doesn't just impact the new list that was introduced here. It also impacts all of the methods that implement this UpdateItem() delegate. They are all required to convert to Object-based interfaces. And, of course, this means that you're stuck, once again, with a scenario that requires each delegate implementation to cast its incoming Object parameter to the appropriate type.

Now, contrast these negatives of this non-generic approach with the generic version. Because the MyList class descended from a generic list type, that list includes a type parameter that allows the UpdateItems() method to work with the specific type being managed by the list. No casts are needed within the implementation of the method, no object data types need to be used in the delegate's interfaces, and no casting is required in the methods that implement the delegate. Overall, this represents a significant improvement.

So, within this one little method call, the major underlying weakness of the non-generic delegates is exposed. You should also see how, in using these generic delegates in combination with other generic types, you get a double bonus — all that simply because you're able to add type parameters to your delegates.

# Event Handling

Event handlers are often forced to take a less than type-safe approach to handling messages. For this reason and others, they make excellent candidates for applying generic delegates. Imagine situations in which you have a non-generic event handler that accepts an Object type to represent each event sender. The declaration of that delegate might appear as follows:

```
[VB code]
Public Delegate Sub EventHandler(ByVal sender As Object, ByVal args As EventArgs)
```

```
[C# code]
public delegate void EventHandler(Object sender, EventArgs args);
```

This usage of an Object type as the type for each sender is no longer necessary with a delegate version of this interface. In fact, with delegates, you can actually create event handling signatures that support the specific models required by your application. If you need another parameter for the event, you can just create a new delegate that adds another type parameter. A generic replacement for this example would be represented as follows:

```
[VB code]
Public Delegate Sub EventHandler(Of I, J)(ByVal sender As I, ByVal args As J)
```

```
[C# code]
public delegate void EventHandler<I, J>(I sender, J args);
```

Now, with this declaration, the implementers of this delegate will be able to eliminate any overhead or baggage that was associated with dealing with the `Object` type that was leveraged in the non-generic version of the delegate.

# Generic Delegates with Generic Methods

Even though generic delegates allow you to reduce the number of delegates you must declare and they certainly add a modicum of type safety, they do not reduce the number of delegate methods you need. In some respects, this seems to reduce the enthusiasm one might have about the value of generic delegates.

Where generic delegates really shine is when they are used in combination with generic methods. Because generic methods allow you to use type parameters in the signature of the implemented method, your delegate implementations can take on an additional dimension of generality on their own. In leveraging generic methods for your delegates, you may find opportunities to reduce the number of methods needed to meet all the requirements of your delegate's functionality.

For examples of how this can be applied, look at the discussion in Chapter 5, "Generic Methods."

# Delegates in the Framework

Given the nature of generic delegates, you can imagine that it is now easier to predefine a series of general-purpose delegates that can service the needs of a wide variety of situations. In fact, as part of introducing generics into the .NET Framework, Microsoft has added a series of generic delegate types into the `System` namespace that are leveraged by the BCL (covered in Chapter 8, "BCL Generics"). These same delegate types are also likely to be of use to you in your own solutions. The goal of this section is to briefly introduce each of these delegate types so you might have a better awareness of what's available out-of-the-box.

> **This section uses the C# notation (`delegate<T>`) to identify each delegate type. Although these delegates are supported by other .NET languages, the documentation seems to most frequently be standardized around the C# notation.**

## *Action<T>*

The `Action<T>` delegate is generally used in situations where you want to perform some action on an object. As an example, the `List<T>` class directly leverages this delegate as part of its `ForEach()` method, allowing you to invoke a delegate on all the items in the list with a single call. This delegate, in fact, would likely be used in place of the delegate that was created in the previous example.

## Comparison<T>

No delegate list would be complete without a generic type that supports the comparison of two objects. The framework fills this void via the `Comparison<T>` delegate which accepts and compares two objects that must both be of type `T`. It returns an integer value indicating if the first object is greater than, less than, or equal to the second object.

## Converter<T, U>

`Converter<T, U>` is used to convert an object from one type to another. The type being converted from is represented by `T` parameter and the type being converted to is represented by the `U` parameter. As an example, the `List<T>` class uses this delegate as part of its `CovertAll()` method to covert each member of the list to a new type. This delegate returns the converted type, `U`, as its result.

## Predicate<T>

The `Predicate<T>` delegate is a highly useful delegate. It is meant to be used in situations where you want to determine if an item of type `T` meets a set of criteria. Implementers of this delegate must return `true` if the item meets the criteria and `false` if it does not. You can imagine using this in a variety of forms to express the criteria you might want applied to retrieve, delete, or otherwise process a specific set of items in a collection. The `List<T>` class, in fact, employs this delegate in a number of its different methods.

## Choosing Your Delegates

I should point out that there are no hard-and-fast rules for how and when these delegates should be used. Instead, they represent placeholders for concepts that you should generally try to conform to in your own solutions. If you have a need, for example, to introduce some delegate behavior that doesn't map well to any of these predefined delegates, you should create a new delegate from scratch. The number of type parameters and signatures are not meant to be the sole criteria used in determining which delegate you should choose.

# Type Coercion

There may be instances where you have a method in a generic class that doesn't *precisely* match the signature of your delegate. For example, assume you have the following class declared:

```
[VB code]
Public Class SimpleClass(Of T)
    Public Sub TestMethod(ByVal t As T, ByVal val As Int32)
        . . .
    End Sub
End Class
```

```
[C# code]
public class SimpleClass<T> {
    public void TestMethod(T t, int val) {
        . . .
    }
}
```

This class is a very simple class that has a single method that uses the type parameter `T` and an `integer` as its parameters. Elsewhere in your code, outside this class, you have a delegate defined that has the following signature:

```
[VB code]
Public Delegate Sub TestDelegate(Of T)(ByVal t As T, ByVal val As Int32)
```

```
[C# code]
public delegate void TestDelegate<T>(T t, int val);
```

Now, consider a scenario in which you have declared an instance of your class (`SimpleClass`) and you've declared an instance of this delegate. In constructing both of these items, you supply a type argument of `Employee`. The question is, can the `TestMethod` from `SimpleClass` be treated as a match for this delegate? Technically, if you take the type argument into consideration, these two instances certainly have the same signature. However, `TestMethod` gets its type for `T` from its surrounding class. To resolve this, let's consider execution of the following code:

```
[VB code]
Dim empDelegate As TestDelegate(Of Employee)
Dim testClass As New SimpleClass(Of Employee)
empDelegate = AddressOf testClass.TestMethod
```

```
[C# code]
TestDelegate<Employee> empDelegate;
SimpleClass<Employee> testClass = new SimpleClass<Employee>();
empDelegate = testClass.TestMethod;
```

So, will the delegate assignment in this example succeed? The answer is: yes. The compiler will actually recognize that these two signatures match and will "coerce" this method into being deemed valid for assignment to the delegate you have declared here.

# Applying Constraints

Like every other generic type, delegates also support the ability to apply constraints to their type parameters. This allows the methods that implement your delegate to invoke type-specific operations on the supplied type arguments. The syntax for declaring a delegate with constraints is fairly straightforward. The following code provides an example of a delegate with constraints applied:

```
[VB code]
Public Delegate Sub TestDelegate(Of T As Employee)(ByVal val As T)
```

```
[C# code]
public delegate void TestDelegate<T>(T val) where T : Employee;
```

With this constraint added to your declaration, you'll find that the compiler will now only allow you to create instances of this delegate using an Employee type (or one of its descendant types).

# Delegates and Anonymous Methods

As part of Visual Studio 2005, C# 2.0 added support for anonymous methods. This new language feature is particularly useful when it comes to implementing delegate methods. Instead of requiring you to write separate, standalone methods for each delegate, anonymous methods allow you to employ a "shorthand" technique where the delegate's implementation and the consumer of that delegate are declared in tandem.

Here's a simple example that declares a method that requires a delegate and the anonymous method that implements that delegate all in one pass:

```
[C# code]
collCustList.Sort(delegate(Customer cust1, Customer cust2) {
    return Comparer<Customer>.Default.Compare(cust1, cust2);
});
```

In this example, you have a generic list that contains customers and you want to sort this list using the list's Sort() method, which accepts a Comparer delegate. Instead of declaring a method that conforms to the Comparer signature, you've simply declared an anonymous method that implements the delegate as part of the call. This method will get created and supplied to the Sort() method all in one, semishort bit of text. In some respects, this improves the readability and maintainability of your code in that it marries the delegate implementation directly to the method using it. It should be very clear, as you read this, how the comparison is going to be performed. If this weren't an anonymous method, you would have to determine what delegate implementation was supplied by the caller.

Of course, this approach presumes that your Sort() method will only need to leverage a single delegate implementation, which will be valid for many scenarios.

# Summary

Generic delegates represent one of those areas where a subtle change to a type can have a significant impact to the overall framework. On their own, generic delegates are just delegates that take type parameters. But in the overall generics scheme where delegates are leveraged by other generic types, their value suddenly goes up. You saw, in this chapter, how generic delegates allow you to create much more abstract representations of your delegates where the signature of your delegate is no longer so tightly bound to specific data types. As part of this discussion, you also saw how other generic types can leverage the generic nature of your delegates in a way that wasn't achievable without generics.

# 7

# Generic Constraints

Generic constraints represent a key component of the .NET generics implementation, allowing you to constrain your type parameters to specific interfaces. Knowing the strengths and limitations that are associated with using constraints is vital to broadening your understanding of what can ultimately be achieved with generic types. This chapter looks at all the different mechanisms that are available to you when deciding how, when, and what types of constraints you want to apply to your type parameters. It also looks at each of the constraint types and discusses some of the ramifications associated with combining constraints. The chapter also considers some of the broader implications that accompany the application of constraints.

## Overview

To understand the role of generic constraints, you must first have a clear picture of why they're needed and how they are applied. With that as goal in mind, let's get started by building a sample that simply extends an existing generic type. For this scenario, let's assume you've decided to introduce your own `DataObjectCollection` that will descend from the `List<T>` collection and will invoke operations on the data objects being managed by the collection. This new class is implemented as follows:

```vb
[VB code]
Public Class DataObjectCollection(Of T)
    Inherits List(Of T)

    Public Sub Print()
        Dim coll As List(Of T).Enumerator = GetEnumerator()
        While (coll.MoveNext())
            Console.Out.WriteLine(coll.Current.ToString)
        End While
    End Sub


    Public Function Lookup(ByVal lookupValue As String) As T
```

```
            Dim retVal As T
            Dim coll As List(Of T).Enumerator = GetEnumerator()
            While (coll.MoveNext())
                If (coll.Current.ToString().Equals(lookupValue) = True) Then
                    retVal = coll.Current
                    Exit While
                End If
            End While
            Return retVal
    End Function
End Class
```

```csharp
[C# code]
public class DataObjectCollection<T> : List<T> {
    public void Print() {
        List<T>.Enumerator coll = GetEnumerator();
        while (coll.MoveNext()) {
            Console.Out.WriteLine(coll.Current.ToString());
        }
    }

    public T Lookup(string lookupValue) {
        T retVal = default(T);
        List<T>.Enumerator coll = GetEnumerator();
        while (coll.MoveNext()) {
            if (coll.Current.ToString().Equals(lookupValue) == true) {
                retVal = coll.Current;
                break;
            }
        }
        return retVal;
    }
}
```

The `DataObjectCollection` class shown here includes a `Print()` method that dumps the contents of the collection. It's also equipped with a `Lookup()` method, which takes a single parameter and locates any data object that matches the value of that parameter. Although the example is a bit contrived, you can imagine how it might be extended to offer a set of operations that could operate, somewhat globally, on a set of domain or database objects. And, in the spirit of generics, it certainly achieves all of this in a type-safe manner.

Now, suppose you want to introduce a new method into this class that will be used to determine if all the items held by the collection are considered valid. To achieve this, the method will iterate over all the items in the collection, calling the `Validate()` method for each item. The new method appears as follows:

```
[VB code]
Public Function IsValid() As Boolean
    Dim retVal As Boolean = False
    Dim coll As List(Of T).Enumerator = GetEnumerator()
    While (coll.MoveNext())
        Dim dataObj As T = coll.Current
        If (dataObj.Validate() = True) Then
            retVal = False
```

```
            Exit While
        End If
    End While
    Return retVal
End Function
```

```
[C# code]
public bool IsValid() {
    bool retVal = false;
    List<T>.Enumerator coll = GetEnumerator();
    while (coll.MoveNext()) {
        T dataObj = coll.Current;
        if (dataObj.Validate() == false) {
            retVal = false;
            break;
        }
    }
    return retVal;
}
```

This method, on the surface, appears to be a perfectly valid addition to the DataObjectCollection class. However, it fails during compilation. If you look closely, you'll notice that the IsValid() method makes an explicit call to Validate() as it processes each object in the collection.

The problem here revolves around the fact that this collection can accept type arguments of *any* type and, although Validate() may be an acceptable method for some type arguments, it certainly cannot be treated as valid for *every* possible type argument. If you construct DataObjectCollection as a collection of integers, for example, the integers will not be able to support a Validate() method as part of their interface. This means that, as implemented here, your collection can only call methods that are valid for all objects. Although this limitation might be fine for data containers that never invoke specific operations on their contained objects, there are certainly times when you will want to overcome this limitation. And, as you might have guessed, constraints represent the construct that allows you to remedy this situation.

Through constraints, you are allowed to add additional qualifiers to your generic declarations, each of which is used to specify the interfaces that must be supported by a given type parameter. In this example, assume that you have an IValidator interface that includes a Validate() method. Now, if you add this interface as a constraint on your class, the IsValid() method in the preceding code will successfully compile. The modified declaration appears as follows:

```
[VB code]
Public Interface IValidator
    Function Validate() As Boolean
    Function ToString() As String
End Interface

Public Class DataObjectCollection(Of T As IValidator)
    ...
    ...
End Class
```

```
[C# code]
public interface IValidator {
    bool Validate();
}

public class DataObjectCollection<T> : List<T> where T : IValidator {
    ...
    ...
}
```

With a constraint, the `IsValid()` method can now resolve its reference to the `Validate()` method. The addition of this constraint also forces all consumers of this generic class to supply type arguments that implement the `IValidator` interface.

As you can see, the introduction of constraints is, well, constraining. Each time you apply constraints to a type parameter you are narrowing the applicability of your generic class, method, and so on. And, in fact, if the constraints become too narrow, you have to ask yourself whether generics really represent a good fit for the problem you're trying to solve. For example, if you have a `Person` object that implements an `IPerson` interface, would it make sense to create the following generic type?

```
[VB code]
Public Class DataObjectCollection(Of T As IPerson)
    ...
End Class
```

```
[C# code]
public class DataObjectCollection<T> : List<T> where T : IPerson {
    ...
}
```

In this scenario, assume for a moment that `Person` is a standalone type that is not participating in any object hierarchy. If that's the case, how is this generic declaration any more valuable than the following non-generic declaration?

```
[VB code]
Public Class PersonCollection
    Inherits ArrayList

    Public Sub Add(ByVal person As IPerson)
        MyBase.Add(person)
    End Sub

    Public Function Lookup(ByVal lookupValue As String) As IPerson
        ...
    End Function
End Class
```

```
[C# code]
public class PersonCollection : ArrayList {
    public void Add(IPerson person) {
        base.Add(person);
    }
```

```
        public IPerson Lookup(string lookupValue) {
            ...
        }
    }
```

If you think about it — even though this class doesn't employ generics — it is really no more restrictive than the generic version you created earlier. The generic version gives you a slight boost of type safety in that it represents your true type in its internal collection. However, that's really its only advantage. As soon as you attached IPerson as a constraint on your type parameter, you have essentially eliminated much of its generic-ness.

This might have you thinking that the addition of *any* constraint makes your generic types useless. That's not the case. Plenty of scenarios certainly exist in which the application of a type parameter constraint still leaves you with a very generic representation. Even in the preceding example, your generic collection could have had value if the Person object was at the base of some larger object hierarchy. Then, even though you're still constrained, your collection would be able to provide a more type-safe approach to managing all the types that descend from the Person object. You may also find yourself leveraging generic types with significant constraints simply to capture performance gains.

The more valuable examples show up in situations where your constraints fall into that pool of broader, more general-purpose interfaces that can be applied to any number of unrelated types. IComparable, for example, is an interface that is applied to any number of different data types. Adding IComparable doesn't, by itself, impose any huge restrictions on the types that can be managed by your generic class. It certainly narrows the population of what can be supplied as a type argument, but not in a way that makes you question the fundamental value of making your class generic.

# Constraint Types

You can express the constraints that will be applied to your type parameters in a number of different ways. If a type exposes any kind of public interface, that interface can typically be used to constrain the signature of your type parameters. The sections that follow look at all the different approaches you can take when constraining your type parameters. Specifically, you'll look at how you can use interfaces, classes, and generic types as constraints. You'll also examine the use of a constructor constraint, which is required to enable applying the new operator to your type parameters. Understanding the implications associated with each of these different constraint types is key to grasping all the nuances of applying constraints.

## Interface Constraints

Because, in most cases, you are expected to use interfaces as a way of separating an object's interface from its implementation, an interface provides you with the most natural mechanism for constraining a type. Interfaces also make a nice vehicle for expressing constraint because they allow your generic types to accept any type argument that happens to implement that interface without binding to any single concrete type. The previous examples leveraged this approach, using the IValidator and IPerson interfaces to constrain their type parameters. You can also imagine how many of the standard framework interfaces might make good candidates to be applied as general-purpose constraints.

## *Class Constraints*

Whereas interfaces may be the preferred model for constraining types, it is not considered invalid to use a class as constraint type. If you were to use a class as a constraint, the public interface of that class will be used to determine which operations will be deemed valid for your type parameters. So, suppose you have the following `DataObject` class defined:

```
[VB code]
Public Class DataObject
    Private _name As String

    Public Property Name() As String
        Get
            Return Me._name
        End Get
        Set(ByVal value As String)
            Me._name = value
        End Set
    End Property

    Public Sub Update()
    End Sub

    Private Sub Convert()

    End Sub
End Class
```

```
[C# code]
public class DataObject {
    private string _name;

    public DataObject() {
    }

    public string Name {
        get { return this._name; }
        set { this._name = value; }
    }

    public bool Update() {
        return false;
    }

    private void Convert() {
    }
}
```

This class exposes a public property of `Name` and a public method of `Update()`. It also includes a private `Convert()` method. Now, apply this class as a constraint on generic class as follows:

```
[VB code]
Public Class MyConstrainedClass(Of T As DataObject)
    Public Sub New(ByVal val As T)
        val.Update()
        val.Name = "Test Name"
    End Sub
End Class
```

```
[C# code]
public class MyConstrainedClass<T> where T: DataObject {
    public MyConstrainedClass(T val) {
        val.Update();
        val.Name = "Test Name";
    }
}
```

With `DataObject` applied as a constraint, you can see that you have full access to the public interface of the class. If you were to attempt to access the private `Convert()` method here, though, you would get a compiler error. You also have the option of mixing interfaces with classes in your type constraints. See the section "Using Multiple Constraints" later in the chapter for additional information on that topic.

## Generic Types as Constraints

Constraints are not limited to non-generic types. In fact, any open or constructed type can be used as a constraint. In reality, generic interfaces and generic classes really just represent another variation on the interface and class constraints discussed earlier. The rules that govern them are mostly identical. The upside here is that the type parameters passed to your generic types can also be applied in the declaration of your constraints. The following sample declarations should give you a better feel for how they might be used:

```
[VB code]
Public Class MyClass1(Of T As IValidator(Of T))
End Class

Public Class MyClass2(Of T As IValidator(Of Int32))
End Class

Public Class MyClass3(Of T As DataObject(Of T))
End Class

Public Class MyClass4(Of K As IValidator(Of V), V As IValidator(Of K))
End Class
```

```
[C# code]
public class MyClass1<T> where T : IValidator<T> {}
public class MyClass2<T> where T : IValidator<int> { }
public class MyClass3<T> where T : DataObject<T> { }
public class MyClass4<K, V> where K : IValidator<V> where V : IValidator<K> { }
```

These declarations employ generic interface and class constraints. The first two classes, `MyClass1` and `MyClass2`, use the generic interface `IValidator<T>`. `MyClass1` uses an open type and `MyClass2` uses a constructed type. The third class here uses a generic class as a constraint. And, finally, `MyClass4` illustrates the application of separate constraints for two different type parameters.

After looking at this example, it should be clear that using generic types is not all that different than the non-generic examples you've already seen. They conform to the same set of basic syntax patterns. At the same time, the ability to leverage generics in this role provides you with the opportunity to express your type constraints in a much more generic-friendly, dynamic manner.

I should also point out that a type parameter cannot, on its own, be used as a constraint. For example, the following would be considered invalid:

```
[VB code]
Public Class MyClass(Of K, V As K)
```

```
[C# code]
public class MyClass<K, V> where V : K { }
```

This example tries to apply the type parameter K as one of the constraints on type parameter V. That won't fly with the compiler.

## Constructor Constraints

Constructor constraints don't really fit the same mold as the other constraint types you've seen so far. In fact, for many, this constraint may easily get overlooked. Consider the following, unconstrained generic class declaration:

```
[VB code]
Public Class MyClass(Of T)
    Private _value As T

    Public Sub New()
        Me._value = New T()
    End Sub
End Class
```

```
[C# code]
public class MyClass<T> {
    private T _value;

    public MyClass() {
        this._value = new T();
    }
}
```

For the sake of this example, suppose you really wanted to keep this class completely general and free from any constraints. At first glance, it would seem as though this class would achieve that objective. It certainly doesn't appear to attempt to access any methods or properties of its type parameter. Still, when you compile this, the line of code that attempts to construct an instance of T throws an error.

It's possible that the disconnect that happens here may be related to the fact that construction isn't always viewed as invoking an operation on your object. Maybe it's just because you see the new operator as one of those universal operations you expect the compiler to be able to resolve, much like it can identify the Object interface (ToString(), GetType(), and so on) for the type parameter T without the assistance of any constraints.

Expectations aside, the compiler still isn't going to allow you to construct an unconstrained type. Instead, your class declaration must be amended with a constructor constraint to make your default constructor accessible within your generic type. The new, amended declaration appears as follows:

```
[VB code]
Public Class MyClass(Of T As New)
    ...
End Class
```

```
[C# code]
public class MyClass<T> where T : new() {
    ...
}
```

This works and, at the same time, gives rise to a new set of questions. Specifically, you may be wondering if this same mechanism can be used to supply constructor constraints that have parameters in their signature. Although this isn't odd to expect, it is not supported at this stage. So, if you expect to be constructing types within your generic classes, make sure they always supply a default constructor.

# Boxing and Constraints

In some cases, the application of type constraints will allow you to eliminate the need to box types as you work with them. Suppose, for example, you had the following interface and structure that you wanted to use to manage stock prices:

```
[VB code]
Public Interface IPriceTicker
    Sub UpdatePrice(ByVal newPrice As Double)
    Function ToString() As String
End Interface

Public Structure Stock
    Implements IPriceTicker
    Private currentPrice As Double

    Public Sub UpdatePrice(ByVal newPrice As Double) _
                            Implements IPriceTicker.UpdatePrice
        Console.Out.WriteLine("Updating With Price: {0}", newPrice)
        currentPrice = newPrice
    End Sub

    Public Overrides Function ToString() As String Implements IPriceTicker.ToString
        Return currentPrice.ToString()
    End Function

End Structure
```

```
[C# code]
public interface IPriceTicker {
    void UpdatePrice(double newPrice);
}

public struct Stock : IPriceTicker {
    Private double currentPrice;

    public void UpdatePrice(double newPrice) {
        Console.Out.WriteLine("Updating With Price: {0}", newPrice);
        currentPrice = newPrice;
    }

    public override string ToString() {
        return currentPrice.ToString();
    }
}
```

The Stock structure introduced here is meant to represent a simple value type that, through its implementation of the IPriceTicker interface, allows clients to change the value of a stock. Now, put together a couple of clients that will create a Stock and feed it some new prices:

```
[VB code]
Public Class PriceTest
    Public Sub ProcessPrices1(Of T As New)(ByVal prices As Double())
        Dim item As New T

        For idx As Int32 = 0 To (prices.Length - 1)
            DirectCast(item, IPriceTicker).UpdatePrice(prices(idx))
            Console.Out.WriteLine("Updated Stock Price: {0}", item.ToString())
        Next
    End Sub

    Public Sub ProcessPrices2(Of T As {IPriceTicker,New})(ByVal prices As Double())
        Dim item As New T

        For idx As Int32 = 0 To (prices.Length - 1)
            item.UpdatePrice(prices(idx))
            Console.Out.WriteLine("Updated Stock Price: {0}", item.ToString())
        Next
    End Sub
End Class
```

```
[C# code]
public class PriceTest {
    public void ProcessPrices1<T>(double[] prices) where T : new() {
        T item = new T();

        for (int idx = 0; idx < prices.Length; idx++) {
            ((IPriceTicker)item).UpdatePrice(prices[idx]);
            Console.Out.WriteLine("Updated Stock Price: {0}", item.ToString());
        }
    }

    public void ProcessPrices2<T>(double[] prices) where T : IPriceTicker, new() {
```

```
        T item = new T();

        for (int idx = 0; idx < prices.Length; idx++) {
            item.UpdatePrice(prices[idx]);
            Console.Out.WriteLine("Updated Stock Price: {0}", item.ToString());
        }
    }
}
```

These two methods are very similar. They both take an array of prices and iterate over that array calling the `UpdatePrice()` method with each new price. The only real difference between these two is the use of constraints. The first method only applies the `new` constraint to its type parameter, whereas the second method constrains its type parameter with the `IPriceTicker` interface.

The absence of a more specific constraint on the first method forces each item to be cast to an `IPriceTicker` type in order to gain access to its `UpdatePrice()` method. The cast is bad enough, but there's a bigger problem here. When you call this method and provide it with a `Stock` type argument, that value type is going to get boxed as a result of your cast. In contrast, the second method — with its `IPriceTicker` constraint — is able to call `UpdatePrice()` without any cast or boxing of your value types.

The boxing that occurs here also impacts the state of your `Stock` objects. Suppose you were to execute the following code:

```
[VB code]
Public Sub BoxingTest()
    Dim testPrices As New PriceTest()
    testPrices.ProcessPrices1(Of Stock)(New Double() {93.33, 321.33, 193.42})
    testPrices.ProcessPrices2(Of Stock)(New Double() {93.33, 321.33, 193.42})
End Sub
```

```
[C# code]
public void BoxingTest() {
    PriceTest testPrices = new PriceTest();
    testPrices.ProcessPrices1<Stock>(new double[] { 93.33, 321.33, 193.42 });
    testPrices.ProcessPrices2<Stock>(new double[] { 93.33, 321.33, 193.42 });
}
```

When you call the first method, the `Stock` object writes out its price as it's being set. It also displays the value assigned to the `Stock` object once it has returned from the `UpdatePrice()` method. The output from calling each of these two methods is as follows:

```
Unconstrained Method:
Updating With Price: 93.33
Updated Stock Price: 0
Updating With Price: 321.33
Updated Stock Price: 0
Updating With Price: 193.42
Updated Stock Price: 0

Constrained Method:
Updating With Price: 93.33
Updated Stock Price: 93.33
```

```
Updating With Price: 321.33
Updated Stock Price: 321.33
Updating With Price: 193.42
Updated Stock Price: 193.42
```

Notice that, with the unconstrained method, your object never actually got updated. Meanwhile, the constrained version, as you would expect, was successfully modified.

# Using Multiple Constraints

Though the examples used so far have all applied a single constraint to each type parameter, you actually have the option (within some boundaries) of applying multiple constraints to a type parameter. Suppose, for example, you wanted to apply the IVisitor constraint to one of your type parameters and, at the same time, you also wanted to provide your class with access to the default constructor for that same type parameter. The syntax for expressing these two constraints together appears as follows:

```
[VB code]
Public Class MyClass(Of T As {IVisitor, New})
    ...
End Class
```

```
[C# code]
public class MyClass<T> where T : IVisitor, new() {
    ...
}
```

You will notice, from this example, that this is one area where VB and C# have taken fairly different approaches to their syntax. Personally, VB's use of curly brackets seems to feel more like a syntactic afterthought. Still, it gets the job done.

Now, as you start to work with multiple constraints, the only issue you're likely to run into is determining what combinations of constraint types are valid. For interfaces, you're actually allowed to apply any number of interfaces to your type parameters. The compiler will simply verify that every attempt to access a member in your generic type can be resolved via at least one of the interfaces provided in your list of constraints. The following provides a simple example where multiple interface constraints are applied to a single type parameter:

```
[VB code]
Public Class MyClass(Of T As {IVisitor, IComparable(Of T), IInspector})
    ...
End Class
```

```
[C# code]
public class MyClass<T> where T : IVisitor, IComparable<T>, IInspector {
    ...
}
```

In this scenario, your class would only be allowed to accept type arguments that implement each of the interfaces referenced in this constraint list. You can also mix class constraints in with these interface constraints. However, with class constraints, you are limited to referencing a single class in your constraints list. As you might expect, this same rule also applies to constructor constraints. So, although it might be unlikely pairing, the following would be considered a valid combination of constraints:

```
[VB code]
Public Class MyClass(Of T As {Person(Of T), IComparable(Of T), IInspector, New})
    ...
End Class
```

```
[C# code]
public class MyClass<T> where T : Person<T>, IComparable<T>, IInspector, new() {
    ...
}
```

This code mixes a class constraint (`Person<T>`), two interface constraints (`IComparable<T>`, `IInspector`), and a constructor constraint. Now, this is anything but a practical example. However, it does provide a clear picture of what's possible when applying multiple constraints to a type parameter.

For C#, the order of these constraints is also significant. C# requires class constraints to always appear first in the list of constraints. It also requires constructor constraints to appear at the end of any constraint list. VB, on the other hand, does not appear to impose any ordering requirements on its constraints.

## Ambiguous Constraints

When you're working with multiple constraints, it is possible to end up with constraints that introduce ambiguity problems. If two constraints expose identical members, the compiler will be unable to determine which of these members should be invoked and, as a result, will throw a compile-time error. Suppose, for example, you have defined the following two interfaces:

```
[VB code]
Public Interface A
    Sub Foo1()
    Sub Foo2()
End Interface

Public Interface B
    Sub Foo1()
    Sub Foo3()
    Sub Foo4()
End Interface
```

```
[C# code]
public interface A {
    void Foo1();
    void Foo2();
}
public interface B {
    void Foo1();
    void Foo3();
    void Foo4();
}
```

Now, take these two interfaces and apply them as constraints to a simple class along with a constructor constraint. The code to achieve this is as follows:

```
[VB code]
Public Class TestClass(Of T As {A, B, New})
    Public Sub New()
        Dim aClass As New T()

        aClass.Foo2()
        aClass.Foo1()
    End Sub
End Class
```

```
[C# code]
public class TestClass<T> where T : A, B, new() {
    public TestClass() {
        T aClass = new T();

        aClass.Foo2();
        aClass.Foo1();
    }
}
```

In this example, the constructor you've implemented first leverages the constructor constraint and creates a new instance of the type T. Then, it proceeds to attempt to make calls to the Foo2() and Foo1() methods. Although these are valid methods for the constraints you've included in your class declaration, the compiler throws an error when it encounters the call to Foo1(). If you look at the two interfaces that are declared in the example, you'll notice that both of these interfaces include a Foo1() method. This creates a problem of ambiguity for the compiler, because it cannot determine which Foo1() it should call here.

It is possible to overcome this error. You certainly could remedy this by casting the object to a specific interface type. However, if you're in a generic mindset, casting is not going to leave a bad taste in your mouth. At the same time, it's your only option if you really need to use constraints with signatures that collide.

## Ambiguity When Mixing Classes and Interfaces

Using class and interface constraints in tandem can also cause ambiguity issues. In this scenario, the compiler will always defer to the members of the class and hide any members from an interface that might overlap with those exposed by the class constraint. Here's a simple example that exhibits this behavior:

```
[VB code]
Public Class C
    Public Sub Foo1()
    End Sub

    Public Sub Foo3()
    End Sub
End Class

Public Class TestClass2(Of T As {C, A, B, New})
    Public Sub New()
        Dim aClass As New T()
```

```
        aClass.Foo1()
        aClass.Foo3()
        aClass.Foo2()
        aClass.Foo4()
    End Sub
End Class
```

```
[C# code]
public class C {
    public void Foo1() { }
    public void Foo3() { }
}

public class TestClass2<T> where T : C, A, B, new() {
    public TestClass2() {
        T aClass = new T();

        aClass.Foo1();
        aClass.Foo3();
        aClass.Foo2();
        aClass.Foo4();
    }
}
```

This example introduces a new class, C, and uses that class as a constraint in combination with the interfaces that were supplied in the previous example. It then attempts to invoke methods that are associated with each of these constraints.

You'll notice here that the Foo1() and Foo3() methods of your class constraint overlap with methods from your interface constraints. And, based on the error in the previous example, you might think this would also generate a similar error. However, with a class constraint, the compiler just resolves this ambiguity in favor of the class constraint. At the same time, the C# version of this class is still able to invoke the Foo2() method from interface A and the Foo4() method from interface B. So, in cases where there wasn't overlap and there is no ambiguity, you are still able to access the methods exposed by these interfaces.

VB's approach to this problem is slightly different. When it encounters a class constraint, it completely hides *all* members associated with the interface constraints, making them virtually useless, it would seem. In general, VB appears to take a much less lenient approach when using class constraints in combination with interface constraints.

# Generic Delegate and Method Constraints

Every generic construct in the .NET Framework provides a mechanism for qualifying its type parameters with constraints. And, from the previous discussion, you've gotten to see plenty of examples where constraints were included as part of a generic class declaration. However, so far, you haven't really seen how constraints are applied to the remaining generic constructs. There's a reason for this. The constraints syntax for each of the remaining constructs is very similar to what you've already seen with generic classes. To illustrate this point, take a quick look at some simple generic delegates and methods with constraints applied to their type parameters:

```
[VB code]
Public Class MyClass
    Public Delegate Sub MyDelegate(Of T As IValidator)(ByVal val As Int32)

    Public Sub Foo(Of T As IValidator)(ByVal val As T)
    End Sub
End Class
```

```
[C# code]
public class MyClass {
    public delegate void MyDelegate<T>(int val) where T : IValidator;

    public void Foo<T>(T val) where T : IValidator {}
}
```

This probably appears just as you would expect. The C# examples offer a bit more variation, but nothing that's all that different than what you saw with generic classes.

# Inheritance and Constraints

Constraints must also be factored into your object hierarchies. The constraints that are applied to your base class directly influence the constraints that must be applied to your descendent classes. Consider, for example, the following two class declarations:

```
[VB code]
Public Class BaseClass(Of K As {IValidator, New}, V)
    Public Sub New()
        Dim val As New K()
    End Sub
End Class

Public Class SubClass1(Of K, V)
    Inherits BaseClass(Of K, V)

    Public Sub New()
        MyBase.New()
    End Sub
End Class
```

```
[C# code]
public class BaseClass<K, V> where K : IValidator, new() {
    public BaseClass() {
        K val = new K();
    }
}

public class SubClass1<K, V> : BaseClass<K, V> {
    public SubClass1() : base() {
        K val = new K();
    }
}
```

In the declaration of BaseClass here, you'll notice that some constraints have been applied to the first type parameter, K. The example then subclasses this class with SubClass1 and, within the constructor of this subclass, attempts to create a new instance of K. Because K already had a constructor constraint added to it as part of the parent class, you might assume that constraint would simply be inherited and applied to your subclass. However, if you attempt to compile this example, you'll discover that the compiler is unhappy with this declaration. The problem here is that, whenever your base class imposes constraints on its type parameters, those same constraints are applied to your type arguments as part of your subclass declaration. In this case, the K that is being supplied as the first type argument to the BaseClass must guarantee that it will meet the constraints that are declared for that parameter as part of the base class. To resolve this, you would change the declaration of the subclass as follows:

```
[VB code]
Public Class SubClass1(Of K As {IValidator, New}, V)
    ...
End Class
```

```
[C# code]
public class SubClass1<K, V> : BaseClass<K, V> where K : IValidator, new() {
    ...
}
```

With this declaration, any constructed type for SubClass1 will be required to implement IVisitor and provide a parameterless constructor for its first type parameter, K. Now, suppose you created a second subclass of BaseClass that declared its inheritance as follows:

```
[VB code]
Public Class SubClass2(Of K As IComparable, V)
    Inherits BaseClass(Of Customer, String)
End Class
```

```
[C# code]
public class SubClass2<K, V> : BaseClass<Customer, string> where K : IComparable {
    public SubClass2() : base() { }
}
```

Here, you'll notice that the constraints are no longer necessary because K is not being passed through to BaseClass as part of the inheritance declaration. Instead, because K isn't even visible to the base class, it gets an entirely different constraint (IComparable) applied to it. At the same time, the constraints in the base class are applied to the incoming Customer type argument. And, because it implements IValidator and supplies a default constructor, it successfully satisfies the constraints.

# Are Generics Generic?

Some would say that the introduction of constraints makes the .NET generics implementation anything but generic. As best as I can tell, this argument seems to emanate primarily from those who have strong ties to templates. And, from that perspective, where a type parameter is truly a placeholder for *any* type, I can see how that would lead one to conclude that constraints somehow detract from the broader definition of a generic type. In that context, being a generic type means having no constraints on your type parameters and the freedom to view those types as being completely devoid of any rules that would impose requirements on their shape or structure. If you share this view, you are likely to believe that generics aren't generic.

The .NET implementation of generics introduced constraints as a tradeoff. Supporting the existing C++ templates model for generics would have required generics to support a compile-time model, where each constructed type would be created as part of compilation. This would have been the only way to retain these fully generic types and still verify that each instance of parameter substitution was fully resolvable. This was certainly a valid option. However, it also brought with it the baggage that is associated with the templates model, including code bloat (see Chapter 3 "Generics ≠ Templates," for a complete comparison of generics and templates). The generics designers wanted to overcome some of the traditional templates-related issues by introducing the concept of run-time generic types. Instead of precompiling all the types, generic types would be introduced into the CLR and each generic instance would be created as it was used at run-time.

This goal of having run-time generic types has lots of upsides. At the same time, with each constructed type being created at run-time, there must also be some way of prevalidating that these types are valid. This is where constraints come in. Through constraints, the compiler is able to guarantee that the operations performed on any supplied type argument can be resolved.

So, the question is, does this idea of requiring constraints to support the run-time model somehow make generics not generic? From my perspective, there is no absolute answer to this question. It really depends on how you want to define the concept of a generic type. If you're looking to the .NET generic implementation as a direct replacement for the generic, metaprogramming concepts that have been traditionally associated with C++ templates, you're likely to conclude that generics aren't generic. However, if you loosen that definition some, and you look at what the generics implementation enables, you might come to a different conclusion. For better or worse, this is how generics are and are likely to be for some time, and whether or not they are truly generic is less important than whether or not they add value. And, in that light, I think most would agree that they add value to the .NET platform.

# Summary

The goal of the chapter was to provide some clear indication of how constraints can be applied to your generic types. As part of this discussion, the chapter looked at how interface, class, and constructor constraints all separately influence the implementation of a generic type. You also saw how these constraint types could be leveraged in combinations. Along the way, you examined some of the side effects of using multiple constraints for your type parameters and explored some scenarios where these constraints could introduce ambiguity. After looking at all the implications of constraints, you should have a much clearer idea about how constraints are likely to influence the choices you make when creating your own generic types.

# 8

# BCL Generics

The potential and power of generics is most fully realized in the implementation of container frameworks. Given this reality, it only made sense that the introduction of generics would also be accompanied by the introduction of a pool of new generic types. In version 2.0 of the .NET Framework, the Base Class Library (BCL) introduces two new namespaces, `System.Collections.Generics` and `System.Collections.ObjectModel`, both of which include generic representations of many of the non-generic containers that already existed in the `System.Collections` namespace long before generics came along. The goal of this chapter is to provide you with an overview of the classes that appear in these namespaces, along with a roadmap for how and when you might want to apply each of these generic types. It also covers many of the key methods and properties that are associated with each of these new types.

## Motivation

Most .NET developers are likely to have some degree of familiarity with the existing collection types. In fact, I suspect that a significant portion of the development community has grown quite comfortable with the idea of collections that manage `Object` data types. Casting, boxing, and unboxing have, for many, become the necessary evils that accompany working with these collections. This was a natural dynamic. There simply weren't any attractive alternatives that didn't also introduce a high degree of code bloat.

My expectation is that generics will trigger a reversal of this trend. After seeing all the advantages of generics, it should be clear why you should favor using generic collections wherever possible. That's not to say that you should consider the contents of the `System.Collections` namespace as being deprecated. It is likely that there are still some scenarios where these classes can and should be applied. At the same time, to make these non-generic types your default choice would be a mistake. The efficiency, expressiveness, and type safety of generics is simply too compelling to be ignored.

# The Big Picture

Before you start looking at the behavior of individual generic classes and interfaces, you need to take a step back and consider the higher-level factors that have influenced the shape and structure of the `System.Collections.Generic` and `System.Collections.ObjectModel` namespaces. If you're going to be able to take full advantage of these types, you really need to have a firm grasp on the role each class and interface plays in the overall scheme. If you understand these concepts, you'll be much better equipped to determine how each of these generic types should be applied in your own solutions.

The section that follows explores the basic organization of the interfaces and types that are part of the BCL. Along the way, it will point out any broader concepts that might be of value to you as a consumer of these generic types.

If you are familiar with the `System.Collections` namespace, you should be able to see all the similarities between the generic types and their non-generic counterparts. In fact, in some cases, the generic versions of these types will have interfaces that closely mirror the non-generic versions. Even with these similarities, it's important for you to see how generics have influenced the overall mechanics and signatures of each type.

## *Generic Collection Interfaces*

The best place to start your exploration of the generics namespace is with interfaces, because they define the signature of what will ultimately be possible with the library's concrete types. The generics namespace currently consists of a fairly compact list of interfaces. Each of these interfaces has a well-defined role that, ultimately, influences the scope and purpose of what appears in the resulting classes.

At the root of the BCL's generic collection interface hierarchy (shown in Figure 8-1) is the `IEnumerable<T>` interface. This interface is as basic as they come. It is limited to supporting iteration over a collection of items and nothing more. You'll also notice that `IEnumerable<T>` extends the non-generic `IEnumerable` interface. This may cause some concern, because the `IEnumerable` interface deals with `object` data types, which is precisely what you're trying to avoid. While this may feel a bit unnatural, it turns out it's not all that limiting. In reality, including this interface for your collections only means that you'll also support a `GetEnumerator()` call that can return objects. Because `IEnumerable` only iterates over and retrieves data, it doesn't introduce any signatures that would compromise type-safety.

The broader question is: Why is `IEnumerable` even needed in this hierarchy? Isn't `IEnumerable<T>` adequate? Well, the rationale here is targeted more at the interoperability of your generic and non-generic types. Because generics need to live alongside their non-generic counterparts (`IList`, `ICollection`, `IEnumerable`, and so on), it's fair to expect that you'd like them to play nicely. It would be nice, for example, to have an `IList` data type be treated as compatible with an `IList<T>` where an `IList` parameter may willingly accept an `IList<T>` data type. This, of course, ends up being mostly a fantasy. Because the `IList<T>` interface supports methods that mutate the collection (via `Add(T)`, for example), they cannot achieve this direct interoperability with the non-generic `IList` interface. `IList` simply wouldn't have any means of enforcing the type-safety that is declared with `IList<T>`. If you started out with an `IList<double>` and assigned that collection to an `IList` data type, there would be nothing that prevented you from adding, for example, a `double` type to the collection that wasn't a `double`.

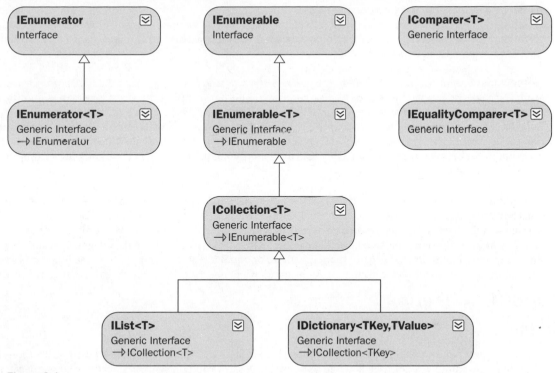

**Figure 8-1**

Okay, if that's the case then, you might be wondering why is IEnumerable<T> allowed to extend IEnumerable? And, as you might suspect, the only thing that allows this is the fact that IEnumerable is a one-way interface. It only allows data to be returned from the collection. As a result, it never needs to deal with the issues that you saw with the IList example. So, even though it would have been nice for all the interfaces to support this added interoperability between generic and non-generic types, it turns out that IEnumerable represents the only class where this can be achieved.

Now, as you move down the interface hierarchy, you'll notice that each of the interfaces that extend IEnumerable<T> adds additional functionality. The ICollection<T> interface, for example, provides members that allow clients to add and remove items from the collection. This, I should note, is not true for the non-generic version of this interface. While ICollection<T> adds some basic add/remove operations, is still does not retain any specific ordering to its items. More specifically, it does not provide any index-based access to its items. That, as you probably figured by now, is what is added by the IList<T> interface. IList<T> includes the idea of an indexer that will allow you to randomly access items based on an index.

> Throughout this section, the C# angle bracket syntax is used to express the names of each interface and class. This follows the convention that has been used in the Visual Studio 2005 documentation. If you're more comfortable with the VB syntax, just mentally replace each instance of <T> with VB's (Of T) syntax.

Finally, no discussion of collection interfaces would be complete without a dictionary interface. The generics namespace provides the classic IDictionary<TKey, TValue> interface that allows you to store items in a collection, each of which is associated with a key. This key can then be used to randomly access the elements of a dictionary.

Somewhat on their own, but no less important, are the IEnumerator<T>, IEqualityComparer<T>, and IComparer<T> interfaces. The IEnumerator<T> interface simply provides a type-safe signature for iterating over a collection of items. This interface also represents the other half of the IEnumerable<T> interface. By implementing the IEnumerable<T> interface, a generic class is essentially enabling iteration via the IEnumerator<T> interface. You'll get a look at this interface in more detail later, but it's important to point it out because it plays such a key role in the implementation of any class that wants to support the standard iteration mechanisms.

The IEqualityComparer<T> interface is used to test the equality of two objects via an Equals() comparison. Similarly, the IComparer<T> interface introduces the common set of operations that are used to compare two objects. The key difference here is that IEqualityComparer<T> will only return a boolean result that indicates whether two objects are equal, while IComparer<T> yields a numeric result that indicates whether an item is greater than, less than, or equal to another item. Both these interfaces are small but heavily used interfaces that provide standard, generic mechanisms for comparing and sorting objects.

## Classes

Now that you have a clearer picture of the generic interfaces exist and what roles they play, it's time to look at the framework classes that use these interfaces. As you will see, the framework assigns very specific roles to each class in the library, and these roles are certainly influenced by the interfaces they implement. And, as someone who's likely to be traversing the library in search of the *right* class, you'll want to have a firm grasp of the functionality and purpose associated with each generic class in the BCL.

The List<T> class probably represents the best place to start off this subject. It certainly stands out as one of the most popular and heavily used generic classes. This class, which is the type-safe, functional replacement for ArrayList, provides you with a powerful set of operations for managing and accessing index-based collections. It is also used, internally, as part of the implementation of some of the other BCL types. In fact, you're likely to find yourself making heavy use of List<T> within the implementation of many of your own classes.

Although the List<T> class is certainly powerful, its implementation was targeted primarily at performance and flexibility. And, as a result, much of its implementation is sealed. This isn't a problem if you're not going to introduce your own custom specializations of this class. However, if you need to subclass any collection, you're going to want to leverage the collection-based classes. Specifically, the Collection<T>, ReadOnlyCollection<T>, and KeyedCollection<TKey, TItem> classes are meant to play this role. They include much more "open" interfaces via a series of protected methods that allows you to override and modify the default behaviors of these collections.

The BCL also includes a small set of classes that are implementations of the IDictionary<TKey, TValue> interface. The first of these, Dictionary<TKey, TValue>, is meant to represent the functional equivalent of the non-generic HashTable. However, some important differences exist between the Dictionary<TKey, TValue> and HashTable classes. You'll get a chance to explore the differences later in this chapter. The other dictionary-based class is SortedDictionary<TKey, TValue>. This class, as its name implies, gives you the best of both worlds in that you get the random access of a dictionary in conjunction with some of the behaviors of an ordered list. The BCL also includes the `SortedList<TKey, TValue>` collection, which provides you with a hybrid of index-based access and a `SortedDictionary<TKey, TValue>`, where items in the container may be accessed by keys and/or by a numeric index.

Of course, no container library would be complete without some of the classic container types. Along these lines, the BCL adds `Queue<T>`, `Stack<T>`, and `LinkedList<T>` classes, which bring the type-safety of generics to these fundamental data structures. The behavior of these classes is very much a direct mapping of the non-generic versions of these classes.

## System.Collections.ObjectModel

The `KeyedCollection<TKey, TItem>`, `ReadOnlyCollection<T>`, and `Collection<T>` classes are not in the `System.Collections.Generic` namespace. These classes were moved to the `System.Collections.ObjectModel` namespace late in the development of version 2.0 of the .NET Framework. The rationale behind this move seemed to come about as a result of concern about creating some confusion for VB developers. The default `Microsoft.VisualBasic` namespace already included a `Collection` class, which meant making the `System.Collections.Generic` namespace a default message would cause IntelliSense to display two separate collection types for VB developers. To resolve this, the BCL team had the choice of renaming the `Collection<T>` class or moving it to a new namespace. This is what gave rise to the new `System.Collections.ObjectModel` namespace.

Moving these classes to this namespace did not come without great debate. Many believe that the rationale behind moving these classes was not exactly sound. In fact, some believe the BCL's organization is being compromised by a desire to reduce confusion for VB6 programmers. And, even if you're okay with the move, there's an even bigger audience that can't understand the thinking behind using the name `ObjectModel` for this new namespace. There's plenty of rationalization behind choosing this name, but I haven't seen anything that brings any clarity to the meaning behind this name. Instead, it feels more like they needed a name in a hurry and just picked one. Still, it's the name we're all left to work with.

## Enumerators

For the most part, each of the generic collection classes provided in the BCL is also accompanied by one or more enumerators. The enumerators provide a standard mechanism for enumerating the contents of each collection. Each collection class achieves this by implementing the `IEnumerable<T>` interface. In doing so, these classes all end up providing a common interface for retrieving an instance of an `IEnumerator<T>` object that supports all the basic set of navigation methods.

For a simple container, the BCL typically just provides an implementation of the `IEnumerable<T>` interface that returns a type-safe `IEnumerator<T>`. You'll notice, for example, that `Stack<T>` includes a `Stack<T>.Enumerator` that is used to iterate over its items. The same holds true for `List<T>`, `Collection<T>`, and so on. The basic idea here is that if a container is managing a single type, it will typically provide a corresponding enumerator.

Now, when you look at some classes in the BCL, you'll find that this basic approach isn't quite adequate. And, in these situations, the BCL has provided more specific enumeration mechanisms for acquiring the contents of a container. The main example of this is the `Dictionary<TKey, TValue>`–related containers. Because these containers manage two different collections of data (keys and values), they require the addition of a few more mechanisms for acquiring a container's data.

In the most general sense, a dictionary is actually managing a collection of `KeyValuePair<TKey, TValue>` objects. And, for this reason, the `Dictionary<TKey, TValue>.Enumerator` implementation returns an `Enumerator<T>` that contains `KeyValuePair<TKey, TValue>` objects. This is what you would expect. However, at times you'll still want the ability to access the keys and values independently. For these cases, the `Dictionary<TKey, TValue>` class adds two additional mechanisms. The `Dictionary.KeyCollection<TKey, TValue>` class provides you with access to a separate collection that just contains the set of keys being managed by the dictionary. And, as you might suspect, the corresponding `Dictionary.ValueCollection<TKey, TValue>` class provides access to the values that are managed by the dictionary. Each of these dictionary types provides an implementation of `IEnumerable<T>` that is used to get an enumerator that will be used to iterate over the keys or values. This same approach is also applied to the `SortedDictionary<TKey, TValue>` class.

This general approach to handling enumeration for containers is clean and consistent. Certainly, if you were to consider introducing your own container or specializations of these containers, it would make sense to continue to comply with this scheme.

The other question you might have is: Why do I need to support `IEnumerable<T>` for my own containers? Well, without support for this interface, you would prevent your C# and VB clients from using the "`for each`" construct to process the items in your collection. This construct makes a client's life much easier and, in my opinion, makes your code much more readable. If that reason isn't enough to convince you, you may simply want to support `IEnumerable<T>` simply to remain consistent with the BCL.

## Using Delegates

As you look more carefully at the generic classes in the BCL, you'll find a number of methods that take delegates as parameters. If you haven't done much work with delegates, you may want to brush up on some of the basic concepts. As you walk through the examples, this knowledge will make it easier for you to have a broader understanding of how delegates are being applied. The information provided on generic delegates in Chapter 6 also provides more details on the specific delegates that are leveraged by the BCL.

# Generic Collection Classes

Now that you have a high-level view of the generics namespaces, it's time to look at the nuts-and-bolts details of each individual class. The idea here is to go through the members of every class and provide an overview of the purpose and usage of each member. Each class in this section is also accompanied by samples that illustrate some of the key concepts associated with that specific class.

## Collection<T>

The `Collection<T>` class is an index-based, dynamically sized collection that provides you with all the fundamental interfaces you need to add, remove, and randomly access the elements of a collection. Its purpose is to provide a lightweight interface for constructing and maintaining a collection that can also serve as the base class for any user-defined, custom collections. The following table shows a complete list of methods and properties for `Collection<T>`.

| Method or Property Name | Description |
| --- | --- |
| Add() | Adds the provided object to the end of the collection. |
| Clear() | Removes all the items from the collection. |
| Contains() | Attempts to find an object in the collection equal to the passed in object. If a matching object is found, the method returns true. |
| CopyTo() | Copies the contents of the collection to an Array. |
| Count | Returns the number of items currently stored in the collection. |
| GetEnumerator() | Gets the IEnumerator<T> enumerator for your collection. |
| IndexOf() | Finds the index of the object equal to the object supplied as a parameter. If no matching object is found, this method returns –1. |
| Insert() | Inserts a new object into the collection at the specified index. If an invalid index is provided, the class throws an ArgumentOutOfRangeException. |
| Item | Indexer that provides index-based access to the elements of collection. If an invalid index is provided, the class throws an ArgumentOutOfRangeException. |
| Remove() | Searches for an object that is equal to the supplied object and removes it. If the object is found and removed, the function returns true. Otherwise, it returns false. |
| RemoveAt() | Removes the object at the specified index. If an invalid index is provided, the class throws an ArgumentOutOfRangeException. |

All of the generic collections included in the BCL use a zero-based indexing scheme.

## Constructing a Collection<T>

The Collection<T> class supports two different modes of construction. Clients can use the default constructor or they can use the overloaded constructor that accepts a list of items. The following snippets of code provide examples of both of these constructors in action:

```
[VB code]
Dim intCollection As New Collection(Of Int32)()

Dim strList As New List(Of String)()
strList.Add("Val1")
strList.Add("Val2")
```

```
Dim strCollection As New Collection(Of String)(strList)

For Each strVal1 As String In strCollection
    System.Console.WriteLine(strVal1)
Next

strList(0) = "Val Changed"

For Each strVal2 As String In strList
    System.Console.WriteLine(strVal2)
Next
```

```
[C# code]
Collection<int> intCollection = new Collection<int>();

List<String> strList = new List<String>();
strList.Add("Val1");
strList.Add("Val2");

Collection<String> strCollection = new Collection<String>(strList);
foreach (String strVal1 in strCollection)
    System.Console.WriteLine(strVal1);

strList[0] = "Val Changed";

foreach (String strVal2 in strCollection)
    System.Console.WriteLine(strVal2);
```

In this example you start by constructing a simple collection of integers to demonstrate use of the default constructor. Then, you construct an instance of a `Collection<T>` class, passing in your list of strings. At this point, you write out the contents of the new collection to demonstrate that it was correctly populated with the contents of the source list.

Once the collection has been populated from the list, you modify the original list to point out a particular pitfall you may not be expecting. You'll notice that the example changes the value of the first item in your original list to "Val Changed". Now, because you only modified your original list, you would expect this to have no impact on your collection. However, when you look at the contents of `strCollection`, you'll discover that the change made to `strList` also modified `strCollection`.

The problem here is that the reference to the list you supplied was retained by the collection during construction. So, while you might have expected a deep copy in this scenario, you didn't get one. And, given this reality, it should be clear that any changes you make to the items in your original list are also going to be reflected in the new collection. They both share the same references so any change to one will impact the other.

## Adding and Updating Items

The `Collection<T>` class supports a series of methods that allow you to populate and maintain the state of your collection. The class's interface gives you the option of modifying the collection via indexed and non-indexed interfaces.

Naturally, in addition to these methods and properties, the `Collection<T>` class also inherits all the methods every class inherits from the `Object` class. The `Collection<T>` class does not define any alternative implementations of these methods. So, if you want to add your own definition of equality or supply your own definition for a hash code, it will be your responsibility to extend the class and add your own implementation of these items.

Now that that's out of the way, let's build an example that demonstrates some of these methods. Specifically, let's start by looking at how you can populate and update your `Collection<T>` class. Before you can do that, though, you'll need an object to put in your collection (collections of `integers` and `strings` get old in a hurry). The following code implements a `Customer` class that will be used by various generic containers throughout this chapter:

```vb
[VB Code]
Public Class Customer
    Implements System.IComparable
    Private _id As Int32
    Private _name As String
    Private _rating As String
    Private Shared _order As SortOrder

    Public Enum SortOrder
        Ascending = 0
        Descending = 1
    End Enum

    Public Sub New(ByVal id As Int32, ByVal name As String)
        Me.New(id, name, "Other")
    End Sub

    Public Sub New(ByVal id As Int32, ByVal name As String, ByVal rating As String)
        Me._id = id
        Me._name = name
        Me._rating = rating
    End Sub

    Public Property Id() As Int32
        Get
            Return Me._id
        End Get
        Set(ByVal value As Int32)
            Me._id = value
        End Set
    End Property

    Public Property Name() As String
        Get
            Return Me._name
        End Get
        Set(ByVal value As String)
            Me._name = value
        End Set
    End Property
```

```vb
        Public Property Rating() As String
            Get
                Return Me._rating
            End Get
            Set(ByVal value As String)
                Me._rating = value
            End Set
        End Property

        Public Shared Property Order() As SortOrder
            Get
                Return _order
            End Get
            Set(ByVal value As SortOrder)
                _order = value
            End Set
        End Property

        Public Overrides Function Equals(ByVal obj As Object) As Boolean
            Dim retVal As Boolean = False
            If (Not obj Is Nothing) Then
                Dim custObj As Customer = DirectCast(obj, Customer)
                If ((custObj.Id = Me._id) And _
                    (custObj._name.Equals(Me.Name)) And _
                    (custObj._rating.Equals(Me.Rating))) Then
                    retVal = True
                End If
            End If
            Return retVal
        End Function

        Public Overrides Function ToString() As String
            Return CStr(Me._id) + ": " + Me._name
        End Function

        Public Function CompareTo(ByVal obj As Object) As Integer Implements
    IComparable.CompareTo

            Select Case _order
                Case SortOrder.Ascending
                    Return Me.Name.CompareTo(CType(obj, Customer).Name)
                Case SortOrder.Descending
                    Return (CType(obj, Customer).Name).CompareTo(Me.Name)
                Case Else
                    Return Me.Name.CompareTo(CType(obj, Customer).Name)
            End Select
        End Function

End Class
```

```csharp
[C# Code]
public class Customer : System.IComparable {
    private int _id;
    private string _name;
    private string _rating;
```

```
    private static SortOrder _order;

    public enum SortOrder {
        Ascending = 0,
        Descending = 1
    }

    public Customer(int id, string name) : this(id, name, "Other") {
    }

    public Customer(int id, string name, string rating) {
        this._id = id;
        this._name = name;
        this._rating = rating;
    }

    public int Id {
        get { return this._id; }
        set { this._id = value; }
    }

    public string Name {
        get { return this._name; }
        set { this._name = value; }
    }

    public string Rating {
        get { return this._rating; }
        set { this._rating = value; }
    }

    public static SortOrder Order {
        get { return _order; }
        set { _order = value; }
    }

    public override bool Equals(Object obj) {
        bool retVal = false;
        if (obj != null) {
            Customer custObj = (Customer)obj;
            if ((custObj.Id == this.Id) &&
                (custObj.Name.Equals(this.Name) &&
                (custObj.Rating.Equals(this.Rating))))
                retVal = true;
        }
        return retVal;
    }

    public override string ToString() {
        return this._id + ": " + this._name;
    }

    public int CompareTo(Object obj) {
```

```
        switch (_order) {
            case SortOrder.Ascending:
                return this.Name.CompareTo(((Customer)obj).Name);
            case SortOrder.Descending:
                return (((Customer)obj).Name).CompareTo(this.Name);
            default:
                return this.Name.CompareTo(((Customer)obj).Name);
        }
    }

}
```

Okay, you now have a basic `Customer` domain object. It holds a customer's id, name, and rating attributes and supplies overrides of the `Equals()` and `ToString()` methods. You'll also notice that it implements the `System.IComparable` interface. Overall, it's a very simple class, but it gives you a nice, self-contained object to put in your collection. And, it's likely to be a simplified representation of the kinds of objects you'll be tossing into your own collections.

From here, you can construct a `Collection<T>` class and start filling it with instances of `Customer` objects. The following code demonstrates a few of the approaches you can take to placing items in your collection:

```vb
[VB code]
Public Sub AddCollectionItemsTest()
    Dim custColl As New Collection(Of Customer)()
    custColl.Add(New Customer(1, "Sponge Bob"))
    custColl.Add(New Customer(2, "Kim Possible"))
    custColl.Add(New Customer(3, "Test Person"))

    custColl.Insert(1, New Customer(4, "Inserted Person"))

    custColl(3) = New Customer(9, "Fat Albert")

    For Each cust As Customer In custColl
        Console.Out.WriteLine(cust)
    Next
End Sub
```

```csharp
[C# Code]
public void AddCollectionItemsTest() {
    Collection<Customer> custColl = new Collection<Customer>();
    custColl.Add(new Customer(1, "Sponge Bob"));
    custColl.Add(new Customer(2, "Kim Possible"));
    custColl.Add(new Customer(3, "Test Person"));

    custColl.Insert(1, new Customer(4, "Inserted Person"));

    custColl[3] = new Customer(9, "Fat Albert");
    foreach (Customer cust in custColl)
        Console.Out.WriteLine(cust);
}
```

This example demonstrates the three separate mechanisms that can be used to place items into an instance of a `Collection<T>` class. It starts out by adding three customers using the `Add()` method. This method simply adds each new item to the end of the list, dynamically increasing the overall size of the collection as needed. You'll typically use this method to initially populate your collection.

The second approach to adding items to the collection is to use the `Insert()` method. This method takes a zero-based index and inserts the passed-in object at that specified position in the collection. All the objects below this new item will automatically have their indexes adjusted to account for the inserted item. If you attempt to insert an item with an index that is outside the currently valid range, the method will throw an exception. There is one slight twist on this, though. You are allowed to insert an item in the last position, essentially appending a new item to the end of the collection. In that instance, you can use an index value that is one greater than the index of the last item in the collection.

Finally, the last method shown in the example uses an indexer, which leverages the underlying `Items` property to randomly access items in the collection as if it were an array. For this example, you assign a new customer, Fat Albert, to the fourth position in your collection. The indexer's approach varies slightly from the `Insert()` method in that it cannot be used to add new items to your collection. It can only be used to modify an existing item in the collection or retrieve its value. As you might expect, if you supply an index that is out of the collection range of valid items, the class will throw an exception.

## Removing Items

The `Collection<T>` class also provides a series of methods that let you remove items from the collection. The following represents some sample code that exercises these interfaces:

```
[VB Code]
Public Sub RemoveCollectionItemsTest()
    Dim custColl As New Collection(Of Customer)()
    custColl.Add(New Customer(1, "Sponge Bob"))
    custColl.Add(New Customer(2, "Kim Possible"))
    custColl.Add(New Customer(3, "George Jetson"))
    custColl.Add(New Customer(4, "Fred Flintstone"))

    Dim success As Boolean = custColl.Remove(New Customer(4, "Bob Smith"))
    custColl.RemoveAt(1)

    For Each cust As Customer In custColl
        Console.Out.WriteLine(cust)
    Next

    custColl.Clear()

    For Each cust As Customer In custColl
        Console.Out.WriteLine(cust)
    Next
End Sub
```

```
[C# code]
public void RemoveCollectionItemsTest() {
    Collection<Customer> custColl = new Collection<Customer>();
    custColl.Add(new Customer(1, "Sponge Bob"));
    custColl.Add(new Customer(2, "Kim Possible"));
```

```
        custColl.Add(new Customer(3, "George Jetson"));
        custColl.Add(new Customer(4, "Fred Flintstone"));

        bool success = custColl.Remove(new Customer(4, "Bob Smith"));
        custColl.RemoveAt(1);

        foreach (Customer cust in custColl)
            Console.Out.WriteLine(cust);

        custColl.Clear();

        foreach (Customer cust in custColl)
            Console.Out.WriteLine(cust);
    }
```

This example demonstrates the three methods that are used to remove data from an instance of a
Collection<T> class. This example populates a collection with an initial set of customers. Then, it
attempts to remove an item from the collection using the Remove() method. This method accepts a
Customer object and searches for a matching Customer in the collection. If a match is found, it is
removed and the method returns true. For this specific scenario, you supplied a Customer that did not
exist in the collection, so the method returns false. Note that your Customer object supplies an implementation of the Equals() method that ends up being used to determine the equality of Customer
objects.

The code also employs the RemoveAt() method to delete an item from its collection using an index. It
removes the second item from the list, passing an index of 1 (remember, the collection uses a zero-based
index). Whereas Remove() returns a boolean status, the RemoveAt() method throws an exception if you
supply an invalid index.

The last removal mechanism, Clear(), is used to remove all items from a collection.

## Accessing and Inspecting Items

The Collection<T> class also includes a variety of methods and properties that can be used to access
the data in the collection and obtain information about the state of the collection. The following example
demonstrates each of these methods and properties:

```vb
[VB code]
Public Sub AccessingCollectionItemsTest()
    Dim custColl As New Collection(Of Customer)()
    custColl.Add(New Customer(1, "Sponge Bob"))
    custColl.Add(New Customer(2, "Kim Possible"))
    custColl.Add(New Customer(3, "George Jetson"))
    custColl.Add(New Customer(4, "Fred Flintstone"))

    Dim custEnum As IEnumerator(Of Customer) = custColl.GetEnumerator()
    While (custEnum.MoveNext())
        Dim cust As Customer = custEnum.Current
        Console.Out.WriteLine(cust)
    End While

    Dim cust1 As New Customer(9, "Fred Rodgers")
    If (custColl.Contains(cust1)) Then
```

```
        custColl.Remove(cust1)
    End If

    Dim custIndex As Int32 = custColl.IndexOf(New Customer(3, "George Jetson"))
    If (custIndex >= 0) Then
        custColl.RemoveAt(custIndex)
    End If

    Dim custArray(custColl.Count) As Customer
    custColl.CopyTo(custArray, 0)

    For Each cust As Customer In custColl
        Console.Out.WriteLine(cust)
    Next
End Sub
```

```
[C# code]
public void AccessingCollectionItemsTest() {
    Collection<Customer> custColl = new Collection<Customer>();
    custColl.Add(new Customer(1, "Sponge Bob"));
    custColl.Add(new Customer(2, "Kim Possible"));
    custColl.Add(new Customer(3, "George Jetson"));
    custColl.Add(new Customer(4, "Fred Flintstone"));

    IEnumerator<Customer> custEnum = custColl.GetEnumerator();
    while (custEnum.MoveNext()) {
        Customer cust = custEnum.Current;
        Console.Out.WriteLine(cust);
    }

    Customer cust1 = new Customer(9, "Fred Rodgers");
    if (custColl.Contains(cust1))
        custColl.Remove(cust1);

    int custIndex = custColl.IndexOf(new Customer(3, "George Jetson"));
    if (custIndex >= 0)
        custColl.RemoveAt(custIndex);

    Customer[] custArray = new Customer[custColl.Count];
    custColl.CopyTo(custArray, 0);
    foreach (Customer cust in custColl)
        Console.Out.WriteLine(cust);
}
```

In order to maximize the coverage of the Collection<T> interface, this example employs both the Contains() and IndexOf() methods to look up items in a collection. The first section of code invokes the Contains() method to determine if the collection includes a reference to the "Fred Rodgers" Customer object. If the object is found (and it's not), it would be removed from the collection. The alternative approach, using the IndexOf() method, is also employed. This method searches for a matching object and returns the index for the item that is found. If no match is found, the method returns –1.

Collection<T> also supports two different modes for enumerating the items in your collection. The most common of these, the "for each" mechanism, provides the fastest and simplest means of iterating over the items in a collection. In rare instances, you may also want to work directly with the underlying enumerator. The example demonstrates both of these approaches. The more manual approach starts by calling the GetEnumerator() method, which returns an instance of an IEnumerator<T> object. Then that enumerator interface is used to iterate over the initially loaded set of Customer objects. At the end of the example, the "for each" construct is used to dump the final contents of the collection. This second option is clearly cleaner and more readable.

Of course, because this is an indexed-based collection, you also have the additional option of using the indexer to grab one or more items out of your collection.

## Specializing Collection<T>

Although the Collection<T> class will frequently support most of your basic collection needs, there will still be times when you'll need to extend its functionality. The Collection<T> was built with this in mind, offering you a series of protected members that allow you to modify or extend the behavior of this class.

With this in mind, let's look at a simple example that examines specializing the Collection<T> class. The following code introduces a new HistoryCollection that intercepts any changes made to the collection and records the collection's "recently deleted" history:

```
[VB code]
Public Class HistoryCollection(Of T)
    Inherits Collection(Of T)
    Private _deletedHistory As Collection(Of T)

    Public Sub New()
        _deletedHistory = New Collection(Of T)
    End Sub

    Protected Overrides Sub InsertItem(ByVal index As Integer, ByVal item As T)
        Console.Out.WriteLine("Added--> " + item.ToString())
        MyBase.InsertItem(index, item)
    End Sub

    Protected Overrides Sub RemoveItem(ByVal index As Integer)
        If ((index >= 0) And (index < Me.Count)) Then
            Dim item As T = Me(index)
            Console.Out.WriteLine("Removed--> " + item.ToString())
            _deletedHistory.Insert(0, item)
            MyBase.RemoveItem(index)
        End If
    End Sub

    Protected Overrides Sub ClearItems()
        For Each item As T In Me
            _deletedHistory.Insert(0, item)
        Next

        Console.Out.WriteLine("All Items Removed")
        MyBase.ClearItems()
    End Sub

    Protected Overrides Sub SetItem(ByVal index As Integer, ByVal item As T)
```

```
        Console.Out.WriteLine("New Value-->", item)
        MyBase.SetItem(index, item)
    End Sub

    Public ReadOnly Property DeletionHistory() As Collection(Of T)
        Get
            Return Me._deletedHistory
        End Get
    End Property
End Class
```

[C# code]
```csharp
public class HistoryCollection<T> : Collection<T> {
    private Collection<T> _deletedHistory;

    public HistoryCollection() {
        _deletedHistory = new Collection<T>();
    }


    protected override void InsertItem(int index, T item) {
        Console.Out.WriteLine("Added--> " + item);
        base.InsertItem(index, item);
    }


    protected override void RemoveItem(int index) {
        if ((index >= 0) && (index < this.Count)) {
            T item = this[index];
            Console.Out.WriteLine("Removed--> " + item);
            _deletedHistory.Insert(0, item);
            base.RemoveItem(index);
        }
    }


    protected override void ClearItems() {
        foreach (T item in this)
            _deletedHistory.Insert(0, item);

        Console.Out.WriteLine("All Items Removed");
        base.ClearItems();
    }

    protected override void SetItem(int index, T item) {
        Console.Out.WriteLine("New Value-->", item);
        base.SetItem(index, item);
    }

    public Collection<T> DeletionHistory {
        get { return this._deletedHistory; }
    }
}
```

This `HistoryCollection` overrides each of the protected methods that are exposed by the `Collection<T>` class and adds logic to keep track of each item as it is deleted. It also writes out information about the state of the collection each time it is modified. This is achieved by inserting code into the `RemoveItem()` and `ClearItems()` methods, each of which intercepts deletion calls and places the deleted items into the `deletedHistory` field that holds the list of all items that have been removed (with the most recently deleted items placed at the top of the list). Clients are allowed to access this list via the `DeletionHistory` property.

Now that you have this new collection, you can put together a simple example that will exercise its interface:

```
[VB code]
Public Sub HistoryCollectionTest()
    Dim custColl As New HistoryCollection(Of Customer)
    custColl.Add(New Customer(1, "Sponge Bob"))
    custColl.Add(New Customer(2, "Kim Possible"))
    custColl.Add(New Customer(3, "George Jetson"))
    custColl.Add(New Customer(4, "Fred Flintstone"))
    custColl.Add(New Customer(5, "Barney Rubble"))

    custColl.RemoveAt(1)
    custColl.RemoveAt(3)

    Console.Out.WriteLine("")
    Console.Out.WriteLine("Deletion History")
    Console.Out.WriteLine("==================")
    For Each cust As Customer In custColl.DeletionHistory
        Console.Out.WriteLine(cust)
    Next
End Sub
```

```
[C# code]
public void HistoryCollectionTest() {
    HistoryCollection<Customer> custColl = new HistoryCollection<Customer>();
    custColl.Add(new Customer(1, "Sponge Bob"));
    custColl.Add(new Customer(2, "Kim Possible"));
    custColl.Add(new Customer(3, "George Jetson"));
    custColl.Add(new Customer(4, "Fred Flintstone"));
    custColl.Add(new Customer(5, "Barney Rubble"));

    custColl.RemoveAt(1);
    custColl.RemoveAt(3);

    Console.Out.WriteLine("\nDeletion History");
    Console.Out.WriteLine("==================");
    foreach (Customer cust in custColl.DeletionHistory)
        Console.Out.WriteLine(cust);
}
```

You'll notice that this example declares an instance of your `HistoryCollection<T>` and adds five items to the collection. Then, to show off the collection's ability to track deleted items, it removes two items from the collection. Finally, the example dumps out the contents of the deleted items history. After running this example, the following output is shown on the console:

```
Added--> 1: Sponge Bob
Added--> 2: Kim Possible
Added--> 3: George Jetson
Added--> 4: Fred Flintstone
Added--> 5: Barney Rubble
Removed--> 2: Kim Possible
Removed--> 5: Barney Rubble

Deletion History
==================
5: Barney Rubble
2: Kim Possible
```

This is a very simple example. However, it illustrates the basic mechanics of creating your own specialization of the Collection<T> class. It also points out those protected methods that are available to you when creating a descendant collection.

## Comparer<T>

When dealing with collections of objects, you need to have a general-purpose mechanism that allows you to compare objects. The BCL achieves this via the Comparer<T> class, which provides a default implementation of the IComparer<T> interface.

You can imagine how having this functionality broken out of the individual collections can come in handy. By separating out this concept, you have the opportunity to provide a variety of different comparison implementations. So, if you want the comparison to be case insensitive, for example, you could create your own implementation of the IComparer<T> interface that supplies this new definition of object equality.

The Comparer<T> class really only has two members that deserve your attention — the Default property and the Compare() method. The Default property is used in determining the default mode of comparing two objects. In fact, the Default property is itself an instance of a Comparer<T> class.

When you invoke the Compare() method, it consults this Default property to determine how it should go about comparing two objects. As part of this process, the default comparer will determine if the type parameter, T, implements IComparable<T>. If it does, that mechanism will be used to perform the comparison. However, if T does not implement this interface, the default comparer will then attempt to use the non-generic IComparable interface to complete the comparison. It is possible that T won't implement either of these interfaces. If this is the case, Compare() will throw an exception.

Now, take a look at how this class might work in a more practical example. In your Customer class, you'll notice that it had the forethought to implement the System.IComparable interface. In doing so, the class was also required to provide an implementation of the CompareTo() method. That method allows you to sort the customers by name in ascending or descending order. Without having provided this interface, the Comparer would have no direct means of sorting Customer objects. You could use a Comparer to sort individual attributes of the customer (Id, Name, and so on), but not the Customer object itself.

Now that you're aware of the Customer object's support for comparisons, here's a look at how Comparer can be applied to sort a collection of customers:

```
[VB Code]
Public Class ComparerTest
    Public Function NameSortDelegate(ByVal cust1 As Customer, _
                                     ByVal cust2 As Customer) As Integer
        Return Comparer(Of Customer).Default.Compare(cust1, cust2)
    End Function

    Public Sub NameSortTest()
        Dim collCustList As New List(Of Customer)()
        collCustList.Add(New Customer(99, "Happy Gillmore", "Platinum"))
        collCustList.Add(New Customer(77, "Billy Madison", "Gold"))
        collCustList.Add(New Customer(55, "Bobby Boucher", "Gold"))
        collCustList.Add(New Customer(88, "Barry Egan", "Platinum"))
        collCustList.Add(New Customer(11, "Longfellow Deeds", "Other"))

        Console.Out.WriteLine("Before Sort:")
        For Each cust As Customer In collCustList
            Console.Out.WriteLine(cust)
        Next

        Customer.Order = Customer.SortOrder.Ascending
        collCustList.Sort(AddressOf NameSortDelegate)

        Console.Out.WriteLine("After Ascending Sort:")
        For Each cust As Customer In collCustList
            Console.Out.WriteLine(cust)
        Next

        Customer.Order = Customer.SortOrder.Descending
        collCustList.Sort(AddressOf NameSortDelegate)
        Console.Out.WriteLine("After Descending Sort:")
        For Each cust As Customer In collCustList
            Console.Out.WriteLine(cust)
        Next
    End Sub
End Class
```

```
[C# Code]
public class ComparerTest {
    public void NameSortTest() {
        List<Customer> collCustList = new List<Customer>();
        collCustList.Add(new Customer(99, "Happy Gillmore", "Platinum"));
        collCustList.Add(new Customer(77, "Billy Madison", "Gold"));
        collCustList.Add(new Customer(55, "Bobby Boucher", "Gold"));
        collCustList.Add(new Customer(88, "Barry Egan", "Platinum"));
        collCustList.Add(new Customer(11, "Longfellow Deeds", "Other"));

        Console.Out.WriteLine("Before Sort:");
        foreach (Customer cust in collCustList)
            Console.Out.WriteLine(cust);

        Customer.Order = Customer.SortOrder.Ascending;
        collCustList.Sort(delegate(Customer cust1, Customer cust2) {
            return Comparer<Customer>.Default.Compare(cust1, cust2);
        });
```

```
                    Console.Out.WriteLine("After Ascending Sort:");
                    foreach (Customer cust in collCustList)
                        Console.Out.WriteLine(cust);

                    Customer.Order = Customer.SortOrder.Descending;
                    collCustList.Sort(delegate(Customer cust1, Customer cust2) {
                        return Comparer<Customer>.Default.Compare(cust1, cust2);
                    });

                    Console.Out.WriteLine("After Descending Sort:");
                    foreach (Customer cust in collCustList)
                        Console.Out.WriteLine(cust);
            }
        }
```

This example uses the `List<T>` collection that is described in great detail later in this chapter. It populates the list and then proceeds to sort it first in ascending order and then, once again, in descending order. For each call to the `Sort()` method, you supply an instance of `Comparer<Customer>` that ends up calling the `CompareTo()` method of your `Customer` object. `CompareTo()` then consults the `Customer.Order` property to determine what sorting scheme should be applied. The output of this example is as follows:

```
Before Sort:
99: Happy Gillmore
77: Billy Madison
55: Bobby Boucher
88: Barry Egan
11: Longfellow Deeds

After Ascending Sort:
88: Barry Egan
77: Billy Madison
55: Bobby Boucher
99: Happy Gillmore
11: Longfellow Deeds

After Descending Sort:
11: Longfellow Deeds
99: Happy Gillmore
55: Bobby Boucher
77: Billy Madison
88: Barry Egan
```

Although the `Comparer` class is not particularly difficult to understand, it should be viewed as a fundamental type that you're likely to leverage anywhere you might be comparing objects. As part of this, it should also be clear that you're going to need to consider implementing the `System.IComparable` interface for many of your own data types.

## Dictionary<TKey, TValue>

The `Dictionary<TKey, TValue>` class is used to map keys to values in a collection. These keys, each of which must be unique, will then allow you randomly access the values that are stored in the collection. As you can imagine, the efficiency and general behavior of the `Dictionary<TKey, TValue>` class makes it a priceless tool that has countless applications.

If you've been working with the System.Collections namespace, you've probably already been using the HashTable class. In the generics namespace, the Dictionary<TKey, TValue> class is the functional equivalent of the HashTable. However, even though it inherits most of the concepts from the HashTable, it represents a mostly revamped implementation. As such, its performance characteristics will not necessarily match those of the HashTable.

The following table summarizes the methods and properties that are part of the Dictionary<TKey, TValue> class.

| Method or Property Name | Description |
|---|---|
| Add() | Adds the supplied key and value to the dictionary. |
| Clear() | Removes all the items from the dictionary. |
| ContainsKey() | Determines if the supplied key exists in the current dictionary, returning true if it is found. |
| ContainsValue() | Determines if the supplied value exists in the current dictionary, returning true if it is found. |
| Count | Returns the number of items currently stored in the dictionary. |
| GetEnumerator() | Returns an enumerated collection of KeyValuePair objects corresponding to the items in the dictionary. |
| GetObjectData() | Retrieves a serialized representation of the dictionary. |
| Item | Indexer property that uses keys to add or update items in the dictionary. |
| Keys | Returns a Dictionary.KeyCollection containing all the keys in the dictionary. |
| OnDeserialization() | Called when deserialization has completed. |
| Remove() | Finds the items that match the passed-in key and removes it. If the item is found, the method returns true. |
| TryGetValue() | Attempts to get the value that corresponds to the supplied key. If the value is found, it is returned. Otherwise, the default value for the value parameter is returned. |
| Values | Returns a Dictionary.ValuesCollection containing all the values in the dictionary. |

## Constructing a Dictionary<TKey, TValue>

Of all the generic classes found in the BCL, the Dictionary<TKey, TValue> class offers the largest menu of overloaded constructors. Of particular interest are those constructors that allow you to provide different Comparer<T> implementations that can be used to customize how keys are evaluated and compared by the dictionary. Here's a simple example that illustrates the use of a few of the Dictionary<TKey, TValue> constructors:

```
[VB code]
Public Sub ConstuctorTest()
    Dim custDict As New Dictionary(Of Int32, Customer)(Comparer(Of Int32).Default)
    custDict(99) = New Customer(99, "Happy Gillmore", "Platinum")
    custDict(77) = New Customer(77, "Billy Madison", "Gold")
    custDict(55) = New Customer(55, "Bobby Boucher", "Silver")
    custDict(88) = New Customer(88, "Barry Egan", "Platinum")

    Dim copyDict As New Dictionary(Of Int32, Customer)(custDict)
    copyDict(55) = New Customer(55, "Longfellow Deeds", "Other")

    Dim custValues As Dictionary(Of Int32, Customer).ValueCollection = _
                                            custDict.Values

    For Each cust As Customer In custValues
        Console.Out.WriteLine(cust)
    Next

    custValues = copyDict.Values
    For Each cust As Customer In custValues
        Console.Out.WriteLine(cust)
    Next

    Dim capacityDict As New Dictionary(Of Int32, Customer)(100)
End Sub
```

```
[C# Code]
public void ConstuctorTest() {
    Dictionary<int, Customer> custDict =
                new Dictionary<int, Customer>(Comparer<int>.Default);
    custDict[99] = new Customer(99, "Happy Gillmore", "Platinum");
    custDict[77] = new Customer(77, "Billy Madison", "Gold");
    custDict[55] = new Customer(55, "Bobby Boucher", "Silver");
    custDict[88] = new Customer(88, "Barry Egan", "Platinum");

    Dictionary<int, Customer> copyDict = new Dictionary<int, Customer>(custDict);
    copyDict[55] = new Customer(55, "Longfellow Deeds", "Other");

    Dictionary<int, Customer>.ValueCollection custValues = custDict.Values;
    foreach (Customer cust in custValues)
        Console.Out.WriteLine(cust);

    custValues = copyDict.Values;
    foreach (Customer cust in custValues)
        Console.Out.WriteLine(cust);

    Dictionary<int, Customer> capacityDict = new Dictionary<int, Customer>(100);
}
```

This example starts out by declaring an instance of Dictionary<TKey, TValue> that supplies a Comparer as one of the parameters provided to the constructor. This Comparer is simply the default Comparer for the integer data type and, as such, it doesn't buy you anything over the default comparer you would have gotten without providing this parameter. It's primarily here to convey the idea that you have the option of supplying your own custom Comparer whenever you construct a

`Dictionary<TKey, TValue>` class. This can be very handy if you have a complex key for your dictionary. However, in many instances, you'll probably be able to leverage the default `Comparer` for your key.

Once the initial dictionary is populated, the example then constructs yet another dictionary, this time supplying the previously constructed dictionary as a parameter. This new dictionary will take this incoming parameter and copy its contents into the new dictionary instance. Now, the question is, does the `Dictionary<TKey, TValue>` class make a deep copy of the incoming dictionary? Well, to determine this, the example modifies one of the items in the new dictionary and dumps the contents of both the original and the new dictionaries. From the output, you'll discover that the original source dictionary was not affected by the changes to the new dictionary, which means the copy was deep.

Finally, the last constructor example includes a parameter for capacity. This parameter allows you to have more control over the initial allocation of the size of items you expect the dictionary to hold. If you're expecting the dictionary to be quite large, you may want to pre-allocate the capacity using this parameter. By pre-setting the capacity, you'll improve the overall performance of your large dictionaries. However, regardless of how this value is set, your dictionary instances will continually grow to accommodate new items.

Although this example covers the highlights of constructing `Dictionary<TKey, TValue>` classes, there are also a few additional permutations of overloaded constructors that simply represent variations on the themes covered here.

## Adding and Updating Items

Maintaining the contents of a `Dictionary<TKey, TValue>` class doesn't follow the same patterns you saw with the collection classes. With dictionaries, your collection has no order. Your items are "poked" somewhere into its internal collection with no guarantee for where they are placed. As such, all of your interactions with a dictionary are achieved through a key that represents the unique index of any given value that has been placed in the dictionary.

The set of methods or properties that are allowed to modify the contents of a dictionary is fairly small. The following example demonstrates these methods and properties in action:

```
[VB code]
Public Sub AddUpdateRetrieveItems()
    Dim custDict As New Dictionary(Of Int32, Customer)()
    custDict(99) = New Customer(99, "Happy Gillmore", "Platinum")
    custDict(77) = New Customer(77, "Billy Madison", "Gold")
    custDict(55) = New Customer(55, "Bobby Boucher", "Silver")
    custDict(88) = New Customer(88, "Barry Egan", "Platinum")

    custDict.Add(11, New Customer(11, "Longfellow Deeds", "Other"))
    custDict.Add(77, New Customer(77, "Test Person", "Gold"))

    custDict(55) = New Customer(55, "Bobby Boucher", "Gold")

    Dim tmpCust As Customer = custDict(88)
    tmpCust.Rating = "Other"
End Sub
```

```
[C# code]
public void AddUpdateRetrieveItems() {
    Dictionary<int, Customer> custDict = new Dictionary<int, Customer>();
    custDict[99] = new Customer(99, "Happy Gillmore", "Platinum");
    custDict[77] = new Customer(77, "Billy Madison", "Gold");
    custDict[55] = new Customer(55, "Bobby Boucher", "Silver");
    custDict[88] = new Customer(88, "Barry Egan", "Platinum");

    custDict.Add(11, new Customer(11, "Longfellow Deeds", "Other"));
    custDict.Add(77, new Customer(77, "Test Person", "Gold"));

    custDict[55] = new Customer(55, "Bobby Boucher", "Gold");

    Customer tmpCust = custDict[88];
    tmpCust.Rating = "Other";
}
```

Whenever you're populating a dictionary, you'll always be expected to supply both a key and a value parameter. This example adds items to your dictionary using both the indexer and the `Add()` method. With the indexer, you simply provide the key as the index value and assign a value to that key. The result is that the item that gets assigned to that index (key) is inserted into your dictionary. The `Add()` method achieves this in the old-fashioned way, accepting key and value parameters and inserting the new item into the dictionary.

So, the question is, why two methods that essentially do the same thing? Well, that's where understanding the difference between the indexer and the `Add()` method is critical. The indexer can actually be used to both add and *update* items in a collection. If you assign a value to a key that already exists, the indexer will simply replace the current item with the new value. The `Add()` method, on the other hand, can *only* be used to add items to a collection. So, if you call `Add()` and provide a key for an item that already exists in the dictionary, the supplied value will not be placed in the collection.

In the example, you'll notice `Add()` is used to attempt to add two new customers to a dictionary. The first customer, with the index of 11, gets added successfully. However, the next line throws an exception because it attempts to add an item with a key that has already been inserted into the dictionary. If you want to update an existing item, you must use the indexer. An example of how that is done is shown in the next line of code, where you update the value for an existing customer by assigning the key of 55 a new customer reference.

Although there are no hard-and-fast rules that surround using indexers and the `Add()` method, the variation in their behavior would suggest that the indexer might best be reserved for retrieving and updating existing dictionary values and the `Add()` method, of course, would only be used to add items (because that's all it can do anyway). This indexer is too prone to introducing ambiguity because you can never be certain if it's adding or updating an item.

The last bit of the example is focused on pointing out how reference types held by a dictionary are managed as, well, reference types. That is to say that if you extract an item from your dictionary that is a reference, any modification of that reference is also modifying the dictionary's reference to that same item. So, when you retrieve the `Customer` with they key of 88 in the example, you are working directly with the same reference that is being held by the dictionary.

## *Looking Up Items*

The `Dictionary<TKey, TValue>` class includes methods that allow you to determine if specific keys *or* values already exist in your dictionary. As you can imagine, methods of this nature play a key role in your management of a dictionary's content.

Here's a simple example of these methods in action. For this next set of sample code, assume there's a class that has a dictionary, `myDictionary`, which was pre-populated with the following `Customer` objects:

```
Customer(99, "Happy Gillmore", "Platinum")
Customer(77, "Billy Madison", "Gold"));
Customer(55, "Bobby Boucher", "Silver")
Customer(88, "Barry Egan", "Platinum")
Customer(11, "Longfellow Deeds", "Other")
```

Now, with this as your current list of customers, you're going to call a series of methods that will be used to determine if items already exist in the collection of customers referenced here. The list you're going to pass into each of these methods contains the following `Customer` objects:

```
Customer(33, "Marvin Hagler", "Platinum")
Customer(11, "Buster Douglas", "Other")
Customer(55, "Bobby Boucher", "Silver")
Customer(51, "Mike Tyson", "Gold")
Customer(77, "Ray Leonard", "Silver")
```

Okay, the stage is finally set. All that's left now is to introduce a set of methods that will operate on these two populations of customers. These methods all use different techniques to locate customers, each with its own approach to locating a value in a dictionary:

```vb
[VB code]
Public Sub AddCustomersByID(ByVal customers As Collection(Of Customer))
    For Each cust As Customer In customers
        If (myDictionary.ContainsKey(cust.Id) = False) Then
            myDictionary.Add(cust.Id, cust)
        Else
            Console.Out.WriteLine("Dupe Customer Id: {0}", cust.Id)
        End If
    Next
End Sub

Public Sub AddCustomersByValue(ByVal customers As Collection(Of Customer))
    For Each cust As Customer In customers
        If (myDictionary.ContainsValue(cust) = False) Then
            If (myDictionary.ContainsKey(cust.Id) = True) Then
                myDictionary(cust.Id) = cust
            Else
                myDictionary.Add(cust.Id, cust)
            End If
        Else
            Console.Out.WriteLine("Dupe Customer Value: {0}", cust.Id)
        End If
    Next
```

```
    End Sub

    Public Function FindDupeCustomers(ByVal customers As Collection(Of Customer)) _
                                                  As Collection(Of Customer)
        Dim retVal As New Collection(Of Customer)()
        For Each cust As Customer In customers
            Dim tmpCust As New Customer(0, "New")
            If (myDictionary.TryGetValue(cust.Id, tmpCust) = True) Then
                retVal.Add(tmpCust)
                Console.Out.WriteLine("Dupe Customer Found: {0}", cust.Id)
            End If
        Next
        Return retVal
    End Function
```

```
[C# code]
public void AddCustomersByID(Collection<Customer> customers) {
    foreach (Customer cust in customers) {
        if (myDictionary.ContainsKey(cust.Id) == false)
            myDictionary.Add(cust.Id, cust);
        else
            Console.Out.WriteLine("Dupe Customer Id: {0}", cust.Id);
    }
}

public void AddCustomersByValue(Collection<Customer> customers) {
    foreach (Customer cust in customers) {
        if (myDictionary.ContainsValue(cust) == false) {
            if (myDictionary.ContainsKey(cust.Id) == true)
                myDictionary[cust.Id] = cust;
            else
                myDictionary.Add(cust.Id, cust);
        } else {
            Console.Out.WriteLine("Dupe Customer Value: {0}", cust.Id);
        }
    }
}

public Collection<Customer> FindDupeCustomers(Collection<Customer> customers) {
    Collection<Customer> retVal = new Collection<Customer>();
    foreach (Customer cust in customers) {
        Customer tmpCust = new Customer(0, "New");
        if (myDictionary.TryGetValue(cust.Id, out tmpCust) == true) {
            retVal.Add(tmpCust);
            Console.Out.WriteLine("Dupe Customer Found: {0}", cust.Id);
        }

    }
    return retVal;
}
```

The first method, AddCustomersById(), takes your second set of customers as a parameter and attempts to add any new incoming customers to your internal dictionary (myDictionary). It calls the ContainsKey() method on myDictionary to look up each customer's Id from the incoming list and, if the Id of the items is not found, the customer is added to the list. Otherwise, if the Id already exists, a message is written to the console.

The next method, `AddCustomersByValue()`, takes a slightly different approach. It requires the `Customer` objects to match on more than their `Ids` to be considered a true match. As it processes each `Customer` from the incoming list, it calls the `ContainsValue()` method on the dictionary, which searches the dictionary for a matching `Customer` object. If a matching object is not found, the method will decide if it needs to update an existing item or add a new one. This approach allows you to update customers who may have the same Id but have changed one or more of their other attributes.

Finally, the last method in this example, `FindDupeCustomers()`, leverages the `TryGetMethod()` to illustrate one last way to extract information from a dictionary. The method simplifies the process of fetching an item from a dictionary in that it eliminates the need to surround your method call with any exception handling or pre-validation logic. From this example, which builds and returns a list of duplicate customers, you can see how this method is used to both check for the existence of a customer and retrieve its contents all in one call and with no need for any exception handling.

So, what happens when you run each of these methods with the data supplied earlier in this section? Well, the `AddCustomersById()` method locates three duplicate customer Ids (11, 55, and 77). The next example, `AddCustomersByValue()`, only reports one duplicate, customer 55. That's because, although 11 and 77 are duplicate Ids, the rest of their data did not match. As such, they were updated and not reported as true duplicates. The `FindDupeCustomers()` method, which serves a slightly different purpose, ends up returning a collection with customers 11, 55, and 77.

## Retrieving Keys and Values

Ultimately, at some point, you're going to want to extract all the information from your `Dictionary<TKey, TValue>` objects. Given that you have both keys and values in your dictionary, you'll need specific methods that will allow you to access the collection of keys, the collections of values, as well as the collection of key/value pairs. Fortunately, the `Dictionary<TKey, TValue>` class equips you with all the methods you need to access all of this information. The following example provides a quick view of how you can access each of these different collections of data:

```
[VB code]
Public Sub GetContents()
    Dim custDict As New Dictionary(Of Int32, Customer)()
    custDict(55) = New Customer(55, "Bobby Boucher", "Silver")
    custDict(88) = New Customer(88, "Barry Egan", "Platinum")
    custDict(11) = New Customer(11, "Longfellow Deeds", "Other")

    Dim custKeys As Dictionary(Of Int32, Customer).KeyCollection = custDict.Keys
    Dim custValues As Dictionary(Of Int32, Customer).ValueCollection = _
                                            custDict.Values

    Dim custEnum As Dictionary(Of Int32, Customer).Enumerator = _
                                            custDict.GetEnumerator()
    While (custEnum.MoveNext())
        Dim custKVP As KeyValuePair(Of Int32, Customer) = custEnum.Current
        Console.Out.WriteLine(custKVP.Value)
    End While
End Sub
```

```
[C# code]
public void GetContents() {
    Dictionary<int, Customer> custDict = new Dictionary<int, Customer>();
    custDict[55] = new Customer(55, "Bobby Boucher", "Silver");
    custDict[88] = new Customer(88, "Barry Egan", "Platinum");
    custDict[11] = new Customer(11, "Longfellow Deeds", "Other");

    Dictionary<int, Customer>.KeyCollection custKeys = custDict.Keys;
    Dictionary<int, Customer>.ValueCollection custValues = custDict.Values;

    Dictionary<int, Customer>.Enumerator custEnum = custDict.GetEnumerator();
    while (custEnum.MoveNext()) {
        KeyValuePair<int, Customer> custKVP = custEnum.Current;
        Console.Out.WriteLine(custKVP.Value);
    }
}
```

As you can see, the `Dictionary<TKey, TValue>` class provides you with some specific classes that are used to hold its keys and values. This example simply demonstrates how to extract each one of these items from an existing, populated dictionary. It accesses both the `Keys` and `Values` properties and places their results into a collection that you can iterate over like any other collection. It also retrieves the dictionary's enumerator with a call to the `GetEnumerator()` and iterates over the results.

Notice that for each of these items you accessed — key, values, and the enumerator — the dictionary returned a specific corresponding construct, `Dictionary<TKey, TValue>.KeyCollection`, `Dictionary<TKey, TValue>.ValueCollection`, and `IEnumerator<KeyValuePair<TKey, TValue>>`.

### Removing Items

The interface for removing items from a `Dictionary<TKey, TValue>` is as simple as they come. Because all keys in the dictionary must be unique, you really only need one method, `Remove()`, to support the deletion of an individual item. This method looks up the passed-in key and removes the item from the collection if it is found. It returns `true` if the removal was successful. The class also includes a `Clear()` method that can be used to remove all items from the dictionary.

### Null Keys

One requirement of the `HashTable` is that all of its keys and values must be represented as objects. This fact means that it could accept null values for both the key and value parameters. With `Dictionary<TKey, TValue>` this is not possible. As part of being generic, the `Dictionary<TKey, TValue>` class must accept both value and reference types. To get around this problem, you can use the `Nullable<T>` class, which will allow you to supply the dictionary with null values for both value and reference types.

## EqualityComparer<T>

When working with generics, you may run into situations where you want to test the equality of two type parameters. Although you might expect this to work, the .NET Framework does not allow you to explicitly compare the equality of two generic parameters. For example, suppose you had the following generic class:

```
[VB code]
Public Class EqualityTest(Of T)
    Private _value As T

    Public Sub New(ByVal value As T)
        If value <> Me._value Then
            Me._value = value
        End If
    End Sub
End Class
```

```
[C# code]
public class EqualityTest<T> {
    private T _value;

    public EqualityTest(T value) {
        if (value != this._value)
            this._value = value;
    }
}
```

This example looks simple enough. However, the equality test that is performed in your constructor will fail because the compiler will not let you directly test the equality of two type parameters. If you think about it, it makes sense that this would be a problem for the compiler. Because type parameters can be both value and reference types, there's no default behavior that equality can apply here to resolve this expression. This is what gave rise to the need for the `EqualityComparer<T>` class. Take a look at how this class can be applied to resolve this problem:

```
[VB code]
Public Class EqualityTest(Of T)
    Private _value As T

    Public Sub New(ByVal value As T)
        If (EqualityComparer(Of T).Equals(value, Me._value) = False) Then
            Me._value = value
        End If
    End Sub
End Class
```

```
[C# code]
public class EqualityTest<T> {
    private T _value;

    public EqualityTest(T value) {
        if (EqualityComparer<T>.Equals(value, this._value) == false)
            this._value = value;
    }
}
```

The application of the `EqualityComparer<T>` class allows you to successfully compare the two type parameters. This is a simple generic helper, but it's an essential tool for implementing many generic types.

# KeyedCollection<TKey, TItem>

The KeyedCollection<TKey, TItem> class plays the same role, at least conceptually, as the Dictionary<TKey, TValue> class. Much like the dictionary, it allows you to map a key to an item in the collection. So, the next question is: Why do you need the KeyedCollection<TKey, TItem> class at all? Why not just use the dictionary?

To answer this, you have to think back to the discussion of the role of the Collection<T> class. If you recall, the Collection<T> class provided a number of protected methods and attributes and, as such, it was meant to play the role of the programmer-extensible collection. In contrast, List<T> offers minimal extensibility. So, although you might use List<T> classes extensively, the BCL is expecting you to favor using Collection<T> classes as the primary class you'd hand off to clients.

Now, with this as a backdrop, you have to look at KeyedCollection<TKey, TItem> and Dictionary<TKey, TValue> in the same light. KeyedCollection<TKey, TItem> offers up a pool of protected properties and methods that allow you to extend and customize the behavior of the collection, whereas Dictionary<TKey, TValue> includes a very minimal set of protected members.

As you look at the following list of properties and methods supported by the KeyedCollection<TKey, TItem>, you'll notice that the majority of its functionality is inherited from the Collection<T> class.

| Method or Property Name | Description |
| --- | --- |
| Add() | Adds the provided object to the end of the collection. |
| Clear() | Remove all the items from the collection. |
| Contains()* | Attempts to find an object in the collection equal to the passed-in object. If a matching object is found, the method returns true. |
| CopyTo() | Copies the contents of the collection to an Array. |
| Count | Returns the number of items currently stored in the collection. |
| GetEnumerator() | Gets the IEnumerator<T> enumerator for your collection. |
| IndexOf() | Finds the index of the object equal to the object supplied as a parameter. If no matching object is found, this method returns –1. |
| Insert() | Inserts a new object into the location at the specified index. If an invalid index is provided, the class throws an ArgumentOutOfRangeException. |
| Item* | Indexer that provides index-based access to the elements of collection. If an invalid index is provided, the class throws an ArgumentOutOfRangeException. |
| Remove()* | Searches for an object that is equal to the supplied object and removes it. If the object is found and removed, the function returns true. Otherwise, it returns false. |
| RemoveAt() | Removes the object at the specified index. If an invalid index is provided, the class throws an ArgumentOutOfRangeException. |

Although this interface mirrors that of the Collection<T> class, you'll notice that some of the methods and properties (those with an asterisk) have been modified to accommodate the introduction of a key. So, the Remove() method, for example, now supports removing items by their key.

If you should decide to create your own specialized KeyedCollection<TKey, TItem> class, you'll find that the exposed protected methods allow you to easily extend and modify the default behavior of this class. You'll also notice that the class actually uses a dictionary as one of its protected properties.

## LinkedList<T>

The LinkedList<T> class is one of the staple Computer Science 101 data structures that you've probably implemented yourself at one time or another. Instead of employing an indexed-based approach to accessing the collection's items, the LinkedList<T> maintains — for each item in the list — a reference to the next item in the stream. Thus, the only way to retrieve items from a linked list is to traverse this linked structure. Because the structure is maintained as a series of references, it is allowed to grow and shrink arbitrarily.

In the BCL, the LinkedList<T> implementation allows you to easily construct a doubly linked list. This means that any given item in the list will have references to both its parent and its child nodes, which allows this list to be traversed in either direction.

The methods and properties of LinkedList<T> are oriented around this concept linkage where you're either inserting or adding a node relative to the position of another node in the list. The following table shows the exposed list of methods and properties for this class.

| Method or Property Name | Description |
|---|---|
| AddAfter() | Adds a new node in the position after the specified node. |
| AddBefore() | Adds a new node in the position before the specified node. |
| AddFirst() | Adds a new node to the start of the list. |
| AddHead() | Adds a new node to the start of the list. |
| AddLast() | Adds a new node to the end of the list. |
| AddTail() | Adds a new node to the end of the list. |
| Clear() | Removes all the nodes from the list. |
| Contains() | Determines if the supplied node exists in the list and returns true if it's found. |
| CopyTo() | Copies the contents of the list to an Array. |
| Count | Returns the number of nodes in the list. |
| Find() | Searches the list for a specific node and returns it as a LinkedList<T> if it's found. |
| FindLast() | Searches the list for the last node that matches the specific node and returns it as a LinkedList<T> if it's found. |
| First | Returns a reference to the first node in the list. |

| Method or Property Name | Description |
|---|---|
| GetEnumerator() | Returns an instance of a LinkedList<T>.Enumerator that can used to iterate over all the items in your list. |
| GetObjectData() | Retrieves a serialized representation of the dictionary. |
| Head | Returns a reference to the first node in the list. |
| Last | Returns a reference to the last node in the list. |
| OnDeserialization() | Called when deserialization has completed. |
| Remove() | Finds the node that matches the passed-in node and removes it from the list. If the item is found, the method returns true. |
| RemoveFirst() | Removes the node that is currently at the head of the list and makes the next node the new head. |
| RemoveHead() | Removes the node that is currently at the head of the list and makes the next node the new head. |
| RemoveLast() | Removes the node that is currently at the tail of the list and makes the previous node the new tail. |
| RemoveTail() | Removes the node that is currently at the tail of the list and makes the previous node the new tail. |
| Tail | Returns a reference to the last node in the list. |

You'll find that some of the methods of this class provide overloaded versions that reference the LinkedListNode<T> class. This class, which is described in the next section, wraps up each item and provides properties for managing the references that are used in traversing instances of LinkedList<T>. All items that are supplied to a linked list are ultimately represented, internally, as a LinkedListNode<T>.

## LinkedListNode<T>

LinkedListNode<T> is simply a type-safe wrapper for any node that might appear in any implementation of a linked list. If, for example, you were to decide to build your own linked list implementation, you might still be able to leverage this class to represent the nodes in your list. Overall, though, this class primarily exists to support the needs of the BCL's LinkedList<T> class.

The following table lists the properties that are exposed by the LinkedListNode<T> class.

| Property Name | Description |
|---|---|
| List | If a node is owned by a LinkedList<T>, this property will hold a reference to that list. |
| Next | Holds a reference to the next node in the linked list. |
| Previous | Holds a reference to the previous node in the linked list. |
| Value | Returns the value (T) that is associated with this node. |

# List<T>

Whereas the Collection<T> class was designed to be the extensible base class for your custom collections, the List<T> collection represents the highly optimized workhorse of the collection classes. It was built from the ground up with an eye on maximizing performance. Just as with the Collection<T> class, the List<T> class shares a rather obvious heritage with the non-generic ArrayList.

The following table summarizes the methods and properties that are part of the List<T> class.

| Method or Property Name | Description |
| --- | --- |
| Add() | Adds the provided object to the end of the collection. |
| AddRange() | Appends an IEnumerable<T> collection to the end of the current collection. |
| AsReadOnly() | Returns a read-only copy of the current collection. |
| BinarySearch() | Performs a binary search on a sorted list and returns the index of the found out. If no match is found, the method returns –1. |
| Capacity | Sets the expected maximum number of items in the collection. |
| Clear() | Removes all the items from the collection. |
| Contains() | Attempts to find an object in the collection equal to the passed-in object. If a matching object is found, the method returns true. |
| ConvertAll<U> | Converts the collection to another type. |
| CopyTo() | Copies the contents of the collection to an Array. |
| Count | Returns the number of items currently stored in the collection. |
| Exists() | Determines if one or more objects in the collection match the supplied criteria. Returns true if a match is found. |
| Find() | Searches for the first object that matches the supplied criteria. If a match is found, the matching object is returned. If no item is found, the default value for T is returned. |
| FindAll() | Finds all objects that match the supplied criteria and returns them as a List<T>. If no items are found, the resulting collection will be empty. |
| FindIndex() | Searches for the first object that matches the supplied criteria. If a match is found, the zero-based index of the object is returned. If no item is found, an index of –1 is returned. |
| FindLast() | Returns the last item that matches the passed-in search criteria. |
| FindLastIndex() | Returns the index of the last item that matches the passed-in search criteria. If no matching item is found, an index of –1 is returned. |

| | |
|---|---|
| ForEach() | Applies the specified `Action<T>` to each item in the collection. |
| GetEnumerator() | Returns the `IEnumerator<T>` for this collection. |
| GetRange() | Gets a shallow copy of a subset of items from the collection. |
| IndexOf() | Returns the zero-based index of the first item that matches the passed-in item. If no matching item is found, -1 is returned. |
| Insert() | Inserts the supplied item at the specified, zero-based index. |
| InsertRange() | Inserts a list of items at the specified index. |
| Item | Indexer property used to retrieve or edit objects in the collection using an index. |
| LastIndexOf() | Returns the zero-based index of the last item that is equal to the passed-in item. If no matching item is found, -1 is returned. |
| Remove() | Removes the supplied item from the collection. If the item is not found, false is returned. |
| RemoveAll() | Removes all the items that match the passed-in criteria and returns a count of the number of items removed. |
| RemoveAt() | Removes the item at the supplied zero-based index. |
| RemoveRange() | Removes a set of items from the collection starting at the supplied, zero-based index and removes the number of items specified. |
| Reverse() | Reverses the order of the items in the collection. |
| Sort() | Sorts the list using the criteria provided by one of its overloaded methods. |
| ToArray() | Coverts the list to an array of items of type `T`. |
| TrimExcess() | Sets the capacity of the collection to the actual capacity if the list is less than 90% full. |
| TrueForAll() | Returns true if all the items in the collection match the supplied criteria. |

As you can see, this is a very complete class, offering you a wide variety of mechanisms for maintaining, ordering, and searching your list. About the only thing that's missing here is an eventing model that fires events as the list changes state (that's found in `BindingList<T>` described later in this chapter).

The sections that follow provide you with some examples of how to use most of these methods and properties. The goal here is to touch on the basic concepts of most of these items. I've attempted to cluster the methods into logical categories of functionality to make it easier to locate specific kinds of operations.

## *Size Matters*

Although the List<T> collection is a dynamic list, there may be times when you would like to pre-allocate the size of the list. This is achieved via the Capacity property, which sets the expected capacity of the list. In situations where you're expecting the list to be quite large, you might want to consider using the Capacity property. Or, you may set the capacity at the time of construction.

Even if you completely ignore capacity, though, the collection still maintains a value for capacity internally. However, as you hit specific thresholds, the class will dynamically increase the capacity to accommodate additional growth. Naturally, if you want to inspect this property at any time, you can. You can also retrieve the total number of items in the collection via the Count property.

As your list is growing and the capacity is being continually grown in chunks, you may reach a point at which you want to trim back the extra items and make the capacity precisely match the count of the items in your collection. This is achieved by applying the TrimExcess method to your collection.

The following code demonstrates some of the size-related methods and properties in action:

```vb
[VB code]
Public Sub SizeTest()
    Dim capacity As Int32 = 2
    Dim custList As New List(Of Customer)(capacity)

    For idx As Int32 = 1 To 12
        custList.Add(New Customer(idx, "Customer" + CStr(idx)))
        If (custList.Capacity > capacity) Then
            Console.Out.WriteLine("Current Count: {0}", custList.Count)
            Console.Out.WriteLine("Old Capacity : {0}", capacity)
            Console.Out.WriteLine("New Capacity : {0}", custList.Capacity)
            Console.Out.WriteLine("")
            capacity = custList.Capacity
        End If
    Next

    Console.Out.WriteLine("Final Count    : {0}", custList.Count)
    Console.Out.WriteLine("Final Capacity : {0}", custList.Capacity)
    custList.TrimExcess()
    Console.Out.WriteLine("After TrimExcess: {0}", custList.Capacity)
End Sub
```

```csharp
[C# code]
public void SizeTest() {
    int capacity = 2;
    List<Customer> custList = new List<Customer>(capacity);

    for (int idx = 1; idx <= 12; idx++) {
        custList.Add(new Customer(idx, "Customer" + idx));
        if (custList.Capacity > capacity) {
            Console.Out.WriteLine("Current Count: {0}", custList.Count);
            Console.Out.WriteLine("Old Capacity : {0}", capacity);
            Console.Out.WriteLine("New Capacity : {0}", custList.Capacity);
            Console.Out.WriteLine("");
            capacity = custList.Capacity;
        }
    }
```

```
        }

    Console.Out.WriteLine("Final Count      : {0}", custList.Count);
    Console.Out.WriteLine("Final Capacity   : {0}", custList.Capacity);
    custList.TrimExcess();
    Console.Out.WriteLine("After TrimExcess: {0}", custList.Capacity);
}
```

This example constructs a list with an initial capacity of two. Then, it proceeds to add 50 items to the list and, along the way, spits out information about how these additions end up influencing the capacity of the collection. The output is as follows:

```
Current Count: 3
Old Capacity : 2
New Capacity : 4

Current Count: 5
Old Capacity : 4
New Capacity : 8

Current Count: 9
Old Capacity : 8
New Capacity : 16
```

You should notice that the capacity just doubles each time the list reaches capacity. Finally, after you reach the end, the example calls `TrimExcess()` and dumps out the size of capacity before and after this call. The output is:

```
Final Count     : 12
Final Capacity  : 16
After TrimExcess: 12
```

Your final capacity ended up at 16 and, after you trimmed, it was adjusted back down to 12 to match the count of items in your collection. If you're working with large collections, setting the capacity can represent an effective means of optimizing your collection's performance. The pre-allocation of the collection's contents and the elimination of the need to continually resize the collection will allow you to reduce the overall overhead associated with populating your class.

The `TrimExcess()` method will only trim the list if the list is less than 90 percent full. The idea here is that the benefits of executing the trim operation may not be realized if list is already nearly full.

## Adding and Updating Items

The `List<T>` collection offers you a variety of methods that can be used to populate it with data or modify the representation of a given item in the collection. In contrast with `Collection<T>`, this class also offers methods that will allow you to insert or append ranges of objects into your collection. These bulk operations can make it much easier to manage the content of your collection. The following sample code illustrates some of these mechanisms:

```
[VB code]
Public Sub AddItemsTest()
    Dim collCustList As New Collection(Of Customer)()
    collCustList.Add(New Customer(99, "Happy Gillmore"))
    collCustList.Add(New Customer(77, "Billy Madison"))

    Dim rangeList As New List(Of Customer)()
    rangeList.Add(New Customer(55, "Bobby Boucher"))
    rangeList.Add(New Customer(44, "Robbie Hart"))

    Dim masterList As New List(Of Customer)(collCustList)
    masterList.AddRange(rangeList)

    masterList.Insert(2, New Customer(33, "Longfellow Deeds"))
    masterList(3) = New Customer(88, "Sonny Koufax")

    For Each cust As Customer In masterList
        Console.Out.WriteLine(cust)
    Next
End Sub
```

```
[C# code]
public void AddItemsTest() {
    Collection<Customer> collCustList = new Collection<Customer>();
    collCustList.Add(new Customer(99, "Happy Gillmore"));
    collCustList.Add(new Customer(77, "Billy Madison"));

    List<Customer> rangeList = new List<Customer>();
    rangeList.Add(new Customer(55, "Bobby Boucher"));
    rangeList.Add(new Customer(44, "Robbie Hart"));

    List<Customer> masterList = new List<Customer>(collCustList);
    masterList.AddRange(rangeList);

    masterList.Insert(2, new Customer(33, "Longfellow Deeds"));
    masterList[3] = new Customer(88, "Sonny Koufax");

    foreach (Customer cust in masterList)
        Console.Out.WriteLine(cust);
}
```

In this example you start out by constructing two separate lists. Your first list, collCustList, assembles a handful of your Customer objects using the Collection<T> class. The example also builds an additional list of customers in the rangeList using an instance of the List<T> class. Because both Collection<T> and List<T> implement the IEnumerable<T> interface, they can be used as parameters to all of your range-based methods. This scenario passes your collection in as one of the parameters to your constructor and it adds the items to your list. The other list, rangeList, ends up being added via the AddRange() method. This method takes the incoming list of items and appends them to the end of the overall collection.

Once the list is fully populated, you can then insert a new item into the middle of the list using the Insert() method. This method accepts a zero-based index as one of its parameters and inserts the new item at that specified position. Finally, the indexer is used to update item three in the list, replacing the Customer at that position in the list with a new Customer instance in the list, which appends the passed-in list to your overall collection.

## Removing Items

If you're going to put data into your list, you're also going to want to be able take it out. The `List<T>` collection is equipped with the standard set of methods that are used to remove its items. Along with the index-based methods, the class also provides methods that support more complex rules for determining what items are removed from your collection. Here's a simple example:

```
[VB Code]
Public Function FindGoldDelegate(ByVal cust As Customer) As Boolean
    Return cust.Rating.Equals("Gold")
End Function

Public Sub RemoveItemsTest()
    Dim collCustList As New List(Of Customer)()
    collCustList.Add(New Customer(99, "Happy Gillmore", "Platinum"))
    collCustList.Add(New Customer(77, "Billy Madison", "Gold"))
    collCustList.Add(New Customer(55, "Bobby Boucher", "Gold"))
    collCustList.Add(New Customer(44, "Robbie Hart", "Other"))
    collCustList.Add(New Customer(22, "Henry Roth", "Deluxe"))
    collCustList.Add(New Customer(88, "Barry Egan", "Platinum"))
    collCustList.Add(New Customer(11, "Longfellow Deeds", "Other"))

    collCustList.RemoveAt(6)
    collCustList.RemoveRange(3, 2)

    Dim numRemoved As Int32 = collCustList.RemoveAll(AddressOf FindGoldDelegate)
    For Each cust As Customer In collCustList
        Console.Out.WriteLine(cust)
    Next

    collCustList.Clear()
End Sub
```

```
[C# Code]
public void RemoveItemsTest() {
    List<Customer> collCustList = new List<Customer>();
    collCustList.Add(new Customer(99, "Happy Gillmore", "Platinum"));
    collCustList.Add(new Customer(77, "Billy Madison", "Gold"));
    collCustList.Add(new Customer(55, "Bobby Boucher", "Gold"));
    collCustList.Add(new Customer(44, "Robbie Hart", "Other"));
    collCustList.Add(new Customer(22, "Henry Roth", "Deluxe"));
    collCustList.Add(new Customer(88, "Barry Egan", "Platinum"));
    collCustList.Add(new Customer(11, "Longfellow Deeds", "Other"));

    collCustList.RemoveAt(6);
    collCustList.RemoveRange(3, 2);

    int numRemoved = collCustList.RemoveAll(delegate(Customer cust) {
        return cust.Rating.Equals("Gold");
    });

    foreach (Customer cust in collCustList)
        Console.Out.WriteLine(cust);

    collCustList.Clear();
}
```

This example exercises each of the methods that can be used to remove data from a `List<T>` collection. The first two methods it calls, `RemoveAt()` and `RemoveRange()`, are very straightforward index-based operations. `RemoveAt()` simply removes the items at the indicated index, and `RemoveRange()` starts at the specified index and removes the number of items specified by its second parameter. `List<T>` also supports an overloaded version of the `Remove()` method that takes an object, looks it up, and removes it if it's found.

The `RemoveAll()` method shown here offers a more flexible approach to deleting items from the collection. It actually accepts a generic delegate (`Predicate<T>`) as one of its parameters. This predicate gives you a more powerful, more type-safe mechanism for describing a filter that can be applied when removing items from the collection.

The `Predicate<T>` delegate is defined as taking a single parameter of type `T` and returning a `boolean` that indicates if the supplied parameter meets your criteria. When you call the `RemoveAll()` method, this delegate is called once for each item in your collection and, if the delegate returns `true`, the method will remove that item. It is the responsibility for your delegate's implementation to supply the rules that will determine which items meet the criteria of your search. For the purpose of this example, your delegate will return true for every `Customer` that has a rating of "Gold," causing all customers with this rating to be removed from the collection.

You'll notice some variation here between how the VB and C# examples supply their delegates. The C# example uses an anonymous method (new to VS 2005) for its delegate implementation. This approach was taken here to point out how handy this mechanism can be, allowing you to place the method's implementation directly within the method that's using it. VB, on the other hand, does not support anonymous methods and, as such, must implement a standalone method (`FindGoldDelegate`) that complies with the signature of the predicate interface. Both are very workable. However, I tend to favor the readability of the C# syntax.

As you look at the rest of the `List<T>` class methods, you'll see how generic delegates are actually used in a variety of roles throughout the class. They primarily serve as type-safe means of expressing the filter criteria that are used to delete, find, or operate upon the items in your list. This application of generic delegates actually serves as a nice example of how you might want to leverage the combination of generics and delegates as part of your own classes.

Finally, as part of looking at how items are removed from a `List<T>` collection, you should consider how removing items might influence the `Capacity` property of your collections. You saw earlier in this chapter how the `Capacity` property was continually doubled to accommodate growth in your collection. So, does it shrink as you remove items? No. If you add 999 items to your list and then remove 998 of them, the `Capacity` property will remain at 999 despite the fact that you only have 1 item remaining in your collection. This is not of concern, but something you will want to keep in mind if you are maintaining lists that may be growing and shrinking by large increments. If you ever decide you want to adjust the capacity, you could simply use the `TrimExcess()` method to reduce the overall capacity of the collection.

## Searching for Items

Although this `List<T>` collection is an index-based collection, it also includes a series of useful methods that allow you to generally search the contents of your collection. Most of these methods employ delegates to express the criteria that are used when searching the collection. You'll notice that these methods have similar behavior. They only vary by their return type or the scope of their search. Overall, though, the interface for these methods is largely the same.

The following is a sample program that will give you a brief glimpse of how each of these methods works in practice:

```
[VB Code]
Public Class ListTest
    Dim targetId As Int32

    Public Function FindGoldDelegate(ByVal cust As Customer) As Boolean
        Return cust.Rating.Equals("Gold")
    End Function

    Public Function FindPlatinumDelegate(ByVal cust As Customer) As Boolean
        Return cust.Rating.Equals("Platinum")
    End Function

    Public Function FindIdDelegate(ByVal cust As Customer) As Boolean
        Return (cust.Id = targetId)
    End Function

    Public Sub SearchTest()
        Dim collCustList As New List(Of Customer)()
        collCustList.Add(New Customer(99, "Happy Gillmore", "Platinum"))
        collCustList.Add(New Customer(77, "Billy Madison", "Gold"))
        collCustList.Add(New Customer(55, "Bobby Boucher", "Gold"))
        collCustList.Add(New Customer(44, "Robbie Hart", "Other"))
        collCustList.Add(New Customer(22, "Henry Roth", "Deluxe"))
        collCustList.Add(New Customer(88, "Barry Egan", "Platinum"))
        collCustList.Add(New Customer(11, "Longfellow Deeds", "Other"))

        targetId = 22
        Dim cust22 As Customer = collCustList.Find(AddressOf FindIdDelegate)
        Console.Out.WriteLine("Find Customer Id 22: {0}", cust22.Name)

        Dim custIndex As Int32 = collCustList.FindIndex(AddressOf FindIdDelegate)
        Console.Out.WriteLine("Find Customer Id 22 Index: {0}", custIndex)

        Dim goldCustomers As List(Of Customer) = _
                        collCustList.FindAll(AddressOf FindGoldDelegate)
        For Each cust As Customer In goldCustomers
            Console.Out.WriteLine("Gold Customer Found: {0}", cust)
        Next

        Dim platCust As Customer = _
                collCustList.FindLast(AddressOf FindPlatinumDelegate)
        Console.Out.WriteLine("Find Last Platinum Customer: {0}", platCust)

        Dim rangeCust As IEnumerable(Of Customer) = collCustList.GetRange(3, 3)
        For Each cust As Customer In rangeCust
            Console.Out.WriteLine("Range Customer: {0}", cust)
        Next
    End Sub
End Class
```

```
[C# Code]
public void SearchTest() {
    List<Customer> collCustList = new List<Customer>();
    collCustList.Add(new Customer(99, "Happy Gillmore", "Platinum"));
    collCustList.Add(new Customer(77, "Billy Madison", "Gold"));
    collCustList.Add(new Customer(55, "Bobby Boucher", "Gold"));
    collCustList.Add(new Customer(44, "Robbie Hart", "Other"));
    collCustList.Add(new Customer(22, "Henry Roth", "Deluxe"));
    collCustList.Add(new Customer(88, "Barry Egan", "Platinum"));
    collCustList.Add(new Customer(11, "Longfellow Deeds", "Other"));


    int targetId = 22;
    Customer cust22 = collCustList.Find(delegate(Customer cust) {
        return cust.Id == targetId;
    });
    Console.Out.WriteLine("Find Customer Id 22: {0}", cust22.Name);

    int custIndex  = collCustList.FindIndex(delegate(Customer cust) {
        return cust.Id == targetId;
    });
    Console.Out.WriteLine("Find Customer Id 22 Index: {0}", custIndex);

    List<Customer> goldCustomers = collCustList.FindAll(delegate(Customer cust) {
        return cust.Rating.Equals("Gold");
    });
    foreach (Customer cust in goldCustomers)
        Console.Out.WriteLine("Gold Customer Found: {0}", cust);

    Customer platCust = collCustList.FindLast(delegate(Customer cust) {
        return cust.Rating.Equals("Platinum");
    });
    Console.Out.WriteLine("Find Last Platinum Customer: {0}", platCust);

    IEnumerable<Customer> rangeCust = collCustList.GetRange(3, 3);
    foreach (Customer cust in rangeCust)
        Console.Out.WriteLine("Range Customer: {0}", cust);

}
```

Four different flavors of `Find` methods are demonstrated in this example, each of which uses the `Predicate<T>` delegate to filter the list of items that are returned by the operation. The `Find()`, `FindLast()`, and `FindIndex()` methods are all used to locate a single item in your collection. The `Find()` and `FindLast()` methods both return an instance of a `Customer` object, and the `FindIndex()` method, as its name implies, returns the zero-based index.

As shown here, the `Find()` and `FindIndex()` methods will find the first matching item in the collection, whereas `FindLast()` will find the last matching item in the collection. However, the `FindIndex()` method provides three overloaded implementations that let you further qualify the range of items to be searched. One version allows you to indicate a starting index, and the other allows you to provide a starting and ending index range for the search.

The last method that is demonstrated here is GetRange(), which uses an index to retrieve a collection of items. It uses the first parameter to determine the starting point for retrieving items and uses the second parameter to determine how many items to return.

## Transforming List<T> Contents

At times, you may need to transform the contents of your List<T> collection to another representation. The List<T> class provides a set of methods that allow you to either copy or covert its contents. The CopyTo() method is especially useful in that there are plenty of situations where you may want to create a copy of some or all of the items in a List<T> collection. The key to the CopyTo() method is that it makes a deep copy of the collection. Here's an example of the CopyTo() and the ConvertAll() methods used in conjunction:

```vb
[VB Code]
Public Function NameRatingsDelegate(ByVal cust As Customer) As String
    Dim retVal As String = cust.Name
    If (cust.Rating.Equals("Platinum")) Then
        retVal = cust.Name + " ****"
    ElseIf (cust.Rating.Equals("Gold")) Then
        retVal = cust.Name + " ***"
    ElseIf (cust.Rating.Equals("Other")) Then
        retVal = cust.Name + " **"
    End If
    Return retVal
End Function

Public Sub UpperCustDelegate(ByVal cust As Customer)
    cust.Name = cust.Name.ToUpper()
End Sub

Public Sub TransformContentsTest()
    Dim collCustList As New List(Of Customer)()
    collCustList.Add(New Customer(99, "Happy Gillmore", "Platinum"))
    collCustList.Add(New Customer(77, "Billy Madison", "Gold"))
    collCustList.Add(New Customer(55, "Bobby Boucher", "Gold"))
    collCustList.Add(New Customer(88, "Barry Egan", "Platinum"))
    collCustList.Add(New Customer(11, "Longfellow Deeds", "Other"))

    Dim custNames As List(Of String) =
                collCustList.ConvertAll(Of String)(AddressOf NameRatingsDelegate)
    For Each custName As String In custNames
        Console.Out.WriteLine(custName)
    Next

    Dim deepNameCopy(custNames.Count) As String
    custNames.CopyTo(deepNameCopy)
    custNames(0) = "CHANGED NAME"

    For Each custName As String In custNames
        Console.Out.WriteLine(custName)
    Next

    For Each custName As String In deepNameCopy
```

```
            Console.Out.WriteLine(custName)
        Next

        collCustList.ForEach(AddressOf UpperCustDelegate)

        For Each cust As Customer In collCustList
            Console.Out.WriteLine(cust.Name)
        Next
    End Sub
```

```
[C# Code]
public void TransformContentsTest() {
    List<Customer> collCustList = new List<Customer>();
    collCustList.Add(new Customer(99, "Happy Gillmore", "Platinum"));
    collCustList.Add(new Customer(77, "Billy Madison", "Gold"));
    collCustList.Add(new Customer(55, "Bobby Boucher", "Gold"));
    collCustList.Add(new Customer(88, "Barry Egan", "Platinum"));
    collCustList.Add(new Customer(11, "Longfellow Deeds", "Other"));

    List<string> custNames =
                collCustList.ConvertAll<string>(delegate(Customer cust) {
        string retVal = cust.Name;
        if (cust.Rating.Equals("Platinum"))
            retVal = cust.Name + " ****";
        else if (cust.Rating.Equals("Gold"))
            retVal = cust.Name + " ***";
        else if (cust.Rating.Equals("Other"))
            retVal = cust.Name + " **";
        return retVal;
    });

    foreach (string custName in custNames)
        Console.Out.WriteLine(custName);

    string[] deepNameCopy = new string[custNames.Count];
    custNames.CopyTo(deepNameCopy);
    custNames[0] = "CHANGED NAME";

    foreach (String custName in custNames)
        Console.Out.WriteLine(custName);

    foreach (string custName in deepNameCopy)
        Console.Out.WriteLine(custName);

    collCustList.ForEach(delegate(Customer cust) {
        cust.Name = cust.Name.ToUpper();
    });

    foreach (Customer cust in collCustList)
        Console.Out.WriteLine(cust.Name);
}
```

The `ConvertAll()` method introduces yet another application of generic delegates. In this case, the `ConvertAll()` method accepts a `Converter<T, U>` delegate as one of its parameters. The `T` parameter is used as the source type you are converting from and corresponds to the `T` that is being managed by the `List<T>` collection. The `U` type parameter corresponds to the type that you are coverting to. For this example, a delegate is provided that converts from `Customer` objects to strings. It takes each incoming `Customer` and creates a string that contains the `Customer` name with a series of asterisks appended that are derived from the customer's rating. So, when you run this example, it yields a collection of customer names that appear as follows:

```
Happy Gillmore ****
Billy Madison ***
Bobby Boucher ***
Barry Egan ****
Longfellow Deeds **
```

After converting the names, you use the `CopyTo()` method to make a deep copy of the new list of names. Whenever you retrieve a collection of items, you should pay attention to whether that collection contains a shallow or a deep copy. If the copy is shallow, any modifications you make to the returned list will also result in changes to the original collection. Obviously, plenty of scenarios exist where this may not be the desired result. In the example, you prove that the copy is deep by modifying the returned collection, setting the value of the first item in the `deepNameCopy` array to "CHANGED NAME". Now, to confirm that your change didn't impact the original source collection, you dump the contents of both lists. The resulting output is as follows:

```
CHANGED NAME
Billy Madison ***
Bobby Boucher ***
Barry Egan ****
Longfellow Deeds **

Happy Gillmore ****
Billy Madison ***
Bobby Boucher ***
Barry Egan ****
Longfellow Deeds **
```

One more method, `ForEach()`, can be used to operate on the items in a collection. This method leverages the `Action<T>` delegate to specify an action that is to be performed on each item. The `Action<T>` delegate is a simple function that takes just a single parameter and, unlike most of the other delegates you've looked at, returns *no* value. Instead, this delegate simply defines a function that will operate — in place — on the supplied item. For the example, your `Action<T>` delegate just converts the name of each `Customer` to uppercase.

## Sorting Items

The `List<T>` class provides two methods that can be used to sort the contents of the collection. The first of these two, the `Sort()` method, includes a set of overloaded versions that support varying approaches to sorting this collection. The second method, `Reverse()`, allows you to invert the order of the collection's items. The following example demonstrates both of these methods:

```
[VB Code]
Public Function SortDelegate(ByVal c1 As Customer, ByVal c2 As Customer) As Integer
    Return Comparer(Of Int32).Default.Compare(c1.Id, c2.Id)
End Function

Public Sub SortTest()
    Dim collCustList As New List(Of Customer)()
    collCustList.Add(New Customer(99, "Happy Gillmore", "Platinum"))
    collCustList.Add(New Customer(77, "Billy Madison", "Gold"))
    collCustList.Add(New Customer(55, "Bobby Boucher", "Gold"))
    collCustList.Add(New Customer(88, "Barry Egan", "Platinum"))
    collCustList.Add(New Customer(11, "Longfellow Deeds", "Other"))

    Console.Out.WriteLine("Before:")
    For Each cust As Customer In collCustList
        Console.Out.WriteLine(cust)
    Next

    collCustList.Sort(AddressOf SortDelegate)

    Console.Out.WriteLine("After:")
    For Each cust As Customer In collCustList
        Console.Out.WriteLine(cust)
    Next

    collCustList.Reverse()

    Console.Out.WriteLine("Reversed:")
    For Each cust As Customer In collCustList
        Console.Out.WriteLine(cust)
    Next
End Sub
```

```
[C# Code]
public void SortTest() {
    List<Customer> collCustList = new List<Customer>();
    collCustList.Add(new Customer(99, "Happy Gillmore", "Platinum"));
    collCustList.Add(new Customer(77, "Billy Madison", "Gold"));
    collCustList.Add(new Customer(55, "Bobby Boucher", "Gold"));
    collCustList.Add(new Customer(88, "Barry Egan", "Platinum"));
    collCustList.Add(new Customer(11, "Longfellow Deeds", "Other"));

    Console.Out.WriteLine("Before:");
    foreach (Customer cust in collCustList)
        Console.Out.WriteLine(cust);

    collCustList.Sort(delegate(Customer cust1, Customer cust2) {
        return Comparer<int>.Default.Compare(cust1.Id, cust2.Id);
    });

    Console.Out.WriteLine("After:");
    foreach (Customer cust in collCustList)
        Console.Out.WriteLine(cust);

    collCustList.Reverse();
```

```
        Console.Out.WriteLine("Reversed:");
        foreach (Customer cust in collCustList)
            Console.Out.WriteLine(cust);
}
```

This example uses the overloaded version of the Sort() method that accepts a Comparer<T> class. To simplify the example, it uses a default Comparer implementation to compare the Customer Ids, which are integers. Naturally, if you had a more complex data type to sort on, you could provide your own implementation of Comparer.

Three other variants of the Sort() method exist that aren't shown here. A "default" version is included. It takes no parameters and uses the default Comparer to determine how to compare the values for the type T. If T implements IComparable<T>, it will be used to compare the items. If it doesn't implement this generic interface, the class will attempt to use the non-generic IComparable interface. If T doesn't implement either of these interfaces, an InvalidOperationException is thrown.

The remaining two implementations of Sort() are similar to the version you saw in the preceding example. One uses the Comparison<T> delegate to perform the sorting of each item. The other allows you to provide a starting and ending index along with an IComparer<T> instance to perform the comparisons.

## Queue<T>

The Queue<T> class is unlike many of the collections you've seen in this chapter. Most of the collections you've seen so far are very centered around indexed or keyed access to the items in your collections. These types of collections have no concern for how the items were originally placed into the collection.

In contrast, the Queue<T> class is much more sensitive to the order items are inserted into the queue. The queue's interfaces reflect that fact. Gone are all those index-oriented methods and properties you saw with Collection<T> and List<T>. Instead, with the Queue<T> class, you're now provided with a small set of first-in-first-out operations that are used to enqueue and dequeue items.

The following table is a breakdown of the methods and properties that are exposed by the Queue<T> class.

| Method or Property Name | Description |
| --- | --- |
| Clear() | Removes all the items from the queue. |
| Contains() | Attempts to find an item in the collection equal to the passed-in object. If a match is found, the method returns true. |
| CopyTo() | Copies the contents of the queue to an Array. |
| Count | Returns the number of items in the queue. |
| Dequeue() | Removes an item from the beginning of the queue. |
| Enqueue() | Adds the supplied item to the end of the queue. |

*Table continued on following page*

| Method or Property Name | Description |
| --- | --- |
| GetEnumerator() | Retrieves an instance of Queue<T>.Enumerator that can be used to iterate over the contents of the queue. |
| Peek() | Retrieves the item at the beginning of the queue without removing it from the queue. |
| TrimExcess() | Reduces the capacity of the queue so that it is equal to the number of items currently in the queue, if the queue is less than 90% full. |

As you can see, there's not much to the interface for this class. The following is an example that demonstrates some of these methods:

```
[VB code]
Dim custQueue As New Queue(Of Customer)()
custQueue.Enqueue(New Customer(99, "Happy Gillmore", "Platinum"))
custQueue.Enqueue(New Customer(77, "Billy Madison", "Gold"))
custQueue.Enqueue(New Customer(55, "Bobby Boucher", "Silver"))
custQueue.Enqueue(New Customer(88, "Barry Egan", "Platinum"))

Dim tmpCust as Customer = custQueue.Dequeue()
Console.Out.WriteLine("Dequeued: {0}", tmpCust)

For Each cust As Customer In custQueue
    Console.Out.WriteLine("Queue Item: {0}", cust)
Next

tmpCust = custQueue.Peek()
Console.Out.WriteLine("Queue Peek: {0}", tmpCust)

custQueue.Enqueue(New Customer(88, "Barry Egan", "Platinum"))

For Each cust As Customer In custQueue
    Console.Out.WriteLine("Queue Item: {0}", cust)
Next
```

```
[C# code]
Queue<Customer> custQueue = new Queue<Customer>(100);
custQueue.Enqueue(new Customer(99, "Happy Gillmore", "Platinum"));
custQueue.Enqueue(new Customer(77, "Billy Madison", "Gold"));
custQueue.Enqueue(new Customer(55, "Bobby Boucher", "Silver"));
custQueue.Enqueue(new Customer(88, "Barry Egan", "Platinum"));

Customer tmpCust = custQueue.Dequeue();
Console.Out.WriteLine("Dequeued: {0}", tmpCust);

foreach (Customer cust in custQueue)
```

```
        Console.Out.WriteLine("Queue Item: {0}", cust);

    tmpCust = custQueue.Peek();
    Console.Out.WriteLine("Queue Peek: {0}", tmpCust);

    custQueue.Enqueue(new Customer(88, "Barry Egan", "Platinum"));

    foreach (Customer cust in custQueue)
        Console.Out.WriteLine("Queue Item: {0}", cust);
```

This example starts by inserting a series of Customer objects using the Enqueue() method. Then, it calls Dequeue(), which removes a Customer from the start of the queue. At that point, it dumps the contents of the queue to verify that the item was actually removed. Finally, it calls the Peek() method to examine the item that is currently at the start of the queue before dumping the list once more to verify that the peek operation did not alter the contents of the queue.

# ReadOnlyCollection<T>

In some instances, when you're returning a collection to a client, you want to ensure that the client has no ability to modify your original collection. You can approach this in two ways. First, you could make a copy of the collection and return that to the client. And, for small collections, that may be an acceptable approach. However, imagine scenarios where you're managing a large set of items. In those situations, it may be prohibitive to make a copy.

To address this need, the BCL includes the ReadOnlyCollection<T> class. This class, as its name implies, restricts the client's ability to modify the collection. The methods and properties it exposes are listed in the following table.

| Method or Property Name | Description |
| --- | --- |
| Count | Returns the number of items in the collection. |
| Contains() | Attempts to find an item in the collection equal to the passed-in object. If a match is found, the method returns true. |
| CopyTo() | Copies the contents of the collection to an Array. |
| GetEnumerator() | Retrieves an instance of IEnumerator<T> that can be used to iterate over the contents of the collection. |
| IndexOf() | Finds the index of the supplied item. If no item is found, this method returns -1. |
| Item | Read-only indexer that fetches individual items from the collection. |

You can see that this interface removes any methods or properties that would allow you to add, update, or otherwise modify the contents of the collection. Here's some sample code that illustrates the usage of the ReadOnlyCollection<T> class:

```
[VB code]
Public Sub BuildReadOnlyCollection()
    Dim collCustList As New List(Of Customer)()
    collCustList.Add(New Customer(99, "Happy Gillmore", "Platinum"))
    collCustList.Add(New Customer(77, "Billy Madison", "Gold"))
    collCustList.Add(New Customer(55, "Bobby Boucher", "Gold"))
    collCustList.Add(New Customer(88, "Barry Egan", "Platinum"))
    collCustList.Add(New Customer(11, "Longfellow Deeds", "Other"))

    Dim roCustColl As New ReadOnlyCollection(Of Customer)(collCustList)

    Dim tmpCust As Customer = roCustColl(1)
    tmpCust.Name = "NAME CHANGED"

    For Each cust As Customer In roCustColl
        Console.Out.WriteLine(cust)
    Next
End Sub
```

```
[C# code]
public void BuildReadOnlyCollection() {
    List<Customer> collCustList = new List<Customer>();
    collCustList.Add(new Customer(99, "Happy Gillmore", "Platinum"));
    collCustList.Add(new Customer(77, "Billy Madison", "Gold"));
    collCustList.Add(new Customer(55, "Bobby Boucher", "Gold"));
    collCustList.Add(new Customer(88, "Barry Egan", "Platinum"));
    collCustList.Add(new Customer(11, "Longfellow Deeds", "Other"));

    ReadOnlyCollection<Customer> roCustColl =
                        new ReadOnlyCollection<Customer>(collCustList);

    Customer tmpCust = roCustColl[1];
    tmpCust.Name = "NAME CHANGED";

    foreach (Customer cust in roCustColl)
        Console.Out.WriteLine(cust);
}
```

Notice here that the example starts out by constructing a list of customers, which are then passed as a parameter to your ReadOnlyCollection<T> class. Because the class is read-only, the only way to populate it is via this constructor.

Because collections often contain references, they cannot be viewed as being completely read-only. In this example, in fact, you obtain an item from the collection and modify its Name property. And, as you might suspect, this change also changes the Customer reference held by the collection. The idea of "read-only" for this collection is only meant to indicate that items cannot be added, removed, or replaced in the collection. So, if your collection contains references, you are allowed to modify the state of those references. At the same time, the class does prevent you from replacing any reference held by the collection with a new reference. This means the following line of code would be invalid:

```
[VB code]
roCustColl(1) = New Customer(99, "New Customer")
```

```
[C# code]
roCustColl[1] = New Customer(99, "New Customer")
```

The indexer for the `ReadOnlyCollection<T>` class is implemented as a read-only property and, as such, will prevent you from modifying or adding a new item.

# SortedDictionary<TKey, TValue>

The `Dictionary<TKey, TValue>` class is quite useful on its own. However, as indicated earlier, the client of the `Dictionary<TKey, TValue>` class has absolutely no control over the order of the items in its collection. And, as long as you're sticking with key-based access to the dictionary, this really never ends up being of any concern.

The problem is that there are times when you want your dictionary to behave like a collection, allowing you to reliably traverse the dictionary's items in specific order. This is where the `SortedDictionary<TKey, TValue>` class comes in. This class, which is somewhat akin to the `SortedList` class from the `System.Collections` namespace, offers very much the same interface you saw with the `Dictionary<TKey, TValue>` class earlier in this chapter (in fact, they both implement the `IDictionary<TKey, TValue>` interface). However, a few subtle differences were introduced into `SortedDictionary<TKey, TValue>` to facilitate ordering of the dictionary.

The following table is a breakdown of the methods and properties that are exposed by the `SortedDictionary<TKey, TValue>` class.

| Method or Property Name | Description |
| --- | --- |
| Add() | Adds the supplied `key` and `value` to the dictionary. |
| Capacity | A count of the maximum number of items allocated for the dictionary. This will automatically resize when the maximum is reached. |
| Clear() | Removes all the items from the dictionary. |
| Comparer | Holds the `Comparer<T>` instance that will be used to sort the keys in the dictionary. |
| ContainsKey() | Determines if the supplied `key` exists in the current dictionary, returning `true` if it is found. |
| ContainsValue() | Determines if the supplied value exists in the current dictionary, returning `true` if it is found. |
| CopyTo() | Copies the `KeyValuePair<TKey, TValue>` item from the dictionary to an array starting at the specified index. |
| Count | Returns the number of items currently stored in the dictionary |
| GetEnumerator() | Returns an enumerated collection of `KeyValuePair` objects corresponding to the items in the dictionary. |
| Item | Indexer property that uses keys to add or update items in the dictionary. |

*Table continued on following page*

| Method or Property Name | Description |
|---|---|
| Keys | Returns a List<T> collection containing all the keys in the dictionary. |
| Remove() | Finds the item that matches the passed-in key and removes it. If the item is found, the method returns true. |
| TryGetValue() | Attempts to get the value that corresponds to the supplied key. If the value is found, it is returned. Otherwise, the default value for the value parameter is returned. |
| Values | Returns a List<T> collection containing all the values in the dictionary. |

This class is mostly a mirror image of the Dictionary<TKey, TValue> class. So, instead of rehashing (no pun intended) all these methods and properties that are essentially duplicates of the Dictionary<TKey, TValue> class, I'll just focus on they key points of difference. In reality, the only real variation here shows up in the Comparer and Keys properties. Because this dictionary supports sorting, this also means the collection associated with the Keys property must be sorted. The order of these keys is determined by the value you end up assigning to the Comparer property.

The following is a quick example that uses a few of these new methods and properties:

```
[VB code]
Public Sub BuildSortedDictionary()
    Dim custDict As New Dictionary(Of Int32, Customer)()
    custDict(99) = New Customer(99, "Happy Gillmore", "Platinum")
    custDict(77) = New Customer(77, "Billy Madison", "Gold")
    custDict(55) = New Customer(55, "Bobby Boucher", "Silver")
    custDict(88) = New Customer(88, "Barry Egan", "Platinum")

    Dim unsortedValues As Dictionary(Of Int32, Customer).ValueCollection
    unsortedValues = custDict.Values
    For Each cust As Customer In unsortedValues
        Console.Out.WriteLine("Customer Name: {0}", cust.Name)
    Next

    Dim sortedDict As New SortedDictionary(Of Int32, Customer)(custDict)

    Dim sortedValues As SortedDictionary(Of Int32, Customer).ValueCollection
    sortedValues = sortedDict.Values
    For Each cust As Customer In sortedValues
        Console.Out.WriteLine("Customer->{0}", cust.Name)
    Next

    sortedDict.Remove(88)

    sortedValues = sortedDict.Values
    For Each cust As Customer In sortedValues
        Console.Out.WriteLine("Customer->{0}", cust.Name)
    Next
End Sub
```

```
[C# code]
public void BuildSortedDictionary() {
    Dictionary<int, Customer> custDict = new Dictionary<int, Customer>();
    custDict[99] = new Customer(99, "Happy Gillmore", "Platinum");
    custDict[77] = new Customer(77, "Billy Madison", "Gold");
    custDict[55] = new Customer(55, "Bobby Boucher", "Silver");
    custDict[88] = new Customer(88, "Barry Egan", "Platinum");

    Dictionary<int, Customer>.ValueCollection unsortedValues = custDict.Values;
    foreach (Customer cust in unsortedValues)
        Console.Out.WriteLine("Customer Name: {0}", cust.Name);

    SortedDictionary<int, Customer> sortedDict;
    sortedDict = new SortedDictionary<int, Customer>(custDict);

    SortedDictionary<int, Customer>.ValueCollection sortedValues;
    sortedValues = sortedDict.Values;
    foreach (Customer cust in sortedValues) {
        Console.Out.WriteLine("Customer->{0}", cust.Name);
    }

    sortedDict.Remove(88);

    sortedValues = sortedDict.Values;
    foreach (Customer cust in sortedValues) {
        Console.Out.WriteLine("Customer->{0}", cust.Name);
    }
}
```

To demonstrate some of the new functionality offered by the `SortedDictionary<TKey, TValue>` class, this example starts out with a regular, unsorted dictionary. This dictionary is populated with a series of customers before the contents are dumped to the console. The output of this first step appears as follows:

```
Customer Name: Happy Gillmore
Customer Name: Billy Madison
Customer Name: Bobby Boucher
Customer Name: Barry Egan
```

As you can see, the values returned from the `Dictionary<TKey, TValue>` class are not sorted. Now, you create a `SortedDictionary<TKey, TValue>` instance and populate it with the contents of your dictionary, passing the existing dictionary as a parameter to the constructor. Your dictionary should now be sorted and, to verify that, you dump the contents of your new sorted dictionary. The output of this step is:

```
Customer->Bobby Boucher
Customer->Billy Madison
Customer->Barry Egan
Customer->Happy Gillmore
```

Notice that your list is now sorted by `Customer` Id. To top it off, the example then employs the `Remove()` method to remove the item at with a key value of `88`. And, to confirm that your operation removed the item you expected, you dump the contents one last time, which yields the following output:

```
Customer->Bobby Boucher
Customer->Billy Madison
Customer->Happy Gillmore
```

Sure enough, the item you expected to be removed is now gone. So, this should give you a feel for how `SortedDictionary<TKey, TValue>` allows you to create an ordered dictionary, while retaining keyed, random access to its values.

# SortedList<TKey, TValue>

The `SortedDictionary<TKey, TValue>` class will likely meet most of your needs if you simply want to sort your dictionary based on its key. However, if you'd like some additional index-based access to your collection, you'll want to consider using the `SortedList<TKey, TValue>` class. This class essentially gives you a semi-hybrid of the `List<T>` and `SortedDictionary<TKey, TValue>` classes. In fact, if you've worked with the non-generic `SortedList` class, this class will probably look familiar to you.

One key difference between this `SortedList<TKey, TValue>` and `SortedDictionary<TKey, TValue>` classes is the interfaces they use to access the container's keys and collections. The `SortedList<TKey, TValue>` class does not employ the `KeyCollection<TKey, TValue>` or `ValueCollection<TKey, TValue>` classes. Instead, keys and values are simply returned as `IList<T>` collections.

The following table is a breakdown of the methods and properties that are exposed by the `SortedList<TKey, TValue>` class.

| Method or Property Name | Description |
| --- | --- |
| Add() | Adds the supplied `key` and `value` to the list. |
| Capacity | A count of the maximum number of items allocated for the list. This will automatically resize when the maximum is reached. |
| Clear() | Removes all the items from the list. |
| Comparer | The `Comparer<T>` that will be used to sort the list's keys. |
| ContainsKey() | Determines if the supplied `key` exists in the current list, returning `true` if it is found. |
| ContainsValue() | Determines if the supplied value exists in the current list, returning `true` if it is found. |
| Count | Returns the number of items currently stored in the list. |
| Clear() | Removes all the items from the list. |
| GetEnumerator() | Returns an enumerated collection of `KeyValuePair` objects corresponding to the items in the list. |
| IndexOfKey() | Returns the zero-based index of the first item that matches the passed-in key. A value of –1 is returned if no match is found. |

| Method or Property Name | Description |
|---|---|
| IndexOfValue() | Returns the zero-based index of the first item that matches the passed-in value. A value of –1 is returned if no match is found. |
| Item | Indexer property that uses keys to add or update items in the list. |
| Keys | Returns a List<T> collection containing all the keys in the list. |
| Remove() | Finds the item that matches the passed-in key and removes it. If the item is found, the method returns true. |
| RemoveAt() | Removes the item at the specified index. An ArgumentOutOfRangeException is thrown if the index is not valid. |
| TrimExcess() | Sets the capacity of the list to the number of items in the list if the number of items is less than 90% of the capacity. |
| TryGetValue() | Attempts to get the value that corresponds to the supplied key. If the value is found, it is returned. Otherwise, the default value for the value parameter is returned. |
| Values | Returns a List<T> collection containing all the values in the list. |

You'll notice that this class essentially adds a set of index-based members that were not available in the SortedDictionary<TKey, TValue> class. For example, you may now use the IndexOfKey() and IndexOfValue() functions to retrieve the index of a specific key or value. The RemoveAt() method also provides an index-based mechanism for removing items from this container.

## Stack<T>

The Stack<T> class falls into the same category as the other classic data structures (LinkedList<T> and Queue<T>) that were discussed earlier in this chapter. It implements a simple last-in-first-out mechanism. As each item is inserted into the list it is "pushed" onto the stack, and as each item is accessed, it is "popped" off the stack. If you understand that concept, you will have mastered all there is to know about the Stack<T> class. The following table lists the properties and methods that are exposed by the Stack<T> class.

| Method or Property Name | Description |
|---|---|
| Clear() | Removes all the items from the stack. |
| Contains | Returns true if the stack contains an item that matches the supplied parameter. |
| Count | Returns the number of items currently stored in the stack. |
| CopyTo() | Copies the current contents of the stack to an Array. |

*Table continued on following page*

| Method or Property Name | Description |
| --- | --- |
| GetEnumerator() | Returns a `Stack<T>.Enumerator` that can be used to iterate over all the items in the stack. |
| Peek() | Returns the item at the top of the stack without popping it off the stack. |
| Pop() | Pops an item off the top of the stack. |
| Push() | Pushes an item onto the top of the stack. |
| ToArray() | Returns an array of items of type `T`. |
| TrimExcess() | Reduces the capacity of the stack to make it match the number of items in the stack if the number of items is less than 90% of the capacity. |

## BindingList<T>

So far, all of the generic types you've looked at have lived in the `System.Collections.Generic` and `System.Collections.ObjectModel` namespaces. However, there is one straggler that didn't quite fit in these namespaces. The `BindingList<T>` generic class, which implements the non-generic `IBindingList` interface, is found in the `System.ComponentModel.Collections.Generic` namespace. This class allows you to have a generic list that can be bound to the various components (`DataGrid`, `DataGridView`, and so on) that are part of the BCL. This ends up being a very helpful addition to the pool of available generics, because developers are very likely to want to bind their generic collections to the existing UI components.

The `BindingList<T>` is implemented as a descendant of the `Collection<T>` class and, as such, inherits a great deal of its implementation from that class. It then adds additional methods and properties to support the rest of what's needed to make it conform to the methods imposed by the `IBindingList` interface. Of particular interest is the introduction of support for events that will notify you when items are added and removed from the collection.

The `BindingList<T>` class is a much more heavyweight class compared to the `List<T>` class. So, unless you really need the extended capabilities offered by `BindingList<T>`, you're better off keeping all the optimization that's offered by the `List<T>` class.

# Testing Equality

Many of the collections described in this chapter include methods that take an object as a parameter and search the collection for a matching object. As an example, the `Collection<T>` class employs a series of methods (`Remove()`, `Contains()`, and so on) that take objects (instead of indexes) as parameters. For these kinds of methods, you may discover that you do not always get the behavior you're expecting. Objects you expect to match sometimes won't.

The confusion surrounding these methods typically stems from the fact that these methods use equality to search for matching objects. Clients of these methods, though, you may not always be aware of how this equality check is being performed. As a result, you may end up expecting objects to match that don't. To eliminate this confusion, you should be certain you have a firm grasp on how your objects are actually being compared. Between `Comparers` and specialized implementations of `IComparable`, you can end up with plenty of unexpected side effects.

# Null Collection Elements

Prior to the introduction of generics, the BCL collection classes represented their elements as objects. As such, developers were able to store and retrieve null values from their collections. However, with generics, you now have the luxury of using value types in your collections.

For clients of generic collections, this means you are no longer allowed to supply "null" values when populating your collection. Well, at least not as directly as you're used to. Instead, you'll need to leverage the `Nullable<T>` type that you saw in Chapter 4. The end result is that you still have a way to use null values in your collections. And you're allowed to get that null behavior without requiring any boxing or unboxing of the elements of your collections.

# More to Come

I think it's fair to assume that the generic classes found in the BCL only represent the tip of the iceberg. I fully expect Microsoft to continue to extend and evolve this namespace, slowly folding in all the generic types the development community will come to demand. In the interim, a groundswell of third-party activity is already focused on the creation of new generic libraries. Many of these libraries are evolving out of the STL-wannabe space where developers who are accustomed to STL are trying to drag all their favorite types forward into the .NET environment. You'll actually get a look at one of these libraries, Power Collections, in detail in Chapter 14. Looking at libraries of this nature serves two purposes. First, it allows you to supplement your generic tool bag with a set of additional generic types. Second, it gives you yet another concrete set of examples for how generics can be applied.

# Summary

The goal of this chapter was to provide a detailed view of the generic types that have been added to the BCL. To meet that objective, this chapter started out by providing a high-level overview of all the classes, interfaces, and enumerators that are part of the library. It also supplied examples and reference information for each of the new generic classes that are part of the BCL. The main idea was to equip you some insight into the basic mechanics of each of these classes. Beyond these mechanics, this chapter also tried to provide some context for how and when you might apply each of these generic types.

# 9

# Reflection, Serialization, and Remoting

The introduction of generics, in some respects, represents an extension of the existing .NET type system. And, of course, whenever types inherit new behavior, the APIs that interact with those types must also evolve to support those concepts. This chapter looks at three specific areas of the .NET Framework — reflection, serialization, and remoting — that are directly influenced by the introduction of generic types. The bulk of this chapter focuses on reflection, describing how generic types are created, examined, and manipulated dynamically via the reflection API. The chapter also looks at how generic types are serialized and the role they can play in solutions that use remoting. Along the way, you'll also see a few scenarios where generics can be applied to create more type-safe interactions with these APIs.

## Reflection

Reflection is one of the more powerful tools that developers can take advantage of as part of the .NET platform. As its name implies, reflection is meant to capture the set of functionality that allows clients to explore all the details about a data type. The most powerful aspect of reflection is its ability to allow programmers to use late-binding to create types on-the-fly at run-time. Developers leverage these reflection mechanisms as the backbone of a whole host of creative solutions.

As you can imagine, reflection is a fairly broad topic that is outside the scope of this book. At the same time, generics represent a fairly significant enhancement of the existing .NET type system and, as such, it's important for developers to understand how to provide specific insight into inspecting, creating, and manipulating generic types via the reflection APIs. Generics definitely throw some new concepts into the mix. The sections that follow explore each of these generic constructs in detail.

## Working with Open and Closed Types

The interfaces for creating, inspecting, and manipulating generic types are loosely divided into those that operate on open types and those that operate on closed types. Chapter 1, "Generics 101," talked about how open types were the conceptual equivalent of a class, whereas closed types could be viewed as objects that are instances of those open types. It's helpful to keep this conceptual view in mind as you look at the reflection interfaces for generics. So, if you're not feeling comfortable with this terminology, I suggest you revisit Chapter 1 to refresh your memory.

## Extending System.Type

A generic type, as you've seen, inherits most of the same behaviors as non-generic types. So, when it comes to reflection, it only makes sense that the generic characteristics of a type be introduced as extensions of the existing `System.Type` class. All of your interactions with reflection, then, are managed through the members associated with this class (and its subordinate classes). This will certainly simplify your transition to using reflection with generic types.

In addition to the members that have been added to `System.Type` to support specific generic characteristics, you'll also find that many of the existing methods and fields can be directly applied to generic types. For example, the `Type.GetType()` method that is used to create non-generic types can also be used in the creation of generic types.

## Determining if a Type Is Generic

Generic types, as you might suspect, throw some new wrinkles into your traditional reflection code. As a result, you certainly run into scenarios where you might need to provide separate logic for processing your generic types, which also means you'll need some way to determine if a given type is generic. This is achieved through the `IsGenericType` property shown here:

```vb
[VB code]
Public Sub TestIsGenericType()
    Dim dict As New Dictionary(Of Int32, Int32)()
    Dim myString As String = "Test"

    Dim testGeneric As Type = dict.GetType()
    If (testGeneric.IsGenericType = True) Then
        Console.Out.WriteLine("Is a generic type")

        testGeneric = myString.GetType()
        If (testGeneric.IsGenericType = True) Then
            Console.Out.WriteLine("Is a generic type")
        End If
    End If
End Sub
```

```csharp
[C# code]
public void TestIsGenericType() {
    Dictionary<int, int> dict = new Dictionary<int, int>();
    String myString = "Test";

    Type testGeneric = dict.GetType();
```

```
        if (testGeneric.IsGenericType == true)
            Console.Out.WriteLine("Is a generic type");

        testGeneric = myString.GetType();
        if (testGeneric.IsGenericType == true)
            Console.Out.WriteLine("Is a generic type");
}
```

For this example, you just create two types — one generic and one not. Then, you inspect the
IsGenericType property for each of these types. If that method returns True, you know the type
is generic.

## Creating Open and Closed Types with Reflection

Developers frequently use reflection to load types at run-time. The basic idea here is that a type can be
loaded dynamically based on its name. This mechanism provides developers with a great deal of flexibility, allowing compiled solutions to be extended at run-time via dynamically loaded types.

Fortunately, generic types are also able to participate in this dynamic scheme. In fact, with the exception
of a few twists, you should find that generic types are created very much like non-generic types. Still, it's
worth seeing what subtle nuances are introduced by generic types. To see this concept in action, let's create a GenericsFactory class that includes a few static methods for dynamically creating generic types.
The code for this factory is as follows:

```
[VB code]
Public Class GenericsFactory
    Private Sub New()
    End Sub

    Public Shared Function CreateOpenType(ByVal typeName As String) As Type
        Dim retVal As Type
        Dim charIdx As Int32 = typeName.IndexOf("`")
        If ((charIdx >= 0) And (charIdx < (typeName.Length - 1))) Then
            Dim arityStr As String
            arityStr = typeName.Substring(charIdx+1, (typeName.Length-charIdx) - 1)
            Dim arityNum As Int32
            If (Int32.TryParse(arityStr, arityNum) = True) Then
                retVal = Type.GetType(typeName)
            End If
        End If

        Return retVal
    End Function

    Public Shared Function CreateOpenType(ByVal typeName As String, _
                                          ByVal arity As Int32) As Type
        typeName = typeName + "`" + CStr(arity)
        Return Type.GetType(typeName)
    End Function
```

```vbnet
    Public Shared Function CreateClosedType(ByVal typeName As String, _
                                ByVal typeArgs As List(Of String)) As Type
        Dim retVal As Type
        Dim openType As Type
        openType = GenericsFactory.CreateOpenType(typeName, typeArgs.Count)

        If ((IsDBNull(openType) = False) And _
            (openType.IsGenericTypeDefinition = True)) Then
            Dim typeArgTypes As New List(Of Type)(typeArgs.Count)

            For Each argTypeName As String In typeArgs
                typeArgTypes.Add(Type.GetType(argTypeName))
            Next

            retVal = openType.MakeGenericType(typeArgTypes.ToArray())
        End If

        Return retVal
    End Function
End Class
```

```csharp
[C# code]
public class GenericsFactory {
    private GenericsFactory() { }

    public static Type CreateOpenType(string typeName) {
        Type retVal = null;
        int charIdx = typeName.IndexOf("`");
        if ((charIdx >= 0) && (charIdx < (typeName.Length - 1))) {
            string arityStr;
            arityStr = typeName.Substring(charIdx+1, (typeName.Length-charIdx)-1);
            int arityNum;
            if (int.TryParse(arityStr, out arityNum) == true)
                retVal = Type.GetType(typeName);
        }

        return retVal;
    }

    public static Type CreateOpenType(string typeName, int arity) {
        typeName = typeName + "`" + arity;
        return Type.GetType(typeName);
    }

    public static Type CreateClosedType(string typeName, List<String> typeArgs) {
        Type retVal = null;
        Type openType = GenericsFactory.CreateOpenType(typeName, typeArgs.Count);

        if ((openType != null) && (openType.IsGenericTypeDefinition == true)) {
            List<Type> typeArgTypes = new List<Type>(typeArgs.Count);

            foreach (String argTypeName in typeArgs)
                typeArgTypes.Add(Type.GetType(argTypeName));
```

```
            retVal = openType.MakeGenericType(typeArgTypes.ToArray());
        }

    return retVal;
    }
}
```

As you can see, this example introduces three methods for creating both open and closed types. Let's start by looking at the methods that support the creation of open types. Typically, when you're creating a non-generic type dynamically, you need only supply the fully qualified type name. However, with generic types, you can "overload" a generic class name by defining separate versions that accept varying numbers of type parameters. So, if you have MyType<T> and MyType<T, U>, you have two types with the same name. The number of parameters for these types (their arity) is what uniquely distinguishes each type. So, where you might have typically just called Type.GetType("MyType") to create this type at run-time, you must now include some additional qualifiers with your type name to indicate which generic type you want created.

For .NET generics, this type-naming issue is resolved by appending the "`" character to each type name along with the number of parameters it accepts. So, MyType`1 is considered the type name for MyType<T> and MyType`2 is the type name for MyType<T, U>. In fact, if you examine these types within the debugger, these are the exact names you'll see associated with your types. It's not exactly elegant, but it works.

Now, with this knowledge, let's examine the two implementations of the CreateOpenType() method that are part of the GenericsFactory class. The first version accepts a single string that represents the type name of the generic type to be created. This method assumes that the client has provided a fully qualified name that includes the arity for the type. In fact, the bulk of this method is dedicated to validating that this information is included as part of the type name. If it's not, it will not attempt to create the type and will return null.

The second version of this method accepts a type name and a parameter that represents the number of type parameters that exist for the type that is to be created. The idea for this method is that the client need only supply the name and the number of parameters and the method will use this information to assemble a valid type name. This method doesn't add lots of value, but does eliminate the client's need to include the "`" character as part of their type names.

The last method in this class, CreateClosedType(), is somewhat more involved. It employs a two-step process that starts with the creation of an open type. Once the open type is created, the type is made "closed" by binding type arguments to its parameters. You'll also notice that the type names supplied to this method cannot include the arity in the name. This is intentional. The list of type arguments that are supplied to this method are used to determine how many type parameters are needed and that number is used to create the appropriate open type.

Let's finish this topic off by assembling a look at a few examples that exercise the methods of this generics factory. First, you'll create a few calls that are used to create generic open types:

```
[VB code]
Public Class SampleType(Of T)
End Class


Public Class SampleType(Of T, U)
End Class
```

```vb
Public Sub DumpGenericArguments(ByVal genericType As Type)
    If (genericType.IsGenericType = True) Then
        Console.Out.WriteLine("Type : {0}", genericType.Name)
        For Each arg As Type In genericType.GetGenericArguments()
            Console.Out.WriteLine("{0,-30} : {1}", arg.Name + _
                                  "->IsGenericParameter", arg.IsGenericParameter)
        Next
    End If
End Sub

Public Sub TestOpenTypeCreation()
    Dim openType As Type
    openType = GenericsFactory.CreateOpenType("Reflection.SampleType`1")
    Console.Out.WriteLine("IsGenericType ={0}", openType.IsGenericType)
    DumpGenericArguments(openType)

    openType = GenericsFactory.CreateOpenType("Reflection.SampleType", 2)
    Console.Out.WriteLine("IsGenericType ={0}", openType.IsGenericType)
    DumpGenericArguments(openType)
End Sub
```

```csharp
[C# code]
Public class SampleType<T> {}
Public class SampleType<T, U> {}

public void DumpGenericArguments(Type genericType) {
    if (genericType.IsGenericType == true) {
        Console.Out.WriteLine("\nType : {0}", genericType.Name);
        foreach (Type arg in genericType.GetGenericArguments())
            Console.Out.WriteLine("{0,-30} : {1}", arg.Name +
                                  "->IsGenericParameter", arg.IsGenericParameter);
    }
}

public void TestOpenTypeCreation() {
    Type openType = GenericsFactory.CreateOpenType("Reflection.SampleType`1");
    Console.Out.WriteLine("IsGenericType={0}", openType.IsGenericType);
    DumpGenericArguments(openType);

    openType = GenericsFactory.CreateOpenType("Reflection.SampleType", 2);
    Console.Out.WriteLine("IsGenericType={0}", openType.IsGenericType);
    DumpGenericArguments(openType);
}
```

This example calls both variations of the CreateOpenType() method. You'll notice the first call supplies a fully qualified name that includes "`1" as part of the class name, indicating that it should create the version of SampleType that accepts a single type parameter. The second block of code creates a version of SampleType that accepts two parameters, passing the simplified type name and a parameter that indicates how many parameters are required. From looking at this, you can see that the second method is somewhat superfluous. Still, I can see how some developers might want to avoid including the "`".

The creation of an open type only creates type definitions. These definitions, by themselves, cannot be constructed. Instead, you would primarily only use an open type to inspect the general characteristics of the type. Or, you might use these type definitions as the basis for creating one or more closed types. The last option would be to create your closed types with one call to the `GenericsFactory`. The following code demonstrates how the factory could be used to create closed types:

```
[VB code]
Public Sub TestClosedTypeCreation()
    Dim args As New List(Of String)(1)
    args.Add("System.Int32")
    Dim closedType1 As Type
    closedType1 = GenericsFactory.CreateClosedType("Reflection.SampleType", args)
    DumpGenericArguments(closedType1)
    Dim newType1 As Object = Activator.CreateInstance(closedType1)

    args.Clear()
    args.Add("System.Int32")
    args.Add("System.String")
    Dim closedType2 As Type
    closedType2 = GenericsFactory.CreateClosedType("Reflection.SampleType", args)
    DumpGenericArguments(closedType2)
    Dim newType2 As Object = Activator.CreateInstance(closedType2)
End Sub
```

```
[C# code]
public void TestClosedTypeCreation() {
    List<String> args = new List<String>(1);
    args.Add("System.Int32");
    Type closedType1;
    closedType1 = GenericsFactory.CreateClosedType("Reflection.SampleType", args);
    DumpGenericArguments(closedType1);
    Object newType1 = Activator.CreateInstance(closedType1);

    args.Clear();
    args.Add("System.Int32");
    args.Add("System.String");
    Type closedType2;
    closedType2 = GenericsFactory.CreateClosedType("Reflection.SampleType", args);
    DumpGenericArguments(closedType2);
    Object newType2 = Activator.CreateInstance(closedType2);
}
```

This example achieves the equivalent of constructing `SampleType<int>` and `SampleType<int, String>`. To pull this off dynamically, it must first create a list of arguments that will then be supplied to the factory. The factory will take these parameters, create the appropriate open type, bind the parameters to the open type, and spit out a closed type. The closed type that is returned from the factory can then be instantiated via the `Activator.CreateInstance()` call. And there you have it, a dynamically loaded generic type.

If you are already familiar with reflection, you will likely find this application of generic flavor of reflection to be very familiar. The truth is, the only real twist introduced by generics here is the variations on the type name based on the number of type parameters. Other than that, the mechanics follow the same themes that are supported for non-generic types.

## *Converting Closed Types to Open Types*

There may be scenarios in which you are given a closed type and want to have access to the open type that is the basis for your closed type. In these situations, you can use the reflection API's `GetGenericTypeDefinition()` to achieve this result. The following provides an example of how this would work:

```vb
[VB code]
Public Function CovertToOpenType(ByVal aType As Type) As Type
    Dim retVal As Type
    If (aType.IsGenericType = True) Then
        retVal = aType.GetGenericTypeDefinition()
    End If
    Return retVal
End Function

Public Sub TestClosedToOpenConversion()
    Dim doubleList As New List(Of Double)()
    Dim doubleListType As Type = doubleList.GetType()
    Console.Out.WriteLine(doubleListType.Name + ".IsOpenType : {0}", _
                        doubleListType.IsGenericTypeDefinition)
    DumpGenericArguments(doubleListType)

    Dim openType As Type = CovertToOpenType(doubleList.GetType())
    Console.Out.WriteLine(openType.Name + ".IsOpenType : {0}", _
                        openType.IsGenericTypeDefinition)
    DumpGenericArguments(openType)
End Sub
```

```csharp
[C# code]
public Type CovertToOpenType(Type aType) {
    Type retVal = null;
    if (aType.IsGenericType == true)
        retVal = aType.GetGenericTypeDefinition();
    return retVal;
}

public void TestClosedToOpenConversion() {
    List<Double> doubleList = new List<Double>();
    Type doubleListType = doubleList.GetType();
    Console.Out.WriteLine(doubleListType.Name + ".IsOpenType : {0}",
                        doubleListType.IsGenericTypeDefinition);
    DumpGenericArguments(doubleListType);

    Type openType = CovertToOpenType(doubleList.GetType());
    Console.Out.WriteLine(openType.Name + ".IsOpenType : {0}",
                        openType.IsGenericTypeDefinition);
    DumpGenericArguments(openType);
}
```

This example starts out by creating a `List<Double>` closed type and dumping the information about that type. It then calls `CovertToOpenType()`, a helper method that checks to see if the supplied type is generic before calling `GetGenericTypeDefinition()`. This last method call returns the type definition of List<T> that is the underlying type that was used to create the closed type. The resulting open type can then be bound to a different parameter to form a new closed type.

## Examining Parameters and Arguments

The introduction of type parameters required a new set of members to be added to the reflection API. These new methods and properties allow clients to acquire and examine the parameters or arguments that are associated with a given generic type. Here's an example where the API is used to explore the parameters of a generic type:

```
[VB code]
Public Sub DumpParamProperties(ByVal aType As Type)
  For Each arg As Type In aType.GetGenericArguments()
    If (arg.IsGenericParameter = True) Then
      Console.Out.WriteLine("Type Param Name : {0}, Position {1}", arg.Name, _
                            CStr(arg.GenericParameterPosition))
            Dim cn As GenericParameterAttributes
      cn = arg.GenericParameterAttributes & _
            GenericParameterAttributes.SpecialConstraintMask

      If ((cn & GenericParameterAttributes.DefaultConstructorConstraint) <> 0) Then
        Console.Out.WriteLine("Has constructor constraint")
      End If

      If ((cn & GenericParameterAttributes.ValueTypeConstraint) <> 0) Then
        Console.Out.WriteLine("Has value constraint")
      End If

      If ((cn & GenericParameterAttributes.ReferenceTypeConstraint) <> 0) Then
        Console.Out.WriteLine("Has reference constraint")
      End If
    Else
      Console.Out.WriteLine("Argument Name : {0}", arg.Name)
    End If

    For Each intface As Type In arg.GetInterfaces()
      Console.Out.WriteLine("Parameter Interface : {0}", intface.Name)
    Next
  Next
End Sub
```

```
[C# code]
public void DumpParamProperties(Type aType) {
  foreach (Type arg in aType.GetGenericArguments()) {
    if (arg.IsGenericParameter == true) {
      Console.Out.WriteLine("Type Param Name : {0}, Position {1}",
                                arg.Name, arg.GenericParameterPosition);
      GenericParameterAttributes cn;
      cn = arg.GenericParameterAttributes &
            GenericParameterAttributes.SpecialConstraintMask;

      if ((cn & GenericParameterAttributes.DefaultConstructorConstraint) != 0)
        Console.Out.WriteLine("Has constructor constraint");
```

```
            if ((cn & GenericParameterAttributes.ValueTypeConstraint) != 0)
                Console.Out.WriteLine("Has value constraint");

            if ((cn & GenericParameterAttributes.ReferenceTypeConstraint) != 0)
                Console.Out.WriteLine("Has reference constraint");
        } else {
            Console.Out.WriteLine("Argument Name : {0}", arg.Name);
        }

        foreach (Type intface in arg.GetInterfaces())
            Console.Out.WriteLine("Parameter Interface : {0}", intface.Name);
    }
}
```

This example creates a `DumpParamProperties()` method that is used to display the properties associated with any type parameter or type argument. This method first retrieves a list of the arguments by calling the `GetGenericArguments()` method on the passed-in type. It then iterates over all the items returned from this call, inspecting and displaying the information about each parameter/argument it finds.

The `IsGenericParameter` property is used here to determine whether each parameter is a type parameter or a type argument. For type parameters, you can inspect the constraints associated with each parameter via the `GenericParameterAttributes` mask. These attributes allow you to get much more detailed information about the characteristics of a parameter, including its position in the parameter list as well as any constraints that may be attached to it. If the argument is a type argument, the example simply displays the parameter's type name.

With this method in place, all that remains is to exercise it with a few different generic types. The following example declares some basic generic types and then passes each of those types into the `DumpParamProperties()` method:

```
[VB code]
Public Interface IValidator
End Interface

Public Interface ITransformer
End Interface

Public Class Person
End Class

Public Class Employee
    Inherits Person
    Implements IValidator
    Implements ITransformer

    Public Sub New()
    End Sub
End Class

Public Class PersonCollection(Of T As {Person, IValidator, ITransformer, New})
End Class
```

```vbnet
Public Class PersonCollection(Of T As {Person, IValidator, ITransformer, New}, _
                                U As {IEnumerable(Of U), IComparable})
End Class

Public Sub TestParameterProperties()
  Dim dict As New Dictionary(Of String, Long)()
  Dim aType As Type = dict.GetType()
  DumpParamProperties(aType)

  aType = GenericsFactory.CreateOpenType("Reflection.PersonCollection`1")
  DumpParamProperties(aType)

  aType = GenericsFactory.CreateOpenType("Reflection.PersonCollection`2")
  DumpParamProperties(aType)
End Sub
```

```csharp
[C# code]
public interface IValidator { }

public interface ITransformer { }
public class Person { }

public class Employee : Person, IValidator, ITransformer {
    public Employee() { }
}

public class PersonCollection<T> where T : Person, IValidator, ITransformer, new()
{}

public class PersonCollection<T, U> where T : Person,IValidator,ITransformer, new()
                                    where U : IEnumerable<U>, IComparable {}

public void TestParameterProperties() {
    Dictionary<String, long> dict = new Dictionary<String, long>();
    Type aType = dict.GetType();
    DumpParamProperties(aType);

    aType = GenericsFactory.CreateOpenType("Reflection.PersonCollection`1");
    DumpParamProperties(aType);

    aType = GenericsFactory.CreateOpenType("Reflection.PersonCollection`2");
    DumpParamProperties(aType);
}
```

You'll notice that the types declared here include various permutations of constraints. These are included to exercise some of the different paths supported by the DumpParamProperties() method. The first call in the test program uses a constructed type. When it's processed, its type arguments (String and long) are displayed. The next two examples use open types with varying constraints. When DumpParamProperties() is called for these types, you'll get information regarding the position of each parameter and its constraints. The output of running this example is as follows:

```
Processing Type : Dictionary`2

Argument Name : String
Parameter Interface : IComparable
```

```
Parameter Interface : ICloneable
Parameter Interface : IConvertible
Parameter Interface : IEnumerable
Parameter Interface : IComparable`1

Argument Name : Int64
Parameter Interface : IComparable
Parameter Interface : IFormattable
Parameter Interface : IConvertible
Parameter Interface : IComparable`1


Processing Type : PersonCollection`1

Type Param Name : T, Position 0
Has constructor constraint
Has value constraint
Has reference constraint
Parameter Interface : ITransformer
Parameter Interface : IValidator


Processing Type : PersonCollection`2

Type Param Name : T, Position 0
Has constructor constraint
Has value constraint
Has reference constraint
Parameter Interface : ITransformer
Parameter Interface : IValidator

Type Param Name : U, Position 1
Has constructor constraint
Has value constraint
Has reference constraint
Parameter Interface : IComparable
Parameter Interface : IEnumerable`1
```

# Reflection and Generic Inheritance

When using reflection with inherited types, you may encounter some unexpected behavior. In the following  example, you'll create a subclass of a generic type and see how that might influence what is returned by the reflection API:

```
[VB code]
Public Class MyCollection(Of T)
End Class

Public Class MyDictionary(Of K, V)
    Inherits MyCollection(Of V)
End Class

Public Sub TestSubclassedTypes()
```

```
        Dim openType As Type
        openType = GenericsFactory.CreateOpenType("Reflection.MyDictionary`2")
        Dim baseClassType As Type = openType.BaseType
        Console.Out.WriteLine("{0}->IsGenericTypeDefinition :{1}", baseClassType.Name,_
                                           baseClassType.IsGenericTypeDefinition)
        DumpGenericArguments(baseClassType)
    End Sub
```

```
[C# code]
public class MyCollection<T> {}

public class MyDictionary<K, V> : MyCollection<V> {}

public void TestSubclassedTypes() {
    Type openType;
    openType = GenericsFactory.CreateOpenType("Reflection.MyDictionary`2");
    Type baseClassType = openType.BaseType;
    Console.Out.WriteLine("{0}->IsGenericTypeDefinition : {1}", baseClassType.Name,
                                        baseClassType.IsGenericTypeDefinition);
    DumpGenericArguments(baseClassType);
}
```

This example introduces the `MyDictionary<TKey, TValue>` type that inherits from `MyCollection<T>`, using its type parameter `TValue` in the inheritance declaration. This would not be an atypical pattern of inheritance. The question is: What will the reflection APIs tell you about this base class? From looking at it, you might assume it would be treated as a type definition. After all, it doesn't appear to have any bound arguments here and it's created like any other open type.

To determine how this base class is represented, you first use reflection to create `MyDictionary<TKey, TValue>` as an open type. You then retrieve its base type and inspect the `IsGenericTypeDefinition` property to determine if this base class is truly "open." This property ends up returning `False`. Even though no type arguments are supplied here, the inherited type is bound indirectly to the `TValue` parameter of the subclass. It's not free to accept any type — only those types that are supplied to its subclass. So, via this constraint, the base class is not considered an "open" type.

## Reflecting on Generic Methods

Generic methods also create the need for some new members in the reflection API. They share many of the same themes that you've already seen with generic classes. However, they obtain the bulk of their information about a generic method from the `MethodInfo` type. Here's an example that explores some of the nuances of reflecting on generic methods:

```
[VB code]
Public Sub DumpMethodProperties(ByVal aMethod As MethodInfo)
    If (aMethod.IsGenericMethodDefinition = True) Then
        Console.Out.WriteLine("Is a generic method")
    End If

    If (aMethod.ContainsGenericParameters = True) Then
        Console.Out.WriteLine("Method has generic parameters")
    End If
```

```
        If (aMethod.IsGenericMethod = True) Then
            Console.Out.WriteLine("Method has generic arguments")
            For Each param As Type In aMethod.GetGenericArguments()
                DumpParamProperties(param)
                If (param.IsGenericParameter = True) Then
                    Console.Out.WriteLine("Param is unbound : {0}", param.Name)
                Else
                    Console.Out.WriteLine("Param is bound : {0}", param.Name)
                End If
            Next
        End If
End Sub

Public Sub TestGenericMethod()
    Dim aSample As New SampleType(Of String)
    Dim aMethodType As Type = aSample.GetType()
    Dim aMethod As MethodInfo = aMethodType.GetMethod("GetItems")
    DumpMethodProperties(aMethod)

    aMethodType = GenericsFactory.CreateOpenType("Reflection.SampleType`1")
    aMethod = aMethodType.GetMethod("GetItems")
    DumpMethodProperties(aMethod)

    Dim typeArgs() As Type = New Type() {GetType(Int32), GetType(Double)}
    aMethod = aMethod.MakeGenericMethod(typeArgs)
    DumpMethodProperties(aMethod)

    aMethod = aMethod.GetGenericMethodDefinition()
    DumpMethodProperties(aMethod)
End Sub
```

[C# code]
```
public void DumpMethodProperties(MethodInfo aMethod) {
    if (aMethod.IsGenericMethodDefinition == true)
        Console.Out.WriteLine("Is a generic method");

    if (aMethod.ContainsGenericParameters == true)
        Console.Out.WriteLine("Method has generic parameters");

    if (aMethod.IsGenericMethod == true) {
        Console.Out.WriteLine("Method has generic arguments");
        foreach (Type param in aMethod.GetGenericArguments()) {
            DumpParamProperties(param);
            if (param.IsGenericParameter == true)
                Console.Out.WriteLine("Param is unbound : {0}", param.Name);
            else
                Console.Out.WriteLine("Param is bound : {0}", param.Name);
        }
    }
}

public void TestGenericMethod() {
    SampleType<String> aSample = new SampleType<String>();
    Type aMethodType = aSample.GetType();
```

```
        MethodInfo aMethod = aMethodType.GetMethod("GetItems");
        DumpMethodProperties(aMethod);

        aMethodType = GenericsFactory.CreateOpenType("Reflection.SampleType`1");
        aMethod = aMethodType.GetMethod("GetItems");
        DumpMethodProperties(aMethod);

        Type[] typeArgs = { typeof(int), typeof(double) };
        aMethod = aMethod.MakeGenericMethod(typeArgs);
        DumpMethodProperties(aMethod);

        aMethod = aMethod.GetGenericMethodDefinition();
        DumpMethodProperties(aMethod);
    }
```

This example creates a `DumpMethodProperties()` method that will take a `MethodInfo` parameter and examine all the generic characteristics of that method. You can see that the general set of generic-focused members added to `MethodInfo` mimic those found on `System.Type`. For example, the `IsGenericMethodDefinition` property referenced here maps conceptually to the `IsGenericTypeDefinition` property that was used in the earlier example for generic classes.

This same theme also carries through to the processing of generic parameters. You call `GetGenericArguments()` on the `MethodInfo` type and it returns an array of types that correspond to each of the type parameters associated with a method. From there, the handling and inspection of these parameters is identical to what can be done with parameters from a generic class. In fact, the example actually calls the same `DumpParamProperties()` method here that was used earlier in the chapter to display information about the attributes for each parameter.

In order to illustrate some of the different attributes that can be associated with a generic method, this example also creates a series of open and closed methods with varying characteristics. These examples also allow you to see how the reflection API can be used to detect bound and unbound parameters for a generic method.

Finally, I should also point out the use of the `MakeGenericMethod()` method here. This call binds type arguments to the type parameters of an open generic method and gives you the option of calling the `Invoke()` method on this dynamically constructed method.

## Obfuscation Reminder

If you're working with dynamically loaded types, you'd normally expect these type names to also be provided at run-time. If your code is referencing the fully qualified name at compile-time, you have to ask yourself why you're even using reflection. Still, there are times when you may end up using literal strings in your code to construct part or all of a type name. And, whenever you use any literal strings to create your open types, the names you reference must be precisely matched at run-time.

So what's the big deal? Well, in environments where you're not obfuscating your code, using these names is perfectly acceptable. However, for obfuscated environments, using these literal strings at compile-time may create a problem. When the `Reflection.MyType`1 class gets processed by the obfuscator, it and all of its references may get renamed to, say, `AAA.BBB`1, which will make your embedded literal string invalid. This problem is usually resolved by forcing the obfuscator to be more selective about what names are obfuscated. It also means you'll typically need to be more strategic about organizing your types into those that may be exposed to via reflection and those that are not.

These obfuscation issues actually apply to *any* solution that's using reflection—with or without generic types. It's just a point that needs to be reiterated as part of any discussion that includes reflection.

# Serialization

If you've been working with objects—on any platform—you've likely already been exposed to the concept of serialization. If you're moving types between systems or you're just persisting a representation of a type, you're likely to be leveraging some form of serialization. Many of the .NET types, in fact, implement the ISerializable interface that allows them to be used in combination with the platform's serialization classes to extract (serialize) or reconstitute (deserialize) the state of your objects from a stream.

Although serialization can be a fairly in-depth topic, the goal here is to focus specifically on how generic types participate in the existing .NET serialization scheme. You need to understand how a generic type is serialized, and you need to consider how generics might be applied to improve your general interactions with the serialization API. The sections that follow address both of these topics.

## Serialization Basics

First, let's start by looking at how basic serialization will work with your generic types. You need to begin by introducing a type that can be successfully serialized. In this case, let's create a SampleCollection<T> class that extends this existing list type. The code for this class is as follows:

```
[VB code]
<Serializable()> _
Public Class SampleCollection(Of T)
    Inherits List(Of T)

    Private _intData As Int32
    Private _stringData As String

    Public Sub New(ByVal intData As Int32, ByVal stringData As String)
        Me._intData = intData
        Me._stringData = stringData
    End Sub

    Public ReadOnly Property IntVal() As Int32
        Get
            Return Me._intData
        End Get
    End Property

    Public ReadOnly Property StrVal() As String
        Get
            Return Me._stringData
        End Get
    End Property
End Class
```

```
[C# code]
[Serializable]
public class SampleCollection<T> : List<T> {
    private int _intData;
    private string _stringData;

    public SampleCollection(int intData, string stringData) {
        this._intData = intData;
        this._stringData = stringData;
    }

    public int IntVal {
        get { return this._intData; }
    }

    public string StrVal {
        get { return this._stringData; }
    }
}
```

To participate in serialization, this type need only add the [Serializable] attribute to its declaration. For this particular class, the example also adds a data member that helps illustrate how its data will get serialized along with the rest of your class. With this class created, let's now consider how clients would go about serializing and deserializing this type. The following example creates an instance of this class, serializes its contents to a stream, and deserializes it in a separate instance:

```
[VB code]
Public Sub TestBasicSerialization()
    Dim strList As New SampleCollection(Of String)(111, "Value1")
    strList.Add("Val1")
    strList.Add("Val2")

    Dim stream As New MemoryStream()
    Dim formatter As New BinaryFormatter()
    formatter.Serialize(stream, strList)
    stream.Seek(0, SeekOrigin.Begin)

    Dim newList As SampleCollection(Of String)
    newList = DirectCast(formatter.Deserialize(stream),SampleCollection(Of String))

    Console.Out.WriteLine("Int Data Member : {0}", newList.IntVal)
    Console.Out.WriteLine("String Data Member : {0}", newList.StrVal)

    For Each listValue As String In newList
        Console.Out.WriteLine("Value : {0}", listValue)
    Next
End Sub
```

```
[C# code]
public void TestBasicSerialization() {
    SampleCollection<string> strList = new SampleCollection<string>(111, "Value1");
    strList.Add("Val1");
    strList.Add("Val2");
```

```
        MemoryStream stream = new MemoryStream();
        BinaryFormatter formatter = new BinaryFormatter();
        formatter.Serialize(stream, strList);
        stream.Seek(0, SeekOrigin.Begin);

        SampleCollection<string> newList;
        newList = (SampleCollection<string>)formatter.Deserialize(stream);
        Console.Out.WriteLine("Int Data Member : {0}", newList.IntVal);
        Console.Out.WriteLine("String Data Member : {0}", newList.StrVal);

        foreach (string listValue in newList)
            Console.Out.WriteLine("Value : {0}", listValue);
    }
```

You'll notice that the deserialization of your stream into your generic type requires a cast to the specific constructed type that was used when this type was originally serialized. This is consistent with the theme that you've seen elsewhere, where the marriage of a generic type and its type arguments represents a unique type. So, in this example, you could not serialize a SampleCollection<Double> and then turn around and attempt to deserialize its stream into a SampleCollection<String>. That would be the conceptual equivalent of serializing a Double and trying to deserialize it into a String. When serializing generic types, the constructed serialized type must *always* match the constructed type being used for deserialization.

## Custom Serialization

At times you may want more explicit control over the serialization of your types. To take control over the serialization process, you must have your generic type implement the ISerializable interface. Through this interface, you'll be allowed to intercept the calls to serialize/deserialize your type and create your own custom serialization stream. Naturally, the stream produced by the serialization process must match, precisely, the stream consumed in the deserialization process.

Again, no special infrastructure was added to the platform to support generic types. It wasn't necessary. Generic types are first-class citizens and can be serialized like any other type in the system. Still, the mechanics of serializing a generic type within the existing framework may not be entirely clear. In the following example, you'll create your own generic type that supports custom serialization to see this mechanism in action:

```
[VB code]
<Serializable()> _
Public Class CustomClass(Of T)
    Implements ISerializable

    Private _intData As Int32
    Private _stringData As String
    Private _genericData As T

    Public Sub New()
    End Sub

    Private Sub New(ByVal serInfo As SerializationInfo, _
                    ByVal context As StreamingContext)
        Dim objValue As Object
```

```vbnet
        objValue = serInfo.GetValue("_intData", GetType(Int32))
        _intData = DirectCast(objValue, System.Int32)

        objValue = serInfo.GetValue("_stringData", GetType(String))
        _stringData = DirectCast(objValue, System.String)

        objValue = serInfo.GetValue("_genericData", GetType(T))
        _genericData = DirectCast(objValue, T)
    End Sub

    Public Sub New(ByVal intData As Int32, ByVal stringData As String, _
                ByVal genericType As T)
        Me._intData = intData
        Me._stringData = stringData
        Me._genericData = genericType
    End Sub

    Public Sub GetObjectData(ByVal serInfo As SerializationInfo, _
                        ByVal context As StreamingContext) _
                        Implements ISerializable.GetObjectData
        serInfo.AddValue("_intData", _intData)
        serInfo.AddValue("_stringData", _stringData)
        serInfo.AddValue("_genericData", _genericData, _genericData.GetType())
    End Sub

    Public ReadOnly Property IntVal() As Int32
        Get
            Return Me._intData
        End Get
    End Property

    Public ReadOnly Property StrVal() As String
        Get
            Return Me._stringData
        End Get
    End Property

    Public ReadOnly Property GenericVal() As T
        Get
            Return Me._genericData
        End Get
    End Property
End Class
```

```csharp
[C# code]
[Serializable]
public class CustomClass<T> : ISerializable {
    private int _intData;
    private string _stringData;
    private T _genericData;

    public CustomClass() { }

    private CustomClass(SerializationInfo serInfo, StreamingContext context) {
        _intData = (int)serInfo.GetValue("_intData", typeof(int));
```

```
            _stringData = (string)serInfo.GetValue("_stringData", typeof(string));
            _genericData = (T)serInfo.GetValue("_genericData", typeof(T));
        }

    public CustomClass(int intData, string stringData, T genericType) {
        this._intData = intData;
        this._stringData = stringData;
        this._genericData = genericType;
    }

    public void GetObjectData(SerializationInfo serInfo, StreamingContext context)
{
        serInfo.AddValue("_intData", _intData);
        serInfo.AddValue("_stringData", _stringData);
        serInfo.AddValue("_genericData", _genericData, _genericData.GetType());
    }

    public int IntVal {
        get { return this._intData; }
    }

    public string StrVal {
        get { return this._stringData; }
    }

    public T GenericVal {
        get { return this._genericData; }
    }
}
```

Two new elements were added to this class to make it support custom serialization. First, the GetObjectData() method was added to support serialization of the object. Its responsibility is to place each of the object's properties you want serialized into the SerializationInfo class. This class is passed in by the framework during the serialization process. You then call the AddValue() method for each property of your class, supplying a name and a data type. And, because the type of your _genericData member is of type T, you must call GetType() at run-time to acquire its type.

To support deserialization, you must supply a constructor that accepts SerializationInfo and StreamContext parameters. Then, within this constructor, you must call GetValue() on SerializationInfo to extract the value for each piece of data that is serialized by your object.

Now, while this default approach certainly works, some elements of how this mechanism can really benefit from the application of generics. If you look closely at the SerializationInfo class, you'll find that it includes a large collection of AddValue() overloads to support each data type that can be serialized. Of more significance is its GetValue() method, which must return Object data types that are then cast to the appropriate types on the way out. This class represents the perfect example of a class that could improve the type safety and clarity of its interface through the application of generics.

Consider how you might morph the behavior of the SerializationInfo class to eliminate some of the type-safety issues that have shown up in the preceding example. Your first thought might be to subclass the SerializationInfo class and add your own members. The class is sealed, though, so that approach is out. Instead, a better solution would be to create a simple TypeSafeSerializer class with a set of static methods for adding and getting serialized values. The code for this helper class is as follows:

```
[VB code]
Public Class TypeSafeSerializer
    Private Sub New()
    End Sub

    Public Shared Sub AddValue(Of T)(ByVal name As String, ByVal value As T, _
                                ByVal serInfo As SerializationInfo)
        serInfo.AddValue(name, value)
    End Sub

    Public Shared Function GetValue(Of T)(ByVal name As String, _
                                    ByVal serInfo As SerializationInfo) As T
        Dim retVal As T = DirectCast(serInfo.GetValue(name, GetType(T)), T)
        Return retVal
    End Function
End Class
```

```
[C# code]
public class TypeSafeSerializer {
    private TypeSafeSerializer() { }

    public static void AddValue<T>(String name, T value,SerializationInfo serInfo){
        serInfo.AddValue(name, value);
    }

    public static T GetValue<T>(String name, SerializationInfo serInfo) {
        T retVal = (T)serInfo.GetValue(name, typeof(T));
        return retVal;
    }
}
```

The generic AddValue() and GetValue() methods provided here are meant to replace the corresponding methods that are part of SerializationInfo. They still take SerializationInfo as a parameter and use it to call AddValue() and GetValue(), but their interface shields you from some of the type issues that surround using this interface directly. To back that point up, take a look at how the constructor and the GetObjectData() members of your previous class would be changed by the inclusion of this new helper class. The new implementation of these methods is as follows:

```
[VB code]
Private Sub New(ByVal serInfo As SerializationInfo, _
            ByVal context As StreamingContext)

    _intData = TypeSafeSerializer.GetValue(Of Int32)("_intData", serInfo)
    _stringData = TypeSafeSerializer.GetValue(Of String)("_stringData", serInfo)
    _genericData = TypeSafeSerializer.GetValue(Of T)("_genericData", serInfo)
End Sub

Public Sub GetObjectData(ByVal serInfo As SerializationInfo,
                        ByVal context As StreamingContext)
                    Implements ISerializable.GetObjectData

    TypeSafeSerializer.AddValue(Of Int32)("_intData", _intData, serInfo)
    TypeSafeSerializer.AddValue(Of String)("_stringData", _stringData, serInfo)
    TypeSafeSerializer.AddValue(Of T)("_genericData", _genericData, serInfo)
End Sub
```

```
[C# code]
private CustomClass(SerializationInfo serInfo, StreamingContext context) {
    _intData = TypeSafeSerializer.GetValue<int>("_intData", serInfo);
    _stringData = TypeSafeSerializer.GetValue<string>("_stringData", serInfo);
    _genericData = TypeSafeSerializer.GetValue<T>("_genericData", serInfo);
}

public void GetObjectData(SerializationInfo serInfo, StreamingContext context) {
    TypeSafeSerializer.AddValue<int>("_intData", _intData, serInfo);
    TypeSafeSerializer.AddValue<string>("_stringData", _stringData, serInfo);
    TypeSafeSerializer.AddValue<T>("_genericData", _genericData, serInfo);
}
```

For the `AddValue()` method, you can see how your generic data type now participates on equal footing with its non-generic counterparts. It no longer requires a separate call to acquire its types. The real bene-factor here, though, is `GetValue()`. The generic `GetValue()` method of the `TypeSafeSerializer` class lets you extract the serialized values for generic and non-generic types without any casting. For both of these cases, the type of the incoming type parameter ends up driving which underlying method of `SerializationInfo` gets called, which means there's no need for a series of methods that are over-loaded on type.

This example should illustrate how custom types are serialized and how generics can be applied to make the serialization a more type-safe experience. This pattern may also help you identify similar scenarios where generics can be leveraged to improve your existing classes.

## Serialization with Web Services

Whenever you're working with web services, you must consider how types will be transported to and from a service. And, with the introduction of generics, you must also consider how generic types will participate in your web service APIs. Specifically, you'll need to think about how a Web service will seri-alize each generic type and transform it into a type that can be represented in a SOAP construct.

In this section you'll create a simple web service that includes references to a few generic types to demon-strate how a generic type will be brokered by a service. The following code represents the implementation of a basic web service:

```
[VB code]
<WebServiceBinding(ConformanceClaims:=WsiClaims.BP10,EmitConformanceClaims:=True)>_
Public Class SampleService
    <XmlType("My{T}List")> _
    Public Class MyList(Of T)
        Inherits List(Of T)
    End Class

    <XmlType("My{T}Collection")> _
    Public Class MyCollection(Of T)
        Inherits Collection(Of T)
    End Class

    <WebMethod()> _
    Public Function GetListValues1() As MyList(Of String)
        Dim list As New MyList(Of String)
```

```vb
        list.Add("Val1")
        list.Add("Val2")
        Return list
    End Function

    <WebMethod()> _
    Public Function GetListValues2() As MyList(Of Double)
        Dim list As New MyList(Of Double)
        list.Add(3223.54)
        list.Add(6436.65)
        list.Add(76.54)
        list.Add(8664.24)
        Return list
    End Function

    <WebMethod()> _
    Public Function GetCollectionValues() As MyCollection(Of Int32)
        Dim coll As New MyCollection(Of Int32)
        coll.Add(123)
        coll.Add(456)
        coll.Add(789)
        Return coll
    End Function
End Class
```

```csharp
[C# code]
[WebServiceBinding(ConformanceClaims=WsiClaims.BP10,EmitConformanceClaims = true)]
public class SampleService {
    [XmlType("My{T}List")]
    public class MyList<T> : List<T> {
    }

    [XmlType("My{T}Collection")]
    public class MyCollection<T> : Collection<T> {
    }

    [WebMethod]
    public MyList<string> GetListValues1() {
        MyList<string> list = new MyList<string>();
        list.Add("Val1");
        list.Add("Val2");
        return list;
    }

    [WebMethod]
    public MyList<double> GetListValues2() {
        MyList<double> list = new MyList<double>();
        list.Add(3223.54);
        list.Add(6436.65);
        list.Add(76.54);
        list.Add(8664.24);
        return list;
    }
```

```
    [WebMethod]
    public MyCollection<int> GetCollectionValues() {
        MyCollection<int> coll = new MyCollection<int>();
        coll.Add(123);
        coll.Add(456);
        coll.Add(789);
        return coll;
    }
}
```

This example exposes three web service methods (`GetListValues1()`, `GetListValues2()`, and `GetCollectionValues()`), each of which returns a different generic type. To be able to cross the web service boundary, each of these types must support serialization. In this case, your types all subclass generic types that already support serialization, which means they can be used as-is.

Now, take a look at how these types end up getting serialized into XML as you call each of these methods. The following represents the XML that would be returned from the calls to the three methods exposed by your web service:

```
<?xml version="1.0" encoding="utf-8" ?>
<MystringList xmlns:xsi=http://www.w3.org/2001/XMLSchema-instance
        xmlns:xsd="http://www.w3.org/2001/XMLSchema" xmlns="http://tempuri.org/">
  <string>Val1</string>
  <string>Val2</string>
</MystringList>

<?xml version="1.0" encoding="utf-8" ?>
<MydoubleList xmlns:xsi=http://www.w3.org/2001/XMLSchema-instance
        xmlns:xsd="http://www.w3.org/2001/XMLSchema" xmlns="http://tempuri.org/">
  <double>3223.54</double>
  <double>6436.65</double>
  <double>76.54</double>
  <double>8664.24</double>
</MydoubleList>

<?xml version="1.0" encoding="utf-8" ?>
<MyintCollection xmlns:xsi=http://www.w3.org/2001/XMLSchema-instance
        xmlns:xsd="http://www.w3.org/2001/XMLSchema" xmlns="http://tempuri.org/">
  <int>123</int>
  <int>456</int>
  <int>789</int>
</MyintCollection>
```

These three message responses all include XML serialized representations of the generic types that were populated and returned from each of your web service calls. You'll notice the names of the tags for each of these types are derived from the attribute naming scheme applied to each of your generic types. For example, the attribute for `MyList<T>` in your web service declaration is represented as `[My{T}List]`, where `{T}` is replaced with the type of the supplied type argument. So, as an example, the XML tag that gets generated for the `MyList<String>` constructed type will be `MystringList`.

# Remoting

Generics can also be incorporated into solutions that access remote objects. In fact, generics have some fairly useful applications for remoting solutions. Consider, for example, the interfaces you define for your remote types. The application of generic interfaces to these types allows you to have a single interface that can support a much broader range of types. So, instead of building separate interfaces or overloading methods heavily, your generic interface can support a wider spectrum of possible data types with a single interface.

To illustrate this point, let's assemble a simple example that employs a generic remote interface. The first step in this process is to create a generic interface that will become the interface you'll use for interacting with a remote object:

```
[VB code]
Namespace RemoteGenericInterfaces
    Public Interface IRemoteGenericInterface(Of T)
        Function RemoteMethod(ByVal param As T) As T
    End Interface
End Namespace
```

```
[C# code]
namespace RemoteGenericInterfaces {
    public interface IRemoteGenericInterface<T> {
        T RemoteMethod(T param);
    }
}
```

This generic interface exposes a single method that accepts a parameter of type T and returns a value of type T. As you can see, this interface is the same as any other generic interface you might have seen. There's certainly nothing you need to do to make it usable for remote objects. Now, let's look at a class that will implement this class on a remote server:

```
[VB code]
Namespace RemoteGenerics
    Friend Class RemoteClass(Of T)
        Inherits MarshalByRefObject
        Implements IRemoteGenericInterface(Of T)

        Public Sub New()
            Console.Out.WriteLine("RemoteClass created.")
        End Sub

        Public Function RemoteMethod(ByVal param As T) As T _
                        Implements IRemoteGenericInterface(Of T).RemoteMethod
            Console.Out.WriteLine("Processing request")
            Console.Out.WriteLine("Param Type   : {0}", param.GetType().ToString())
            Console.Out.WriteLine("Param Value  : {0}", param.ToString())
            Return param
        End Function
    End Class
End Namespace
```

```
[C# code]
namespace RemoteGenerics {
    internal class RemoteClass<T> : MarshalByRefObject, IRemoteGenericInterface<T>{
        public RemoteClass() {
            Console.Out.WriteLine("RemoteClass created.");
        }

        T IRemoteGenericInterface<T>.RemoteMethod(T param) {
            Console.Out.WriteLine("Processing request");
            Console.Out.WriteLine("Param Type  : {0}", param.GetType().ToString());
            Console.Out.WriteLine("Param Value : {0}", param.ToString());
            return param;
        }
    }
}
```

This class serves two purposes. First, its constructor displays a message each time an instance of this object is created. Then, as clients make calls to its RemoteMethod() method, it will display information about the type that it is supplied and the value assigned to that type. Finally, on the server side, you must provide an application that registers instances of this method that will be available to consumers. The code for this console application is as follows:

```
[VB code]
Namespace RemoteGenerics
    Public Class RemoteGenericServer
        <STAThread()> _
        Public Shared Sub Main()
            Dim remoteType As Type
            Dim mode As WellKnownObjectMode = WellKnownObjectMode.SingleCall

            remoteType = GetType(RemoteClass(Of Double))
            RemotingConfiguration.RegisterWellKnownServiceType(remoteType, _
                                                    "RemoteDouble.rem", mode)

            remoteType = GetType(RemoteClass(Of Int32))
            RemotingConfiguration.RegisterWellKnownServiceType(remoteType, _
                                                    "RemoteInt.rem", mode)

            remoteType = GetType(RemoteClass(Of String))
            RemotingConfiguration.RegisterWellKnownServiceType(remoteType, _
                                                    "RemoteString.rem", mode)

            Dim channel As New IpcChannel("RemoteServer")
            ChannelServices.RegisterChannel(channel)

            Console.Out.WriteLine("Connection Established. Waiting for clients.")
            Console.ReadLine()
        End Sub
    End Class
End Namespace
```

```
[C# code]
namespace RemoteGenerics {
    class RemoteGenericServer {
        [STAThread]
```

```
        static void Main(string[] args) {
            Type remoteType;
            WellKnownObjectMode mode = WellKnownObjectMode.SingleCall;

            remoteType = typeof(RemoteClass<Double>);
            RemotingConfiguration.RegisterWellKnownServiceType(remoteType,
                                              "RemoteDouble.rem", mode);

            remoteType = typeof(RemoteClass<Int32>);
            RemotingConfiguration.RegisterWellKnownServiceType(remoteType,
                                                "RemoteInt.rem", mode);

            remoteType = typeof(RemoteClass<string>);
            RemotingConfiguration.RegisterWellKnownServiceType(remoteType,
                                             "RemoteString.rem", mode);

            IpcChannel channel = new IpcChannel("RemoteServer");
            ChannelServices.RegisterChannel(channel);

            Console.Out.WriteLine("Connection Established. Waiting for clients.");
            Console.ReadLine();
        }
    }
}
```

If you've worked with remoting at all, this should look fairly familiar. This example makes a series of calls to `RegisterWellKnownServiceType()` and, for each method you want to expose, it assigns a name that clients must use when binding to your class. You'll notice that you are required to register specific constructed types during this process. This means that your server will only be able to accept calls for those constructed types. In this case, the `RemoteClass<Double>`, `RemoteClass<int>`, and `RemoteClass<string>` types are all registered. Once each of these instances of `RemoteClass` are `registered`, you can then create a channel with a port name and register that channel. After these steps are completed, your server is ready to start receiving requests.

With the server up, all that remains is to create a client that will access these registered `RemoteClass` types. The following code provides an example of some basic client calls to the remote server:

```
[VB code]
Public Class GenericClient
    Private Const _svr = "ipc://RemoteServer/"
        <STAThread()> _
        Public Shared Sub Main()
            Dim remoteType As Type

            remoteType = GetType(IRemoteGenericInterface(Of Double))
            Dim remoteDoubleObj As Object
            remoteDoubleObj = Activator.GetObject(remoteType, _svr + _
                                                    "RemoteDouble.rem")

            remoteType = GetType(IRemoteGenericInterface(Of Int32))
            Dim remoteIntObj As Object
            remoteIntObj = Activator.GetObject(remoteType, _svr + "RemoteInt.rem")
```

```
            remoteType = GetType(IRemoteGenericInterface(Of String))
            Dim remoteStringObj As Object
            remoteStringObj = Activator.GetObject(remoteType, _svr + _
                                                  "RemoteString.rem")

            Dim remoteDouble As IRemoteGenericInterface(Of Double)
            remoteDouble = remoteDoubleObj

            Dim remoteInt As IRemoteGenericInterface(Of Int32)
            remoteInt = remoteIntObj

            Dim remoteString As IRemoteGenericInterface(Of String)
            remoteString = remoteStringObj

            Console.Out.WriteLine("Call to remote double: {0}", _
                            remoteDouble.RemoteMethod(323.443).ToString())
            Console.Out.WriteLine("Call to remote int   : {0}", _
                            remoteInt.RemoteMethod(423).ToString())
            Console.Out.WriteLine("Call to remote string: {0}", _
                            remoteString.RemoteMethod("Called Remote Server"))
    End Sub
End Class
```

[C# code]

```
public static class GenericClient {
    private const string _svr = "ipc://RemoteServer/";

    [STAThread]
    public static void Main(string[] args) {
        Type remoteType;

        remoteType = typeof(IRemoteGenericInterface<double>);
        object remoteDoubleObj;
        remoteDoubleObj = Activator.GetObject(remoteType, _svr+"RemoteDouble.rem");

        remoteType = typeof(IRemoteGenericInterface<int>);
        object remoteIntObj;
        remoteIntObj = Activator.GetObject(remoteType, _svr + "RemoteInt.rem");

        remoteType = typeof(IRemoteGenericInterface<string>);
        object remoteStringObj;
        remoteStringObj = Activator.GetObject(remoteType, _svr+"RemoteString.rem");

        IRemoteGenericInterface<double> remoteDouble;
        remoteDouble = remoteDoubleObj as IRemoteGenericInterface<double>;

        IRemoteGenericInterface<int> remoteInt;
        remoteInt = remoteIntObj as IRemoteGenericInterface<int>;

        IRemoteGenericInterface<string> remoteString;
        remoteString = remoteStringObj as IRemoteGenericInterface<string>;

        Console.Out.WriteLine("Call to remote double: {0}",
                            remoteDouble.RemoteMethod(323.443).ToString());
```

```
        Console.Out.WriteLine("Call to remote int   : {0}",
                              remoteInt.RemoteMethod(423).ToString());
        Console.Out.WriteLine("Call to remote string: {0}",
                              remoteString.RemoteMethod("Called Remote Server"));
    }
}
```

This sample client calls `Activator.GetObject()` for each of the constructed types that are supported by the remote server. This method call returns an `Object` type. So, before the client can call your method, this object must be converted to an `IRemoteGenericInterface<T>` reference. You then proceed to make calls to `RemoteMethod()` for each of the three argument types, `Double`, `integer`, and `String`.

After looking at this code, you might also notice that these remoting interfaces can also benefit from the application of generics. You can imagine how you could create a wrapper for the `Activator` to make a generic version of the `GetObject()` method that would improve readability and general type safety of this client code.

# Summary

The goal of this chapter was to look at how reflection, serialization, and remoting have all been impacted by the introduction of generics. The chapter explored, in detail, how reflection can be used to create open and closed generic types. As part of looking at reflection, the chapter explored techniques for examining the attributes of generic types. It also looked at generic serialization, explaining how to serialize generic types and, more specifically, how to implement custom serialization for generic types. Finally, the chapter finished off with a look at how generic interfaces can be used in remoting-based solutions.

# 10

# Generics Guidelines

With each significant new language feature also comes a set of guidelines that dictate how and when that feature should be applied. Generics are no different. This chapter assembles a set of guidelines that attempt to address some of the common practices that should be applied or given consideration when consuming or constructing generic types. As part of this effort, it provides an item-by-item breakdown of the guidelines and, where necessary, digs into the pros and cons associated with a given guideline. The goal here is to bring together, in one place, all those generics practices that are being discussed, debated, and adopted by the development community.

## An Evolving List

Although generics can't be classified as *new*, they certainly will be showing up on the desktops of a whole new group of programmers with the release of Visual Studio 2005. With generics being unfolded to a broader audience and with .NET introducing its own new variations on the generics theme, it's easy to see why generics require the introduction of some new guidelines. It's also fair to assume that this list of guidelines is very much in its infancy. Once developers are using generics in full force, I would expect the list of generics guidelines to continue to grow and mature.

To kick-start this process, Microsoft has been assembling a preliminary list of items that shape much of the thinking on guidelines at this stage. The goal of this chapter is to distill that list, add new items, and generally provide a more thorough examination of rationale behind applying these guidelines. Overall, this effort will produce a more formalized look at the factors that are likely to influence some aspects of your generic thinking.

## Defining Guidelines

As guidelines, I would also expect there to be some level of disagreement about these items. If you can't get programmers to agree on tabs versus spaces, you're certainly not going to get them to reach consensus on areas that have even higher levels of grey matter. So, as you review this list, you need to keep in mind that these are only guidelines and are not being represented as rules that are set in stone. Guidelines can and *should* be violated under certain circumstances. They exist purely to help you define the rules that should shape your general process for deciding how and when to use a generic type. When you find exceptions to the rule, by all means—violate the rule. Just be sure that you can defend each violation and, if you can, you'll be fulfilling the spirit of what the guideline is trying to achieve.

# Organization

In general, when you're assembling a list of guidelines, they don't always fall into natural categories. However, as I looked at the list I had, I did see some items fitting into specific clusters that seemed to conform to a specific theme. Within each cluster, I simply list each item with a number, which provides me with a simple mechanism for referencing each item individually.

# Identifying Generic Opportunities

This first set of guidelines is focused on describing a specific set of scenarios where you should consider leveraging generics. These items represent areas where you would want to consider refactoring existing code or they may just be patterns you'll want to consider when you're introducing new code. Some of these may be somewhat obvious based on other topics covered elsewhere in this book. However, the goal is to assemble all of these items in one place as a list that you can easily consult as you're working with generics.

## Item 1: Use Generic Collections

Data collections are typically one of the most heavily used data types. You likely already have `ArrayLists` and `HashTables` strewn throughout your existing code. You were also likely—before generics—to make heavy use of these `System.Collections` data structures in new code you would be writing. However, with generics, there's really no good reason to continue to use the collections from this namespace.

If there is one area where generics add unquestionable value, it is in the area of collections. Without generics, producers and consumers of non-generic collections were forced to represent contained types as objects. This, of course, meant your code was littered with casts and general type coercion to covert each object to its actual type. It also meant that value types needed to be boxed to be represented as object types. Even in cases where you may have tried to limit the impact of non-generic collections, you were still typically forced to bloat your code with type-specific collection wrappers. For these reasons and a hundred others sprinkled throughout this book, it should be clear that there are few compelling reasons to cling to these old, non-generic collections. In fact, I would argue that generic collections represent the single most compelling usage of generics and, if you're not sold on the value of using generic collections, you're not likely to be sold on *any* of the value generics can bring to your code.

Although I think the arguments for using generic collections are compelling, not every solution may have the luxury of fully replacing non-generic collections with their generic counterparts. If you expose a public API and have clients that currently bind to that non-generic API, you're going to need to figure out how to transition your API to generics. In these instances, it would still seem valuable to leverage generic collections within your implementation and, over time, ease generics into your API.

# Item 2: Replace Objects with Type Parameters

Before generics, programmers in search of generality typically found themselves relying on the `object` type as the universal solution to achieving generality. If you had a class or methods that had common functionality that could be applied to disparate types, you had few options at your disposal. If you didn't have a common base class or interface, your only alternative was to use a least common denominator type, the `object` type. For example, suppose you had the following method to send messages:

```
[VB code]
Public Function SendMsg(ByVal sender As Object, ByVal param As Object) as Object
End Function
```

```
[C# code]
public object SendMsg(object sender, object param) {}
```

This method provides a very general-purpose mechanism for sending a message from any `object` type with any parameter type and any return type. By using the `object` type throughout this method, you've allowed this method to be used with a wide spectrum of types. Of course, you've also completely traded off type safety for generality here.

As you can imagine, generics are a perfect fit for solving the type-safety issues introduced by this method. Through generics, you can strike a balance between type safety and generality, which is exactly what you're looking for in this scenario. The generic version of this method would appear as follows:

```
[VB code]
Public Function SendMsg(Of I, J, K)(ByVal sender As I, ByVal param As J) as K
End Function
```

```
[C# code]
public K SendMsg<I, J, K>(I sender, J param) {}
```

You can see here that the `SendMsg()` method has been converted into a generic method that uses type parameters in each of the slots where it had previously used `object` types.

This example illustrates just one instance where `object` types can be made type-safe through the use of generics. You may be using `object` data types in a variety of different contexts and, for each of those, you should be considering swapping out these `object` types with some flavor of generic solution.

The basic rule of thumb here is that, with generics, there should be a much lower incidence of `object` types showing up in your code. Wherever you spot an `object` you should be asking yourself if generics can be applied to eliminate the dependency on this `object` type. Generics should make least common denominator programming the anomaly instead of the norm.

# Item 3: Replace System.Type with Type Parameters

In some instances, you may have used references to `System.Type` in the signature of your methods, allowing you to alter the behavior of your method based on a supplied type. For example, it wouldn't be all that uncommon in the pre-generic era to find a method that used a type parameter as follows:

```
[VB code]
Public Function FindPerson(ByVal personType As Type, ByVal Int32 As id) As Object
End Function
```

```
[C# code]
public object FindPerson(Type personType, int id) {}
```

This method takes a System.Type type as an incoming parameter and searches for people that have an id that matches the supplied id. If it finds a match, it will construct an object that corresponds to the supplied type (Customer, Employee, and so on) and return that as the output of this function call. This method might come in handy in scenarios where you have specialized Person objects, each of which has a unique id. It allows you to find and construct any descendant Person type without requiring separate methods to support each type.

Before generics, this would not have been an unreasonable piece of code to find. However, with generics, you shouldn't find yourself needing to rely on the System.Type nearly as much. In fact, this method could be made much cleaner by making it a generic method and retrofitting it with type parameters as follows:

```
[VB code]
Public Function FindPerson(Of T)(ByVal personType As T, ByVal Int32 As id) As T
End Function
```

```
[C# code]
public T FindPerson<T>(T personType, int id) {}
```

This makes for a cleaner interface and likely reduces the complexity of this method's implementation. It also means that consumers of this method won't be forced to cast this method's return value to a specific type.

## Item 4: Use Type Parameters for Ref Types (C# Only)

Item 2 talked about the general strategy of replacing object types with type parameters. There is one variant of this rule that seems relevant enough to warrant the introduction of a new item. For this item, the focus is on the use of object data types as reference parameters. With C#, a reference parameter will only accept references that match, exactly, the type identified by the reference parameter. Consider, for example, the following method that accepts a reference parameter:

```
[C# code]
public void Sort(ref object param1, ref object param2) {}
```

This method was created to sort objects of any type. And, as such, it took the least common denominator approach of using an object type as the reference it accepts for its two parameters. The fact that these two parameters are identified as object types wouldn't seem like a real problem. Here's a look at what happens when you construct two Person objects and call this Sort() method:

```
[C# code]
public void processItems() {
    Person person1 = new Person(424);
    Person person2 = new Person(190);

    Sort(ref person1, ref person2);
}
```

On the surface, this would appear to be fine. The Person objects, which are rooted in object, will simply get cast to an object and passed successfully as parameters to this method. And, if this method didn't specify these parameters as reference types, that logic would be fine. However, as mentioned earlier, with reference types the compiler will require the supplied parameters to match the precise type that is called out in the signature of the method. And, in this example, `Person` will not match `object`.

Now, you could solve this with a handy dandy cast, casting each `Person` object to an `object` type. However, that's not necessary. You can resolve this problem by making your `Sort()` method generic and using type parameters in place of the `object` types. The new version would appear as follows:

```
[C# code]
public void Sort<T>(ref T param1, ref T param2) {}
```

This change makes your types match exactly and, because types can be inferred, the previous sample client code for this method can remain untouched.

VB seems to handle this scenario more gracefully. It does not appear to require the incoming types to match the precise signature of the types declared in the method. Still, even with VB, you should see that it still makes sense to use a generic method here. In the spirit of Item 2, you should still be looking for opportunities to rid your code of `object` types.

In many respects, this rule may appear to be a duplicate of Item 2. And, in the general sense, it is a duplicate. However, the added twist associated with using reference types seems to stand out as one more variation that's worth considering in isolation.

# Item 5: Genericize Types That Vary Only by a Data Type

If you look across all of your existing classes, interfaces, delegates, and methods, you are likely to identify code that varies primarily by the types it contains and/or manages. In these cases, you need to consider whether generics can be applied, allowing a single implementation to service the needs of multiple data types. Applying generics in these scenarios can produce a variety of positive side effects, including reducing code size, improving type safety, and so on. The following sections provide examples of some of these refactoring themes.

## Eliminating Redundant Data Containers

By far, data containers represent one of the most common, straightforward areas where you will want to do some generic refactoring. Most solutions have at least one or two examples where, in your distaste for the compromised type safety of an `ArrayList`, you created your own type-safe wrapper classes. It would not be uncommon, for example, to find pre-generic code that might appear as follows:

```
[VB code]
Public Class PersonCollection
    Private _persons As ArrayList

    Public Sub New()
        _persons = New ArrayList()
    End Sub

    Public Sub Add(ByVal person As Person)
        _persons.Add(person)
    End Sub
```

```
        Public ReadOnly Property Item(ByVal Index As Int32) As Person
            Get
                Return DirectCast(_persons(Index), Person)
            End Get
        End Property
End Class

Public Class OrderCollection
    Private _orders As ArrayList

    Public Sub New()
        _orders = New ArrayList()
    End Sub

    Public Sub Add(ByVal Order As Order)
        _orders.Add(Order)
    End Sub

    Public ReadOnly Property Item(ByVal Index As Int32) As Order
        Get
            Return DirectCast(_orders(Index), Order)
        End Get
    End Property
End Class
```

```
[C# code]
public class PersonCollection {
    private ArrayList _persons;

    public PersonCollection() {
        _persons = new ArrayList();
    }

    public void Add(Person person) {
        _persons.Add(person);
    }

    public Person this[int index] {
        get { return (Person)_persons[index]; }
    }
}

public class OrderCollection {
    private ArrayList _orders;

    public OrderCollection() {
        _orders = new ArrayList();
    }

    public void Add(Order order) {
        _orders.Add(order);
    }
```

```
        public Order this[int index] {
            get { return (Order)_orders[index]; }
        }
    }
```

These two classes wrap an `ArrayList` and expose a type-safe interface that shields clients from the object-reality that comes along with using a non-generic container. After looking at these two classes, it should be obvious that they are perfect candidates for generic refactoring. And, while each of these classes can be improved through the application of generics, there are broader issues to consider here.

Outside of the data types being managed here, `Person` and `Order`, there's nothing different in their actual implementation. And, whenever this is the case, you know you have a situation that is crying out for the application of generics. In fact, the `Collection<T>` container that is provided as part of `System.Collections.Generic` would eliminate the need for any of this code to exist. By simply declaring `Collection<Person>` and `Collection<Order>`, you would get all the type safety and functionality that's provided in the preceding example.

If your collection classes had introduced functionality that was not directly supported by `Collection<T>`, you would still simply create a new class that subclassed `Collection<T>` and added any new custom members.

This example is straight out of the Generics 101 bible. As such, it may have already been evident. Still, to overlook this scenario in the context of generic guidelines would be a mistake — especially because this should be one of the areas where generics will deliver the most value.

### Identifying Candidate Methods

Finding methods that are candidates for generic refactoring is a more subtle, less exact science. The fundamentals are still the same. You essentially want to look for sets of methods that vary, primarily by the data type they are processing. The most common examples that seem to show up here are those methods that perform very basic operations on whole objects without calling specific methods. The following examples fall into this category:

```
[VB code]
Public Shared Sub Swap(ByRef val1 As String, ByRef val2 As String)
    Dim tmpObj As String = val2
    val2 = val1
    val1 = tmpObj
End Sub

Public Shared Sub Swap(ByRef val1 As Double, ByRef val2 As Double)
    Dim tmpObj As Double = val2
    val2 = val1
    val1 = tmpObj
End Sub

Public Shared Function Max(ByVal val1 As Int32, ByVal val2 As Int32) As Int32
    Dim retVal As Int32 = val1
    If (val2 > val1) Then
        retVal = val2
    End If
    Return retVal
End Function
```

```
Public Shared Function Max(ByVal val1 As String, ByVal val2 As String) As String
    Dim retVal As String = val1
    If (val2.CompareTo(val1) > 0) Then
        retVal = val2
    End If
    Return retVal
End Function
```

```
[C# code]
public static void Swap(ref String val1, ref String val2) {
    String tmpObj = val2;
    val2 = val1;
    val1 = tmpObj;
}

public static void Swap(ref Double val1, ref Double val2) {
    Double tmpObj = val2;
    val2 = val1;
    val1 = tmpObj;
}

public static int Max(int val1, int val2) {
    int retVal = val1;
    if (val2 > val1)
        retVal = val2;
    return retVal;
}

public static String Max(String val1, String val2) {
    String retVal = val1;
    if (val2.CompareTo(val1) > 0)
        retVal = val2;
    return retVal;
}
```

These examples include implementations of the `Swap()` and `Max()` methods. Methods of this nature are meant to invoke a general-purpose operation on an object without concern for its interface. `Swap()`, for example, simply causes two objects to trade places. `Max()` just determines and returns the maximum value of the two supplied parameters. However, in order to maintain type safety and avoid any boxing overhead for your value types, you are required to provide a series of overloaded versions of each of the methods.

In looking at these two methods, it's clear that expanding your list of overloads to embrace all types would be time consuming, would bloat your code, and would introduce maintenance overhead. However, using `object` types here would also be a mistake. It would introduce a host of other problems. It would also violate the spirit of Item 2.

This, of course, means the best option here is to make generic versions of these methods. The following represents generic implementations of the `Swap()` and `Max()` methods:

```
[VB code]
Public Shared Sub Swap(Of T)(ByRef val1 As T, ByRef val2 As T)
    Dim tmpObj As T = val2
    val2 = val1
```

```
        val1 = tmpObj
    End Sub

    Public Shared Function Max(Of T)(ByVal val1 As T, ByVal val2 As T) As T
        Dim retVal As T = val1
        If (Comparer(Of T).Default.Compare(val1, val2) < 0) Then
            retVal = val2
        End If
        Return retVal
    End Function
```

```
    [C# code]
    public static void Swap<T>(ref T val1, ref T val2) {
        T tmpObj = val2;
        val2 = val1;
        val1 = tmpObj;
    }

    public static T Max<T>(T val1, T val2) {
        T retVal = val1;
        if (Comparer<T>.Default.Compare(val1, val2) < 0)
            retVal = val2;
        return retVal;
    }
```

There's nothing earth-shattering about how generics make these methods better. These examples are only intended to represent a sample of a pattern you're going to want to look for in your own code. Essentially, anytime you find yourself overloading a method's signature to support variations of parameter types, you have to ask yourself if that method might be better implemented as a generic method. You'll also want to look at the body of these methods to determine how tightly they are coupled to the types that appear in their parameter lists.

As part of considering whether to make methods of this nature generic, you should also consider how constraints might be used to expose some minimal interfaces of your type parameters. If, for example, you were to constrain a method using IComparable<T>, you would be allowing the method to access the comparable interface without significantly narrowing the capabilities of the method. If your objects implement many of these general-purpose interfaces, these interfaces can then be leveraged as constraints and further expose the capabilities of your type parameters.

The thrust here, though, is to focus your energy on making cleaner, more type-safe replacements of existing methods. Any time you can reduce the size of code and simultaneously improve its type-safety, you need to seize the opportunity.

## Replacing Multiple Delegates with One Generic Delegate

The introduction of generic delegates should fundamentally change how and when you create your own delegates. Delegates represent one of the most fundamental and natural applications of generics. As such, I have trouble imagining any situation where you would ever want to use a non-generic delegate. It is also possible that you may already have delegates in your code that could be improved via generics. Suppose, for example, you had the following non-generic delegates in your application:

```vb
[VB code]
Public Delegate Sub MyDel1(ByVal x As Int32, ByVal y As String)
Public Delegate Sub MyDel2(ByVal x As Int32, ByVal y As Double)
Public Delegate Sub MyDel3(ByVal x As Int32, ByVal y As Long)

Public Delegate Sub MyDel4(ByVal x As Int32, ByVal y As String, ByVal z As Double)
Public Delegate Sub MyDel5(ByVal x As Int32, ByVal y As Double, ByVal z As Double)
```

```csharp
[C# code]
public delegate void MyDel1(int x, string y);
public delegate void MyDel2(int x, double y);
public delegate void MyDel3(int x, long y);

public delegate void MyDel4(int x, string y, double z);
public delegate void MyDel5(int x, double y, double z);
```

Here you have two sets of delegate signatures. The first set accepts two parameters and varies only by the type of the second parameter. The second set has three parameters and also varies only by its second parameter. Now, with these delegates in place, you can start declaring methods that implement these delegates. The question is, do you really need all of these declarations? No. You can actually replace all of these declarations with the following pair of generic delegates:

```vb
[VB code]
Public Delegate Sub MyDel(Of T, U)(ByVal x As T, ByVal y As U)
Public Delegate Sub MyDel(Of T, U, V)(ByVal x As T, ByVal y As U, ByVal z As V)
```

```csharp
[C# code]
public delegate void MyDel<T, U>(T x, U y);
public delegate void MyDel<T, U, V>(T x, U y, V z);
```

These two generic delegate declarations will accept any permutation of types for your two- and three-parameter delegates, eliminating the need to declare a new delegate for each new method signature. This also improves the expressive qualities of those methods that accept delegates. The following code provides a few simple examples of how these generic delegates impact your interactions with methods that accept delegates:

```vb
[VB code]
Public Sub Func1(ByVal x As Int32, ByVal y As String)
End Sub

Public Sub Func4(ByVal x As Int32, ByVal y As String, ByVal z As Double)
End Sub

Public Sub AcceptDelegate(ByVal MyDel As MyDel(Of Int32, String))
End Sub

Public Sub AcceptDelegate(ByVal MyDel As MyDel(Of Int32, String, Double))
End Sub

Public Sub CallWithDelegate()
    AcceptDelegate(AddressOf Func1)
    AcceptDelegate(AddressOf Func4)
End Sub
```

```
[C# code]
public void Func1(int x, string y) {}
public void Func4(int x, string y, double z) { }

public void AcceptDelegate(MyDel<int, string> MyDel) { }
public void AcceptDelegate(MyDel<int, string, double> MyDel) { }

public void CallWithDelegate() {
    this.AcceptDelegate(Func1);
    this.AcceptDelegate(Func4);
}
```

Here, in your `AcceptDelegate()` method, you can see how your generic delegate is used to express the signature of methods that it will accept. This, from my perspective, clearly identifies the kinds of methods that can be supplied and makes it easier for you to change delegate method signatures directly at the spot where they are being used. In a non-generic model, you'd have to hunt down the delegate signature elsewhere to modify it.

The main idea here is that, for your existing code, you may have delegates that can be removed and replaced with generic delegates. There are certainly upsides here—especially in scenarios where you're looking for an approach that allows you to more clearly convey the signature of a delegate at the point where it is referenced.

### Using Generic Methods as Delegate Methods

The methods that you supply as the implementation of a delegate may also be generic. These two constructs—used in combination—offer you a number of opportunities to reshape your approach to how you define and implement delegates in your solutions. At a minimum, as you look at each method that implements a given delegate, you should also consider whether a collection of delegate methods could be replaced by a single generic method. If this is the case, this would represent yet another opportunity to use generics to reduce the size and improve the maintainability of your delegate methods. It also puts you in a position where your delegate is prepared to support a broader set of types without any additional enhancement. Less can certainly translate into more in this scenario.

### Introducing Generic Interfaces

Because interfaces don't contain implementation, they can represent a very natural target for applying generic concepts. The basic idea here, as it has been throughout this section, is to make more abstract representations of your interfaces that allows them to be applied to a broader set of data types. This is especially useful with interfaces that are more general in nature. In your own code, you should be looking for any interfaces that might benefit from the application of generics. Any interface that varies only by the type it leverages may be a candidate for generic refactoring.

The `IComparable<T>` and `IEnumerable<T>` interfaces make great examples of small, focused interfaces that leverage generics while remaining globally applicable to a wide variety of types. This characteristic also makes these same interfaces excellent candidates for being applied as constraints.

# Balancing Readability with Expressiveness

Some view the syntactic constructs introduced by generics as a welcome addition to the language. This crowd looks at the type arguments that accompany a generic declaration and sees them as providing a very precise, undeniably clear definition of each data type. For them, generics eliminate any confusion that might have been associated with using non-generic APIs.

Meanwhile, another population views generics as imposing on the readability of their code. They see type parameters and constraints and new keywords as muddying the image of what was an otherwise perfectly clean, uncluttered block of code. Many in this group see generics as undermining the general usability and maintainability of their code.

The challenge here is striking a balance between these two groups. If everyone can agree on the general value of generics, the only issue that remains is how to introduce them without creating code that is so confusing that it requires a decoder ring to decipher the text. The goal of this section is to offer up some guidelines that can establish some fundamental boundaries that give developers the freedom to leverage generics without leaving behind a trail of unreadable code.

## Item 6: Use Expressive, Consistent Type Parameter Names

During the beta cycle for Visual Studio 2005, early adopters focused a significant portion of venom and debate on naming conventions for type parameters. Because type parameters are littered throughout your generic types, it makes sense that developers would be concerned about how these type parameters could be named in a manner that could accurately convey their intended use.

There are basically two camps of thought on this subject. One camp prefers single-letter type parameter names simply because they reduce the overall size of the signature of your generic declarations. This is a model that is employed by most C++ template libraries, which may contribute to the mindset of those who prefer to continue this tradition. The other camp finds these one-letter type parameters simply too terse. They don't see how a single letter can really adequately convey the nature of a type parameter. This group, as you might suspect, prefers lengthier, more expressive naming conventions. The following declarations illustrate the tradeoffs that are associated with these competing mindsets:

```
[VB code]
Public Class Dictionary(Of K, V)
End Class

Public Class Dictionary(Of TKey, TValue)
End Class
```

```
[C# code]
public class Dictionary<K, V> {}
public class Dictionary<TKey, TValue>
```

The first declaration is short and sweet, but hardly expressive. The second option uses full names, prepending a T to each name to designate it as a type parameter. In this scenario, the second of these two options seems like it might be the preferred model. However, consider this same approach as it might be applied to a generic method or delegate declaration with constraints applied. An example of this nature might appear as follows:

```
[VB code]
```

```
Public Function Foo(Of TKey As IComparable, TValue)(ByVal key As TKey, _
                                        ByVal val As TValue) As TValue
End Function

Public Function Foo(Of K As IComparable, V)(ByVal key As K, ByVal val As V) As V
End Function

[C# code]
public TValue Foo<TKey, TValue>(TKey key, TValue val) where TKey : IComparable {}
public TValue Foo<K, V>(K key, V val) where K : IComparable {}
```

In this example, the longer names can get slightly more unwieldy. Naturally, the opposition would say the second of these two starts to resemble more of an algebraic equation than a method. At the same time, the full names certainly make this feel more like the signatures conform to a pattern that you might be more comfortable digesting.

## The Naming Compromise

As you can imagine, there's no one guideline I can suggest that will suddenly resolve the preferences of either of these approaches. In the end, it's mostly subjective. Do you like spaces or tabs in your files? Do you indent your code two spaces or four? It almost falls into that area of debate that really ends up being more a matter of personal preference. Still, there are some guidelines in this area that should, at a minimum, establish some parameters for how you might standardize your approach.

The best compromise appears to be to use single-letter type parameters when a single letter adequately captures the nature of your type parameter. If, for example, you have a generic collection, the name MyCollection<T> would be considered acceptable. The use of T in this scenario is adequate, because a longer name can't really convey anything extra about the type parameter's intent or role. The truth is, in any scenario where you have a single un-constrained type parameter, the single-letter use of T will likely suffice.

However, cases exist where you have multiple type parameters playing specific, identifiable roles. In these situations, you should select longer, more expressive names that clearly convey the role of each type parameter. With a generic dictionary class, for example, you know its first type parameter represents a key and its second parameter represents a value. Given these roles, the guidelines suggest that you should declare this dictionary as Dictionary<TKey, TValue>. Here, you've added meaning to the names and conformed to the standard of pre-pending a T to each type parameter name.

## Using Constraints to Qualify Names

If you're using constraints with your generic types, those constraints provide more information about the nature of the type parameters they constrain. Suppose, for example, you have the following declaration:

```
[VB code]
Public Class TestClass(Of T As IValidator)
    Private _myType As T
End Class

[C# code]
public class TestClass<T> where T : IValidator {
    private T _myType;
}
```

This example has a single type parameter that is constrained as being of the type IValidator. Now, as you reference the type parameter in the body of your class, the references to the type parameter as T does little to convey the fact that T is being used as an IValidator type. To remedy this, you should make the constraint name part of the type parameter name. The new, improved version of this declaration would appear as follows:

```
[VB code]
Public Class TestClass(Of TValidator As IValidator)
    Private _myType As TValidator
End Class
```

```
[C# code]
public class TestClass<T> where TValidator : IValidator {
    private TValidator _myType;
}
```

Now, as you reference your type parameter in the body of your class, the type parameter name provides significantly more insight into its nature. This will work for a number of scenarios. However, if you're using multiple constraints, you may opt to stick with a simple T as your type parameter name.

## Generic Methods in Generic Classes

One area that seems to get left out of the naming debate is the name of type parameters for generic methods that appear within a generic class. Consider the following simple example:

```
[VB code]
Public Class TestClass(Of T)
    Public Sub Foo(Of T)(ByVal val As T)
        Dim localVar As T
    End Sub
End Class
```

```
[C# code]
public class TestClass<T> {
    public void Foo<T>() {
        T localVar;
    }
}
```

In conforming to the "use T when you have a single parameter" guideline, you have used T as the name of the type parameter for your class *and* you've used T as the type parameter for the method that appears within your class. Although this compiles, using the same type parameter name for both your class and the Foo() method creates a situation where your method will not be able to access the type parameter from its surrounding class.

This calls for another naming guideline that requires method type parameters to always be named in a consistent manner that will prevent methods from hiding access to the type parameters of their surrounding class. In cases where your method accepts a single parameter, I suggest that you use a consistent replacement for T that will be used across all your generic methods.

## Being Consistent

Though I can espouse the value of naming conventions, I often doubt whether the masses can be persuaded to adopt a universal approach. That said, I do think there's room for agreement on the topic of consistency. No matter what scheme you adopt, it's essential that you be consistent with that theme throughout your code. Consistency will contribute as much to the readability of your generic types as any guideline. Of course, if you're exposing your generic types as part of a public API, your choice of naming convention schemes gets more complicated. Ideally, you'd like your generic signatures and documentation to conform to a broader standard. This will simplify matters for the consumers of your API. So, in that light, you should place added value on making sure your naming conventions are keeping up with what, at this stage, is likely to continue to be a bit of a moving target.

## Item 7: Use Aliasing for Complex or Frequently Used Types

In some cases, you may have a rather lengthy generic type declaration that is used heavily throughout a block of code. In these situations, you may find the bulky nature of your generic type as imposing on the overall readability of the rest of your code. Consider, for example, the following code:

```
[VB code]
Public Sub ProcessItem(ByVal value As MyType1(Of Long, Double, String), _
                                             ByVal status As Int32)
    Dim x As New MyType1(Of Long, Double, String)
    If (status = 1) Then
        Dim y As MyType1(Of Long, Double, String) = value
    Else
        Dim z As New Nullable(Of MyType1(Of Long, Double, String))
    End If
End Sub
```

```
[C# code]
public void ProcessItem(MyType1<long, double, string> value, int status) {
    MyType1<long, double, string> x = new MyType1<long, double, string>();
    if (status == 1) {
        MyType1<long, double, string> y = value;
    } else {
        Nullable<MyType1<long, double, string>> z =
                              new Nullable<MyType1<long, double, string>>();
    }
}
```

This method continually references the generic type MyType1 and, with its three type arguments, it starts polluting the esthetics of your code in a hurry. Fortunately, for scenarios like this, you have the option of creating an alias that can act as a placeholder for these more heavyweight declarations. This detracts some from the expressiveness of your types but is worth it if the readability of your code is being compromised. Here's a quick look at how the aliased version of this function would improve the situation:

```
[VB code]
Imports MType = MyType1(Of Long, Double, String)

Public Class Aliasing
    Public Sub ProcessItem(ByVal value As MType, ByVal status As Int32)
        Dim x As New MType
        If (status = 1) Then
            Dim y As MType = value
        Else
            Dim z As New Nullable(Of MType)
        End If
    End Sub
End Sub
```

```
[C# code]
using MType = MyType1<long, double, string>;

public void ProcessItem(MType value, int status) {
    MType x = new MType();
    if (status == 1) {
        MType y = value;
    } else {
        Nullable<MType> z = new Nullable<MType>();
    }
}
```

An aliasing statement is added to the top of this example that now declares `MType`, which serves as a placeholder for the full generic declaration of `MyType1` throughout the implementation of your code. The result is certainly a more readable version of your method.

## Item 8: Don't Use Constructed Types as Type Arguments

Although you may be embracing the splendor of generics, you still need to make sure you're not going overboard with your generic types. You can, if you choose, introduce generic types that can make construction a less than graceful process. Consider, for example, a generic type that accepts two constructed types as parameters:

```
[VB code]
Public Class MyComplexType(Of T, U)
End Class

Public Class MyType2(Of T, U, V)
End Class

Public Class MyType3(Of T, U)
End Class

Public Class TestClass
    Public Sub foo()
        Dim x As New MyComplexType(Of MyType2(Of Int32, String, Double), MyType3(Of
String, String))
    End Sub
End Class
```

```
[C# code]
public class MyComplexType<T, U> { }

public class MyType2<T, U, V> { }

public class MyType3<T, U> { }

public class TestClass {
    public void foo() {
      MyComplexType<MyType2<int, string, double>, MyType3<string, string>> x =
        new MyComplexType<MyType2<int, string, double>, MyType3<string, string>>();

    }
}
```

This example declares a generic class, `MyComplexClass`, which takes two type parameters. It also creates a couple of additional generic types that are then used as type arguments in the construction of an instance of `MyComplexClass`. You can see, from looking at this, that using constructed types as type arguments has a serious impact on the readability of your code. As a rule of thumb, you should avoid scenarios of this nature. This is not to say that you should completely abandon passing constructed types as parameters. It just means you should construct some intermediate representation and pass that declared type as your parameter. It's all about making your code more readable—not limiting what types can be used as parameters.

## Item 9: Don't Use Too Many Type Parameters

The more type parameters you add to your generic types, the more difficult they will be to use and maintain. The reality is that there probably aren't too many situations where you will need to leverage more than two type parameters. This fact and the reality that using more than two type parameters is likely to negatively impact the usability of your generic types would suggest that, as a guideline, it would make sense to generally constrain the number of type parameters you use to two or less.

## Item 10: Prefer Type Inference with Generic Methods

One of the best features of generic methods is their ability to infer the types of their type parameters. This feature eliminates the need to explicitly provide type arguments for each call to a generic method and, as a result, has a significant impact on the overall maintainability and readability of your code. The following example illustrates type inference in action:

```
[VB code]
Public Class TypeInference
    Public Sub MyInferenceMethod(Of I, J)(ByVal param1 As I, ByVal param2 As J)
    End Sub

    Public Sub MakeInferenceCall ()
        MyInferenceMethod("TestVal", 122)
        MyInferenceMethod(122, "TestVal")
        MyInferenceMethod(New Order(), 833.22)
    End Sub
End Class
```

```
[C# code]
public class TypeInference {
    public void MyInferenceMethod<I, J>(I param1, J param2) { }

    public void MakeInferenceCall () {
        MyInferenceMethod("TestVal", 122);
        MyInferenceMethod(122, "TestVal");
        MyInferenceMethod(new Order(), 833.22);
    }
}
```

From this example you can see how type inference makes the generic-ness of your method completely transparent. Each call that is made here is no different than the calls you might make to a non-generic method. It's as if you've overloaded this method with every combination of possible data types. Given this upside, it's only natural to have a guideline that suggests that consumers of generic methods should, as a rule of thumb, always prefer type inference to explicitly specified type arguments.

There are also times when the declaration of your generic methods will prohibit you from inferring the types of your parameters. Consider the following:

```
[VB code]
Public Function MyNonInferenceMethod(Of I, J)() As I
End Function
```

```
[C# code]
public I MyNonInferenceMethod<I, J>() { }
```

The absence of references to type parameters in the signature of this method means there's no way to supply types that could then be used to infer type information for your type parameters. This isn't necessarily wrong or even common. However, you should still be aware of the fact that clients of this method will not be able to leverage type inference when making their calls.

## Item 11: Don't Mix Generic and Non-Generic Static Methods

If you are using static methods in a generic class that also includes static *generic* methods, you may end up creating some ambiguity in the interface of your class. The following example illustrates a simple case where this could be a problem:

```
[VB code]
Public Class TestClass(Of T)
    Public Shared Sub Foo()
    End Sub

    Public Shared Sub Foo(Of T)()
    End Sub
End Class
```

```
[C# code]
public class TestClass<T> {
    public static void Foo() {}
    public static void Foo<T>() {}
} Okay - MAS
```

You'll notice that this generic class includes a static method Foo() in addition to a static generic method also named Foo(). Given these two methods, imagine the confusion this would generate for consumers of this class. The following provides an example of calls to both of these methods:

```
[VB code]
TestClass(Of String).Foo()
TestClass.Foo(Of String)()
```

```
[C# code]
TestClass<string>.Foo();
TestClass.Foo<string>();
```

The presence of both of these static methods, as you can see, ends up creating some general confusion. Fortunately, you're not likely to end up in many scenarios like this one. Or, if you do, you could easily overcome this by altering your method names.

# Using BCL Generic Types

The System.Collections.Generic and System.Collections.ObjectModel namespaces introduce a whole host of out-of-the-box generic types. Chapter 8, "BCL Generics," looks at each of these types in great detail. However, there are also some simple guidelines you need to keep in mind as you work with these types. The items that follow point out a few key areas you'll want to consider as part of working with this set of types.

## Item 12: Custom Collections Should Extend Collection<T>

At some point you're likely to want to introduce your own generic custom collections. These collections are typically implemented as extensions to one of the existing collection classes. This allows them to inherit all the behavior of the existing collection and supplement or amend that functionality with new operations that are targeted at addressing the specific requirements of your solution.

In these situations, you may be tempted to have your custom collections be implemented as an extension of the List<T> class. List<T> is certainly the most robust and powerful of the containers found in the System.Collections.Generic namespace. However, to achieve its optimizations, this class also prevents clients from overriding or altering most of its behavior. Suppose, for example, you wanted to amend the list class and record some additional data each time an item was added to or removed from a list. With the List<T> class, you would not be allowed to override the methods that clients use to add and remove items.

So, although List<T> may be one of your favorite classes to consume, it is not intended to serve as the base class for your custom collections. Instead, the Collection<T> class is meant to play this role. Although it doesn't have all the capabilities of List<T>, it exposes a key set of protected members that you can freely override in your descendent types.

The System.Collections.ObjectModel namespace provides two additional collection implementations that should be lumped into this category with the Collection<T> class. The ReadOnlyCollection<T> and KeyedCollection<TKey, TItem> classes provide specific variations of the Collection<T> class and both are intentionally open to further specialization. The theme here is that this family of xxxxCollection classes are all meant to serve as the common foundation for any custom collection classes you might want to introduce. This, I believe, is part of the rationale behind having these types appear in their own, separate namespace.

As you create specializations of these collection classes, you should attempt to apply a naming scheme that allows each new collection class to continue to convey the nature of the class. A descendant of KeyCollection<TKey, TItem>, for example, might be called MyKeyedCollection<TKey, TItem>. This makes the role of the collection very explicit to consumers of that collection.

## Item 13: Use the Least Specialized Interface in Your APIs

The collections included in the System.Collections.Generic namespace implement a series of different interfaces that provide varying levels of support for interacting with and managing your collections. When using these types in your own APIs, you should give special consideration to which interface best suits your requirements. As a rule of thumb, you should select the least specialized interface in these scenarios. If, for example, you're just going to iterate over the collection's items sequentially, you only need the IEnumerable<T> interface. However, if you want index-based access, you may want to consider using IList<T>. If you'll be modifying the state of the collection, you may need to consider using ICollection<T>.

The basic idea here is that, by choosing the least specialized interfaces, you're able to limit the constraints placed on the clients of your types. You should always factor this into your thinking when selecting a generic interface for inclusion in your own APIs. This guideline is really a more general, OOP guideline. However, it seems worth highlighting again in the context of generics.

## Item 14: Enable "for each" Iteration with IEnumerable<T>

The System.Collections.Generic namespace includes an IEnumerable<T> interface. This interface provides a standard mechanism for iterating over the items in a collection. However, its role is more significant than the other collection-based interfaces that are part of the framework. This interface is what enables, indirectly, the mechanism that is employed by the foreach construct.

In general, the foreach construct is often viewed as the preferred mechanism for sequentially processing the items in a collection, providing a cleaner, more readable approach to processing the items in a collection. Given these realities, it's fair to assume that consumers of your custom collections are going to expect you to provide support for foreach-based iteration. So, as a general rule of thumb, you should always consider implementing the IEnumerable<T> interface on any custom type that needs to support iteration.

# Applying Constraints

Anytime you choose to apply constraints to your generic types, you're narrowing the applicability and reusability of that type. And, via constraints, you're also influencing heavily the scope of what can be achieved within the implementation of your generic types. The next set of items point out some specific topics you'll want to consider as you apply constraints to your type parameters.

## Item 15: Select the Least Restrictive Constraints

In selecting an appropriate constraint for a type parameter, you should attempt to choose the constraint that gives you the minimum level of accessibility you need without imposing any unneeded, additional constraints on your type parameters. Here's a quick example that illustrates how a constraint might be overly restrictive:

```
[VB code]
Public Interface IPerson
    Sub Validate()
End Interface

Public Interface ICustomer
    Inherits IPerson
End Interface

Public Interface IEmployee
    Inherits IPerson
End Interface
```

```
Public Class TestClass(Of T As ICustomer)
    Public Sub New(ByVal val As T)
        val.Validate()
    End Sub
End Class
```

```
[C# code]
public interface IPerson {
    void Validate();
}

public interface ICustomer : IPerson { }

public interface IEmployee : IPerson { }

public class TestClass<T> where T : ICustomer {
    public TestClass(T val) {
        val.Validate();
    }
}
```

In this example, you have a hierarchy of interfaces where IPerson is at the base and has descendent interfaces for ICustomer and IEmployee. Now, in your TestClass, you're currently expecting it to primarily work with Customer types and, because you need to call Validate() on each customer in the constructor, you've applied the ICustomer constraint to your type parameter to enable access to this method.

This certainly works. However, it also overly constrains your type parameter. Because all you're accessing at this point is the Validate() method and that method is part of the IPerson interface, you should have used IPerson to constrain your type parameter. That opens up your type to support other types that implement IPerson. The rule of thumb here is that you want to select the least constraining interface that still allows you to satisfy the compile-time validation of your type. If you need to be more restrictive, you can always alter the constraints as your solution evolves.

## Item 16: Don't Impose Hidden Constraints

Even though you may have a type that does not include any constraints in its declaration, that does not mean that your type can't impose "hidden" constraints within its implementation. You can imagine how, through a cast or through calls to the GetType() method, you could create code within your generic type that builds in some assumptions about the nature of its type parameters. In these situations, you are still imposing, indirectly, constraints on your type parameter — they're just not being explicitly declared. In the end, these are still viewed as constraints and they're still considered a bad idea.

## Item 17: Avoid Multiple Constraint Ambiguity

When you're working with constraints, you have the option of applying multiple constraints to any type parameter. In fact, you can combine a single class constraint with multiple interface constraints. As you start to mix and match multiple constraints, you can end up introducing ambiguity within the scope of your generic type. Consider the following example:

```
[VB code]
Public Interface I
    Sub Foo1()
    Sub Foo3()
End Interface

Public Class C
    Public Sub Foo1()
    End Sub
End Class

Public Class TestClass(Of T As C, I)
End Class
```

```
[C# code]
public interface I {
    void Foo1();
    void Foo3();
}

public class C {
    public void Foo1() {}
}

public class TestClass<T> where T : C, I { }
```

This example declares a class that employs class and interface constraints, both of which share a common method, `Foo1()`. Though rules exist that will essentially force the class constraints to take precedence over the interface constraints here, this situation is still ambiguous at best. From my perspective, this represents a scenario you should attempt to avoid. Fortunately, applying constraints that are likely to overlap in this manner should be rare.

## *Item 18: Provide Parameterless Constructors*

Whenever you're introducing your own types, you want to consider how those types will behave when used as a type argument. Obviously, the interfaces you choose to implement will play a key role in how that type can be constrained. At a minimum, every type you want to use as a type argument should include support for parameterless construction. By supporting this constraint, you enable your type to be supplied as a type argument to any generic type that includes a constructor constraint.

Plenty of instances exist where supporting parameterless construction adds value to your interface — for generic and non-generic solutions. If you've worked at all with any variant of the factory pattern, you've probably already provided a parameterless constructor. And, with generics, the list of scenarios where this adds value just gets longer. Suppose, for example, you had the following generic method that retrieved a collection of items from the database:

```
[VB code]
Public Function GetDataObjects(Of T As New)() As IEnumerable(Of T)
End Function
```

```
[C# code]
public IEnumerable<T> GetDataObjects() where T : new() {}
```

This method looks up data objects and returns them in a generic collection. It leverages the incoming type parameter to populate this collection with specific types. However, it would not be able to achieve this without being able to apply the constructor constraint to your incoming type parameter. So, any type you want to use with this method must support a parameterless constructor.

# The Kitchen Sink

In addition to the guidelines discussed previously, a handful of items also exist that don't necessarily fit into any specific categories. The items that appear in the sections that follow fall into this grab bag of miscellaneous items.

## Item 19: Use Static Data Members with Caution

Outside of generics, the behavior of static data members is well understood. Basically, when a data member is static, this indicates that there is one and only one instance of that data member for *all* instances of that class. This is where the VB "shared" keyword almost conveys the concept better than "static" in that these members are actually shared by all instances of the class.

With generics, the behavior of static data members may not actually match what you're expecting. Take a look at a small example that illustrates how generics manage static data:

```
[VB code]
Public Class StaticData(Of T)
    Private Shared _staticData As Int32 = 0

    Public Sub IncrementCount()
        _staticData = _staticData + 1
    End Sub
End Class

Public Sub TestStaticData()
    Dim instance1 As New StaticData(Of String)()
    instance1.IncrementCount()

    Dim instance2 As New StaticData(Of Int32)()
    instance2.IncrementCount()

    Dim instance3 As New StaticData(Of String)()
    instance3.IncrementCount()
End Sub
```

```
[C# code]
public class StaticData<T> {
    private static int _staticData = 0;

    public void IncrementCount() {
        _staticData++;
    }
}
```

```
public void TestStaticData() {
    StaticData<String> instance1 = new StaticData<String>();
    instance1.IncrementCount();

    StaticData<int> instance2 = new StaticData<int>();
    instance2.IncrementCount();

    StaticData<String> instance3 = new StaticData<String>();
    instance3.IncrementCount();
}
```

This example uses a simple generic class that has a static data member. In the `TestStaticData()` method, you declare three separate instances of this class and increment the count held by the static data member. Now, for a non-generic class, the static data member would end up being shared among all instances of the `StaticData` class. At the end of executing this code, the static data member would have been incremented to a value of 3.

With generic types, though, static data members are static for all constructed types that have the same type arguments. Looking back at the example, you'll notice that `instance1` uses a `string` type argument and `instance2` supplies an `integer` type argument. So, these two instances each have their own static data member and, therefore, their values are also incremented separately.

The last instance declared here, `instance3`, uses the same type argument as `instance1`. In this case, because the type arguments of these two instances match, they will end up sharing a common static data member. This means the increment performed on `instance3` will bump the count up to 2.

Once you understand what's going on here, it makes sense. At the same time, if you just look at the code, this side effect may not always be anticipated. And, if you distribute these calls out across a larger body of more complex code, you can imagine scenarios in which this could introduce some difficult-to-detect bugs. I'm not sure if it's completely accurate to classify this as a guideline. However, in the spirit of "good practices," you're likely to want to be especially careful about how you use static data members with generic types.

## Item 20: Use Interfaces in Lieu of Classes

The non-generic APIs you've constructed and consumed have probably relied heavily on the use of interfaces. It's a common practice. An interface allows you to express the signature of a type without binding to any specific implementation of that type. As such, an interface is especially useful in terms of how it shapes your API, enabling its types to be expressed in the manner that allows a single signature to accept multiple implementations.

This pre-existing idea of preferring interfaces to classes in your APIs carries forward into the world of generics. Consider, for example, the following scenario:

```
[VB code]
Public Class DataAccessMgr(Of T, U)
    Public Function FindItems(ByVal id As Int32) As List(Of T)
    End Function

    Public Sub AddChildren(ByVal parent As T, ByVal dataObjects As List(Of U))
    End Function
End Class
```

```
[C# code]
public class DataAccessMgr<T, U> {
    public List<T> FindItems(int id) {}
    public void AddChildren(T parent, List<U> dataObjects) {}
}
```

There's nothing outright wrong with the methods in this class. However, you'll notice that this class makes the mistake of referencing the List<T> in its interface. Using List<T> here forces all clients of this class to use List<T> classes in their interactions with the API.

If, within the body of the AddChildren() method, you're just iterating over the items in the list, you don't really need to be bound directly to the concrete List<T> class. Instead, you can change the signature of this method to use one of the generic collection interfaces, say IEnumerable<T>, and still have no impact on the internal implementation of this method. This allows your method to accept multiple implementations of IEnumerable<T> without restricting what can be achieved within the implementation of your method.

The real focus here is on providing API interfaces that allow type safety without somehow imposing artificial restrictions on your API. You should familiarize yourself with all the interfaces that are part of the System.Collections.Generic namespace so you'll have a better feel for which interfaces convey the meaning you want expressed by your API. You should also keep this general guideline in mind as you create your own generic interfaces.

## Item 21: Use Comparer<T> for All Type Comparisons

Comparer<T> is one of those nice, type-safe utility classes that you almost get for free when you add generics to a language. Comparer<T> should be viewed as the replacement for all the previous modes of type comparison that have been historically used in the pre-generic era.

## Item 22: Use Nullable<T> for Optional Values

When working with value types, there's no standard that defines a state that represents "empty" or "null." Each solution is left to its own devices for defining this state. As discussed before, Nullable<T> allows you to overcome this, providing you with a standardized mechanism for determining if a value type has actually been assigned a value.

As a guideline, it's fair to say that you should consider using Nullable<T> for any value type where you may need to determine its null state. A variety of common scenarios exist where this type can be applied. When working with databases, for example, you might want to use Nullable<T> to determine if a column is empty or null. Or, if you're working with a list of properties, you may apply Nullable<T> to accurately capture the state of a given property. These are just a couple of the more obvious applications of this type. I'm sure, from your own experiences, you can imagine a whole host of situations where you could see yourself leveraging this type.

## Item 23: Use EventHandler<T> for All Events

Item 5 talked about the general value of using a single generic delegate as a replacement for many separate, non-generic delegate declarations. And, because delegates are used as part of eventing, this same idea ends up generating a related guideline around the use of the EventHandler<T> type. This type

241

will allow you to declare event handler delegates without having to create one-off declarations for each delegate. This solution is much cleaner than using non-generic event handlers and should be used as the default for all event handling declarations.

# Summary

The goal of this chapter was to introduce a series of guidelines that could help provide some general rules that would help refine your approach to consuming or constructing generic types. This chapter looked at some specific patterns where generics might be applied as alternatives to existing, non-generic solutions. It also looked at guidelines in the areas of usability, applying constraints, and using BCL generic types. It's important to note that these guidelines are just that — guidelines. They are not accepted standards or hard-and-fast rules. Instead, they represent suggestions for common themes you want to consider as you begin to exercise generic types. As generics mature, however, you can expect these guidelines to evolve, grow, and ultimately become more widely accepted as industry standards.

# 11

# Under the Hood

If you're going to be working with generics, you're also likely to have some interest in understanding how they're managed by the CLR. This chapter looks at all the inner workings of generic types. It examines how generic types are instantiated at run-time, how they're represented in IL, and how the CLR attempts to optimize their size and performance. It also explores some of the key motivating factors that influenced the overall design characteristics employed as part of the .NET generics implementation. The chapter wraps up by looking at some of the performance gains that can be achieved through the use of generics. By the time you reach the end, you should have a much better feeling for the underlying concepts that directly influence how you go about creating and consuming generics.

## Overview

The .NET generics implementation clearly borrows from the many generic implementations that have preceded it. At the same time, it also introduces some new concepts and strategies that have not been employed as part of any prior implementation.

Certainly, being in a single-vendor, managed environment gave the .NET generics visionaries a fair amount of latitude in determining how they could best go about introducing generics into the platform. The .NET Framework's support for true multilanguage development provided Microsoft with the rare chance to bite off a generics solution that could span multiple languages and achieve a degree of interoperability around generic types that had never been fully realized before.

The sections that follow look at some of the key characteristics that distinguish the .NET generics implementation. By understanding these details, you're likely to get a much better sense of factors that shaped the resulting implementation. This view of generics should also provide you with a clearer picture of the trade-offs that were made as part of the .NET generics implementation. Although understanding generics at this level is not vital, having this broader view does help frame some of the rules that govern the definition and consumption of generic types.

# Assumptions

The following sections explore the details of how generic types are represented in IL as well as probe the internal representation of generic types. Though I don't view this material as being overly advanced, it can be daunting if you've never devoted any time to poking your way around in IL and basic CLR concepts. So, if you really want to maximize your understanding of the concepts that follow, you may want to first familiarize yourself with some of the fundamentals of the CLR and how code is transformed into IL at run-time.

# High-Level Goals

When the generics gurus sat down to spell out a strategy for their generics implementation, they established some very key high-level goals that, in a more general sense, shaped some of the resulting, fundamental structure of generics. The following is a brief breakdown of the guiding principles that appear to have played a key role in influencing the overall design of .NET generics.

## Validate at Declaration

For any generics implementation, you must choose between validating generic types at their point of declaration or at their point of instantiation. So, if you define a List<T> generic type and you choose to validate it at the point of declaration, you essentially need to be able to verify that the List<T> generic type will be valid for all type arguments that it could ultimately be supplied as a type parameter.

In contrast, if you choose to validate at the point where each type is used, you are only required to verify that each individual specialization can be successfully compiled. Even if there are declarations that *could* be invalid, they are not factored into the validation of the class at compile-time. Only instances that are actually declared in code will be considered. Although this approach offers a somewhat broader palette of possibilities, it also requires the precompilation of all the existing instances in advance of their use.

For .NET generics, the decision was made to require validation at the point of declaration. The rationale behind this choice will be clearer as you get more familiar with the run-time capabilities and efficiencies that were enabled as a result of choosing this option.

## Simplicity

Generic technologies have historically had a bad reputation in terms of their general complexity. Some developers almost instinctively cringe when they think about the possibility of using or creating generics. Generics have this baggage attached to them that seems to suggest that any generic solution must require developers to mangle their code with cryptic symbols and compile-time code expansion that can make debugging a true nightmare.

I believe this stereotype of complexity was likely, or at least partially, an influencing factor that had some degree of impact on what ultimately became .NET generics. While maximum power and flexibility certainly has its place, the .NET generics approach favors trading a modicum of power for marked improvement in readability and maintainability. There's no clear-cut, objective means by which you can measure the extent to which this is achieved. However, as developers get comfortable with generics, I believe they will find them to be significantly more usable than prior offerings.

## Platform Conformity

Generics are a fundamental construct that are likely to be used on an ever-increasing basis throughout the .NET platform. At the same time, generics needed to be introduced without requiring any significant changes to the existing framework. It was essential that .NET generics be created as a natural extension of the existing concepts that were already part of the platform. The key point here is that the CLR needed to evolve to add support for generics while, at the same time, continuing to support all the existing code that was running against prior versions of the CLR. In looking at the resulting implementation, I think it's fair to say that this goal was achieved.

## Language Agnostic Generics

Supporting generics is a great achievement for the .NET platform. However, if this feature had been introduced as a language-specific solution, it would have violated the basic goals of language interoperability that are such a key element of the .NET mantra. By supporting generics completely within the CLR, Microsoft has allowed generics to play a much broader role in the .NET platform. APIs and libraries will be allowed to embrace generics without concern for breaking the language agnostic model. The importance of multilanguage support was further emphasized when generics were formally made part of the CLS specification. With generics being made part of the CLS, developers will be able to fully leverage this functionality with the confidence that generic types will be consumable by any CLS-compliant language. If generics were not part of the CLS, developers may have hesitated to use them and this could have impacted their overall adoption rate.

## No Boxing

Boxing and unboxing is expensive. However, in dealing with value types, many generic solutions require each value type to be boxed to be managed generically. Consider, for example, an `ArrayList` of 10,000 integers. In order for this collection to manage integer types, it must first convert (box) each of these integer types into an `object` representation. Then, as the data is extracted from the `ArrayList`, each object must get unboxed. The overhead associated with this boxing and unboxing can be significant.

With the .NET generics implementation, Microsoft set out to eliminate the need to box value types. Instead, with .NET generics, each value type remains in its native representation at run-time, eliminating the overhead of boxing and reducing the amount of memory needed to store each value type.

This may seem like no great achievement and, given the CLR's support for run-time generic types, it would seem to come for free. However, in looking at what the .NET generics implementation achieves, this is no small feat. Eliminating boxing is a key advantage .NET generics have over the non-generic alternatives.

Boxing also represents one key area of difference between the .NET and Java implementations of generics. Java generics can only manage reference type arguments and, as such, they are still forced to coerce all value types to objects. This means that Java generics suffer from all the same boxing and unboxing overhead that you've absorbed when working with non-generic types.

## No Meta-Programming

Sometimes, to clarify the goals for a solution you must also clarify what it is *not* trying to achieve. And, given the natural tendency for developers to try and map generics to templates, it's probably important to make it clear that the .NET generics implementation is *not* trying to be a one-for-one replacement for templates. Certainly, generics and templates have some aligned goals. But, the architects for .NET generics have made it clear that their design is not meant to be seen as precisely matching the functionality or intent of templates.

The primary area of difference here is the area of meta-programming. In the world of C++ templates, where validation is done at the point of instantiation, developers are free to create an entirely different breed of types. Support for this mode of generic programming was not seen as being within the scope of what .NET generics was trying to achieve.

# IL Representation of Generic Types

To understand how generics are implemented within the .NET platform, you must first look at how they are represented in the IL that is managed by the CLR. The .NET approach to supporting generic types in IL plays a key role in determining how this IL will ultimately be transformed into executable code. The IL representation of generics also ends up heavily influencing many of the policies and optimizations that end up being associated with the overall implementation.

Because each generic type must be able to be fully validated at the point of its declaration, this also means that these generic types can be directly represented — in their generic form — in the CLR. A .NET generic class requires no advance awareness of instances that might be created with that class. This reality means that generic types can be treated more like traditional classes, where instances are simply created on an as-needed basis.

This idea of representing generic types at run-time is one of the key distinguishing characteristics of the .NET implementation. To get a better idea for what a generic type looks like, you need to look at the IL that gets generated for a generic type. To achieve that goal, though, you must first have a generic type to explore. For the purposes of this example, you'll start with the following simple generic class:

```
[VB code]
Public Class TestClass(Of T)
    Private _data As T

    Public Sub New(ByVal data As T)
        Me._data = data
    End Sub

    Public Function getData() As T
        Return Me._data
    End Function
End Class
```

```
[C# code]
public class TestClass<T> {
    private T _data;

    public TestClass(T data) {
        this._data = data;
    }
```

```
        public T getData() {
            return this._data;
        }
    }
```

Now, when you compile this class — whether it's written in VB or C# — it's going to get compiled into an IL representation of your generic type. This IL form of your generic type shares many of the conceptual traits of a generic class. If you look at the following IL closely, you can see how it introduces specific extensions that allow it to support the idea of placeholders for each generic type parameter:

```
.class public auto ansi beforefieldinit TestClass<(object) T>
    extends object
{
    .field private !0 _data
}

.method public hidebysig specialname rtspecialname instance void .ctor(!0 data)
    cil managed
{
    // Code Size: 16 byte(s)
    .maxstack 8
    L_0000: ldarg.0
    L_0001: call instance void object::.ctor()
    L_0006: nop
    L_0007: ldarg.0
    L_0008: ldarg.1
    L_0009: stfld !0 TestClass`1<!0>::_data
    L_000e: nop
    L_000f: ret
}

.method public hidebysig instance !0 getData() cil managed
{
    // Code Size: 11 byte(s)
    .maxstack 1
    .locals (!0 local1)
    L_0000: ldarg.0
    L_0001: ldfld !0 TestClass`1<!0>::_data
    L_0006: stloc.0
    L_0007: br.s L_0009
    L_0009: ldloc.0
    L_000a: ret
}
```

You can see here how the generic characteristics of your class simply carried forward into this IL. To support this concept, the IL is essentially taking on the same generic constructs that have been added to each of the .NET languages to support generics. By extending IL in this manner, you can see how it's now possible to have generic types at run-time.

This one facet of the .NET generics implementation lays the fundamental foundation for all of the efficiencies and Just-in-Time concepts that are supported by .NET generics. It also allows generic types to participate as first-class citizens within the CLR.

# Specialization and Sharing

Okay, so now you have a better idea of what a generic type looks like in IL. The next concept to consider here is how *instances* of these generic types are managed by the CLR. The process of translating generic types into specific instances is at the epicenter of every generics implementation. Naturally, it's safe to assume that the strategies and policies that are adopted for this translation heavily influence the overall footprint and performance characteristics of any generics implementation. To understand what's at stake here, let's start by considering the two models that have been traditionally employed by prior generics-based solutions.

## *Code Specialization*

Code specialization is the term used to describe the creation of specialized types for each instance of a generic type. If you have declared a generic class, say List<T>, then for each instance of this class that appears in your code (List<int>, List<string>, and so on) the complier will actually generate a unique, standalone specialization for each of these types. This is the strategy that is employed, for example, by C++ templates and is typically criticized for bloating the run-time representation of generic types. It is also lauded for its support for meta-programming models, its handling of value types, and some of the general performance gains it achieves.

## *Code Sharing*

Code sharing is the term used to describe the model where generic instances share their underlying implementation at run-time. So, if you create a generic class List<T>, the compiler will generate a single run-time representation of this class and reuse this implementation for each instance it encounters. This overcomes the issue of bloat but removes some of the flexibility that can be achieved through code specialization. The real problem that has traditionally been associated with code sharing is its inability to gracefully handle value types. In order to share code, every type argument must be able to be represented as a reference. And, to make value types into references, they must be boxed. It's that, or remove support for value types entirely—not the best set of options.

## *The .NET Hybrid Model*

After looking at the two prevailing approaches, you can see how both have their strengths *and* their weaknesses. Instead of leveraging one of these two approaches and accepting its baggage, the .NET generics implementation decided to take a hybrid approach. The fundamental idea here was to employ a mixture of both code specialization and code sharing that could strike a balance between these two competing models. And, although the resulting implementation isn't able to achieve nirvana and support all the characteristics of specialization, it does come as close as it can without compromising on some of the guiding principles discussed earlier.

This hybrid model for specialization and sharing is made possible by the CLR. With its support for dynamic loading and compilation, the CLR provided the .NET generics architects with a natural segue to a solution that could support a more strategic approach to choosing when to specialize and when to share code. In fact, it's hard to imagine how generics could have made any kind of graceful move into the .NET platform without the mechanisms that are enabled by the CLR.

# Just-in-Time Specialization

Through the CLR, the .NET generics implementation is actually able to provide what is referred to as "just-in-time" or "lazy" specialization. Both of these terms accurately convey the CLR's approach to specialization, which is to always favor delaying the creation of any specialized type or method until that type is needed at run-time.

So, suppose you have a List<T> generic class. And, sprinkled throughout your code are a number of different specializations of List<T>, say List<int>, List<cat>, and so on. Now, for a given workflow within your code, there may be paths that never exercise any of these specializations. So, it would be wasteful to create them in advance. Instead, the CLR will wait until it encounters an actual instance of List<T> before it generates code for that type. This same concept is also applied to methods. Although this model is certainly more efficient in terms of limiting the creation of unused types or methods, it causes the initial creation of generic types to absorb some additional overhead.

## Generic Classes and Shared Code

Whenever possible, the CLR will attempt to share the underlying code for "compatible" instantiations of a given generic class. Before looking at how this is achieved, this section looks at what goes into determining if two instantiations of a generic class are deemed compatible.

The compatibility of generic classes is primarily determined by the nature of the type arguments that are used in their construction. Take a look at a handful of declarations and consider whether each of these instances can share any of its implementation. To simplify matters, this first set of classes looks only at how sharing is achieved with classes that use value (primitive) types:

```
[VB code]
Dim intList1 As New List(Of Int32)
Dim intList2 As New List(Of Int32)
Dim boolList As New List(Of Boolean)

intList1.Add(123)
intList2.Add(987)
boolList.Add(True)
```

```
[C# code]
List<int> intList1 = new List<int>();
List<int> intList2 = new List<int>();
List<bool> boolList = new List<bool>();

intList1.Add(123);
intList2.Add(987);
boolList.Add(true);
```

This example declares three different instances of the List<T> class. When intList1 is created, the CLR will first determine if an instance of List<int> already exists. For this example, assume it doesn't. So, as a result of this declaration, the JIT compiler will end up generating a representation of List<int>. Now, for the declaration of intList2, the CLR will follow this same process. However, this time, it will discover that an instance of List<int> already exists and it will reuse the representation that was already created for this type. And, as you can imagine, the final declaration of boolList also forces the JIT compiler to emit a new set of code because there's no existing instance of the List<bool> type that has already been loaded.

The compilation of the methods within a generic class is also done on a just-in-time basis. So, when the first call to `intList1.Add(123)` is invoked, the compiler will determine that this `Add()` method has not been previously compiled and it will force the generation of the code that corresponds to this method. On the subsequent call to `intList2.Add(987)`, the code now exists and is successfully reused. The `boolList.Add(true)` also forces new code for the `bool` instance to be generated.

Okay, that covers value types, but what happens with reference types? Suppose you have the following set of declarations that use reference types as their type arguments:

```
[VB code]
Dim strList1 As New List(Of String)
Dim strList2 As New List(Of String)
Dim dogList As New List(Of Person)
```

```
[C# code]
List<string> strList1 = new List<string>();
List<string> strList2 = new List<string>();
List<Person> boolList = new List<Person>();
```

These declarations are essentially a duplicate of the set used in the previous example. However, this time you've supplied `String` and `Person` reference types as your type arguments. Although it might seem like this scenario would follow the same pattern as the value declarations in the previous example, it does not. The first set of declarations both use `List<string>` and, once code is generated from this first declaration, it is found and reused for the next declaration of `List<string>`. This is exactly as you might suspect. However, when the CLR encounters the `List<Person>` declaration, it does *not* force the generation of any new code. Instead, it reuses the same code that was created for `List<string>`. In fact, any additional declaration of `List<T>` that supplies a reference type argument will be able to reuse the code that was generated for `List<string>`.

So, why are reference types able to share code spanning all instances? To understand this, you need to think about how value types and reference types are represented internally. Each value type can potentially have a different internal representation of itself. Although two value types may be the same in size, their internal field layout could be different. This fact means each value type must require its own code. Meanwhile, with reference types, the CLR doesn't need to be concerned with the internal representation of the type. As long as it can represent the pointer to the object, it's happy. Thus, all reference types can share a single implementation.

The last type to consider is struct. In general, all user-defined structs are treated as being compatible if their internal layouts are considered equivalent.

## Code Sharing Structures

A number of alternative structural models can be used to represent the shared code of a class, each of which has its own performance and efficiency considerations. The model that .NET generics settled on is one where the vtable for each shared instance is replaced with a pointer to the common vtable that contains the shared code for each instance.

In Figure 11-1, you can see how this shared model is represented for a scenario where you've declared two separate instances of the generic class `MyCollection<T>`. Both of these instances are declared using reference parameters (`Person` and `Order`) which, based on the previous discussion, means they will share common code.

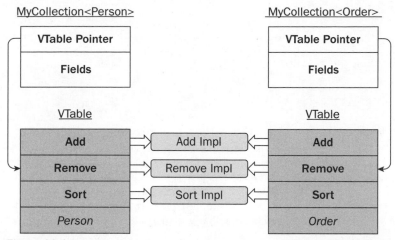

**Figure 11-1**

The challenge here is to introduce a structure that allows each instance to have its own data and still share a common vtable for dispatching method calls. The .NET generics architects settled on the scheme that limits the amount of indirection needed to make each call. To achieve this, they had each instance reference its own combined vtable-and-instantiation data structure. This data structure then provides references to the actual method implementations.

This approach makes the assumption that it is better to provide this duplicate structure for each instance in exchange for better performance on each method call. The design also presumes that there are likely to be only a few unique instantiations, which means the impact of this duplication is also likely to be minimal.

## Open Types in Shared Code

With the shared code model, the .NET generics implementation also had to consider how it would handle the appearance of open types within the methods of a generic type. The following declaration provides an example of this scenario:

```
[VB code]
Public Class TestClass(Of T)
    Public Sub Foo1()
        Dim myList As New List(Of T)
        . . .
    End Sub

    Public Sub Foo2()
        Dim myStack As New Stack(Of T)
        . . .
    End Sub
End Class

[C# code]
Public class TestClass<T> {
    Public void Foo1() {
        List<T> myList = new List<T>();
```

```
        . . .
    }

    Public void Foo2() {
        Stack<T> myStack = new Stack<T>();
        . . .
    }
}
```

In this example, methods Foo1() and Foo2() both include open type declarations. If CLR delayed processing of these types, it would have to lookup the type handles for each of these types at run-time. This lookup would add significant overhead to these methods. So, for the .NET generics implementation, these type handles are actually precomputed. For the example, suppose you were to declare an instance of TestClass<String>. In this scenario, the open types of your two methods (Foo1() and Foo2()) would be precomputed to be List<string> and Stack<string>, respectively. These precomputed type handles are managed with a dictionary that is associated with the TestClass<T> type.

## Generic Methods and Shared Code

Generic methods also support code sharing. In fact, conceptually, they leverage most of the same code sharing techniques that are used to represent generic classes. At the same time, a generic method certainly has a much smaller set of issues to resolve when determining how and *when* to share its code.

The code sharing policies for generic methods are also directly influenced by the nature of the type arguments they are supplied. As you might expect by now, value and reference type arguments each impose a separate set of requirements on the code sharing model that is employed for generic methods. The basic rule here is that each value type will get its own separate x86 representation at execution time, whereas each reference instance will share its implementation with other reference types. The following example provides some insight into how code sharing will work for generic methods by looking at the internals of a generic method that uses reference types:

```
[VB code]
Imports System.Runtime.CompilerServices

Public Class TestClass
    <MethodImpl(MethodImplOptions.NoInlining)> _
    Public Sub Foo(Of T)()
        Console.WriteLine(GetType(T))
    End Sub

    Public Sub TestFoo()
        Foo(Of Double)()
        Foo(Of String)()
        Foo(Of Object)()
    End Sub
End Class

[C# code]
using System.Runtime.CompilerServices;

public class TestClass {
```

```
            [MethodImpl(MethodImplOptions.NoInlining)]
            public void Foo<T>() {
                Console.WriteLine(typeof(T));
            }

            public void TestFoo() {
                Foo<Double>();
                Foo<string>();
                Foo<Object>();
            }
        }
```

This example includes a generic method that is called with various reference types. Now, look at how this same method ends up being represented in IL. The following is the IL listing for the Foo() method as produced by ILDASM:

```
.method public instance void  Foo<T>() cil managed noinlining
{
  // Code size       19 (0x13)
  .maxstack  8
  IL_0000:  nop
  IL_0001:  ldtoken     !!T
  IL_0006:  call        class [mscorlib]System.Type
[mscorlib]System.Type::GetTypeFromHandle(valuetype
[mscorlib]System.RuntimeTypeHandle)
  IL_000b:  call        void [mscorlib]System.Console::WriteLine(object)
  IL_0010:  nop
  IL_0011:  nop
  IL_0012:  ret
} // end of method TestClass::Foo
```

Here, your type parameter is represented by !!T. You can imagine, from looking at this IL, the x86 code needed to represent the IL will be nearly identical for any reference type argument that is supplied to this method. In fact, during the JIT process, the only variable element in this equation is the type of the reference. So, in recognition of this reality, the JIT will actually create a single block of x86 code that will be shared by all reference-based invocations of this method. And, to account for each reference, the JIT process simply replaces the !!T placeholder with a pointer to the method's reference type argument.

In order to support this model, the JIT-compiled Foo() method needs some mechanism that will allow it to receive each object's reference pointer. This required the introduction of a "hidden" parameter, much like the "this" parameter that accompanies each method in a class. This hidden parameter, which is packaged in the MethodDesc run-time data structure, is supplied as part of the generic method call.

Now, turn your attention back to the example and consider how this would play out. With your first call to the method as Foo<Double>(), the method would get JIT'ed and, during the process, your !!T placeholder will be replaced with the information from the MethodDesc that represents Foo<Double>(). Once this process is completed one time, your subsequent calls will only need to deal with acquiring the different type information contained in the MethodDesc structures for Foo<string>() and Foo<object>().

# Exact Run-Time Types

The .NET generics implementation attempts to make generic types behave like any other type you might employ. This means that the marriage of a generic type and its type arguments should represent an actual type that can be evaluated like any other type. Consider the following example:

```
[VB code]
Public Class TestClass1(Of T)
End Class

Public Class TestClass2(Of T)
End Class

Public Class TestExactTypes

    Public Sub CompareTypes()
        Dim type1 As New TestClass1(Of Int32)
        Dim type2 As New TestClass1(Of String)
        Dim type3 As New TestClass2(Of Int32)

        CompareTypes(type1)
        CompareTypes(type2)
        CompareTypes(type3)
    End Sub

    Public Sub CompareTypes(ByVal aType As Object)
        If (TypeOf (aType) Is TestClass1(Of Int32)) Then
            Console.Out.WriteLine("Instance of TestClass1(Of Int32)")
        ElseIf (TypeOf (aType) Is TestClass1(Of String)) Then
            Console.Out.WriteLine("Instance of TestClass1(Of String)")
        ElseIf (TypeOf (aType) Is TestClass1(Of Double)) Then
            Console.Out.WriteLine("Instance of TestClass1(Of Double)")
        ElseIf (TypeOf (aType) Is TestClass2(Of Int32)) Then
            Console.Out.WriteLine("Instance of TestClass2(Of Int32)")
        End If
    End Sub
End Class
```

```
[C# code]
public class TestClass1<T> { }

public class TestClass2<T> { }

public class TestExactTypes {
    public void CompareTypes() {
        TestClass1<int> type1 = new TestClass1<int>();
        TestClass1<string> type2 = new TestClass1<string>();
        TestClass2<int> type3 = new TestClass2<int>();

        CompareTypes(type1);
        CompareTypes(type2);
        CompareTypes(type3);
    }
```

```
    public void CompareTypes(object aType) {
        if (aType is TestClass1<int>)
            Console.Out.WriteLine("Instance of TestClass1<int>");
        else if (aType is TestClass1<string>)
            Console.Out.WriteLine("Instance of TestClass1<string>");
        else if (aType is TestClass1<double>)
            Console.Out.WriteLine("Instance of TestClass1<double>");
        else if (aType is TestClass2<int>)
            Console.Out.WriteLine("Instance of TestClass2<int>");
    }
}
```

This example creates two generic classes and proceeds to declare a few separate instances of these classes. It then passes each of these constructed types to a method that takes the passed in object and compares it to another generic type. The goal here is to illustrate how, in declaring an instance of TestClass1<string>, for example, you have essentially introduced a new type that is considered different than TestClass1<int>. Each combination of type arguments supplied to your class ends up representing a separate, unique type that can be operated on like any other type you might inspect. The key point here is: Comparing generic types is really no different than comparing non-generic types. This may already be obvious, but it's still worth emphasizing.

This same concept is also extended to casting, where a generic type is allowed to be accurately cast from one type to another (as if casting were a good thing). Consider the following example:

```
[VB code]
Public Class TestClass1(Of T)
End Class

Public Class TestClass3(Of T)
    Inherits TestClass1(Of T)
End Class

Public Sub CastTypes()
    Dim type1 As New TestClass1(Of String)
    Dim type2 As TestClass3(Of String)
    Dim type3 As TestClass1(Of String) = New TestClass3(Of String)()
    Dim type4 As New TestClass1(Of Double)

    type1 = TryCast(type2, TestClass1(Of String))
    type1 = type3
    type1 = TryCast(type4, TestClass3(Of String))
End Sub

[C# code]
public class TestClass1<T> { }

public class TestClass3<T> : TestClass1<T> { }

public void CastTypes() {
    TestClass1<string> type1 = new TestClass1<string>();
    TestClass3<string> type2 = new TestClass3<string>();
    TestClass1<string> type3 = new TestClass3<string>();
    TestClass1<double> type4 = new TestClass1<double>();
```

```
        type1 = (TestClass1<string>)type2;
        type1 = (TestClass1<string>)type4;
}
```

This example introduces a pair of simple generic classes that are instantiated in a few different flavors to show off how casting is applied to generic types. The first thing you should notice here is that the variable `type3` is declared as being of the type `TestClass1<string>`. So, even though `type3` is declared with the type `TestClass3<string>`, it is somehow successfully assigned an instance of `TestClass1<string>`. This declaration is considered valid because `TestClass3` subclasses `TestClass1` *and* the declaration uses the same type argument (`string`) for both specializations.

Along these same lines, this example includes a cast that casts the `type2` variable to an instance of `TestClass1<string>`. The subclassing of your generic types also allows this cast to succeed. The only difference here is that a cast is used to assign this instance of `TestClass3<string>` to a variable that is an instance of its superclass, which is declared as `TestClass1<string>`. The final cast example here actually fails. Because the `type4` variable is declared as an instance of `TestClass1<double>`, it cannot be cast to a `TestClass1<string>` type. Fortunately, the compiler catches this error for you.

I should also point out the irony of using casts to illustrate a use of generic types here. After all my preaching about the importance of type safety and the evils of casting, it seems odd to even be mixing casts and generics in the same context. Still, for this purpose, casts are particularly useful for showing off how the generic types are represented.

Overall, the type behaviors in the .NET implementation of generics conform to the patterns you would normally expect from your non-generic types. This aspect of .NET generics — the idea of having exact run-time types — certainly makes generics more approachable and easier to use.

# Support for Polymorphic Recursion

Another upside of the .NET generics implementation is its support for polymorphic recursion. Through polymorphic recursion, you are allowed to call generic methods recursively, supplying alternate type parameters for each recursive call. Here's an example that illustrates this concept in action:

```
[VB code]
Public Class RecursionClass
    Public count As Int32 = 0
    Public Sub Foo(Of T)(ByVal val As T)
        If (count <= 1) Then
            count = count + 1
            Console.Out.WriteLine("Type = {0}", val.GetType())
            Me.Foo(Of String)("String Param")
        End If
    End Sub

    Public Sub DumpTypes()
        Me.Foo(Of Int32)(123)
    End Sub
End Class
```

```
[C# code]
public class RecursionClass {
    public int count = 0;
    public void Foo<T>(T val) {
        if (count <= 1) {
            count++;
            Console.Out.WriteLine("Type = {0}", val.GetType());
            this.Foo<String>("String Param");
        }
    }

    public void DumpTypes() {
        this.Foo<int>(123);
    }
}
```

This class includes a generic `Foo()` method that simply displays the type name of the supplied type parameter before recursively calling itself again with a `string` type argument. You'll notice that this method is invoked by the `DumpTypes()` method, which actually supplies an `integer` type argument. The key point here is that the `Foo()` method was able to call itself recursively with a type argument that had a type that was different from the type that was initially received. This ability to achieve recursion with varying types of arguments is quite powerful and an important byproduct of the .NET generic implementation.

# NGen and Generic Types

The .NET SDK includes the NGen tool that allows developers to generate native x86 versions of their code. Developers might choose to use this tool for a variety of reasons. And, of course, there's also a great deal of debate that surrounds how and when—or even if—NGen should be applied. Regardless of what's motivating your desire to use NGen, you're likely to want to understand how the tool will process the generic code that's part of your solutions.

With NGen, there can't be anything "lazy" about how generics are instantiated. Instead, NGen must create representations of every generics instance it could encounter. The CLR won't be around to JIT anything. So, after all the discussion of avoiding code bloat and taking advantage of CLR's run-time optimizations, NGen takes all those values and turns them on their collective heads.

Even with NGen, though, there can be some degree of code sharing. Reference types, for example, can still share code. So, while you still get the code bloat associated with precompiling every instance, you get some efficiency out of the fact that these reference types will still be using shared code.

For value types, where you can't share code, there's more motivation to avoid precompiling those types that are not needed. To achieve this, NGen will compute the set types that are required for a given assembly (using transitive closure) and precompile just those instances. This will minimize the amount of bloat you'll take on for instances that will never get created at run-time.

Here's a simple example that illustrates how both reference and value types get processed by NGen:

```vb
[VB code]
Namespace AssemblyB

    Public Class MyCollection(Of T)
    End Class

    Public Class SampleClass
        Private _intColl As New MyCollection(Of Int32)
        Private _strColl As New MyCollection(Of String)
    End Class

End Namespace
Imports NGenAssembly.AssemblyB
Namespace AssemblyA
    Public Structure aStruct
        Dim myVal As Int32
    End Structure

    Public Class TestClass
        Private _intColl As New MyCollection(Of Int32)
        Private _bollColl As New MyCollection(Of Boolean)
        Private _structColl As New MyCollection(Of aStruct)
        Private _personColl As New MyCollection(Of Person)

    End Class
End Namespace
```

```csharp
[C# code]
namespace AssemblyB {
    public class MyCollection<T> { }

    public class SampleClass {
        private MyCollection<int> _intColl = new MyCollection<int>();
        private MyCollection<String> _strColl = new MyCollection<String>();
    }
}

using AssemblyB;
namespace AssemblyA {
    public struct aStruct {
        int myVal;
    }

    public class TestClass {
        private MyCollection<int> _intColl = new MyCollection<int>();
        private MyCollection<bool> _boolColl = new MyCollection<bool>();
        private MyCollection<aStruct> _stuctColl = new MyCollection<aStruct>();
        private MyCollection<Person> _personColl = new MyCollection<Person>();
    }
}
```

This goal of this example is to declare reference and value instances spanning two separate assemblies. You create MyCollection<T> in AssemblyA and declare MyCollection<int> and MyCollection<String> instances of that collection in that same assembly. Then, in AssemblyB, you create MyCollection<int>, MyCollection<bool>, MyCollection<aStruct>, and MyCollection<Person> instances.

Now, consider what happens when you run these two assemblies through NGen. In Figure 11-2, you'll notice that AssemblyA will end up generating for the MyCollection<int> and MyCollection<String> instances. Where things get more interesting is when AssemblyB is processed. Even though it declares four separate instances of MyCollection<T>, it only yields code for two instances (MyCollection<bool> and MyCollection(aStruct>).

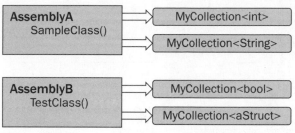

**Figure 11-2**

Because AssemblyA already created code for MyCollection<int>, the declaration in AssemblyB does not require the generation of a new instance. However, the bool and aStruct value types are both new and both require new code to be generated. You'll notice that no code gets generated for MyCollection<Person>. It's using a reference type argument and, as such, it can share code with the instance generated for the reference MyCollection<String> that was already declared in AssemblyA.

# Performance

Although there are a number of advantages to using generics, their performance benefits may represent their most compelling characteristic. In environments where you're trying to eke every last millisecond out of your algorithms, you'll find generics can actually provide significant performance gains — especially when it comes to populating and accessing large data containers.

The primary factor that impacts the performance of existing structures is their dependency on representing all contained types as objects. If, for example, you've got some structure you're using to represent the points on a chart and you're holding a collection of 300,000 of these items in an ArrayList, you're paying a stiff penalty as you move data into this list *and* as you access data in that structure.

Each time a value type is placed into an ArrayList, that list must box each value type. Then, as you access the data for that type, you're going to take on the overhead of unboxing it as it morphs from an object back into its original value representation. You might think the performance hit associated with this boxing and unboxing is nominal — it's not.

As a point of comparison, consider how these same 300,000 value types would be managed by a generic List<T> collection. With a generic collection, there's no need for any boxing. Instead, the value types are represented in IL in the native form for their entire life cycle. The chart in Figure 11-3 attempts to provide some more concrete assessment of the impact generics can have in this scenario.

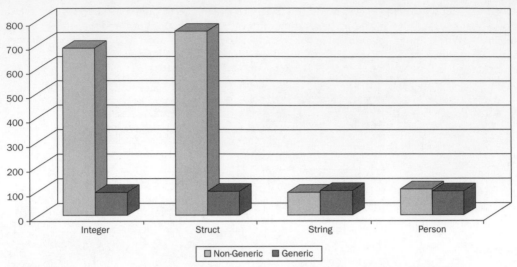

**Figure 11-3**

This chart examines the performance characteristics of populating ArrayList and List<T> collections with various data types. The goal here is to provide a side-by-side comparison of overhead associated with populating ArrayList and List<T> collections with both value and reference types. For this example, integer, struct, string, and Person types were added to ArrayList and List<T> containers and the total time required to populate each of these containers was calculated. Each bar in the diagram represents the total time required to process all of the add() operations. Overall, the numbers for the value types (Integer and Struct) are what really jump out at you. You can see here that the extra boxing overhead that was taken on to convert these types has a significant impact on the performance profiles of these two collections.

If you look at the reference types in this chart, however, you'll notice that the generic collection didn't necessarily buy much. And, if you think about it, that makes sense. After all, if you already have an object representation of the type you're adding to your collection, there's really no significant difference between placing that object in an ArrayList or a List<T> collection.

So, does this mean that you'll really only see a performance boost when you use generic collections with value types? No. The chart in Figure 11-3 only considers the overhead of adding items to a collection. There's also overhead associated with extracting items from an existing collection. And, in this realm, generic collections offer better performance for both value *and* reference types. The chart in Figure 11-4 illustrates this point.

For this example, the same collections that were populated in for the prior benchmark were randomly accessed to extract individual items. So, for this test, both ArrayList and List<T> containers were populated with integer, struct, string, and Person data types. With this structure populated, the test then performed a number of index-based lookups to randomly pull items from each container type. Each bar in the chart represents the total time needed to acquire data from each container type. For the non-generic ArrayList, this meant that each of the value types had to be unboxed. And, for the reference types, it meant a cast needed to be invoked to convert each item to its preferred representation.

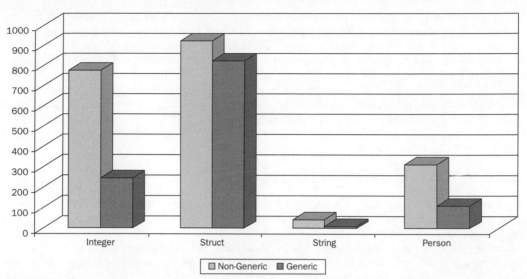

**Figure 11-4**

The results for these tests were more mixed than I would have expected. There are certainly environmental factors that can make these numbers vary more wildly. The key point here isn't to obsess over the specific values yielded from these benchmarks. Instead, from a broader perspective, you should conclude that the general performance of collections is — in some cases — dramatically enhanced with generic containers. As a rule of thumb, it's expected that value types will see a general gain of almost 200 percent, whereas reference types will hover more around the 100 percent number. Combine these figures with type safety and you can understand why some developers are fairly excited about the prospect of using generics.

Now, this is not to say that generics outperform non-generics in *every* scenario. There are plenty of cases where you can find evidence to the contrary. For example, if you populate an ArrayList with a smaller set of items, it can exhibit slightly better performance than a non-generic collection. This is attributed to the larger default initial capacity employed by the ArrayList class. Still, in the grand scheme, generics are typically going to out-perform their non-generic counterparts.

# Memory Footprint

Generic types don't just perform better than non-generic types — they also consume less memory. Let's stick with the theme of ArrayList versus List<T> that was used in the previous set of examples. When you use an ArrayList to hold value types, these value types get boxed and placed on the heap. For each of these boxed items on the heap, there must also be a corresponding object reference added to the ArrayList. The overhead of these references and the heap allocations do not end up being trivial for any reasonably sized ArrayList.

In contrast, the List<T> is able to do away with all this added overhead. Each value type it holds is placed directly into an internal array that holds that value in its native representation. That means no heap allocation and no references.

A nonscientific look at the run-time memory profile of `ArrayList` and `List<T>` suggests that the difference in memory consumption is actually quite profound. I created a test that populated both data containers with a collection of 200,000 integers. The `ArrayList` required 39MB to represent these values whereas the `List<T>` instance appeared to only consume 16MB. That's a difference of 244 percent.

So, with all the attention focused on type safety and expressiveness, it may end up being the case that performance actually represents the single most significant advantage offered by generics. Performance gains of this magnitude are simply too compelling to ignore.

# Backward Compatibility

It should be clear by now that a great deal of the elegance offered by the .NET generics implementation was achieved through modifications to IL extensions. Of course, anytime you're talking about changing IL, you're also talking about changing the CLR and — more importantly — you're talking about giving up on any hope of backward compatibility. So, what does this mean in a practical sense? Well, if you're building solutions that must run with prior versions of the CLR, you won't be able to take advantage of generics. Any code you deploy with generics is going to require version 2.0 of the .NET Framework.

For most, this lack of backward compatibility will not be a significant issue. However, for some environments, it may pose a temporary migration problem. In the grand scheme, though, any hit that generics may impose on backward compatibility is well worth some interim pain. The truth is, the generics examples you've seen in this chapter — with all their optimizations and general efficiencies — would not have been achievable without introducing changes at the IL level.

# Summary

The goal of this chapter was to examine some of the more detailed facets of the .NET generics implementation. The chapter looked at many of the factors that played a role in shaping the overall vision for introducing generics into the .NET platform. Beyond that, it also looked at how generics are represented in IL and managed by the CLR at run-time. The chapter devoted a significant amount of time to discussing the generics code sharing scheme. It also looked at some basic performance metrics of generics to provide a clearer view of the performance gains you can expect to achieve with generic types.

# 12

# Using Generics with C++

At this stage, it should be clear that generics and templates are different beasts. And, even though the syntax of C++ templates shares similarities with generics, significant syntactic differences exist between the two. The goal of this chapter, then, is to provide an overview of the syntax that's associated with creating and consuming generic types in C++. This chapter briefly touches on all the fundamental generic elements, including C++ generic examples of classes, methods, interfaces, and delegates. The chapter also explains how generics and templates can be combined to strike a balance between the power of templates and the interoperability of generics.

## Templates or Generics?

If you're a C++ programmer, you may be asking yourself why you should even concern yourself with generics. After all, you already have full access to the power of templates and you'll probably view generics as narrowing the scope of your generic landscape. However, there are still plenty of good reasons for a C++ programmer to take an interest in generics.

Even though templates offer some added power that's not achievable in generics (see Chapter 3, "Generics ≠ Templates"), this power also comes with some baggage. And, given some of the efficiencies and strengths of generics, it seems to make sense for C++ programmers to at least take a step back and reconsider how generics might influence their overall approach to using or consuming generic types.

The main point here isn't to say generics should be used in lieu of templates. Instead, the point is only that generics bring a new set of parameters to the equation that may — or may not — change how and when you choose to use templates and generics. Clearly, if you're in a more controlled environment, you're likely to stick with a pure, template-based approach. However, if you have more specific size and interoperability requirements, you may want to consider how the use of generics might bring added value to your solutions.

# Blurring the Lines

The C++ language had undergone some major changes as part of the Visual Studio 2005. It has added significant new functionality to support the development of managed code in C++, adding a series of new keywords that allow developers to interact more intuitively with managed types.

The plan, in fact, is to bring the power of C++ to the CLI while bringing the capabilities of the CLI to C++. This should allow C++ to become the language of choice for systems programming on the .NET platform (if it wasn't already). Ultimately, there should be no lower-level language than C++.

The result of all these changes makes C++ a much more appealing offering to developers who are building managed solutions. These language enhancements certainly equip C++ programmers with a rich set of constructs that make C++ a much more inviting environment for first-time C++ developers. This is all achieved, of course, without eliminating access to any of the raw power that is traditionally associated with C++.

As you might imagine, these C++ enhancements have a direct impact on how you create and consume generics within C++. In fact, with all these managed code constructs at your disposal, you're likely to be quite impressed with how closely the C++ implementation of generics matches that of C#. From a pure managed code perspective, the syntactic lines start to get awfully blurry.

# No Limits

The sections that follow demonstrate how each of the generic constructs can be implemented and consumed with C++. As you look at each of these generic constructs, you'll quickly discover that the C++ implementation of generics is very complete. In fact, except for a few mild variations, the C++ language supports all the functionality that is available to VB and C# developers.

As part of supporting all the same generic capabilities you've seen with VB and C#, you'll also discover that the C++ implementation inherits all the same rules and constraints that are associated with these other languages. It's clear that each of these languages is attempting to support a uniform vision of generics as a part of their compliance with the CLS specification.

So, as you examine the examples that follow, you'll find that they intentionally avoid re-iterating the global set of rules that accompany each generic construct. Those rules are littered throughout the other chapters of this book. The goal here is to focus exclusively on the C++ generics nuances without rehashing all the same, common issues that are already covered elsewhere.

# Generic Classes in C++

Writing a generic class in C++ looks very much like a C# generic class. Still, as you look at the code in the following sample class, you'll notice that generic classes also have clear syntactic roots in the world of templates:

```
using namespace System;

generic <typename T, typename V>
```

```
ref class SampleClass {
public:
    T _param1;
    V _param2;

    SampleClass(T param1, V param2) {
        _param1 = param1;
        _param2 = param2;
    }

    T GetValue1() {
        return _param1;
    }

    V GetValue2() {
        return _param2;
    }

    void DisplayValues() {
        Console::WriteLine(L"Type Param1: {0}", _param1->ToString());
        Console::WriteLine(L"Type Param2: {0}", _param2->ToString());
    }
};
```

The first item that stands out here is the introduction of the generic keyword. This keyword identifies your class as being a managed, generic type. This keyword is followed by a set of type parameters enclosed in the already familiar angle brackets. This list of parameters is different than what you've seen with VB and C#. It includes the keyword typename, which is paired with the name for each type parameter. The keyword class can also be used interchangeably with typename in your parameter list.

The other syntax twist here is the ref keyword that precedes the class declaration. This ref keyword is not unique to a generic declaration. It is used to identify any reference managed type — generic or not. So, because your generic type here is a reference managed type, it required the addition of this qualifier.

Within the implementation of this generic class, you'll also notice that the -> operator is used to access the members of your generic types. The rest of your class implementation should resemble the syntax you may have seen with C++ templates.

## Consuming Generic Classes

Now that you've created a generic class, the next item to consider is how to consume that generic class in C++. The syntax for consuming generics in C++ can throw you a curve. The following sample code constructs a few instances of the SampleClass declared in the preceding code and calls its methods:

```
SampleClass<double, long>^ test1 = gcnew SampleClass<double, long>(392.939, 932);
test1->DisplayValues();

SampleClass<String^, int>^ test2 = gcnew SampleClass<String^, int>("Value1", 123);
String^ strVal = test2->GetValue1();
int intVal = test2->GetValue2();
test2->DisplayValues();
```

When creating a constructed type in C++ you must place each of your type arguments in a set of angle brackets that are appended to the class name. This matches the syntax of C# and J#. Where C++ diverges is in its application of unique managed code operators. For example, you'll notice that the ^ character appears in this example in a few different contexts. This symbol was added to C++ as part of Visual Studio 2005 and is referred to as an object handle. This handle indicates that a declared type is a managed type, allowing you to clearly distinguish managed types from unmanaged, heap-based pointers that use the * character in their declarations.

With this in mind, let's look at some of the situations where handles are used in this example. First, you'll notice that the type (`SampleClass<double, int>`) used in your first declaration has the ^ handle character appended to the type name. The reason is that your generic type is a handle that will be managed by the CLR. This handle may also appear with reference type arguments. In the second declaration of the example, your `String` type argument also requires a handle as part of its name because it is a reference type. In general, if the type of an argument cannot be resolved, the compiler will assume it's a reference type and, as such, will require the handle character appended to its name.

The `gcnew` operator employed here may also stand out to you. It too is new to C++. Like the handle syntax, this `gcnew` operator is used to allocate garbage-collected types that are managed by the CLR. All generic types must be created with this operator because they are all considered managed types.

Finally, a few calls are made to the methods of these generic types just to round out this example. The syntax of these calls should be very straightforward.

## Inheritance

It's worth taking a quick peek at how inheritance is implemented with generic classes in C++. All C++ generic classes can descend from both generic and non-generic types and may use type parameters or type arguments in declaring their inheritance from a base class. Following are a few examples that provide some basic insight into how these different flavors of inheritance are represented in C++:

```
generic <typename T>
ref class BaseClass {
public:
    BaseClass(T val1) {}
};

generic <typename T, typename U>
ref class TestClass1 : BaseClass<U> {
public:
    TestClass1(T val1, U val2) : BaseClass<U>(val2) {
    }
};

generic <typename T, typename U>
ref class TestClass2 : BaseClass<String^> {
public:
    TestClass2(T val1, U val2) : BaseClass<String^>("Test Value") {
    }
};
```

This example creates a generic base class that accepts a single type parameter. Then, it creates two separate subclasses of this type. The first subclass, `TestClass1`, uses the type parameter `U` in its inheritance declaration, indirectly constraining this base class to whatever type is supplied for this parameter in the subclass. `TestClass2`, on the other hand, uses a string in declaring its inheritance from `BaseClass`. The only bit of variation you might notice here would be the initializer list, which must include the type arguments and any parameters. If you're used to C++, though, this syntax is likely to match your expectations.

## Nested Classes

C++ provides full support for nested generic classes and essentially conforms to all the rules that are attached to nested classes in VB and C#. However, the syntax for accessing nested classes has a distinct C++ flavor that's worth illustrating. The following provides an example of a generic class with a nested generic class along with some client code to exercise this nested class:

```
generic <typename T>
ref class Class0 {
public:
    Class0() {}

    generic <typename U>
    ref class ClassI {
    private:
        T _dataMember;
        static int _counter = 0;
    public:
        ClassI() {}

        void IncrementCounter() {
            _counter++;
        }

        int GetCount() {
            return _counter;
        }
    };
};

void TestNestedClass() {
    Class0<int>::ClassI<int>^ type1 = gcnew Class0<int>::ClassI<int>();
    Class0<String^>::ClassI<int>^ type2 = gcnew Class0<String^>::ClassI<int>();

    type1->IncrementCounter();
    type1->IncrementCounter();
    Console::WriteLine(L"Counter Value = {0}", type1->GetCount());

    type2->IncrementCounter();
    Console::WriteLine(L"Counter Value = {0}", type2->GetCount());
}
```

The nested class declaration shown here should follow the patterns you're accustomed to with C++. This example creates an outer class (`Class0`) and declares a nested, inner class (`ClassI`) within it. It also includes a data member in the inner class to demonstrate how type parameters from the outer class are accessible within the inner class (as long as the type parameter name for the inner class doesn't collide with the name used for the outer class).

Now, in your client code, the example creates two separate instances of this inner class. Once you've created these two instances, you proceed to call the `IncrementCounter()` method which, in turn, increments a static data member. Because this data member is static, you would think that it will be incremented to a value of 3 after a third and final call to `IncrementCounter()`. Because these inner classes are both instances of `ClassI<int>`, it would seem logical for them to share this static member. However, because each of these instances has a different type argument for its outer class, the two instances are considered unique and separate.

## Methods in Generic Classes

A C++ generic class imposes no specific constraints on its methods. Any method that could be included in a non-generic class can also be included in a generic class. As with the other .NET languages that support generics, you are free to include references to type parameters anywhere within the signature of your non-generic methods. Your method's parameters, its return types, and its internal implementation are all able to leverage the type parameters that are part of their surrounding generic class.

You're also allowed to include generic methods within the scope of your generic C++ classes. All the same rules that were identified for generic classes in Chapter 4, "Generic Classes," are applied to your C++ generic methods. Instead of rehashing the rules for overloading and parameter naming here, I suggest you revisit Chapter 4 for a more complete explanation of what can and cannot be achieved with generic methods.

## Default Types

In C#, you saw how the `default()` operator was used to obtain a default value for a type parameter. In C++, the default value for a type parameter is acquired via the `()` operator. The following example demonstrates the syntax for using this operator:

```
generic <typename T>
ref class DefaultClass {
public:
    DefaultClass(T val) {
        T testVal = T();
        Console::WriteLine(L"Default Value : {0}", testVal->ToString());
    }
};
```

Here, in the constructor of your generic class, you use the `()` operator on the `T` type parameter and assign the result to an instance of `T`. Naturally, the default value that is returned here will vary based on the kind of type argument that is used to construct this class. An `int`, for example, will return a `0`. If the type parameter is a reference type, the default value will be `null`. These returned values are referred to as "default initializers."

# Generic Methods in C++

In C# and VB, every method that you write must appear within a type. Namespaces are not allowed to directly contain methods or fields. In C++, however, methods do not have this same constraint. So, the question is: Can these standalone methods be made generic within C++? And, of course, the answer is:

Yes. This C++ feature certainly extends the flexibility of generic methods, because it may be preferable at times to have your generic methods exist entirely on their own. Consider the following examples:

```
generic <typename T>
T GenericMethod(T val) {
    Console::WriteLine(L"Value is: {0}", val->ToString());
    return val;
}

generic <typename T>
T GenericMethod(T paramVal, String^ stringVal) {
    Console::WriteLine(L"Param1 Value is: {0}", paramVal->ToString());
    Console::WriteLine(L"Param2 Value is: {0}", stringVal);
    return paramVal;
}

// fails at compile-time
generic <class U>
U GenericMethod(U val) {
    Console::WriteLine(L"Value is: {0}", val->ToString());
    return val;
}
```

These generic method declarations employ the same syntax constructs that you saw in the discussion of generic classes earlier. The method name is preceded by a declaration of the type parameter signature followed by the method that freely references any of the supplied type parameters.

In looking at these three methods, you'll notice that they are all overloaded representations of the `GenericMethod()` method. They are included here to simply reiterate some of the overloading concepts that are discussed more thoroughly in Chapter 5, "Generic Methods." The second declaration in this sample overloads the first method by adding a `string` parameter to its signature. The last declaration attempts to overload the method by using an alternate type parameter name (U). However, this last method fails during compilation. Varying the type parameter name does not adequately distinguish this method from the first method that appears in this example.

Generic methods can also appear within a class, and their behavior within the class follows all the rules that were explored in Chapter 5. However, for the purposes of examining the syntax of these generic methods in C++, let's look at a quick example of a class that includes a few generic methods. Some sample client code is also included that exercises these methods as well to demonstrate how generic methods are consumed by clients:

```
generic <typename T>
ref class TestClass {
public:
    TestClass() {}

    generic <typename U>
    void TestMethod(U param) {
        Console::WriteLine(L"Value is: {0}", param->ToString());
    }
```

```
    generic <typename U, typename V>
    void TestMethod(U param) {
        Console::WriteLine(L"Value is: {0}", param->ToString());
    }
};

void TestGenericMethods() {
    GenericMethod<String^>("String Parameter");
    GenericMethod<int>(457, "String Parameter");

    TestClass<int>^ sampleClass = gcnew TestClass<int>();
    sampleClass->TestMethod<double>(521.121);
    sampleClass->TestMethod<int, String^>(922);
}
```

The generic class created here includes a generic method, `TestMethod()`, that is overloaded. In this scenario, the method is overloaded by supplying an additional type parameter in the second of these two methods.

# Generic Interfaces in C++

Generic interfaces are the most basic of the generic constructs you'll run into with C++. At the same time, as you begin to look at mixing generics and templates (discussed later in this chapter), you'll find these generic interfaces taking on added significance. For now, though, take a look at how a generic interface is declared in C++:

```
generic <typename T>
interface class IDBObject {
    bool IsValid();
    T GetObject(int id);
    List<T>^ FindObjectsById(int id);
    List<T>^ FindObjectByName(String^ name);
    bool InsertObject(T dataObject);
    bool InsertObjects(List<T>^ dataObjects);
    T UpdateObject(T dataObject);
};
```

This interface declaration is almost identical to the syntax that was used to declare your generic class. You'll notice that references to the type parameter are sprinkled all throughout this interface. The only other distinguishing C++ characteristic is the addition of the handles for the `List<T>` and `String` reference types that are part of this interface declaration.

I should also point out the inclusion of the `List<T>` from the `System::Collections::Generic` namespace. C++ has full access to the types that are included in this library. Of course, within C++, using these types takes on more meaning because they compete with the STL types that provide similar functionality. Which containers you choose to use will likely have a lot to do with whether or not your code interacts with or is part of a managed solution.

# Constraints

Constraints represent the single most significant point of distinction between generics and templates. In fact, in the world of C++ templates, there is no concept of constraints. So, this is one area where you'll see concepts that have no mapping to templates.

Constraints are used to qualify the interfaces that are supported by a given type parameter. Without constraints, your type parameters would be limited to accessing only those methods exposed by the System::Object data type. And, outside of data containers, being constrained to that interface alone may not be practical. In order to extend the capabilities of your type parameters within your classes or methods, you must add a where clause to your generic declarations. Here's an example of how an interface would be applied to a generic class declaration as a constraint:

```
interface class IValidator {
    bool IsValid();
};


generic <typename T>
where T : IValidator
ref class DataObjectCollection : List<T> {
public:
    DataObjectCollection() {}

    bool Validate() {
        bool retVal = true;
        for (int idx = 0; idx < Count; idx++) {
            T dataObject = this[idx];
            if (dataObject->IsValid() == false) {
                retVal = false;
                break;
            }
        }
        return retVal;
    }
};
ref class DataObject : IValidator {
private:
    int _id;
    int _status;
    double _salary;
public:
    DataObject() : _id(0) {}

    DataObject(int id)
        : _id(id) {}

    DataObject(int id, int status, double salary)
        : _id(id), _status(status), _salary(salary) {}

    virtual bool IsValid() {
        bool retVal = false;
        if (_id > 0)
            retVal = true;
```

```
                return retVal;
        }

        int GetStatus() {
            return this->_status;
        }

        void SetStatus(int status) {
            this->_status = status;
        }

        double GetSalary() {
            return this->_salary;
        }

        void SetSalary(double salary) {
            this->_salary = _salary;
        }
};
```

As you can see, this example creates a basic `IValidator` interface that supports a single `IsValid()` method that is meant to be applied to any class that needs a uniform interface for validating objects. Next, it creates a generic `DataObjectCollection<T>` class that applies the `IValidator` interface as a constraint on its type parameter. The `where` clause that appears immediately after the type parameter declaration can contain one or more constraints. The syntax here mimics, precisely, the syntax employed by C#.

The last step in this example is to provide a class that can be placed in the `DataObjectCollection<T>`. The `DataObject` class included here is made valid through its implementation of the `IValidator` interface. To keep things simple, the implementation of the `IsValid()` method in `DataObject` returns `false` for any object that has an `Id` that is less than or equal to 0.

Now that all the planets are aligned, the only remaining step is to exercise this new collection and confirm that it behaves as expected. The following client code serves this purpose:

```
void TestGenericConstraints() {
    DataObjectCollection<DataObject^>^ coll;
    coll = gcnew DataObjectCollection<DataObject^>();
    coll->Add(gcnew DataObject(23));
    coll->Add(gcnew DataObject(212));
    coll->Add(gcnew DataObject());
    bool isValid = coll->Validate();
}
```

This client code creates an instance of the `DataObjectCollection<T>`, populates it with three `DataObjects`, and then calls `Validate()` on the collection. This will cause the collection to iterate over all the items in the collection to determine if they all return `true` for each call to `IsValid()`. If one item is invalid, the `Validate()` method will return `false`. And, in this example, the last item in the collection has an `Id` of 0, which causes the collection to return `false`.

This example should give you a general feel for how constraints are applied in C++. As you work with constraints in C++, you will find that C++, C#, and VB all vary mildly in this area. C++, for example, imposes no ordering rules on its constraints list. You can supply class and interface constraints together in the order of your choosing. This is not true with some of the other .NET languages. Also of note is the absence of support for value constraints, which are supported by C#.

# Generic Delegates in C++

Generic delegates, like interfaces, are a very simple generic construct. A generic delegate uses type parameters to create a single delegate signature that can be used as the delegate type for a myriad of delegate implementations. This eliminates the need to create separate delegate declarations to support each of the possible delegate signatures you may need to support in your application. So, although there's not a lot of complexity to generic delegates, they are extremely useful. Here's a small delegate sample that shows how generic delegates are represented in C++:

```cpp
generic <typename T>
delegate void MyDelegate(T param);

void UpdateStatus(DataObject^ dataObj) {
    if (dataObj->GetStatus() <= 2) {
        Console::WriteLine("Status updated");
        dataObj->SetStatus(999);
    }
}

void UpdateSalary(DataObject^ dataObj) {
    double salary = dataObj->GetSalary();
    Console::WriteLine("Salary Before : {0}", salary);
    salary *= 1.2;
    Console::WriteLine("Salary After  : {0}", salary);
    dataObj->SetSalary(salary);
}

generic <typename T>
ref class DataObjects : List<T> {
private:
    MyDelegate<T>^ _delegate;
public:
    DataObjects(MyDelegate<T>^ aDelegate) : _delegate(aDelegate) {
    }

    void SetUdpater(MyDelegate<T>^ newDelegate) {
        this->_delegate = newDelegate;
    }

    void UpdateItems() {
        for (int idx = 0; idx < Count; idx++) {
            T dataObj = this[idx];
            _delegate->Invoke(dataObj);
        }
    }
};
```

This example has three basic elements. First, and most significant here, is the declaration of the delegate `MyDelegate<T>`. This declaration defines a delegate that has a single parameter in its signature. Next, you'll see a pair of methods that both accept a `DataObject` parameter (created in an earlier example).

These two methods perform different operations on the supplied `DataObject` to update its state. Finally, the example defines a generic collection class `DataObjects<T>` that accepts a `MyDelegate<T>` delegate and uses that delegate in its `UpdateItems()` method to invoke the delegate for each item in the collection.

The last step in this process is to create a client that will make use of these delegates. The following example constructs instances of the two delegates defined in the preceding code and invokes the `UpdateItems()` method, which leverages these delegates in its implementation:

```
void TestDelegates() {
    MyDelegate<DataObject^>^ statusDel;
    statusDel = gcnew MyDelegate<DataObject^>(&UpdateStatus);

    DataObjects<DataObject^>^ coll;
    coll = gcnew DataObjects<DataObject^>(statusDel);

    coll->Add(gcnew DataObject(1, 3, 9292.33));
    coll->Add(gcnew DataObject(2, 1, 7383.99));
    coll->Add(gcnew DataObject(3, 2, 989.939));
    coll->UpdateItems();

    MyDelegate<DataObject^>^ salaryDel;
    salaryDel = gcnew MyDelegate<DataObject^>(&UpdateSalary);
    coll->SetUdpater(salaryDel);
    coll->UpdateItems();
}
```

# Mixing Generics and Templates

The C++ language includes support for mixing generic and template technologies in a way that attempts to acknowledge the relative value of both technologies. It achieves this by allowing class templates to implement generic interfaces. This means that you can create and expose a generic interface for your types while still leveraging all the power of templates for their implementation. To understand how significant and powerful this is, this section builds an example that exploits this very feature. You start by defining the following generic interface:

```
generic <typename T>
interface class IDataCollection {
    int GetNumItems();
    void AddItem(T newItem);
    T GetItem(int index);
    bool Validate();
};
```

This interface defines a basic data collection interface that can now be used in the declaration of a C++ class template. An example template that implements this interface might appear as follows:

```
template <class T>
ref class TemplateDataCollection : IDataCollection<T> {
private:
    List<T>^ _items;
public:
    TemplateDataCollection() {
        _items = gcnew List<T>();
    }

    virtual int GetNumItems() {
        return this->_items->Count;
    }

    virtual void AddItem(T newItem) {
        this->_items->Add(newItem);
    }

    virtual T GetItem(int index) {
        return this->_items[index];
    }

    virtual bool Validate() {
        bool retVal = true;
        for (int idx = 0; idx < _items->Count; idx++) {
            T item = _items[idx];
            if (item->IsValid() == false) {
                retVal = false;
                break;
            }
        }
        return true;
    }
};
```

As you can see, your class template is allowed to inherit from the generic interface you defined and provide its implementation. This may seem like a minor accomplishment, but it's extremely powerful. Through this mechanism you are afforded all the luxuries and power that come with a C++ template, while still exposing this template to the outside world through a generic interface.

To fully understand the value of this achievement, you need to construct an implementation of this generic interface that employs a generic class for its implementation of the same IDataCollection<T> interface. The methods within this class would be identical to what's shown in the preceding code. In fact, all that would vary would be the declaration and the class name. Here's an abbreviated version of how the generic version of this same collection would be represented:

```
generic <class T>
where T : IValidator
ref class GenericDataCollection : IDataCollection<T> {
private:
    List<T>^ _items;
public:
    GenericDataCollection () {
        _items = gcnew List<T>();
```

```
    }

    ...
    ...
};
```

At this stage, you're probably looking at these two implementations and wondering what's so different about them. Certainly, their implementations are almost identical. The reality of what's really achieved here doesn't really set in until you start to use these two collections. The following sample code should provide the last bit of data needed to bring this point home:

```
interface class IValidator {
    bool IsValid();
};

ref class DataObject : IValidator {
private:
    int _id;
public:
    DataObject(int id) : _id(id) {}

    virtual bool IsValid() {
        bool retVal = false;
        if (_id > 0)
            retVal = true;
        return retVal;
    }
};

ref class TestObject {
public:
    TestObject() {}
    bool IsValid() { return false; }
};

void TestGenericsTemplateHybrid() {
    IDataCollection<DataObject^>^ coll1;
    coll1 = gcnew TemplateDataCollection<DataObject^>();
    coll1->AddItem(gcnew DataObject(1));
    coll1->AddItem(gcnew DataObject(2));
    coll1->Validate();
    Console::WriteLine(L"Num items in collection : {0}", coll1->GetNumItems());

    IDataCollection<TestObject^>^ coll2;
    coll2 = gcnew TemplateDataCollection<TestObject^>();
    coll2->AddItem(gcnew TestObject());

    IDataCollection<DataObject^>^ coll3;
    coll3 = gcnew GenericDataCollection<DataObject^>();
    coll3->AddItem(gcnew DataObject(3));
    coll3->Validate();

    IDataCollection<TestObject^>^ coll4;
    coll4 = gcnew GenericDataCollection<TestObject^>();
}
```

This code first creates two different objects that will be managed by your collections. The `DataObject` class implements the `IValidator` interface and, as a result, is required to include the `IsValid()` method as part of its implementation. The other object here, `TestObject`, also provides an `IsValid()` method. However, this `TestObject` does *not* implement the `IValidator` interface.

With these classes created, the example then proceeds to create a `TemplateDataCollection <DataObject^>` constructed type, placing the resulting reference in an `IDataCollection <DataObject^>` interface handle. This step illustrates that your generic collection can be used successfully to reference instances of template classes. This same process is repeated again, storing `TestObject` references in a separate constructed template class.

As you can see, the `TemplateDataCollection<T>` type was able to successfully manage both `DataObject` and `TestObject` types. Now, consider how this same scenario would play out using the `GenericDataCollection<T>` type. For this collection, you'll discover that it succeeds in managing `DataObject` references but fails when compiling the `GenericDataCollection<TestObject^>` type.

To understand why this fails, you need to re-examine the contents of the `Validate()` method that appears in both of these collection classes. This method iterates over the items in the collection, calling `IsValid()` for each item it finds. How the collection resolves the reference to this method is at the core of the problem.

For the template collection, the compiler verified — at compile-time — that the `IsValid()` method existed for both the `DataObject` and `TestObject`. Because the method existed, the compiler was able to treat both of these collections as being valid. However, with your generic version of this collection, the compiler must be able to verify that any run-time specialization of this collection will be valid. So, in order to make the `IsValid()` method accessible within your generic collection, you needed to add the `IValidator` constraint to the collection's declaration. This allowed the generic collection to manage any type that supported the `IValidator` interface. And, because `DataObject` implements this interface, it was able to be used as a type parameter when constructing the generic collection. However, because `TestObject` does not implement the `IValidator` interface, it cannot be managed by the collection and, therefore, fails during compilation.

Seeing this generics limitation should make it clear why mixing templates and generics is so powerful. By supporting generic interfaces for template classes, you're able to have generic types that can still employ the unconstrained power of a C++ class template. Being able to get around the use of constraints while remaining generic is a real bonus. Combine that with the side effect of exposing your template classes as generic types and you can see why this feature is likely to be very popular.

# STL.NET

With version 2.0 of the .NET Framework, the C++ language also inherits a new library that is being referred to as STL.NET. This library represents a new implementation of the popular and widely adopted STL template library that includes a wide array of useful templates. This new library provides an implementation of the STL library that leverages both C++ templates and generics.

Naturally, the presence of this library raises a number of questions. Although STL.NET will likely strike a balance between generics and templates, it will also create some confusion around interoperability and standardization. Should you, as a developer, use STL.NET or should you confine yourself to the

`System.Collections.Generic` namespace and view that as the de facto standard? Although there's plenty of debate surrounding this topic, I'm not sure there's any black-and-white answer for C++ developers on this question. Like everything else in the world of development, the real answer is: It depends.

Controversy and standardization aside, STL.NET appears to represent an interesting and powerful approach to making a .NET variant of STL that has the freedom to take full advantage of the .NET platform. In this light, STL.NET represents a significant breakthrough for C++ developers.

# Summary

This chapter should have given you a glimpse of how generics can be created and consumed by C++. The examples included here were not intended to be comprehensive. Instead, the chapter attempted to provide a broad overview of all the generic constructs and point out areas where C++ might vary in its syntax and underlying implementation. You also saw some examples of how generics and templates can be combined in a way that would allow other managed languages to interact with templates. Overall, you should find the managed generic syntax of C++ to be fairly easy to write and digest. In fact, the managed evolution of C++ combined with its raw performance makes it a compelling alternative to both VB and C#.

# 13

# Using Generics with J#

Throughout this book, the majority of the examples have used either C# or Visual Basic. These are certainly two of the more heavily used languages of the .NET platform. At the same time, the J# language also includes support for generics, and its generics nuances are certainly worth exploring. This chapter looks at how J# can be used with many of the generic constructs (classes, methods, and so on). It revisits some of the key generic concepts and explains how they take shape within the J# language. The main idea here is to explore the fundamentals of J# generics and provide some concrete examples of J# generics in action. Because many J# programmers are Java transplants, this chapter also points out some of the differences between the Java and .NET generics implementations. Overall, after looking at some of the sample code in this chapter, you'll likely discover that using generics with J# isn't all that different from the other languages of the .NET platform.

## J# Generic Limitations

The fact that generics are part of the CLS specification might lead you to believe that *all* of the .NET languages have equal generic capabilities. Unfortunately, this assumption is not valid. To conform to this specification, a .NET language must only be able to *consume* generic types. Support for the creation of generic types, therefore, is not required. This reality is especially significant to J# developers, because the J# language will only support the consumption of generic types in the initial release of version 2.0 of the .NET Framework.

The inability to create generic types will certainly be viewed as a significant limitation if you use J# as your primary development language. That said, having the ability to fully consume generic types and reference generic interfaces within your J# code is still quite powerful. Without this fundamental functionality, J# would have faced some serious challenges. My expectation is that generics will be showing up in more and more public .NET APIs, and any language that isn't able to at least consume generics is likely to lose some of its appeal.

Even though the current J# implementation lacks support for producing generics, I would expect a subsequent version to overcome this weakness in the not-too-distant future.

# Migrating from Java Generics

Most programmers who have worked with Java tend to find the migration to J# fairly straightforward. Microsoft has done a great job at making J# look and feel very much like Java. In fact, depending on the nature of your application, the move to J# can be fairly transparent. To date, the J# language specification has appeared to mostly mimic many of the syntactic tendencies of Java. Now, with the Java platform introducing generics as part of its 1.5 (Tiger) release, this is a point where J# and Java will diverge more than they have in the past.

If you look at the rationale for introducing generics into Java and .NET, you get the idea that both teams were certainly motivated by a common set of objectives. Both platforms seemed to view the lack of parameterized types as representing a shortcoming they'd both like to overcome. And, if you've been using generics under Java, you'll likely find the transition to J# generics to be relatively painless. The generics syntax for each Java and J# syntax certainly share a number of similarities. That said, generics is one area where you'll find more variation in syntax than you might be expecting.

The similarities between Java and J# generics definitely come to a hard stop at syntax. The underlying implementations of Java and .NET generics are very different ideologically. When generics were introduced into the Java platform, they were done so in a manner that attempted to limit the impact on the existing VM. Meanwhile, the .NET implementation was centered on the whole idea of having generics represented in IL. This fundamental point of divergence between these two technologies led to very different run-time characteristics. Certainly, without treading too heavily into the Java and .NET religious turf, the .NET approach does appear to offer some significant advantages over the current Java implementation.

The key point here is that, while Java and J# have been historically similar, generics represent one area where migrating Java developers may find a higher degree of variation in syntax, performance, and general efficiency.

# Consuming Generic Types

The J# syntax for consuming generic types is very similar to the generics syntax that is used with C#. This section takes a quick look at a few simple generic declarations to provide you with a better feel for the basic syntax of consuming generics with J#:

```
[J# code]
import System.Collections.ObjectModel.*;
import System.Collections.Generic.*;

public void TestTypeConstruction(Object param1) {
    Collection<int> intList = new Collection<int>();
    intList.Add(123);

    Dictionary<String, Integer> aDict = new Dictionary<String, Integer>();
    aDict.Add("Key", new Integer(123));

    ICollection<String> strCollection = new Collection<String>();
    strCollection.Add("Test");

    if (param1 instanceof ICollection<String>)
```

```
        System.out.println("Instance matched");

    IEnumerable<String> strEnum = (IEnumerable<String>)strCollection;
}
```

This example uses some of the generic types that are supplied by the `System.Collection.Generic` namespace. If you've looked at C# generics at all, you may be doing a double take as you look at this code. The syntax in this example is actually identical to the C# generics syntax. You'll notice that J# uses the angle brackets to enclose the list of type arguments that are supplied when constructing a generic type. As you construct each type in this example, you'll also notice that the default, parameterless constructor is used, which is represented by the closed parentheses at the end of each declaration.

Constructed generic types behave like any other J# type you might use and, if you look closely at the last few lines of this method, you'll see two more examples of some scenarios that drive this point home. The first item that stands out here is the `if` statement that uses the `instanceof` operator to determine if the method's incoming parameter matches a specific generic type. And, in the next block of code, you'll also see where a cast is used to cast an instance of a collection to an `IEnumerable<String>`. Both of these examples should make it clear that J# generic types can be used in the same context as any other non-generic J# type.

It's also worth noting that any J# primitive or reference type can be used as a type argument when constructing a generic type. And, unlike Java generics, the value types you supply here will not need to be boxed and unboxed. Because generics are represented in IL, any generic type constructed in J# will benefit from all the same efficiencies that are associated with other languages in the .NET platform.

# Leveraging Cross-Language Support

Even though you can't create generics directly in J#, you do have other options available to you for creating your own generic types. The beauty of the CLR is its ability to easily support the mix-and-match of languages within a single solution. So, if you are determined to stick with J# for much of your coding but want to create the occasional custom generic type, your best option is to hop on over to one of the other .NET languages.

Here's a quick example that demonstrates this concept in action. It starts by creating some very simple generic types that are just subclasses of existing generic types. And, to further demonstrate the cross-language nature of generics and to show I don't play favorites, this example includes classes that are implemented in both C# and Visual Basic. The code for these classes is as follows:

```
[VB code]
Imports System.Collections.Generic

Public Class MyVBDictionary(Of K, V)
    Inherits Dictionary(Of K, V)
End Class

Public Class MyVBCollection(Of T)
    Inherits List(Of T)

    Public Sub New()
```

```
        MyBase.New()
    End Sub

    Public Sub New(ByVal initialCapacity As Int32)
        MyBase.New(initialCapacity)
    End Sub
End Class
```

```
[C# code]
using System.Collections.Generic;

namespace CSharpTypes {
    public class MyCSharpCollection<T> : List<T> {
        public MyCSharpCollection() {}

        public MyCSharpCollection(int initialCapacity) : base(initialCapacity) {}
    }
}
```

These classes are as simple as they come, but they serve our purpose here. Now, with these types created, all that remains is for you to construct these types in J# and start populating them. The following J# code does just that:

```
[J# code]
import CSharpTypes.*;
import VBTypes.*;

public class CrossLanguageTest {
  public CrossLanguageTest() {
      MyCSharpCollection<int> csharpColl1 = new MyCSharpCollection<int>();
      csharpColl1.Add(123);
      csharpColl1.Add(456);
      csharpColl1.Add(789);

      MyCSharpCollection<String> csharpColl2 = new MyCSharpCollection<String>();
      csharpColl2.Add("ABC");

      MyVBCollection<int> vbColl = new MyVBCollection<int>();
      vbColl.Add(123);
      vbColl.Add(456);
      vbColl.Add(789);

      MyVBDictionary<String, double> vbDict = new MyVBDictionary<String, double>();
        vbDict.Add("test", 23.32);
    }
}
```

There aren't any real surprises in this code. It should be just what you were expecting. The generic types defined in VB and C# are imported like any other type and, after that, you are free to construct and exercise all aspects of each generic type without concern for the language that was used for its creation.

In this scenario, the .NET platform's language agnostic approach really helps overcome what could be viewed as a significant issue for J# developers. Although you may prefer to do all your work in J#, an occasional foray into one of the other .NET languages should allow you to strike a reasonable balance while you're waiting for J# to support this functionality directly.

> In general it's considered a good idea to avoid using wildcards when importing data types. However, under J#, the only way to import a generic type is through the use of a wildcard. So, in this one instance, you'll likely have to relax your "no wildcards" requirements.

# Working with Interfaces

As consumers of generic types, J# developers are likely to find themselves working heavily with the generic interfaces that participate in these APIs. Given this reality, let's take a moment to consider how J# will work with these interfaces. To see these interfaces in action, you'll first need to create some generic types that leverage generic interfaces. This is achieved in the following example, which creates a general-purpose DataAccessManager class (in VB) that supports a basic interface for retrieving, inserting, updating, and deleting database objects:

```
[VB code]
Public Enum DataObjectStatus
    Active
    Inactive
    Unknown
End Enum

Public Interface IDataObject
    Property Id() As Int32
    Property Name() As String
    Property Satus() As DataObjectStatus
End Interface

Public Interface IDataObjectCollection(Of T As IDataObject)
    Inherits ICollection(Of T)
    Function getObjectsById(ByVal id As Int32) As T
    Function getObjectsByName(ByVal id As String) As ICollection(Of T)
    Function getObjectsByStatus(ByVal id As DataObjectStatus) As ICollection(Of T)

End Interface

Public Class DataAccessManager(Of T As IDataObject)
    Public Function findObjects(ByVal status As DataObjectStatus) As
                                            IDataObjectCollection(Of T)
        ...
    End Function

    Public Function insertObject(ByVal dataObject As T) As Boolean
        ...
    End Function

    Public Sub updateObjects(ByVal dataObjects As IDataObjectCollection(Of T))
```

```
        ...
    End Sub

    Public Sub deleteObjects(ByVal dataObjects As IDataObjectCollection(Of T))
        ...
    End Sub
End Class
```

As you can see, this class makes heavy use of the IDataObjectCollection<T> throughout its API. This interface provides clients with a specialized collection interface that allows data objects to be retrieved from the collection using a set of specific, custom methods. Using an interface in the API here keeps clients from binding to any specific implementation of this API, which means your generic interface will remain in conformance with the same standards that are typically applied to non-generic interfaces.

Now, with these basics in place, you can use this DataAccessManager class with any data object that implements the IDataObject interface. All that's left is to look at how your J# code will work with these classes and interfaces. The following provides a brief look at how these interfaces are used in J# as you make calls into the class created preceding code:

```
[J# code]
import VBTypes.*;
import System.Collections.ObjectModel.*;
import System.Collections.Generic.*;

DataAccessManager<Customer> dataMgr = new DataAccessManager<Customer>();
IDataObjectCollection<Customer> actCusts =
                            dataMgr.findObjects(DataObjectStatus.Active);
ICollection<Customer> bobCusts = actCusts.getObjectsByName("Bob");

Customer cust = new Customer(1, "Test Person1", DataObjectStatus.Active);
dataMgr.insertObject(cust);

IDataObjectCollection<Customer> custColl = new DataCollection<Customer>();
cust = new Customer(2, "Test Person2", DataObjectStatus.Active);
custColl.Add(cust);

cust = new Customer(3, "Test Person3", DataObjectStatus.Active);
custColl.Add(cust);

dataMgr.deleteObjects(custColl);
```

This example happens to use Customer objects with the DataAccessManager API. It calls a few of the methods on this API just to give you a general feel for how the J# syntax works with interfaces. You can see here how a generic interface really ends up servicing the same need as a non-generic interface. Generic interfaces simply add another dimension of abstraction to the existing model for using interfaces. Other than that, they should be used just as you would any other interface you would have traditionally used.

You may have also noticed that the IDataObjectCollection<T> interface used in this example includes generic interfaces as part of its signature. Two of the calls included in this API return ICollection<T> interfaces that constrain subsets of data objects found within the overall collection.

This ICollection<T> is one of several heavily used interfaces that are part of the BCL. As a pure consumer of generic types, you'll want to be sure you're familiar with all of the interfaces — and classes — that are part of the Sytstem.Collections.Generic namespace. They're likely to play a big role in any scenarios where you're planning to leverage generic types.

# Complying with Constraints

Constraints (covered in Chapter 7, "Generic Constraints") allow you to further qualify the nature of type parameters. When defining any generic type, the author of that type has the option of including type constraints that will require all incoming type arguments to match those constraints.

All consumers of generic types must consider the impact of these constraints and how it may impact what can be supplied as a type argument. This may be slightly more relevant to you if you're a J# developer and all of the generic types you use are defined externally. The only other language-specific issue you might run into here would be if someone were to impose a type constraint that was somehow incompatible with J#. Other than that, the J# approach to complying with constraints follows all the same rules and patterns that are applied as part of the other .NET languages.

In this section you build a basic example that provides a look at how constraints might influence the type arguments you use within a J# environment. First, though, you'll need to declare a generic type that includes type constraints. The following C# class declares a custom collection class that imposes two separate type constraints on its incoming type arguments:

```
[C# code]
public interface IValidator {
    bool IsValid();
}

public interface IProperty<K> {
    String GetProperty(K key);
    void AddProperty(K key, String value);
    void RemoveProperty(K key);
}

public class DataObjectCollection<T> : Collection<T>
                                where T : IValidator, IProperty<String> {
    public DataObjectCollection() {}

    public bool Validate() {
        bool retVal = false;
        foreach (T item in this.Items) {
            if (item.IsValid() == false) {
                retVal = false;
                break;
            }
        }
        return retVal;
    }

    public bool SetProperty(int index, String key, String value) {
```

```
        bool retVal = false;
        try {
            T item = Items[index];
            item.AddProperty(key, value);
        } catch (Exception e) {
            Console.Out.WriteLine("Error Setting Property");
        }
        return retVal;
    }

    public String GetProperty(int index, String key) {
        String retVal = null;
        try {
            T item = Items[index];
            retVal = item.GetProperty(key);
        } catch (Exception e) {
            Console.Out.WriteLine("Error Getting Property");
        }
        return retVal;
    }
}
```

Let's start with the two interfaces that are declared at the top of this block of code. These interfaces are meant to represent the sort of "utility" interfaces (IValidator and IProperty<T>) that have fairly broad applicability. The idea here was to introduce a set of interfaces that could be logically applied in tandem.

Now, with these two interfaces in place, the example creates a DataObjectCollection<T> class that uses these interfaces to constrain its type parameter. This constraint is applied by adding the where clause to your class declaration, which indicates that every type argument supplied to this class must implement both of your new interfaces. Without these constraints, you would not be able access any of the specialized behaviors associated with your type parameters within the body of your collection.

As a consumer of the DataObjectCollection<T> in J#, the constraints give you some extra factors to consider. Specifically, if you're planning on passing any of your own J# types as type arguments to this class, you're going to have to be sure your class can fully comply with the requirements imposed by the IValidator and IProperty<T> constraints. To achieve this, you need only provide an implementation of each of these interfaces on the J# types you want to use with this collection. The following J# DataObject class does just that:

```
[J# code]
import CSharpTypes.*;
import System.Collections.Generic.*;

public class DataObject implements IValidator, IProperty<String> {
    private boolean _isValid = false;
    private Dictionary<String, String> _props = null;

    public DataObject() {
        this._isValid = false;
        this._props = new Dictionary<String, String>();
    }

    public void SetIsValid(boolean isValid) {
```

```
        this._isValid = isValid;
    }

    public boolean IsValid() {
        return this._isValid;
    }

    public void AddProperty(String key, String value) {
        _props.Add(key, value);
    }

    public String GetProperty(String key) {
        return _props.get_Item(key);
    }

    public void RemoveProperty(String key) {
        _props.Remove(key);
    }
}
```

This `DataObject` now complies with all the requirements that are imposed by the constraints that are applied as part of the `DataObjectCollection<T>` class. All that remains is to construct this collection and start filling it with `DataObjects`. The code that follows illustrates this last step in this process:

```
[J# code]
DataObjectCollection<DataObject> testColl = new DataObjectCollection<DataObject>();
testColl.Add(new DataObject());
boolean isValid = testColl.Validate();
testColl.SetProperty(0, "Name", "Test Person");
```

This example successfully creates an instance of the collection, adds an object, and makes a few calls to illustrate that your `IValidator` and `IProperty<T>` interfaces are available and working properly.

To get a more complete view of all the issues that surround the topic of constraints, you're going to want to read Chapter 7. The example provided here only scratches the surface of constraints. It was included solely for the purpose of providing a complete, front-to-back example of how constraints are implemented within a J# environment.

# Calling Generic Methods

There are no limitations on J#'s ability to consume generic methods. In fact, your J# code can even leverage the type inference mechanism that is supported by C# and VB. Take a look at an example of J# calling a generic method so you can get a feel for the general syntax:

```
public void CallGenericMethods() {
    TestClass.Foo1<int>(123);
    TestClass.Foo2<String, double>("Val1", 939.39);

    TestClass testClass = new TestClass();
    testClass.Foo3<DataObject>();
```

```
    TestClass.Foo2(123, 939.39);
    TestClass.Foo2(true, "Val2");
}
```

If you're already familiar with C#, this should be starting to feel like déjà vu. The syntax here precisely mimics the C# syntax. The example starts out by calling the static methods `Foo1()` and `Foo2()`, passing type arguments that are enclosed in angle brackets. It then declares an instance of `TestClass` and calls its one non-static generic method, `Foo3()`. This method includes an `IValidator` constraint for its type parameter, which your `DataObject` parameter (from the prior example) satisfies as part of its implementation.

Finally, to wrap it up, the example makes two calls to `Foo2()` without supplying any type arguments. And, as is true with the other .NET languages, the types of this method's two type parameters get successfully inferred from the types of the incoming parameters.

# Java Type Arguments

The J# language includes support for a series of additional types that are intended to ease the transition for Java developers. In fact, the .NET platform has fairly complete support for many of the types you find included in Java's JDK.

Now, given this presence of these additional data types, you might wonder how these types will behave when used as type arguments in the construction of a generic type. Because J# is ultimately just transformed into IL, it seems safe to assume that these types wouldn't incur any specific restrictions when being used as type arguments. To verify this, let's create an example that mixes generics and these Java types:

```
[J# code]
public void CreateGenericJavaParamTypes() {
    Stack<Vector> myStack = new Stack<Vector>();
    myStack.Push(new Vector(100));

    Dictionary<HashMap, Applet> myDict = new Dictionary<HashMap, Applet>();
    myDict.Add(new HashMap(), new Applet());

    List<char> charList = new List<char>();
    charList.Add('a');

    Vector myVector = new Vector();
    myVector.addElement(charList);
}
```

This code compiles and runs as suspected. In reality, the reference types here aren't any different to generics than the reference types that are supplied by any other .NET language. The value types, `List<char>`, would have been the only possible area where there could have been some issues. However, the platform has already resolved all the necessary type translations, and generics appear to be yet another benefactor of this type transparency.

# Calling Generic Delegates

Generic delegates cannot be defined within J#. However, in sticking with our "consumer-only" theme, they are allowed to be constructed and used with J#. To illustrate this point, you must first define a delegate in one of the generic-producer languages (C# for this example). Its declaration appears as follows:

```
[C# code]
public delegate void SampleDelegate<T, U>(T val1, U val2);
```

With this delegate defined, you can then import and use it freely throughout your J# solutions. The following example represents an example of this delegate being employed with J#:

```
[J# code]
public class TestGenericDelegates {
    public TestGenericDelegates() { }

    public void ProcessItems(SampleDelegate<String, double> aDelegate) {
        aDelegate.Invoke("Param1", 929.00);
    }

    public void Processor(String val1, double val2) {
        System.out.println(val1);
        System.out.println(val2);
    }

    public void CallMethodWithDelegate() {
        SampleDelegate<String, double> myDelegate =
                          new SampleDelegate<String, double>(Processor);
        ProcessItems(myDelegate);
    }
}
```

You'll notice the `ProcessItems()` method here references the `SampleDelegate<T, U>` as the type for its parameter. The `Processor()` method is then declared with a signature that matches that of the declared delegate, allowing it to be successfully instantiated and passed as a parameter in the `CallMethodWithDelegate()` method.

# Arrays of Generic Types

The J# language allows you to create arrays of generic types. As stated earlier in this chapter, a constructed generic type inherits the same set of qualities and capabilities that are associated with any other type you might use. Given this reality, you can imagine how an array of generic types will be declared. The following provides an example of this concept in action:

```
[J# code]
imports System.Collections.Generic.*;

public void DeclareGenericArrays() {
    List<int>[] intListArray = new List<int>[2];
    intListArray[0] = new List<int>();
```

```
        intListArray[1] = new List<int>();

        List<int> tmpIntList = intListArray[1];
        tmpIntList.Add(123);

        List<int> intList = intListArray[1];
        int intVal = intList.get_Item(0);
    }
```

There's no magic here. As you can see, the syntax conforms to the same model you see with non-generic types. Still, since arrays are such a vital structure, I thought it might be helpful to see how they are used with generics.

# Summary

This chapter provided you with a number of examples of how generic classes, methods, interfaces, and delegates can be used within the J# environment. Through these examples, you should have gotten a clearer picture of the J# generics syntax and general mechanics. The chapter also pointed out some factors you'll want to keep in mind as you're consuming externally defined generic types.

Although the J# language is certainly lagging behind C# and VB in its support for generics, the generic capabilities it does support in version 2.0 of the .NET Framework still represent a significant addition to the language. The ability to simply consume generic types is a big step forward for the language. It should be clear that the mere ability to leverage the built-in BCL containers will bring a greater level of type safety, expressiveness, and performance to your existing J# solutions.

# 14

# Power Collections

The .NET platform already provides developers with a rich set of generic types. And, though this collection represents a good start, there's always going to be room for improvement. In fact, a handful of teams have already been hard at work compiling their own generic libraries. Of all of these offerings, the Power Collections framework — the focus of this chapter — appears to have the most momentum and support from Microsoft. This library appears to draw its inspiration from a combination the C++ Standard Template Library and community input, extending the Base Class Library (BCL) with an `Algorithms` class and a series of new containers. This chapter digs into the details of this open source, continually evolving library. It starts with a high-level, conceptual view of all the types in the library and follows that up with a detailed look at the mechanics of using each type.

## A Little History

The origins of the Power Collections framework are somewhat interesting. In traversing the blogs, it appears as though there was some fairly early cooperation between members of the Microsoft and Power Collections teams. Microsoft was essentially looking for new generic types that could be used to extend the BCL and they approached the Power Collections team with the idea of launching a community-based project that would focus on the creation of .NET generic types.

Since this effort was launched, Microsoft has continued to participate in the evolution of this framework. This, of course, has some wondering if the types from the Power Collections library will ultimately find their way into the BCL. There are two schools of thought on this subject. One camp believes moving these types into the BCL will promote the standardization of a broader set of generic types. Others seem to think the Power Collections library should remain independent and free to advance on its own. My belief is that the Power Collections framework will continue to be a proving ground for the continued evolution of generic types, with portions of the library eventually migrating into the BCL.

# The Big Picture

Before getting into the details of the Power Collections, it will be helpful to step back and take a more conceptual view of the framework (this chapter references version 1.0 of the Power Collections library). Understanding this broader view will make it easier for you to determine the general roles that are played by each class in the library. This perspective should also provide you with a better idea for where and how you might want to introduce your own classes that extend the library.

The Power Collections library breaks down, logically, into base classes, containers, algorithms, delegates, and data structures. The sections that follow examine each of the constructs and explains, in more detail, the role each of these constructs might play in your solutions.

In many respects, the classes that appear in the Power Collections library have their roots in classes that have been the staples of existing generic libraries. Specifically, you'll notice that the library borrows from concepts found in the Standard Template Library (STL) that is very popular among the C++ templates crowd. Naturally, though, with the constraints model employed by the .NET generics implementation, the library cannot offer a one-for-one mapping of the STL classes.

## Base Classes

The Power Collections library introduces new types of data containers that offer alternative approaches to organizing and accessing data. The BCL's `Collection<T>` class, for example, implements an indexed collection that may be adequate as a base class. However, its implementation is fairly complete and, in fact, may be too complete for some scenarios.

In order to maximize flexibility, the Power Collections library includes a set of base classes that represent pared down, abstract implementations of each of the key generic collection interfaces. These classes give you a head start on creating your own implementations of these classes without requiring you to inherit all the specifics of the existing BCL implementations. And, in some cases, the BCL implementation has been sealed. So, without these classes as a starting point, you'd have to create your own implementation from scratch.

There are two different groups of base classes to consider. The first set of bases classes, shown in Figure 14-1, parallel the collection classes found in the BCL. The `CollectionBase<T>` abstract class serves as the superclass for the `ListBase<T>`, `DictionaryBase<TKey, TValue>`, and `MultiDictionaryBase<TKey, TValue>` classes. Each of these classes provides the shell of an abstract implementation of the `ICollection<T>`, `IList<T>`, and `IDictionary<TKey, TValue>` interfaces that are defined as part of the BCL.

The library also includes a set of read-only versions of these base classes. They are represented in the diagram shown in Figure 14-2. These classes remove any members that could be used to modify the state of the class. The BCL also includes a `ReadOnlyCollection<T>`. You'll want to keep this class in mind as you decide which base class to subclass when you introduce your own specializations of read-only collections.

In sticking with the theme introduced with the mutable versions described earlier, each of these read-only abstract classes implements either the `ICollection<T>`, `IList<T>`, or `IDictionary<TKey, TValue>` interfaces. In fact, you'll generally find that the Power Collections library does an excellent job of building upon the existing set of standard .NET interfaces.

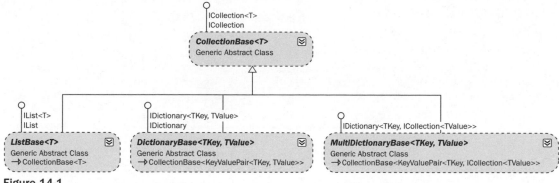

Figure 14-1

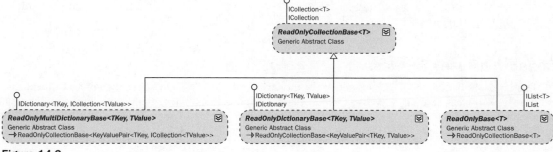

Figure 14-2

# Containers

Power Collections also introduces some new containers that offer some alternative approaches to managing and operating on collections of data. Each of these collections leverages the library's abstract base classes described in the preceding section. The sections that follow provide a brief overview of each of these classes, describing their general behavior as well as their role within the overall library.

## ListBase<T> Classes

The ListBase<T> abstract class serves as the base class for two concrete containers that are included in the Power Collections library. These two collections are shown in Figure 14-3.

The library's BigList<T> class, as its name implies, is a traditional indexed collection that has been optimized to support larger sets of data. Its operations have all been implemented with a slant toward managing collections of greater than 100 items, improving performance by limiting the need to continually adjust the contents of the list as items are inserted or removed.

The other class in this diagram, Deque<T>, represents another variation of the BCL's Queue<T>. It provides you with a double-ended queue, which is simply a queue that allows items to be added to both the head and the tail of the queue.

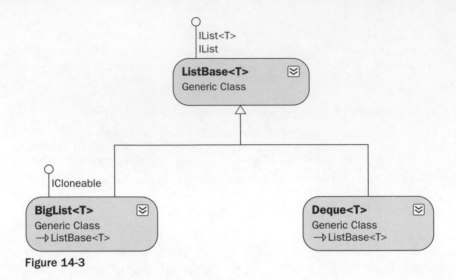

Figure 14-3

## CollectionBase<T> Classes

The CollectionBase<T> class is one of the more heavily used base classes in the Power Collections library. This class actually serves as the base class for four classes. These classes are shown in Figure 14-4.

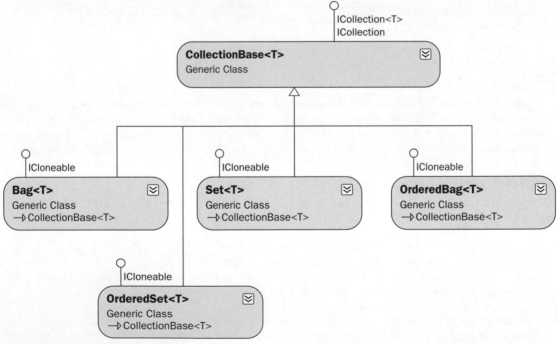

Figure 14-4

The two primary classes added here are Bag<T> and Set<T>. The two containers also serve as the basis for the OrderedBag<T> and OrderedSet<T> containers, which simply bring ordering to the Bag and Set classes. The primary difference between these two is that a Set must contain unique items, whereas the items in a Bag are not required to be unique. These classes also provide operations that allow you to compare and generally operate on all of its items collectively (instead of focusing on individual items).

### Dictionary Base Classes

The Power Collections library offers two different flavors of the dictionary base classes Dictionary Base<TKey, TValue> and MultiDictionaryBase<TKey, TValue> (shown in Figure 14-5). The MultiDictionaryBase<TKey, TValue> class provides all the fundamental elements needed to manage a collection of keys and their corresponding values. MultiDictionaryBase<TKey, TValue> serves a similar purpose. However, this class requires a different data structure and slightly different interface, allowing it to store multiple values for a single key in the dictionary.

You'll notice in Figure 14-5 that these class are further specialized by some of the containers in the Power Collections library. OrderedDictionary<TKey, TValue> specializes DictionaryBase<TKey, TValue>, adding ordering to the keys that appear in this container. MultiDictionaryBase<TKey, TValue> provides the foundation for two additional classes, MultiDictionary<TKey, TValue> and OrderedMultiDictionary<TKey, TValue>.

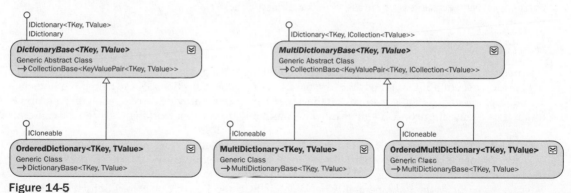

**Figure 14-5**

# Algorithms Class

The Power Collections framework includes a single Algorithms class that provides access to a wide variety of generic utility methods that are used to operate on and manipulate generic containers. The idea here is to introduce a set of generic-aware algorithms that provide type-safe processing of your generic types. If you're planning on using the Power Collections framework, you're going to want to familiarize yourself with the functionality offered by this class.

# Generic Structures

When working with generic types, it's helpful to have classes that serve as general-purpose data containers that can, through their genericness, contain any number of data types. Two specific, somewhat unimaginative classes have traditionally been used to serve this purpose. The Pair<TFist, TSecond> and Triple<TFirst, TSecond, TThird> types play this role in the Power Collections library, allowing you to create sets of arbitrary data types. Suppose, for example, that you wanted to have a dictionary that held Customer/Vendor pairs. Typically, you'd have to create a new structure that held Customers and Vendors. With the `Pair<TFirst, TSecond>` class, though, you don't need to create a custom structure. Instead, you can just construct an instance of `Pair<Customer, Vendor>` and store that object as the value in your dictionary. Naturally, if you had three items to associate, you would use the `Triple` class.

## Delegates

The Power Collections framework also includes a new delegate type. The `BinaryPredicate<T>` delegate is used to represent any method that accepts and compares two parameters of the same type. The definition of the binary comparison is completely user-defined. This is a natural addition that seems so fundamental that it will ultimately find its way into the BCL.

# Class Reference

This section focuses on providing a more detailed examination of the classes that make up the Power Collections library. The goal here is to hit on the key elements of each class and provide examples that exercise these concepts. This should give you a good feeling for how these types are used and address any general requirements that are associated with using these classes.

## Algorithms

Whereas much of the focus of Power Collections is on supplying new data containers, it also includes support for a set of utility methods that are used to operate on collections. These helper methods, which are all implemented as static methods on the `Algorithms` class, provide developers with a natural home for all those general-purpose methods that are commonly used when working with generic containers.

You'll also notice that these `Algorithms` methods are not limited to working on just those collections that are part of the Power Collections library. Instead, these methods heavily leverage the interfaces from the BCL, which allows these algorithm methods to be applied to a much broader spectrum of data types. This also maximizes the interoperability between the BCL and Power Collections library, which was one of the key goals that influenced the overall vision for Power Collections library. Before digging into some of the mechanics of working with the `Algorithms` methods, let's take a high-level look at all the methods that are included in the `Algorithms` class. The following table represents an alphabetically sorted list of all the methods included as part of this class.

| Method | Description |
|---|---|
| `BinarySearch<T>` | Performs a binary search on the supplied collection, using `IComparable<T>` to compare each item in the collection. |
| `CartesianProduct<TFirst, TSecond>` | Takes two collections and computes all the possible points of intersection between the points in the collection, returning the results as a collection of `Pair<TFirst, TSecond>` objects. |

| Method | Description |
|---|---|
| Concatenate<T> | Concatenates all the items from the supplied array of collections into a single collection. All the items being collected must be of the same type. |
| Convert<TSource, TDest> | Converts a collection of TSource items into a collection of TDest items, leveraging a delegate to perform each conversion. |
| Copy<T> | Copies some or all of the source collection to an array. This method provides a number of overloads for specifying the destination index, number of items, and so on. |
| Count<T> | Returns a count of the number of items in a collection. |
| CountEqual<T> | Looks for all the items in a collection that match the supplied item type and returns a count representing the total number of matches that were identified. |
| CountWhere<T> | Returns a count of the number of items in a collection that meets the criteria of the specified predicate. |
| DisjointSets<T> | Returns true if the supplied collections are disjoint. Collections are deemed disjoint if they do not share any common points of intersection. |
| EqualCollections<T> | Determines if two collections are considered equal, returning true if they contain the same items and those items appear in the same order. |
| EqualSets<T> | Determines if two sets are consider equal, returning true if the sets contain the same collection of items. The order of plays no role in determining the equality of the two sets. |
| Exists<T> | Determines if one or more items in a collection matches the rule specified by the supplied predicate. If at least one item is found, the method returns true. |
| Fill<T> | Fills all the items in a collection with the supplied value. |
| FillRange<T> | Fills all the items within the specified range with the supplied value. |
| FindFirstIndexWhere<T> | Finds the index of the first item in a collection that satisfies the criteria of the supplied predicate. A -1 will be returned if no match is found. |
| FindFirstWhere<T> | Finds the first item that satisfies the criteria of the supplied predicate. |

*Table continued on following page*

| Method | Description |
| --- | --- |
| FindIndicesWhere<T> | Finds the indices of all the items that satisfy the criteria of the supplied predicate. The indices are returned in as an IEnumerable<T> collection. |
| FindLastIndexWhere<T> | Finds the index of the last item in a collection that satisfies the criteria of the supplied predicate. A –1 will be returned if no match is found. |
| FindLastWhere<T> | Finds the last item that satisfies the criteria of the supplied predicate. |
| FindWhere<T> | Gets the IEumerable<T> collection that contains all items that match the supplied predicate. |
| FindConsecutiveEqual<T> | Finds occurrences of consecutive items, returning the index of the first of the consecutive items. Clients are allowed to specify how many items must appear consecutively before the consecutive condition is considered satisfied. |
| FindConsecutiveWhere<T> | Finds occurrences of consecutive items, returning the index of the first of the consecutive items. A client-supplied predicate is used to evaluate each item. |
| FindIndexOf<T> | Finds the index of the first item in a collection that matches a supplied item. |
| FindIndexOfMany<T> | Finds the index of the first item that matches at least one of the items from a supplied collection of possible values. |
| ForEach<T> | Iterates over each of the items in a collection, applying the user-supplied Action<T> to each item. |
| GetPermutations<T> | Gets a collection of all the possible permutations of the values that appear in the supplied collection. |
| GetSortedPermutations<T> | Gets a collection of all the possible permutations of the values in lexicographical orders, ensuring that each permutation is will not be generated more than once. |
| GetCollectionEqualityComparer<T> | Gets an EqualityComparer<T> implementation that can be used to compare collections of the same type. |
| GetComparerFromComparison<T> | Given a valid comparison delegate, retrieves the IComparer<T> that can be used to perform that comparison. |
| GetComparisonFromComparer<T> | Uses an IComparer<T> to retrieve its corresponding Comparer<T> instance. |
| GetDictionaryConverter<TKey, TValue> | Uses an IDictionary<TKey, TValue> instance to retrieve a Converter<TKey, TValue> that can convert a dictionary's keys to values. |

| Method | Description |
|---|---|
| `GetIdentityComparer<T>` | Gets an `IEqualityComparer<T>` that can be used to compare the identity of two objects. |
| `GetLexicographicalComparer<T>` | Gets an `IComparer<T>` that is used to perform comparisons of ordered sequences of type `T`. |
| `GetReverseComparer<T>` | Gets the `IComparer<T>` that is the inverse of the supplied `IComparer<T>`. |
| `GetReverseComparison<T>` | Gets the `Comparison<T>` that is the inverse of the supplied `Comparison<T>`. |
| `GetSetEqualityComparer<T>` | Gets an `IEqualityComparer<T>` that can be used to test the equality of sets. |
| `IndexOfMaximum<T>` | Gets the index of the maximum value in the current collection. |
| `IndexOfMinimum<T>` | Gets the index of the minimum value in the current collection. |
| `IndicesOf<T>` | Gets the indices of all the items that are equal to the supplied item. |
| `IndicesOfMany<T>` | Gets the indices of each item in a collection that is equal to at least one of the items in a supplied collection. |
| `IsProperSubsetOf<T>` | Returns `true` if one collection is considered a proper subset of another. |
| `IsSubsetOf<T>` | Returns `true` if one collection is considered a subset of another. |
| `LastIndexOf<T>` | Gets the index of the last item in a collection that is equal to the supplied item. |
| `LastIndexOfMany<T>` | Gets the indices of last items in a collection that is equal to at least one of the items in a supplied collection. |
| `LexicographicalCompare<T>` | Performs a lexicographical comparison of two collections to determine the equality of the values found in two collections. |
| `Maximum<T>` | Gets the item from a collection that is considered the maximum value. |
| `MergedSort<T>` | Merges a collection of collections and sorts the resulting, merged collection. |
| `Minimum<T>` | Gets the item from a collection that is considered the minimum value. |
| `NCopiesOf<T>` | Generates a collection that contains n copies of the supplied item. |

*Table continued on following page*

| Method | Description |
|---|---|
| Partition<T> | Partitions a collection using a predicate to move all the items that satisfy the criteria of a predicate to the top of the resulting collection T. |
| RandomShuffle() | Randomly reorders the contents of a collection and return the results to the client as a new collection. |
| RandomShuffleInPlace<T> | Randomly reorders the contents of a collection, modifying the current collection. |
| RandomSubset<T> | Gets a random subset of n items from a collection and return the resulting subset in random order. |
| Range<T> | Gets a range of items from a collection. |
| ReadOnly<T> | Gets a read-only representation of the supplied collection. |
| ReadOnly<TKey, TValue> | Gets a read-only representation of the supplied dictionary. |
| ReadWriteList<T> | Creates a read/write collection that wrappers an array data type. |
| RemoveDuplicates<T> | Returns a collection to the client that has all the duplicates removed from the supplied collection. |
| RemoveDuplicatesInPlace<T> | Removes all the duplicate items from the current collection. |
| RemoveWhere<T> | Removes all the items from a collection that meet the criteria defined by the supplied predicate. |
| Replace<T> | Replaces all the items in a collection with the specified value and returns the resulting collection. |
| ReplaceInPlace<T> | Performs an in-place replacement of all the items in the current collection, replacing all the items with the passed in value. |
| Reverse<T> | Reverses the order of all the items in the passed in collection and returns the resulting collection. |
| ReverseInPlace<T> | Reverses the order of the items in the current collection. |
| Rotate<T> | Rotates the contents of a collection, using the specified index as the rotation point, returning the resulting collection. |
| RotateInPlace<T> | Rotates the contents of the current collection, using the specified index as the rotation point. |
| SearchForSubsequence() | Searches a collection for a pattern, returning the index of the item that is at the start of the pattern. |

| Method | Description |
|---|---|
| SetDifference() | Gets all the items that appear in the first set and not in the second. |
| SetIntersection() | Gets all the items that are common to two collections. |
| SetSymmetricDifference() | Gets all the items that appear in either of two collections. The number of times an item appears in each collection also factors into determining what's different between the two collections. If the number of instances is different, this equates to a difference. |
| SetUnion<T> | Creates a collection that represents the union of two sets. |
| Sort<T> | Sorts all the items in a collection and returns the resulting collection. |
| SortInPlace<T> | Sorts the current collection in place. |
| StablePartition<T> | Creates a partition and, within that partition, retains the relative position of the items in the collection. |
| StableSort<T> | Sorts the items in a collection and, where items are equal, retains their original, relative positions. |
| StableSortInPlace<T> | Sorts the items in place in the current collection and, where items are equal, retains their original relative postions. |
| ToArray<T> | Creates an array representation of all the items contained within a collection. |
| ToString<T> | Gets a string that represents all the items the items in a collection. |
| ToString<TKey, TValue> | Gets a string that represents all the items that appear in a dictionary. |
| TrueForAll<T> | Determines if all the items within a collection match the rule supplied by the specified predicate. If all items match, the method returns true. |
| TryFindFirstWhere<T> | Gets the first item in a collection that meets the criteria defined by the supplied predicate. |
| TryFindLastWhere<T> | Gets the last item in a collection that meets the criteria defined by the supplied predicate. |
| TypedAs<T> | Generates generic wrappers for non-generic data types. |

Looking at the list, you'll notice that the Algorithms class ends up being a convenient place for the Power Collections library to house a wide variety of standalone, static methods. While some of these methods are certainly true to the spirit of the Algorithms name, others actually seem more like they just landed here because there wasn't anywhere better for them to live. This makes explaining the nature of the Algorithms class more complicated because its contents aren't all focused on one well-defined theme. In fact, I often wonder if this class isn't already in need of some refactoring purely to provide a better organization of its methods.

In order to try to bring some order to this rather daunting set of methods, I've tried to group some of the methods into clusters of logically related operations. This grouping is my own, but it seems to make it easier to help digest the scope of what the `Algorithms` class has to offer. Within each of these sections, I provide examples of code that exercise most of the methods in that area. However, my goal is not provide an exhaustive set of examples that demonstrate *every* method. Instead, I'll try to provide you with just enough code to give you a feel for how some of the key methods behave.

## Inspecting Collection Contents

The first set of methods focuses on those operations that are used to examine the contents of collections. These methods provide you with all the fundamental tools and utilities you'll need to assess the state of any collection. The following example illustrates the usage of these methods:

```vb
[VB code]
Public Function EndsWithN(ByVal searchString As String) As Boolean
    Return searchString.EndsWith("n")
End Function

Public Function FirstNameMary(ByVal searchString As String) As Boolean
    Return searchString.StartsWith("Mary")
End Function

Public Function ContainsSpace(ByVal searchString As String) As Boolean
     Return searchString.Contains(" ")
End Function

Public Sub InspectingCollections()
    Dim coll As New List(Of String)
    coll.Add("Mary Jensen")
    coll.Add("Pat Healy")
    coll.Add("Ted Stroehmann")
    coll.Add("Norman Phipps")
    coll.Add("Pat Healy")
    coll.Add("Mary Jones")

    ' Count operations
    Dim cnt As Int32 = 0
    cnt = Algorithms.CountEqual(coll, "Norman Phipps")
    Console.WriteLine("Num Equal To Norman Phipps: {0}", cnt)

    cnt = Algorithms.CountEqual(coll, "Pat Healy", StringComparer.CurrentCulture)
    Console.WriteLine("Num Equal To Pat Healy   : {0}", cnt)

    cnt = Algorithms.CountWhere(coll, AddressOf EndsWithN)
    Console.WriteLine("Num items ending with N : {0}", cnt)

    cnt = Algorithms.CountWhere(coll, AddressOf FirstNameMary)
    Console.WriteLine("Num items with name Mary: {0}", cnt)

    ' Boolean operations
    Dim success As Boolean = False
    success = Algorithms.Exists(coll, AddressOf FirstNameMary)
```

```
        Console.WriteLine("Has item with first name Mary: {0}", success)

        success = Algorithms.TrueForAll(coll, AddressOf ContainsSpace)
        Console.WriteLine("All items contain a space: {0}", success)

        ' Min/Max operations
        Dim maxPerson As String = Algorithms.Maximum(coll)
        Console.WriteLine("Maximum item value: {0}", maxPerson)

        Dim minPerson As String = Algorithms.Minimum(coll)
        Console.WriteLine("Minimum item value: {0}", minPerson)
        Dim maxIdx As Int32 = Algorithms.IndexOfMaximum(coll)
        Console.WriteLine("Minimum item index: {0}", maxIdx)

        Dim minIdx As Int32 = Algorithms.IndexOfMinimum(coll)
        Console.WriteLine("Maximum item index: {0}", minIdx)
End Sub
```

```
[C# code]
public bool EndsWithN(string searchString) {
    return searchString.EndsWith("n");
}

public bool FirstNameMary(string searchString) {
    return searchString.StartsWith("Mary");
}

public bool ContainsSpace(string searchString) {
    return searchString.Contains(" ");
}

public void InspectingCollections() {
    List<string> coll = new List<string>();
    coll.Add("Mary Jensen");
    coll.Add("Pat Healy");
    coll.Add("Ted Stroehmann");
    coll.Add("Norman Phipps");
    coll.Add("Pat Healy");
    coll.Add("Mary Jones");

    // Count operations
    int cnt = 0;
    cnt = Algorithms.CountEqual(coll, "Norman Phipps");
    Console.WriteLine("Num Equal To Norman Phipps: {0}", cnt);

    cnt = Algorithms.CountEqual(coll, "Pat Healy", StringComparer.CurrentCulture);
    Console.WriteLine("Num Equal To Pat Healy   : {0}", cnt);

    cnt = Algorithms.CountWhere(coll, EndsWithN);
    Console.WriteLine("Num items ending with N : {0}", cnt);

    cnt = Algorithms.CountWhere(coll, FirstNameMary);
    Console.WriteLine("Num items with name Mary: {0}", cnt);

    // Boolean operations
    bool success = false;
```

```
            success = Algorithms.Exists(coll, FirstNameMary);
            Console.WriteLine("Has item with first name Mary: {0}", success);

            success = Algorithms.TrueForAll(coll, ContainsSpace);
            Console.WriteLine("All items contain a space: {0}", success);

            // Min/Max operations
            string maxPerson = Algorithms.Maximum(coll);
            Console.WriteLine("Maximum item value: {0}", maxPerson);

            string minPerson = Algorithms.Minimum(coll);
            Console.WriteLine("Minimum item value: {0}", minPerson);

            int maxIdx = Algorithms.IndexOfMaximum(coll);
            Console.WriteLine("Minimum item index: {0}", maxIdx);

            int minIdx = Algorithms.IndexOfMinimum(coll);
            Console.WriteLine("Maximum item index: {0}", minIdx);
    }
```

This example populates a List<T> collection with a series of strings. This collection will serve as the basis for all the ensuing calls that are made on the Algorithms class. You'll notice, as mentioned earlier, that all the methods exposed by the Algorithms class are static. The example also attempts to use type inference wherever possible when calling these methods.

The first method that is called here is CountEqual(), which determines how many items in the collection match the value of "Norman Phipps." In this case, only one string in this collection matches this value so the method returns a value of 1. A second call is also made to CountEqual() to find instances that match "Pat Healey." And, for that call, the example also provides a Comparer<T> that is used to determine how comparisons are made. In this case, it simply uses the built-in StringComparer. For this call, you get a result of 2 because the collection contains two matches for "Pat Healey."

Next, the example uses two overloaded variations of the CountWhere() method. This method is really just another variation on the CountEqual() method, allowing you to supply a predicate that is used to determine which items are deemed a match. In this case, two methods are created that serve as the predicates for each call. The EndsWithN() method finds matches for all strings ending in the letter "n," while the FirstNameMary() locates all items that have the name Mary.

The next two items here are the Exists() and TrueForAll() methods. Exists() searches the collection for any item that matches the supplied predicate and returns True if a match is found. Only one item in the collection must match for this method to return True. TrueForAll(), on the other hand, also employs a predicate but it requires every item in the collection to match the criteria of the predicate before it can return True.

Finally, the example wraps up by using some minimum and maximum methods. There are two flavors of min/max calls: those that return the actual items in the collection and those that return an index of an item. So, when the example calls Minimum() and passes in the collection of names, this method will compare all the names and return the item that would be the first item in a sorted representation of the list. MinimumIndexOf(), on the other hand, would find this same item and return its current index within the collection. Naturally, each of these minimum functions also has a corresponding maximum counterpart.

## Comparing, Copying, and Converting Collections

The `Algorithms` class also includes methods that are used to compare, copy, and convert entire collections. These methods provide you with a set of basic mechanisms for operating on collection types as a whole. The following code provides an example of how these methods can be applied to your collections:

```
[VB code]
Public Function DoubleToString(ByVal doubleVal As Double) As String
    Return doubleVal.ToString()
End Function
Public Sub ComparingCopyingAndConvertingCollections()
    Dim coll1 As New List(Of Double)
    coll1.Add(122.33)
    coll1.Add(434.22)

    Dim coll2 As New Collection(Of Double)
    coll2.Add(122.33)
    coll2.Add(434.22)

    Dim coll3 As New Collection(Of Double)
    coll3.Add(32.75)
    coll3.Add(984.24)
    coll3.Add(1.93)

    ' Comparing
    Dim success As Boolean = False
    success = Algorithms.EqualCollections(coll1, coll2)
    Console.WriteLine("Coll1 equals Col12    : {0}", success)

    success = Algorithms.EqualCollections(coll1, coll3)
    Console.WriteLine("Coll1 equals Col13: {0}", success)

    ' Copying
    Dim copies As IEnumerable(Of Double)
    copies = Algorithms.NCopiesOf(3, 9142.902)
    For Each val As Double In copies
        Console.WriteLine("Copied double val: {0}", val)
    Next

    Algorithms.Copy(coll1, coll3, 0)
    For Each val As Double In coll3
        Console.WriteLine("Copied double val: {0}", val)
    Next

    ' Converting
    Dim doubleArray As Double() = Algorithms.ToArray(Of Double)(coll3)
    For Each val As Double In doubleArray
        Console.WriteLine("Array double val: {0}", val)
    Next

    Dim convertedColl As IEnumerable(Of String)
    convertedColl = Algorithms.Convert(Of Double, String)(coll3, _
                              AddressOf DoubleToString)
    For Each val As String In convertedColl
```

```
                    Console.WriteLine("Converted string item: {0}", val)
        Next

End Sub
```

```csharp
[C# code]
public string DoubleToString(double doubleVal) {
    return doubleVal.ToString();
}
public void ComparingCopyingAndConvertingCollections() {
    List<double> coll1 = new List<double>();
    coll1.Add(122.33);
    coll1.Add(434.22);

    Collection<double> coll2 = new Collection<double>();
    coll2.Add(122.33);
    coll2.Add(434.22);

    Collection<double> coll3 = new Collection<double>();
    coll3.Add(32.75);
    coll3.Add(984.24);
    coll3.Add(1.93);

    // Comparing
    bool success = false;
    success = Algorithms.EqualCollections(coll1, coll2);
    Console.WriteLine("Coll1 equals Coll2    : {0}", success);

    success = Algorithms.EqualCollections(coll1, coll3);
    Console.WriteLine("Coll1 equals Coll3: {0}", success);

    // Copying
    IEnumerable<double> copies;
    copies = Algorithms.NCopiesOf(3, 9142.902);
    foreach (double val in copies)
        Console.WriteLine("Copied double val: {0}", val);

    Algorithms.Copy(coll1, coll3, 0);
    foreach (double val in coll3)
        Console.WriteLine("Copied double val: {0}", val);

    // Converting
    double[] doubleArray = Algorithms.ToArray<double>(coll3);
    foreach (double val in doubleArray)
        Console.WriteLine("Array double val: {0}", val);

    IEnumerable<string> convertedColl = new Collection<string>();
    convertedColl = Algorithms.Convert<double, string>(coll3, DoubleToString);
    foreach (string val in convertedColl)
        Console.WriteLine("Converted string item: {0}", val);

}
```

This example starts out by creating three separate collection doubles. These collections are then fed to the EqualCollections() method, which is used to determine if the contents of the collections are considered equivalent. For this method to return `True` the collections must have the same number of items, in the same order, with each item matching identically. And, for the first call to the method, these conditions are satisfied and the method does return `true`. The next call to `EqualCollections()` returns `false` because the two collections being compared are completely different.

The example also includes two methods that are used for performing copy operations. The `NCopiesOf()` method shown here simply makes n copies of the supplied item type. Meanwhile, `Copy()` is used to copy the contents of one collection to another, allowing clients to provide an index that will be used to determine where the data will start copying into the target collection. There's no magic to these calls, but they're quite useful.

The `Algorithms` class also includes mechanisms for converting entire collections. The simplest variant of conversion, if you can call it that, is the `ToArray()` method, which converts a collection of items to an array of items. The other conversion method, aptly named `Convert()`, actually uses a delegate to perform the conversion from one the source type to the destination type. So, in this example, the `Convert()` method is used to convert a collection of doubles to strings. It invokes the `DoubleToString()` delegate to perform the conversion of each item in the collection.

## Lexicographical Comparison of Collections

One of the more powerful methods included in the `Algorithms` class is `LexicographicalCompare()`. This method allows you to compare the items in a collection in the same way that you might lexicographically compare two strings, where each character within the string would correspond to an entry in a collection. Here's a quick example that compares a variety of different collections:

```
[VB code]
Public Sub LexicographicalComparison()
    Dim coll1 As New Collection(Of Char)
    Dim coll2 As New Collection(Of Char)
    Dim coll3 As New Collection(Of Char)
    coll3.Add("A")
    coll3.Add("B")

    Dim coll4 As New Collection(Of Char)
    coll4.Add("A")
    coll4.Add("B")

    Dim coll5 As New Collection(Of Char)
    coll5.Add("A")
    coll5.Add("C")

    Dim coll6 As New Collection(Of Char)
    coll6.Add("A")
    coll6.Add("C")
    coll6.Add("D")

    Dim result As Int32 = 0
    result = Algorithms.LexicographicalCompare(Of Char)(coll1, coll2)
    Console.WriteLine("Coll1 Compared To Coll2 returns : {0}", result)

    result = Algorithms.LexicographicalCompare(Of Char)(coll3, coll2)
    Console.WriteLine("Coll3 Compared To Coll2 returns : {0}", result)

    result = Algorithms.LexicographicalCompare(Of Char)(coll5, coll4)
```

```
        Console.WriteLine("Coll5 Compared To Coll4 returns : {0}", result)

        result = Algorithms.LexicographicalCompare(Of Char)(coll4, coll3)
        Console.WriteLine("Coll4 Compared To Coll3 returns : {0}", result)

        result = Algorithms.LexicographicalCompare(Of Char)(coll6, coll5)
        Console.WriteLine("Coll6 Compared To Coll5 returns : {0}", result)
        result = Algorithms.LexicographicalCompare(Of Char)(coll5, coll6)
        Console.WriteLine("Coll5 Compared To Coll6 returns : {0}", result)
    End Sub
```

```
[C# code]
public void LexicographicalComparison() {
    Collection<char> coll1 = new Collection<char>();
    Collection<char> coll2 = new Collection<char>();
    Collection<char> coll3 = new Collection<char>();
    coll3.Add('A');
    coll3.Add('B');

    Collection<char> coll4 = new Collection<char>();
    coll4.Add('A');
    coll4.Add('B');

    Collection<char> coll5 = new Collection<char>();
    coll5.Add('A');
    coll5.Add('C');

    Collection<char> coll6 = new Collection<char>();
    coll6.Add('A');
    coll6.Add('C');
    coll6.Add('D');

    int result = 0;
    result = Algorithms.LexicographicalCompare<char>(coll1, coll2);
    Console.WriteLine("Coll1 Compared To Coll2 returns : {0}", result);

    result = Algorithms.LexicographicalCompare<char>(coll3, coll2);
    Console.WriteLine("Coll3 Compared To Coll2 returns : {0}", result);

    result = Algorithms.LexicographicalCompare<char>(coll5, coll4);
    Console.WriteLine("Coll5 Compared To Coll4 returns : {0}", result);

    result = Algorithms.LexicographicalCompare<char>(coll4, coll3);
    Console.WriteLine("Coll4 Compared To Coll3 returns : {0}", result);

    result = Algorithms.LexicographicalCompare<char>(coll6, coll5);
    Console.WriteLine("Coll6 Compared To Coll5 returns : {0}", result);

    result = Algorithms.LexicographicalCompare<char>(coll5, coll6);
    Console.WriteLine("Coll5 Compared To Coll6 returns : {0}", result);
}
```

You'll notice that this example creates various collections that are populated with individual characters. This was done to make it easier to see how the contents of these collections will get compared. Each time the comparison method is called, it will return a 0 if the collections are equal, 1 if the first collection is greater than the second, and -1 if the first collection is less than the second collection.

So, when this sample program is executed, you will get the following output:

```
Coll1 Compared To Coll2 returns : 0
Coll3 Compared To Coll2 returns : 1
Coll5 Compared To Coll4 returns : 1
Coll4 Compared To Coll3 returns : 0
Coll6 Compared To Coll5 returns : 1
Coll5 Compared To Coll6 returns : -1
```

Collections 1 and 2 are both empty collections. When these two collections are compared they are considered equal, which means the call to `LexicographicalCompare()` ends up returning 0. Now, when you end up comparing collection 3 to collection 2, the method returns 1 because collection 3 contains items and collection 2 does not.

This all seems to make sense. It gets slightly more interesting when you look at the comparison of collections 5 and 4. Here, both collections have two items. However, collection 5 contains the characters "A" and "C," whereas collection 4 is populated with the characters "A" and "B." Because the "C" in collection 5 is lexicographically greater than the "B" in collection 4, the method deems collection 5 as being greater than collection 4.

The last scenario to consider here is the comparison of collections of different sizes, which is illustrated by the comparison of collections 5 and 6. Because collection 6 has more items, it is considered greater than collection 5.

## Modifying and Arranging Collection Contents

Some of the most valuable methods in the `Algorithms` class are those that allow you to modify and rearrange the contents of a collection. The `Algorithms` class provides a myriad of different methods that will let you slice and dice and order your collections. The following example illustrates some of the methods in action:

```vb
[VB code]
Public Function FindInt333(ByVal val As Int32) As Boolean
    Return (val = 333)
End Function


Public Sub ModifyingCollections()
    Dim coll1 As New List(Of Int32)
    coll1.Add(111)
    coll1.Add(4)
    coll1.Add(111)
    coll1.Add(999)

    Dim coll2 As New List(Of Int32)
    coll2.Add(111)
    coll2.Add(4)
    coll2.Add(323)

    ' Concatenation
    Dim concatColls As IEnumerable(Of Int32)() = {coll1, coll2}
    Dim concatColl As IEnumerable(Of Int32)
    concatColl = Algorithms.Concatenate(concatColls)
    For Each val As Int32 In concatColl
        Console.WriteLine("Concatentated Item: {0}", val)
```

```
        Next

        ' Reversing items
        Algorithms.ReverseInPlace(coll1)
        For Each val As Int32 In coll1
            Console.WriteLine("Reversed Item: {0}", val)
        Next

        ' Rotating items
        Algorithms.RotateInPlace(coll1, 2)
        For Each val As Int32 In coll1
            Console.WriteLine("Rotated Item: {0}", val)
        Next

        ' Replacing items
        Algorithms.ReverseInPlace(coll1)
        For Each val As Int32 In coll1
            Console.WriteLine("Concatentated Item: {0}", val)
        Next

        ' Fill
        Algorithms.Fill(coll1, 8888)
        For Each val As Int32 In coll1
            Console.WriteLine("Filled Item: {0}", val)
        Next

        Algorithms.FillRange(coll1, 1, 2, 333)
        For Each val As Int32 In coll1
            Console.WriteLine("Range Filled Item: {0}", val)
        Next

        ' Remove
        Dim tmpColl As New Collection(Of String)
        tmpColl.Add("aaa")
        tmpColl.Add("aaa")
        tmpColl.Add("bbb")
        Dim dupelessColl As IEnumerable(Of String)
        dupelessColl = Algorithms.RemoveDuplicates(tmpColl)
        For Each val As String In dupelessColl
            Console.WriteLine("RemovedDupe item: {0}", val)
        Next

        Dim removedItems As IEnumerable(Of Int32)
        removedItems = Algorithms.RemoveWhere(coll1, AddressOf FindInt333)
        For Each val As Int32 In removedItems
            Console.WriteLine("RemoveWhere item: {0}", val)
        Next

End Sub
```

```
[C# code]
public bool FindInt333(int intVal) {
    return (intVal == 333);
}

public void ModifyingCollections() {
```

```
ILIst<int> coll1 = new List<int>();
coll1.Add(111);
coll1.Add(4);
coll1.Add(111);
coll1.Add(999);

ILIst<int> coll2 = new List<int>();
coll2.Add(111);
coll2.Add(4);
coll2.Add(323);

// Concatenation
IEnumerable<int>[] concatColls = { coll1, coll2 };
IEnumerable<int> concatColl;
concatColl = Algorithms.Concatenate(concatColls);
foreach (int val in concatColl)
    Console.WriteLine("Concatentated Item: {0}", val);

// Reversing items
Algorithms.ReverseInPlace(coll1);
foreach (int val in coll1)
    Console.WriteLine("Reversed Item: {0}", val);

// Rotating items
Algorithms.RotateInPlace(coll1, 2);
foreach (int val in coll1)
    Console.WriteLine("Rotated Item: {0}", val);

// Replacing items
Algorithms.ReverseInPlace(coll1);
foreach (int val in coll1)
    Console.WriteLine("Concatentated Item: {0}", val);

// Fill
Algorithms.Fill(coll1, 8888);
foreach (int val in coll1)
    Console.WriteLine("Filled Item: {0}", val);

Algorithms.FillRange(coll1, 1, 2, 333);
foreach (int val in coll1)
    Console.WriteLine("Range Filled Item: {0}", val);

// Remove
Collection<string> tmpColl = new Collection<string>();
tmpColl.Add("aaa");
tmpColl.Add("aaa");
tmpColl.Add("bbb");
IEnumerable<string> dupelessColl;
dupelessColl = Algorithms.RemoveDuplicates(tmpColl);
foreach (string val in dupelessColl)
    Console.WriteLine("RemovedDupe item: {0}", val);

IEnumerable<int> removedItems;
removedItems = Algorithms.RemoveWhere(coll1, FindInt333);
```

```
        foreach (int val in removedItems)
            Console.WriteLine("RemoveWhere item: {0}", val);
}
```

This code provides example of methods that support concatenating, reversing, rotating, replacing, and removing collection items. As you can see from these examples, the execution of any one of these methods is not all that involved. You simply supply a collection, and the method does the rest.

In looking at these examples, you should notice that the methods of this nature typically come in two flavors. For example, the rotate operation can be called as `Rotate()` or `RotateInPlace()`. The `Rotate()` method takes the incoming collection and returns a rotated collection without ever touching your original collection. `RotateInPlace()`, on the other hand, will actually directly modify the collection it receives. This naming scheme is applied to most of the methods that are able to modify a collection's contents.

Let's touch, quickly, on some of what is achieved here. First, the `Concatenate()` method simply takes a collection of collections and joins them all together into a single collection. Each collection is just appended to the end of the next. So, when `Concatentate()` is called in the example and is given a collection containing `coll1` and `coll2`, the contents of `coll2` will be concatenated to the `coll1`. The resulting collection contents appear as follows:

```
Concatentated Item: 111
Concatentated Item: 4
Concatentated Item: 111
Concatentated Item: 999
Concatentated Item: 111
Concatentated Item: 4
Concatentated Item: 323
```

The `ReverseInPlace()` method is equally simple. It just reverses the current order of the items in the collection. In the example, `ReverseInPlace()` is applied to `coll1` and the contents of the collection after this call end up as follows:

```
Reversed Item: 999
Reversed Item: 111
Reversed Item: 4
Reversed Item: 111
```

The `Rotate()` method is not as straightforward. It is used to move the rotate the positions of the items in a collection. This method takes a rotation position parameter and, based on the sign of that position, determines how to rotate the collection. If the rotation amount is positive, the number will be used as an offset from the top of the collection. If the number is negative, that number will be used as the offset from the bottom of the collection. Once a rotation point is identified, that item at that point is moved to the top of the collection and the positions of the remaining items are updated to reflect this change.

To clarify this, consider how rotation was applied in the example. After successfully reversing the contents of you collection, the items in your collection were ordered as follows:

```
999
111
4
111
```

Then, the example applied Rotate() to this collection with a rotation index of 2. Because the rotation point is positive, the target index is relative to the top of the collection. In this case, the point 2 (zero-based) represents the third item in this list (the item with the value of 4). That will be the rotation point, and that item will be moved to the top, with all the other items rotating in a sort of virtual circle to accommodate the move. So, as 4 moves up one, 999 moves to the bottom of the list. And, as it moves up again, 111 then moves to the bottom of the list. The resulting collection is:

```
4
111
999
111
```

The Fill() and FillRange() methods are also both shown in the example. Fill() simply fills all the entries in your collection with the specified value. For this example, then, the entire contents of the supplied collection will be filled with the value 8888. The FillRange() method is similar, filling a client-specified range within the collection with a given value.

Finally, the last bit of this example provides two examples how items might be removed from a collection using methods from the Algorithms class. The RemoveDuplicates() method, as its name implies, removes any duplicate entries from a collection. The RemoveWhere() method uses a user-supplied predicate to evaluate and remove any items that meet the predicate's criteria.

## Searching Collections

If you're going to put data in generic collections, you're also going to need some standard tools to search the contents of those collections. Fortunately, instead of having to write lots of your own searching utilities, the Algorithms class is equipped with a number of different methods that should support most of your basic needs. The following example covers many of the different types of searches that can be performed with the Algorithms class:

```vb
[VB code]
Public Sub SearchingCollections()
    Dim coll As New Collection(Of String)
    coll.Add("Pat Healy")

    Dim foundVal As String
    Dim success As Boolean
    success = Algorithms.TryFindFirstWhere(coll, AddressOf FirstNameMary, foundVal)

    coll.Add("Mary Jensen")
    coll.Add("Ted Stroehmann")
    coll.Add("Norman Phipps")
    coll.Add("Pat Healy")
    coll.Add("Mary Jones")

    success = Algorithms.TryFindFirstWhere(coll, AddressOf FirstNameMary, foundVal)
```

```vbnet
    Dim foundVals As IEnumerable(Of String)
    foundVals = Algorithms.FindWhere(coll, AddressOf FirstNameMary)
    For Each val As String In foundVals
        Console.WriteLine("Found item: {0}", val)
    Next

    Dim foundIdx As Int32
    foundIdx = Algorithms.FindFirstIndexWhere(coll, AddressOf EndsWithN)
    Console.WriteLine("Found index: {0}", foundIdx)

    foundIdx = Algorithms.FirstIndexOf(coll, "Norman Phipps")
    Console.WriteLine("Found index: {0}", foundIdx)

    Dim foundIndices As IEnumerable(Of Int32)
    Dim targetItems As New Collection(Of String)
    targetItems.Add("Pat Healy")
    targetItems.Add("Mary Jones")
    foundIndices = Algorithms.IndicesOfMany(coll, targetItems)
    For Each val As Int32 In foundIndices
        Console.WriteLine("Found item: {0}", val)
    Next

    Dim conColl As New Collection(Of String)
    conColl.Add("aaa")
    conColl.Add("bbb")
    conColl.Add("aaa")
    conColl.Add("aaa")
    conColl.Add("ccc")
    foundIdx = Algorithms.FirstConsecutiveEqual(conColl, 2)
    Console.WriteLine("Found index: {0}", foundIdx)
End Sub
```

[C# code]

```csharp
public void SearchingCollections() {
    Collection<string> coll = new Collection<string>();
    coll.Add("Pat Healy");

    string foundVal;
    bool success = Algorithms.TryFindFirstWhere(coll, FirstNameMary, out foundVal);

    coll.Add("Mary Jensen");
    coll.Add("Ted Stroehmann");
    coll.Add("Norman Phipps");
    coll.Add("Pat Healy");
    coll.Add("Mary Jones");

    success = Algorithms.TryFindFirstWhere(coll, FirstNameMary, out foundVal);

    IEnumerable<string> foundVals;
    foundVals = Algorithms.FindWhere(coll, FirstNameMary);
    foreach (string val in foundVals)
        Console.WriteLine("Found item: {0}", val);

    int foundIdx = Algorithms.FindFirstIndexWhere(coll, EndsWithN);
```

```
            Console.WriteLine("Found index: {0}", foundIdx);

            foundIdx = Algorithms.FirstIndexOf(coll, "Norman Phipps");
            Console.WriteLine("Found index: {0}", foundIdx);

            IEnumerable<int> foundIndices;
            Collection<string> targetItems = new Collection<string>();
            targetItems.Add("Pat Healy");
            targetItems.Add("Mary Jones");
            foundIndices = Algorithms.IndicesOfMany(coll, targetItems);
            foreach (int val in foundIndices)
                Console.WriteLine("Found item: {0}", val);

            Collection<string> conColl = new Collection<string>();
            conColl.Add("aaa");
            conColl.Add("bbb");
            conColl.Add("aaa");
            conColl.Add("aaa");
            conColl.Add("ccc");
            foundIdx = Algorithms.FirstConsecutiveEqual(conColl, 2);
            Console.WriteLine("Found index: {0}", foundIdx);
    }
```

A number of different searching techniques are shown in this example. The first one that's used here is the `TryFindFirstWhere()` method, which looks for the first item that meets the criteria specified by the predicate you supply. If an item is found, it will be returned in the third parameter. The nice feature of this method is that it's very safe. Instead of tossing exceptions for failed search conditions, it will simply return a `false` if no item is found. The example demonstrates this. It first searches for a person with the first name "Mary" and finds none (because none exist in the collection yet). Then, more names are added and the function is called again, this time returning `true`.

If you want to search for multiple matching values, you'll most likely want to consider using the `FindWhere()` method. This method takes a collection and predicate and finds all the items in the collection that match the criteria applied within your predicate. The found items are returned as a collection. The example calls this method with a collection containing the same set of names and uses a predicate, `EndsWithN`, that returns true for any value that has the letter "n" at the end.

The searching methods also provide the option of retrieving the specific indices of items. `FindFirstIndexWhere()`, for example, will return the index of the first item in the supplied collection that matches the criteria applied by your predicate. Meanwhile, `FindIndexOf()` provides a twist on this, accepting the value to be searched for (instead of using a predicate). For this example, it searches for "Norman Phipps" and returns and index value of 3. A third approach is also shown here, the `IndicesOfMany()` method. This method accepts a collection of values to search for and returns a collection containing the indices of any item where a match is found.

A more exotic search can be achieved with the `FirstConsectutiveEqual()` method. This method doesn't search for individual matches. In fact, it's not trying to find specific matches at all. Instead, its goal is to find patterns of consecutive values in a collection. When you call this method, you provide the collection to search and the number of consecutive instances you're looking for. It then searches for the first location within that collection where it finds that many consecutive instance of a value and returns the index of the first item in that sequence. For the example, I created a collection of string that had consecutive values of "aaa" appearing in the second and third index positions of the collection. And, because the example called `FirstConsectutiveEqual()` and told it to find two consecutive instances, the method returned an index of 2, which was the index of the first consecutive instance of "aaa" in the collection. You can imagine how this might come in handy when you're trying to process lists that may have duplicate items.

The Power Collections library also supports a `BinarySearch()` mechanism, which is not shown within this example.

## Sorting Collections

The `Algorithms` class also provides a small set of methods that are used to sort the order of the items that appear in a collection. There isn't a whole lot of complexity to these methods, but you're still likely to make heavy use of them. Considering this reality, it's worth taking a quick look at the mechanics of these sort methods. The following example builds and sorts a collection using the `Sort()`, `Partition()`, and `MergeSort()` methods:

```
[VB code]
Public Sub SortingCollections()
    Dim coll As New Collection(Of String)
    coll.Add("Pat Healy")
    coll.Add("Mary Jensen")
    coll.Add("Ted Stroehmann")
    coll.Add("Norman Phipps")
    coll.Add("Pat Healy")
    coll.Add("Mary Jones")

    ' Before sort
    For Each val As String In coll
        Console.WriteLine("Unsorted item: {0}", val)
    Next

    Dim sortedList As String()
    sortedList = Algorithms.Sort(coll)

    ' After sort
    For Each val As String In sortedList
        Console.WriteLine("Sorted item: {0}", val)
    Next

    Dim partitionIdx As Int32
    partitionIdx = Algorithms.Partition(coll, AddressOf FirstNameMary)
    Console.WriteLine("Partition index: {0}", partitionIdx)

    Dim coll2 As New Collection(Of String)
    coll2.Add("Adam Abrams")
    coll2.Add("Zany Henderson")
    coll2.Add("Chuck Thompson")
    Algorithms.SortInPlace(coll2)

    Dim collections As IEnumerable(Of String)() = {coll, coll2}

    Dim mergedColl As IEnumerable(Of String)
    mergedColl = Algorithms.MergeSorted(collections)
```

```
        For Each val As String In mergedColl
            Console.WriteLine("Merged item: {0}", val)
        Next

    End Sub
```

```csharp
[C# code]
public void SortingCollections() {
    Collection<string> coll = new Collection<string>();
    coll.Add("Pat Healy");
    coll.Add("Mary Jensen");
    coll.Add("Ted Stroehmann");
    coll.Add("Norman Phipps");
    coll.Add("Pat Healy");
    coll.Add("Mary Jones");

    // Before sort
    foreach (string val in coll)
        Console.WriteLine("Unsorted item: {0}", val);

    string[] sortedList;
    sortedList = Algorithms.Sort(coll);

    // After sort
    foreach (string val in sortedList)
        Console.WriteLine("Sorted item: {0}", val);

    int partitionIdx;
    partitionIdx = Algorithms.Partition(coll, FirstNameMary);
    Console.WriteLine("Partition index: {0}", partitionIdx);

    Collection<string> coll2 = new Collection<string>();
    coll2.Add("Adam Abrams");
    coll2.Add("Zany Henderson");
    coll2.Add("Chuck Thompson");
    Algorithms.SortInPlace(coll2);

    IEnumerable<string>[] collections = { coll, coll2 };

    IEnumerable<string> mergedColl;
    mergedColl = Algorithms.MergeSorted(collections);
    foreach (string val in mergedColl)
        Console.WriteLine("Merged item: {0}", val);

}
```

Once again, the example builds the now familiar list of strings. Then, it sorts this collection of strings using the Sort() method. This example doesn't fully demonstrate all the nuances of sorting. If the default sorting behavior is not what you want, you may provide alternate comparers to sort your collections.

This example also includes a call to the Partition() method. This method is somewhat unusual in that it partitions your data into those items that meet your search criteria and those that don't. When you call this method, you provide a predicate, and all the items that meet the criteria of this predicate will be placed at the "top" of the collection. An index is also returned, indicating the location within the collection where there the data is partitioned.

The example calls `Partition()` with the `FirstNameMary` predicate, which returns `true` for any person with the name "Mary." As result, all the items with that match this condition should be placed at the top of your collection. The following represents the contents of the collection that is returned from this specific call:

```
Mary Jones
Mary Jensen
Ted Stroehman
Norman Phipps
Pat Healy
Pat Healy
```

As you can see, the two items with the name "Mary" appear at the top of the collection. The index that is returned here is 2, which is the index of the first item that did *not* meet the criteria of the predicate. Conceptually, at least, the result is a "partitioned" collection of items.

The last sorting option shown in the example is `MergeSort()`. This method allows you to combine and sort multiple collections with a single call. You just provide it with a collection of collections, and it will do the rest. The example does this by creating a new collection, placing it and the original collection of names into a collection that is then passed to `MergeSort()`. After this call, the resulting collection will be organized as follows:

```
Adam Abrams
Chuck Thompson
Mary Jones
Mary Jensen
Ted Stroehmann
Norman Phipps
Pat Healy
Pat Healy
Zany Henderson
```

## Set Operations

Collections represent, at some level, sets of data. Thus, it only seems logical that you might want to perform some of the traditional set-based operations on these collections. The Power Collections library, which already embraces set-based operations as part of some of its new data containers, also includes a group of generic set-based methods (as part of `Algorithms`) that can be applied to your collections. The following example provides an example of some of these set operations in action:

```
[VB code]
Public Sub SetOperations()
    Dim coll1 As New Collection(Of Int32)
    coll1.Add(1)
    coll1.Add(3)
    coll1.Add(5)

    Dim coll2 As New Collection(Of Int32)
    coll2.Add(7)
    coll2.Add(3)
    coll2.Add(3)
    coll2.Add(5)
```

```vbnet
        Dim items As IEnumerable(Of Int32)
        items = Algorithms.SetIntersection(coll1, coll2)
        For Each val As Int32 In items
            Console.WriteLine("Intersection item: {0}", val)
        Next

        items = Algorithms.SetUnion(coll1, coll2)
        For Each val As Int32 In items
            Console.WriteLine("Union item: {0}", val)
        Next

        items = Algorithms.SetDifference(coll2, coll1)
        For Each val As Int32 In items
            Console.WriteLine("Difference item: {0}", val)
        Next

        items = Algorithms.SetSymmetricDifference(coll1, coll2)
        For Each val As Int32 In items
            Console.WriteLine("Symmetric Difference item: {0}", val)
        Next

        Dim cartProdColl As IEnumerable(Of Pair(Of Int32, Int32))
        cartProdColl = Algorithms.CartesianProduct(coll1, coll2)
        For Each val As Pair(Of Int32, Int32) In cartProdColl
            Console.WriteLine("Cartesian item: {0}", val)
        Next

        If (Algorithms.EqualSets(coll1, coll2) = True) Then
            Console.WriteLine("Sets are equal")
        End If

        Dim coll3 As New Collection(Of Int32)
        coll3.Add(7)
        If (Algorithms.IsSubsetOf(coll3, coll2) = True) Then
            Console.WriteLine("Coll3 is subset of coll2")
        End If

End Sub
```

[C# code]
```csharp
public void SetOperations() {
    Collection<int> coll1 = new Collection<int>();
    coll1.Add(1);
    coll1.Add(3);
    coll1.Add(5);

    Collection<int> coll2 = new Collection<int>();
    coll2.Add(7);
    coll2.Add(3);
    coll2.Add(3);
    coll2.Add(5);

    IEnumerable<int> items;
    items = Algorithms.SetIntersection(coll1, coll2);
    foreach (int val in items)
```

```
            Console.WriteLine("Intersection item: {0}", val);

    items = Algorithms.SetUnion(coll1, coll2);
    foreach (int val in items)
        Console.WriteLine("Union item: {0}", val);

    items = Algorithms.SetDifference(coll2, coll1);
    foreach (int val in items)
        Console.WriteLine("Difference item: {0}", val);

    items = Algorithms.SetSymmetricDifference(coll1, coll2);
    foreach (int val in items)
        Console.WriteLine("Symmetric Difference item: {0}", val);

    IEnumerable<Pair<int, int>> cartProdColl;
    cartProdColl = Algorithms.CartesianProduct(coll1, coll2);
    foreach (Pair<int, int> val in cartProdColl)
        Console.WriteLine("Cartesian item: {0}", val);

    if (Algorithms.EqualSets(coll1, coll2) == true)
        Console.WriteLine("Sets are equal");

    Collection<int> coll3 = new Collection<int>();
    coll3.Add(7);
    if (Algorithms.IsSubsetOf(coll3, coll2) == true)
        Console.WriteLine("Coll3 is subset of coll2");
}
```

This example exercises the majority of the set-based operations that are part of the `Algorithms` class, including `SetIntersection()`, `SetUnion()`, `SetDifference()`, `SetSymmetricDifference()`, and `CartesianProduct()`. The example creates two collections of integers and then uses these collections to demonstrate the behavior of each of these set operations. Each of the set operations included in the `Algorithms` class conforms to the existing, well-understood definitions for these operations. Still, it's worth reviewing these items briefly for those that may not be as familiar with set-based concepts.

Let's start by looking at the use of `SetIntersection()` in this example. The collection returned by this call includes the values 3 and 5. These two values are returned because they represent the points that are common to both collections. The `SetUnion()` method creates a new collection that is guaranteed to include all of the items that appear in either of the two collections. In this case, the union of the two sample collections yields the values 1, 5, 7, 3, and 3. In contrast, the `SetDifference()` method identifies just those items that appear in the first collection that are not in the second. So, when applying this method to the collections, the method will return the values 7 and 3 because these values are in `coll2` and are not in `coll1`.

The `SetSymmetricDifference()` method attacks this problem differently. When this set operation is performed, it returns 1, 7, and 3. The difference with this method is that it looks at *any* difference between either of the two collections. With this definition, it probably makes sense that the 1 and 7 were returned, but you may wonder why the value 3 was included. After all, it already appears in both collections. This value is included because the number of instances of a value also influences the outcome of this set operation. In this case, because the value 3 shows up twice in one collection and only once in the other, this is seen a "difference," and this causes 3 to be added to the results.

The last set operation to consider here is the `SetCartesianProduct()` method, which finds all the points of intersection between two collections. The results from this call are returned as collection of `Pair<T, T>` objects, where each instance of `Pair<T, T>` represents one of the points of intersection.

You'll also notice that the example includes two methods to evaluate sets. The `EqualSets()` method is self-explanatory. It just compares two sets and returns `true` if they are the same. The other method, `IsSubsetOf()`, returns `true` if the first collection is a valid subset of the second.

## Comparers and Comparisons

As you work with generic collections, you'll often find that you need to create specific instances of `Comparer<T>` and `IComparable<T>` objects to be used as part of different operations you may want to perform on a given collection. The `Algorithms` class includes a set of helper methods that are meant to simplify the creation of some of these objects. Each of the methods with the `GetXXXComparer()` and `GetXXXComparison()` signature are meant to serve in this role.

## Radomizing Collections

If you're interested in mixing things up — literally — you'll want to also take a look at the set of collection randomizing methods that are part of the `Algorithms` class. The `RandomShuffle()` and `RandomShuffleInPlace()` methods are both used to use randomly reorganize the items in a collection. A `RandomSubset()` method is also provide. This method returns a subset of a user-specified size, which contains a random set of items from the supplied collection.

# Bag<T>

A `Bag`, in many respects, is the most basic of all the collections. This collection only guarantees that it will hold whatever item you give it. Whereas most collections have some imposed order or indexed access scheme, a `Bag<T>` class doesn't concern itself with order. It's more focused on the treatment of a collection of items as a whole.

Before getting into some examples of how you can evaluate and manipulate `Bags`, the following table examines the full set of methods and properties that are associated with this class.

| Method or Property | Description |
| --- | --- |
| `Add()` | Adds the supplied item to the Bag and, if the item already exists, increments the instance count for that item. |
| `AddMany()` | lection to the Bag. |
| `AddRepresentative()` | Adds the supplied item to the Bag and treats it as the representative item. |
| `ChangeNumberOfCopies()` | Changes the number of items that exist for the supplied item type to the number provided. |
| `Clear()` | Empties the contents of the Bag. |
| `Clone()` | Creates and returns a shallow copy of all the items in the Bag. |
| `CloneContents()` | Creates and returns a deep copy of all the items in the Bag. |

*Table continued on following page*

| Method or Property | Description |
|---|---|
| Comparer | Returns the IEqualityComparer<T> currently associated with this Bag. |
| Contains() | Determines if the Bag contains the specified item. If a match is found, the method returns true. |
| Count | Property that returns the number of items currently in the Bag. |
| Difference() | Computes the difference between the contents of this Bag and the Bag that is supplied. This difference is determined based on the difference in the number of instances of each item in this Bag and the passed-in Bag. A Bag containing the computed difference is returned. |
| DifferenceWith() | Computes the difference between the contents of this Bag and the Bag that is supplied. The current Bag is modified in place to represent the difference between the current Bag and the supplied Bag. |
| DistinctItems() | Retrieves an IEnumerable<T> collection that contains all the unique items that are currently in this Bag. |
| GetEnumerator() | Gets an IEnumerator<T> representation of the items in the Bag. |
| GetRepresentativeItem() | Retrieves the representative item that matches the specified item type. This method also returns the total number of items in the Bag that match the supplied type. |
| Intersection() | Computes the intersection between this Bag and another Bag and returns a new Bag that contains the items in this intersection. |
| IntersectionWith() | Computes the intersection between this Bag and another Bag and modifies this Bag to contain the items that are in this intersection. |
| IsEqualTo() | Determines if two Bags are considered equal. |
| IsDisjointFrom() | Determines if one collection is considered disjoint from another. |
| IsProperSubsetOf() | Determines if the supplied Bag is a valid subset of this Bag. If all the items in the passed-in Bag are in this Bag, this method returns true. To be a "proper" subset, this Bag must have fewer items than the supplied Bag. |
| IsProperSupersetOf() | Determines if the supplied Bag is a valid superset of this Bag. If all the items in the supplied Bag are also in this Bag, this method returns true. To be a "proper" superset, this Bag must have more items than the supplied Bag. |

| Method or Property | Description |
|---|---|
| IsSubsetOf() | Determines if all the items in this bag are valid members of the supplied Bag. If every member in the current Bag exists in the supplied Bag, this method returns true. |
| IsSupersetOf() | Determines if this Bag is the superset of the supplied Bag. If all the items in the supplied Bag are also in this Bag, this method returns true. |
| NumberOfCopies() | Gets a count of the number of duplicate items that exist in the Bag that match the supplied item. |
| Remove() | Removes the item that is equal to the supplied item. |
| RemoveAll() | Removes all items from the Bag that are equal to those items in the supplied collection. |
| RemoveAllCopies() | Removes all duplicate items that match the supplied item. |
| RemoveMany() | Removes all the items in the Bag. |
| Sum() | Merges all the items of the supplied Bag with this Bag, yielding a new Bag that contains all the items from both Bags. |
| SumWith() | Accepts a Bag of items and adds these items to this Bag. The supplied Bag is not modified as a result of calling this method. |
| SymmetricDifference() | Compares the supplied Bag and this Bag, identifying those items that are unique to each Bag. To qualify, an item must exist in one of these two Bags, but may not appear in both. The resulting difference will be placed in a new Bag and returned from this method. The supplied Bag and this Bag remain unchanged. |
| SymmetricDifferenceWith() | Compares the supplied Bag and this Bag, identifying those items that are unique to each Bag. To qualify, an item must exist in one of these two Bags, but may not appear in both. The resulting difference will be placed in this Bag. |
| Union() | Creates a new Bag that represents the union of this Bag and the supplied Bag. Items that are duplicated in each of the two Bags are also duplicated the same number of times in the returned Bag. This Bag and the supplied Bag remain unchanged. |
| UnionWith() | Modifies this Bag replacing its contents with the union of this Bag and the supplied Bag. Items that are duplicated in each of the two Bags are also duplicated the same number of times in the returned Bag. |

## *Construction and Population*

Creating and populating a `Bag` object is a relatively straightforward process. In addition to supporting a default constructor, the `Bag` class provides a constructor that accepts an initial set of items that will be used to populate the `Bag`. The following example provides a basic look at how `Bags` are constructed and populated with data:

```vb
[VB Code]
Public Sub DumpItems(Of T)(ByVal aList As IEnumerable(Of T))
    Console.WriteLine("")
    Dim idx As Int32 = 1
    For Each val As T In aList
        Console.WriteLine("{0}. Value : {1}", idx, val)
        idx = idx + 1
    Next
End Sub

Dim doubleList As New List(Of Double)()
doubleList.Add(124.23)
doubleList.Add(9203.93)
Dim doubleBag1 As New Bag(Of Double)(doubleList)
DumpItems(Of Double)(doubleBag1)

Dim doubleBag2 As Bag(Of Double)
doubleBag2 = New Bag(Of Double)(doubleList, EqualityComparer(Of Double).Default)
DumpItems(Of Double)(doubleBag2)

Dim intList As List(Of Int32)
intList = New List(Of Int32)(New Int32() {23, 522, 9831})
Dim intBag As New Bag(Of Int32)()
intBag.AddMany(intList)

DumpItems(Of Int32)(intBag)
Dim strBag As Bag(Of String)
Dim strList As New List(Of String)(New String() {"Item1", "Item2", "Item3",_
                                                 "Item3", "Item4"})
strBag = New Bag(Of String)(strList)
strBag.Add("Item1")
strBag.Add("Item2")
strBag.Add("Item5")
strBag.AddRepresentative("Item3")
DumpItems(Of String)(strBag)
```

```csharp
[C# code]
public void DumpItems<T>(IEnumerable<T> aList) {
    Console.WriteLine("");
    Int32 idx = 1;
    foreach (T val in aList) {
        Console.WriteLine("{0}. Value : {1}", idx, val);
        idx++;
    }
}

List<Double> doubleList = new List<Double>();
doubleList.Add(124.23);
doubleList.Add(9203.93);
```

```
Bag<Double> doubleBag1 = new Bag<Double>(doubleList);
DumpItems(doubleBag1);

Bag<Double> doubleBag2;
doubleBag2 = new Bag<Double>(doubleList, EqualityComparer<Double>.Default);
DumpItems(doubleBag2);

List<Int32> intList;
intList = new List<Int32>(new Int32[] { 23, 522, 9831 });
Bag<Int32> intBag = new Bag<Int32>();
intBag.AddMany(intList);

DumpItems(intBag); Bag<String> strBag;
strBag = new Bag<String>(new String[] {"Item1", "Item2", "Item3",
                                        "Item3", "Item4"});
strBag.Add("Item1");
strBag.Add("Item2");
strBag.Add("Item5");
strBag.AddRepresentative("Item3");
DumpItems(strBag);
```

The first block of code here illustrates how a Bag object can be constructed using a collection of objects. This example creates a List<Double> collection and passes that list to the Bag during its construction. In reality, the Bag constructor can be populated with any collection that implements the IEnumerable<T> interface.

You'll also notice that an example of another constructor is included here that accepts both a collection of items and an IComparer<T> reference. This constructor allows you to provide your own custom IComparer<T> implementation that will be used by the Bag when determining the equality of its objects. If no comparer is supplied, the Bag will use the default comparer associated with your type argument.

> The code that is used throughout this section uses a DumpItems() method (from the preceding example) to dump the contents of collections. This method simply iterates over the contents of collections, displaying their contents.

Finally, the code provides some basic examples of the methods that can be used to add data to a Bag. The Bag class supports all the interfaces you'd expect to find with any data container, including an Add() method and an AddAll() method that accepts collections of objects.

The one method that stands out here is AddRepresentative(). The idea of a "representative" object is unique to Bag collections. Although the Bag class can hold duplicate items, it doesn't hold separate instances for each duplicated item it contains. Instead, for efficiency, it keeps a single instance of each unique item and simply maintains a count of the number of instances that exist for a given item. Still, at some level, the bag is holding a specific reference of an item and that reference is considered the "representative" item So, if you just use the Add() method, the first item you add will become the "representative" item and, as duplicates of that item are added, they will simply cause the count to be incremented. However, if you call the AddRepresentative() method, the item being added will become the representative item. In most scenarios, you should find yourself using Bags without concern for which item is the representative item. Still, there could be cases where this could be important to your implementation.

## *Accessing Items*

Now that you've seen how a `Bag` gets populated, let's take a look at the members the class provides for accessing the contents of a `Bag`. The following code includes a smattering of those common methods that you would use to retrieve one or more items from a `Bag`:

```vb
[VB code]
Public Function FindGreaterThan50(ByVal d As Double) As Boolean
    Dim retVal As Boolean = False
    If (d > 50.0) Then
        retVal = True
    End If
    Return retVal
End Function

Public Sub GetItemsTests()
    Dim doubleBag As Bag(Of Double)
    Dim doubleList As New List(Of Double)(New Double() {232.23, 1.12, 99.21, _
                                                        14.42, 99.21, 1.12})

    doubleBag = New Bag(Of Double)(doubleList)

    Dim foundItems As IEnumerable(Of Double) = _
                            doubleBag.FindAll(AddressOf FindGreaterThan50)
    DumpItems(Of Double)(foundItems)

    Dim count As Int32 = doubleBag.CountWhere(AddressOf FindGreaterThan50)
    Console.WriteLine("Num Items > 50 {0}", count)

    Dim found As Boolean = doubleBag.Exists(AddressOf FindGreaterThan50)
    Console.WriteLine("Items > 50 returns {0}", found)

    Dim uniqueDoubles As IEnumerable(Of Double)
    uniqueDoubles = doubleBag.DistinctItems()
    DumpItems(uniqueDoubles)

    Dim doubleVal As Double
    Dim repItem As Double = doubleBag.GetRepresentativeItem(99.21, doubleVal)
    Console.WriteLine("Representative Item: {0}", doubleVal)
End Sub
```

```csharp
[C# code]
public bool FindGreaterThan50(Double d) {
    bool retVal = false;
    if (d > 50.0)
        retVal = true;
    return retVal;
}

public void GetItemsTests() {
    Bag<Double> doubleBag;
    doubleBag = new Bag<Double>(new Double[] {232.23, 1.12, 99.21, 14.42, 99.21,
                                              1.12});

    IEnumerable<Double> foundItems = doubleBag.FindAll(FindGreaterThan50);
    DumpItems(foundItems);
```

```
        int count = doubleBag.CountWhere(FindGreaterThan50);
        Console.WriteLine("Num Items > 50 {0}", count);

        bool found = doubleBag.Exists(FindGreaterThan50);
        Console.WriteLine("Items > 50 returns {0}", found);

        IEnumerable<Double> uniqueDoubles = doubleBag.DistinctItems();
        DumpItems(uniqueDoubles);

        Double doubleVal;
        Double repItem = doubleBag.GetRepresentativeItem(99.21, out doubleVal);
        Console.WriteLine("Representative Item: {0}", doubleVal);
    }
```

When working with a `Bags` (and `Sets`), you'll tend to find yourself operating more on the container as a whole. So, even though the `Bag` supports an `Item` interface for accessing the container's individual items, the example here focuses more on those methods that return a set of items that meet specific criteria.

The call to `FindAll()`, for example, supplies a `Predicate<T>` delegate that finds all items in the collection that have a value greater than 50. In this scenario, this method will actually return the following values:

```
1. Value : 232.23
2. Value : 99.21
3. Value : 99.21
```

You'll notice that, because `Bags` can contain duplicate values, this call actually returns a separate item for each entry in the `Bag` — even if it's a duplicate. This explains why the example returns two entries with the value of 99.21.

The `CountWhere()` and `Exists()` methods are also included in this example, both of which use a `Predicate<T>` delegate to evaluate the contents of the `Bag`. `CountWhereTrue()` returns a count of the number of items (including duplicates) that meet the criteria specified by the predicate while `Exists()` simply returns `true` if any item in the `Bag` meets the predicate's criteria.

There may also be times when you'll be interested in ignoring the duplicates that might exist in a `Bag`. In these situations, you can use the `DistinctItems()` method, which will return a collection containing a single item for each unique object in a `Bag`.

The last bit of this example employs the `GetRepresentativeItem()` method to retrieve the representative instance of a specific item in the `Bag`. This method accepts the target item as its first parameter and returns the found value in the second parameter.

## Removing Items

The `Bag` class supports the `Remove()`, `Clear()`, and `RemoveAll()` methods that you'd typically expect to find as part of any container. The usage of these methods conforms to the rules and patterns that you've seen with the DCL classes. Still, here's a quick look at these methods in action:

```
[VB code]
Public Function HasWordItem(ByVal str As String) As Boolean
    Dim retVal As Boolean = False
    If (str.Contains("Item") = True) Then
        retVal = True
    End If

    Return retVal
End Function

Public Sub RemoveItemsTests()
    Dim strBag As Bag(Of String)
    Dim strList As New List(Of String)(New String() {"Item1", "Item2", "Item3", _
                                                     "Item3", "Item4", "Item4"})

    strBag = New Bag(Of String)(strList)

    Dim removed As Boolean = strBag.Remove("Item1")
    Console.WriteLine("Items was removed: 0}", removed)

    Console.WriteLine("Bag contents before call")
    DumpItems(Of String)(strBag)
    strBag.RemoveAllCopies("Item4")
    DumpItems(Of String)(strBag)
    Console.WriteLine("Bag contents after call")

    Dim removedItems As IEnumerable(Of String) = _
                                strBag.RemoveAll(AddressOf HasWordItem)
    DumpItems(removedItems)
End Sub
```

```
[C# code]
public bool HasWordItem(String str) {
    bool retVal = false;
    if (str.Contains("Item") == true)
        retVal = true;
    return retVal;
}

public void RemoveItemsTests() {
    Bag<String> strBag;
    strBag = new Bag<String>(new String[] { "Item1", "Item2", "Item3", "Item3",
                                            "Item4", "Item4"});

    bool removed = strBag.Remove("Item1");
    Console.WriteLine("Items was removed: {0}", removed);

    Console.WriteLine("Bag contents before call");
    DumpItems(strBag);
    strBag.RemoveAllCopies("Item4");
    DumpItems(strBag);
    Console.WriteLine("Bag contents after call");

    IEnumerable<String> removedItems = strBag.RemoveAll(HasWordItem);
    DumpItems(removedItems);
}
```

The only real twist introduced here is the `RemoveAllCopies()` method. Because `Bag` objects can include duplicate objects, the `Bag` class needs to provide a mechanism to remove all the items for a specific value. So, this example calls `RemoveAllCopies()` with the "Item4" value, which causes both instances of "Item4" to be removed from the `Bag`.

## Performing Set Operations

Much of the real value in using `Bags` is encompassed in the collection of set-based methods that are supported by the class. In fact, without this set of methods, the `Bag` class would be just another variant of `Collection<T>`. The whole point in selecting a `Bag` as a container is to enable you to perform operations that evaluate the contents of the container as a group.

To better understand what I'm getting at here, take a look at some examples that exercise the set-related methods that are part of the `Bag` class:

```
[VB code]
Dim strBag1 As Bag(Of String)
Dim strList As New List(Of String)(New String() {"Item1","Item2","Item3","Item3"})
strBag1 = New Bag(Of String)(strList)
DumpItems(Of String)(strBag1)


Dim strBag2 As Bag(Of String)
strList = New List(Of String)(New String() {"Item1", "Item2", "Item3", _
                                            "Item3", "Item3", "Item4"})
strBag2 = New Bag(Of String)(strList)
DumpItems(Of String)(strBag2)


Dim isSubset As Boolean = strBag1.IsSubsetOf(strBag2)
Dim isSuperset As Boolean = strBag2.IsSupersetOf(strBag1)


Dim unionBag As Bag(Of String) = strBag1.Union(strBag2)
DumpItems(Of String)(unionBag)


strBag1.UnionWith(strBag2)
DumpItems(Of String)(strBag1)


Dim doubleBag1 As Bag(Of Double)
Dim doubleList As New List(Of Double)(New Double() {232.23, 1.12, 99.21, 14.42, _
                                                    99.21, 1.12})
doubleBag1 = New Bag(Of Double)(doubleList)


Dim doubleBag2 As Bag(Of Double)
doubleList = New List(Of Double)(New Double() {321.42, 14.42, 1.12, 74.32, _
                                               232.23, 9010.4{1})
doubleBag2 = New Bag(Of Double)(doubleList)


Dim sumBag As Bag(Of Double) = doubleBag1.Sum(doubleBag2)
DumpItems(Of Double)(sumBag)


Dim intersectionBag As Bag(Of Double) = doubleBag1.Intersection(doubleBag2)
DumpItems(Of Double)(intersectionBag)


Dim symmetricDiffBag As Bag(Of Double) = doubleBag1.SymmetricDifference(doubleBag2)
DumpItems(Of Double)(symmetricDiffBag)
```

```
[C# code]
Bag<String> strBag1;
strBag1 = new Bag<String>(new String[] { "Item1", "Item2", "Item3", "Item3" });
DumpItems(strBag1);

Bag<String> strBag2;
strBag2 = new Bag<String>(new String[] { "Item1", "Item2", "Item3",
                                         "Item3", "Item3", "Item4" });
DumpItems(strBag2);

bool isSubset = strBag1.IsSubsetOf(strBag2);
bool isSuperset = strBag2.IsSupersetOf(strBag1);

Bag<String> unionBag = strBag1.Union(strBag2);
DumpItems(unionBag);

strBag1.UnionWith(strBag2);
DumpItems(strBag1);

Bag<Double> doubleBag1;
doubleBag1 = new Bag<Double>(new Double[] {232.23,1.12,99.21,14.42,99.21,1.12});

Bag<Double> doubleBag2;
doubleBag2 = new Bag<Double>(new Double[]{321.42,14.42,1.12,74.32,232.23,9010.41});

Bag<Double> sumBag = doubleBag1.Sum(doubleBag2);
DumpItems(sumBag);

Bag<Double> intersectionBag = doubleBag1.Intersection(doubleBag2);
DumpItems(intersectionBag);

Bag<Double> symmetricDiffBag = doubleBag1.SymmetricDifference(doubleBag2);
DumpItems(symmetricDiffBag);
```

This example starts out by creating and populating two Bags that are used with the IsSubsetOf() and IsSupersetOf() methods. IsSubsetOf() takes the items from strBag1 and determines if these items represent a valid subset of strBag2. Because each of the items in strBag1 can also be found in strBag2, this method returns true. This also means the call to IsSupersetOf() will return true.

Now, when evaluating the subset or superset of a Bag with duplicate entries, the rules are fairly relaxed. As long as at least one matching item is found in the corresponding collection, the method will still return true. However, if you want to be more precise, you can use the IsProperSubsetOf() and IsProperSupersetOf() methods. These two methods require the number of items in each Bag to match exactly.

These same two Bags (strBag1 and strBag2) are also operated on by the Union() and UnionWith() methods. Union() will create a new bag that represents the union between two Bags, where every item in the two Bags is placed into the resulting Bag. It's important to note that a union between two Bags with duplicate items will not result in the sum of the items in each of the two Bags. The preceding example illustrates how this gets handled. The result of the union of strBag1 and strBag2 is as follows:

```
1. Value : Item1
2. Value : Item2
3. Value : Item3
4. Value : Item3
5. Value : Item3
6. Value : Item4
```

Even though one instance of "Item3" existed in `strBag1` and three instances of "Item3" were in `strBag2`, the resulting union only yielded three instances of "Item3." The union operation determines which `Bag` has the greatest number of duplicate items and uses that new count as the number of items that will appear in the newly created `Bag`. `UnionWith()` performs the same operation but places the resulting union in the contents of the calling `Bag`. So, for this example, the call to `strBag1.UnionWith(StrBag2)` ends up replacing `strBag1`'s contents with the union of the two bags.

> The Power Collections library often provides two variants of each method that operates on a `Bag`. For example, it includes both `Union()` and `UnionWith()` methods. The `xxxWith()` method always modifies the calling object, whereas the "non-with" methods will always leave the calling object in tact.

The `Sum()` method, on the other hand, simply does a complete merge of all the items in the two `Bags`. So, in the preceding example, the call to sum two `Bags` (each with six items) yields a new bag that contains 12 items. In this case duplicates don't matter. The result of this sum, then, produces the following output:

```
 1. Value : 232.23
 2. Value : 232.23
 3. Value : 14.42
 4. Value : 14.42
 5. Value : 1.12
 6. Value : 1.12
 7. Value : 1.12
 8. Value : 74.32
 9. Value : 9010.41
10. Value : 99.21
11. Value : 99.21
12. Value : 321.42
```

Next, take a look at the `Intersection()` method. This method identifies only those items that are common to the two `Bags`, returning a single entry for each item that is identified. Given this definition, consider what will be produced from the preceding example:

```
1. Value : 232.23
2. Value : 14.42
3. Value : 1.12
```

Notice that—even though 1.12 appears multiple times in one of the `Bags`—it only appears once in the resulting `Bag`.

Whereas the `Intersection()` method is focused finding points in common between `Bags`, the `SymmetricDifference()` method is used to determine the differences between two `Bags`. When it calculates the difference between the `Bags` in the previous example, it yields the following:

```
1.  Value : 9010.41
2.  Value : 321.42
3.  Value : 1.12
4.  Value : 74.32
5.  Value : 99.21
6.  Value : 99.21
```

You'll notice that this list only contains items that belong, exclusively, to one of the two Bags. The value 9010.41, for example, only appears in one of the two Bags and therefore meets the difference criteria. The same is true for 321.42 and 74.32. What about the other values that appear here, though? Why does 1.12 appear here? It's in both Bags after all. Well, the difference method looks at the counts for each unique item. In this example, because the value 1.12 appears twice in one Bag and only once in the other, the difference between the two Bags will be one item. The value 99.21 also appears twice in just one of the Bags, which accounts for it showing up twice here.

# BigList<T>

The name of the BigList<T> class says it all. This class is very similar to the List<T> class that is found in the System.Collections.Generic namespace. However, its underlying implementation is optimized for managing large lists (greater that 100 items).

The BigList<T> class attempts to overcome some of the typical performance issues associated with lists. Lists do fine with small data, but their need to continually readjust the items in the collection tends to get expensive as the size of the collection grows.

In order to enhance performance for larger collections, the BigList<T> class had to make some trade-offs that impact its efficiency when dealing with smaller collections. So, the rule of thumb here is: don't use BigList<T> for collections with fewer than 100 items.

The following table is an alphabetical listing of all the methods and properties that are associated with the BigList<T> class.

| Method or Property | Description |
| --- | --- |
| Add() | Adds a single item to the end of the collection. |
| AddRange() | Adds a collection of items to the end of the collection. |
| AddRangeToFront() | Adds a collection of items to the front of the collection. |
| AddToFront() | Adds a single item to the front of the collection. |
| BinarySearch() | Performs a binary search on the list for the specified item. |
| Clear() | Empties the contents of the collection. |
| Clone() | Creates and returns a shallow copy of all the items in the collection. |
| CloneContents() | Creates and returns a deep copy of all the items in the list. |
| Count | Gets the number of items in the collection. |
| GetEnumerator() | Gets an IEnumerator<T> representation of the items in the collection. |

| Method or Property | Description |
| --- | --- |
| GetRange() | Gets a subset of the items from the collection starting at specified index. |
| Insert() | Inserts a single item into the collection at the specified index. |
| InsertRange() | Inserts a collection of items into the collection at the specified index. |
| Item | Index-based access to retrieve or update items in the collection. |
| RemoveAt() | Removes the item at the specified index. |
| RemoveRange() | Removes a range of items starting at the specified index. |
| Reverse() | Reverse the order of the items in the list. |
| Sorts() | Sorts the items in the list. |

## Construction and Population

The constructors for the BigList<T> class offer some additional overloaded options that come in handy when creating large collections. The primary addition you'll discover here is the ability to have the constructor add multiple copies of a given collection as part of its construction. Here's a brief look at a few of these constructors just to show what they enable:

```
[VB code]
Dim doubleList1 As BigList(Of Double)
Dim doubleList As New List(Of Double)(New Double() {12.32, 939.39, 3.99})
doubleList1 = New BigList(Of Double)(doubleList)
DumpItems(Of Double)(doubleList1)

Dim doubleList2 As BigList(Of Double)
doubleList2 = New BigList(Of Double)(doubleList1, 3)
DumpItems(Of Double)(doubleList2)

Dim strValues As String() = New String() {"val1", "val2", "val3"}
Dim strList As BigList(Of String)
strList = New BigList(Of String)(strValues, 2)
DumpItems(Of String)(strList)

strList.Add("val4")
DumpItems(Of String)(strList)

strList.AddToFront("frontVal")
DumpItems(Of String)(strList)

Dim listVals As New List(Of String)(New String() {"frontVal1", "frontVal2"})
strList.AddRangeToFront(listVals)

[C# code]
BigList<Double> doubleList1;
doubleList1 = new BigList<Double>(new Double[] { 12.32, 939.39, 3.99 });
DumpItems(doubleList1);
```

```
BigList<Double> doubleList2;
doubleList2 = new BigList<Double>(doubleList1, 3);
DumpItems(doubleList2);

String[] strValues = new String[] {"val1", "val2", "val3"};
BigList<String> strList;
strList = new BigList<String>(strValues, 2);
DumpItems(strList);

strList.Add("val4");
DumpItems(strList);

strList.AddToFront("frontVal");
DumpItems(strList);

strList.AddRangeToFront(new String[] { "frontVal1", "frontVal2" });
DumpItems(strList);
```

The example starts by creating a simple BigList<Double> collection that is then populated with a list of double values. The BigList object supports construction with any collection that implements the IEnumerable<T> interface.

Once you have this initial collection created and populated, you use it to call yet another version of the constructor. This version accepts an IEnumerable<T> collection as well as a second parameter that indicates how many copies of this first collection should be inserted. So, in this example, you have three items in your collection and you've indicated that you want three copies of that collection to be placed into your new BigList collection.

The remaining calls here should be relatively straightforward. The Add() method just adds a new item to the end of the list, and AddToFront() inserts an item into the front of the collection. An example of the AddRangeToFront() method is included to illustrate how a set of items can be added to a specific position within the collection.

## Accessing Items

BigList<T> does a good job supporting all the common mechanisms that are used for accessing the contents of the collection. It also provides a few additional methods that are worth highlighting. They appear in the following example:

```
[VB code]
Dim strList As New BigList(Of String)()

If (strList.Count = 0) Then
    Console.WriteLine("Empty List")
End If

Dim strList2 As New List(Of String)(New String() {"Bob", "Joe", "Bill"})
strList.AddRange(strList2)

Dim str As String = strList(1)
Console.WriteLine("Item 1 = {0}", str)

Dim strVals As IEnumerable(Of String) = strList.GetRange(1, 2)
DumpItems(strVals)
```

```
For Each strVal As String In strList
    Console.WriteLine("Val = {0}", strVal)
Next
```

```
[C# code]
BigList<String> strList = new BigList<String>(); ;

if (strList.Count == 0)
    Console.WriteLine("Empty List");

strList.AddRange(new String[] {"Bob", "Joe", "Bill"});

String str = strList[1];
Console.WriteLine("Item 1 = {0}", str);

IEnumerable<String> strVals = strList.GetRange(1, 2);
DumpItems(strVals);

foreach (String strVal in strList)
    Console.WriteLine("Val = {0}", strVal);
```

You'll notice this example uses the count property to determine if any items are in the list. The example also uses the familiar index-based Item property to demonstrate the fact that this interface is still accessible for retrieving and updating individual list elements.

The last item here, GetRange(), allows you to get a subset of items from the list starting at a specific index. For this scenario, you get two items starting at an index of 1.

## Removing Items

To wrap up the discussion of BigList<T>, you need to look at the methods that can be used to remove one or more items from your list. The methods that are used for removing items follow the same patterns you've seen in the previous examples. The Remove() method finds an item that matches the supplied item parameter and removes it from the list. In contrast, the RemoveAt() method allows you to remove items based on their index. The last option is to remove multiple items with the RemoveRange() method. This method removes the specified number of items starting at the indicated index. The following provides a basic example of these methods in action:

```
[VB code]
Dim intList As BigList(Of Int32)
Dim listVals As New List(Of Int32)(New Int32() {13, 883, 92})
intList = New BigList(Of Int32)(listVals)
intList.Insert(1, 444)
intList.Insert(1, 333)

listVals = New List(Of Int32)(New Int32() {111, 883, 0})
intList.InsertRange(3, listVals)

intList.Remove(883)
DumpItems(Of Int32)(intList)
```

```
intList.RemoveAt(2)
DumpItems(Of Int32)(intList)

intList.RemoveRange(0, 3)
DumpItems(Of Int32)(intList)
```

```
[C# code]
BigList<Int32> intList;
intList = new BigList<Int32>(new Int32[] { 13, 883, 92 });
intList.Insert(1, 444);
intList.Insert(1, 333);

intList.InsertRange(3, new Int32[] { 111, 883, 0 });

intList.Remove(883);
DumpItems(intList);

intList.RemoveAt(2);
DumpItems(intList);

intList.RemoveRange(0, 3);
DumpItems(intList);
```

# BinaryPredicate<T> (Delegate)

The BinaryPredicate<T> delegate is simply an alternative version of the Predicate<T> delegate that is part of the System.Collections.Generic namespace. Whereas Predicate<T> only accepts one type parameter as part of its signature, the BinaryPredicate<T> class accepts two, both of which are of type T.

# CollectionBase<T>

CollectionBase<T> is an abstract base class implementation of the ICollection<T> interface that provides you with a good basis for implementing your own custom collections. The primary goal of this class is to provide an implementation of the common concepts that are typically shared by collections without imposing any restrictions on your derived classes.

At a minimum, all classes that extend this base class must implement the GetEnumerator(), Clear(), Remove(), Add(), and Count members. Essentially, you're responsible for implementing any member that operates on the collection's underlying representation of the data.

The following table is an alphabetical listing of all the methods and properties that are associated with the CollectionBase<T> class.

| Method or Property | Description |
|---|---|
| Add() | Adds an item to the collection. This member must be overridden. |
| AsReadOnly() | Returns a read only representation of the collection. |
| Clear() | Removes all items from the collection. This member must be overridden. |

| Method or Property | Description |
| --- | --- |
| Contains() | Returns true if the collection contains the specified item, using IComparable<T>.Equals or Object.Equals to identify matching items. |
| ConvertAll<TOutput>() | Converts all the items in the collection to the type specified by TOutput, using the supplied Converter to perform the conversion of each item. |
| CopyTo() | Copies all the items in the collection into the provided array. |
| Count | Returns the number of items in the collection. |
| CountWhere() | Returns the number of items in the collection that meet the criteria defined by the supplied predicate. |
| Exists() | Determines if the collection contains at least one item that meets the criteria defined by the supplied predicate. |
| FindAll() | Finds every item in the collection that meet the criteria defined by the supplied predicate. |
| ForEach() | Applies the supplied action to each item in the collection. |
| GetEnumerator() | Gets an IEnumerator<T> iterator that can be used to iterate over all the values from the list. This member must be overridden. |
| Remove() | Removes the specified item from the collection. This member must be overridden. |
| RemoveAll() | Removes all the items in the collection that meet the criteria defined by the supplied predicate. |
| ToArray() | Uses CopyTo() to create an array of all the items in the collection. |
| ToString() | Creates a string that represents all the items in the collection. |
| TrueForAll() | Returns true if all the items in the collection meet the criteria defined by the supplied predicate. |

## Deque<T>

The System.Collections.Generic namespace provides a Queue<T> class, but it doesn't include a double-ended queue. Fortunately, the Power Collections library fills this gap with its Deque<T> class. This class was primarily introduced as an alternative to a list-based implementation. In the same way that the BigList<T> class was added to provide efficiencies for large collections, Deque<T> was also added to overcome similar performance issues. Each time an item is inserted into the head of a list, for example, all the items in the collection must be adjusted to account for this item. Deque's purpose in life is to overcome this inefficiency.

The following table is an alphabetical listing of all the methods and properties that are associated with the Deque<T> class.

| Method or Property | Description |
|---|---|
| Add() | Adds a new item to the end of the Deque. |
| AddManyToBack() | Adds a collection of item to the end of the Deque. |
| AddManyToFront() | Adds a collection of items to the head of the Deque. |
| AddToBack() | Adds a single item to the end of the Deque. |
| AddToFront() | Adds a single item to the front of the Deque. |
| Capacity | The number of items that can be placed in the Deque before its size must be adjusted to accommodate new items. |
| Clear() | Removes all items from the Deque. |
| Clone() | Returns a new Deque that is a copy of the current Deque. |
| CloneContents() | Makes a deep copy of the Deque. |
| CopyTo() | Copies the contents of the Deque to an array. |
| Count | Returns the number of items in the Deque. |
| GetAtBack() | Retrieves a single item from the end of the Deque. |
| GetAtFront() | Retrieves a single item from the head of the Deque. |
| GetEnumerator() | Gets an IEnumerator<T> iterator that can be used to iterate over all the values from the Deque. |
| Insert() | Inserts new items into the Deque at the specified index. |
| InsertRange() | Inserts a collection of items into the Deque at the specified index. |
| Item | Index-based access to retrieve or update an individual item in the Deque. |
| RemoveAt() | Removes the item at the specified index. |
| RemoveFromBack() | Removes the item that is at the end of the Deque. |
| RemoveFromFront() | Removes the item that is at the front of the Deque. |
| RemoveRange() | Removes the indicated number of items starting at the specified index. |
| TrimToSize() | Reduces the capacity to make it match the current number of items in the Deque. |

## Adding Items

When populating a Deque<T> class, you typically find yourself wanting to append items to the front or back of the queue. To accommodate this pattern, the Deque<T> class supplements the traditional Add() method with AddToFront() and AddToBack() methods that provide a quick a and easy way to work with both ends of the queue. Here's an example that exercises these methods:

```
[VB code]
Dim personDeque As New Deque(Of Person)()

personDeque.Add(New Person("Napolean", 111))
personDeque.Add(New Person("Kip", 321))
personDeque.Add(New Person("Jon", 423))
personDeque.Add(New Person("Effren", 732))
DumpItems(Of Person)(personDeque)

personDeque.AddToFront(New Person("Sandy", 931))
personDeque.AddToBack(New Person("Tina", 131))
DumpItems(Of Person)(personDeque)

personDeque.AddManyToFront(New Person() {New Person("Diedrich", 323), _
                                         New Person("Haylie", 329)})
DumpItems(Of Person)(personDeque)

personDeque.InsertRange(2, New Person() {New Person("Ellen", 14), _
                                         New Person("Bracken", 762)})
DumpItems(Of Person)(personDeque)
```

```
[C# code]
Deque<Person> personDeque = new Deque<Person>();

personDeque.Add(new Person("Napolean", 111));
personDeque.Add(new Person("Kip", 321));
personDeque.Add(new Person("Jon", 423));
personDeque.Add(new Person("Effren", 732));
DumpItems(personDeque);

personDeque.AddToFront(new Person("Sandy", 931));
personDeque.AddToBack(new Person("Tina", 131));
DumpItems(personDeque);

personDeque.AddManyToFront(new Person[] {new Person("Diedrich", 323),
                                         new Person("Haylie", 329)});
DumpItems(personDeque);

personDeque.InsertRange(2, new Person[] { new Person("Ellen", 14),
                                          new Person("Bracken", 762) });
DumpItems(personDeque);
```

For this example, you populate your initial Deque with a series of calls to the Add() method where each new item added is appended to the back of the queue. You then employ AddToFront() and AddToBack() to add individual items to the front and back of the queue, respectively. A call to AddManyToFront() is included to illustrate how a collection of items can be selectively added to the Deque.

The last portion of this example uses the InsertRange() method to demonstrate how items can be inserted directly into the middle of a Deque.

## Accessing and Removing Items

Deque<T> also includes a set of queue-friendly methods for accessing and removing items. The signatures of these methods map fairly directly to the methods that were used in the previous example. Specifically, the class includes GetAtFront() and GetAtBack() methods for accessing data and

`RemoveFromFront()` and `RemoveFromBack()` methods for deleting items from the queue. The following provides an example of the application of these methods:

```
[VB code]
Dim personDeque As New Deque(Of Person)()
personDeque.Add(New Person("Napolean", 111))
personDeque.Add(New Person("Kip", 321))
personDeque.Add(New Person("Jon", 423))
personDeque.Add(New Person("Shondrella", 482))
personDeque.Add(New Person("Tina", 131))

Dim dequePerson As Person = personDeque(1)
Console.WriteLine("Person = {0}", dequePerson)

dequePerson = personDeque.GetAtFront()
Console.WriteLine("Person = {0}", dequePerson)

dequePerson = personDeque.GetAtBack()
Console.WriteLine("Person = {0}", dequePerson)

personDeque.RemoveAt(1)
personDeque.RemoveFromBack()
personDeque.RemoveFromFront()

personDeque.RemoveRange(0, 2)
DumpItems(Of Person)(personDeque)
```

```
[C# code]
Deque<Person> personDeque = new Deque<Person>();
personDeque.Add(new Person("Napolean", 111));
personDeque.Add(new Person("Kip", 321));
personDeque.Add(new Person("Jon", 423));
personDeque.Add(new Person("Shondrella", 482));
personDeque.Add(new Person("Tina", 131));

Person dequePerson = personDeque[1];
Console.WriteLine("Person = {0}", dequePerson);

dequePerson = personDeque.GetAtFront();
Console.WriteLine("Person = {0}", dequePerson);

dequePerson = personDeque.GetAtBack();
Console.WriteLine("Person = {0}", dequePerson);

personDeque.RemoveAt(1);
personDeque.RemoveFromBack();
personDeque.RemoveFromFront();
DumpItems(personDeque);

personDeque.RemoveRange(0, 2);
DumpItems(personDeque);
```

There are no real special caveats associated with using these methods. To round things out, the example also leverages the `Item` interface to randomly access a single item with the queue. There are also additional options for removing items in the example. `RemoveAt()` and `RemoveRange()` both employ an index-based approach to removing items, allowing you to remove a single item or subset of items at a given index position.

# DictionaryBase<TKey, TValue>

Dictionary<TKey, TValue>, which extends the library's CollectionBase<T> class, provides developers with an abstract implementation of the IDictionary<TKey, TValue> interface. Its goal is to serve as a good starting point for any derived dictionary types you may choose to implement. For the Power Collections library, it serves as the base class for the OrderedDictionary<TKey, TValue> collection.

At a minimum, all classes that extend this base class must implement the GetEnumerator(), Clear(), Remove(), TryGetValue(), and Item members. Essentially, your descendant class is responsible for implementing any member that operates on the dictionary's underlying representation of the data.

The following table is an alphabetical listing of all the methods and properties that are associated with the DictionaryBase<TKey, TValue> class.

| Method or Property | Description |
| --- | --- |
| Add() | Adds a new key/value pair to the dictionary. |
| AsReadOnly() | Returns a read only representation of this dictionary. |
| Clear() | Removes all items from the dictionary. This method must be overridden. |
| Contains() | Returns true if the collection contains and item that matches the key that is supplied as a key/value pair. This method uses Object.Equals to compare the key values. |
| ContainsKey() | Returns true if the collection contains and item that matches the supplied key. This method uses Object.Equals to compare the key values. |
| Item | Indexer that is used to access or update individual items in the dictionary. This member must be overridden. |
| Keys | Returns an ICollection<T> collection containing all the keys in the dictionary. |
| Remove() | Removes the specified item (key or key/value pair) from the dictionary. This method must be overridden. |
| ToString() | Creates a string that represents all the items in the dictionary. |
| TryGetValue() | Attempts to get the value associated with the supplied key. This method must be overridden. |
| Values | Returns an ICollection<T> collection containing all the values in the dictionary. |

# ListBase<T>

The ListBase<T> class, which extends CollectionBase<T>, provides an abstract implementation of the IList<T> interface. It serves as the base class for both the BigList<T> and Deque<T> classes in the Power Collections library and represents a good starting point for introducing any of your own list-based derived types.

At a minimum, all classes that extend this base class must implement the Clear(), RemoveAt(), Insert(), Count, and Item indexer members. Essentially, your descendant class is responsible for implementing any member that operates on the dictionary's underlying representation of the data.

The following table is an alphabetical listing of all the methods and properties that are associated with the List<T> class.

| Method or Property | Description |
|---|---|
| Add() | Adds a new item to the end of the list. |
| AsReadOnly() | Returns a read-only representation of this list. |
| Clear() | Removes all items from the list. This method must be overridden. |
| Contains() | Returns true if the list contains an item that matches the supplied item. |
| CopyTo() | Copies the items from this list to an array, retaining the current order of the items. |
| Count | Gets the number of items in the list. This method must be overridden. |
| Find() | Finds the first item in the list that meets the criteria defined by the supplied predicate. |
| FindIndex() | Finds the index of the first item in the list that meets the criteria defined by the supplied predicate. |
| FindLast() | Finds the last item in the list that meets the criteria defined by the supplied predicate. |
| FindLastIndex() | Finds the index of the last item in the list that meets the criteria defined by the supplied predicate. |
| GetEnumerator() | Gets an IEnumerator<T> iterator that can be used to iterate over all the values from the list. |
| IndexOf() | Gets the index of the first item in the list that is equal to the specified item. |
| Insert() | Inserts the supplied item at the specified index. This method must be overridden. |
| Item | Indexer that is used to access or update individual items in the list. This member must be overridden. |
| LastIndexOf() | Finds the index of the last item in the list that is equal to the supplied item. |

| Method or Property | Description |
|---|---|
| Range() | Returns a subset of items within the collection that fall within the specified range. |
| Remove() | Finds the first item that is equal to the specified item and removes it from the list. This method must be overridden. |
| RemoveAt() | Removes the item at the specified index. |
| TryFind() | Attempts to find the first item in the list that meets the criteria defined by the supplied predicate. |
| TryFindLast() | Attempts to find the last item in the list that meets the criteria defined by the supplied predicate. |

# MultiDictionary<TKey, TValue>

The MultiDictionary<TKey, TValue> class provides you with yet another twist on the dictionary container. Although a traditional dictionary allows you to associate a single value with each key, the MultiDictionary<TKey, TValue> allows you to associate multiple values with a key.

The following table is an alphabetical listing of all the methods and properties that are included in the MultiDictionary<TKey, TValue> class:

| Method or Property | Description |
|---|---|
| Add() | Adds a new item to the dictionary. |
| Clear() | Removes all entries from the dictionary. |
| Clone() | Returns a shallow copy of all the items in the dictionary. |
| CloneContents() | Returns a deep copy of all the items in the dictionary. |
| Contains() | Returns true if the dictionary contains an item that matches the supplied item. |
| ContainsKey() | Returns true if the dictionary contains an item that matches the supplied key. |
| Count | Gets the number of items in the dictionary. Each key/value combination (for a single key) is counted as a separate item. |
| KeyComparer | Returns the IEqualityComparer<T> that is used when comparing keys in this dictionary. |
| Remove() | Removes the entry associated with the specified key. If a value is supplied with that key, the value associated with that key is removed from the values collection that corresponds to that key. |
| ValueComparer | Returns the IEqualityComparer<T> that is used when comparing values in this dictionary. |

The signature of this dictionary doesn't look all the different than that of the Dictionary<TKey, TValue> class. The differences really show up in the underlying behavior. Let's look at a simple example to see how these differences influence your interaction with the dictionary.

```vb
[VB code]
Public Sub LoadAndAccessDictionary()
    Dim dict As New MultiDictionary(Of String, String)(False)

    dict.Add("Key1", "Val1")
    dict.Add("Key1", "Val1")
    dict.Add("Key1", "Val2")
    dict.Add("Key1", "Val3")
    dict.Add("Key1", "Val4")

    Dim values As IEnumerable(Of String)
    values = dict.Values
    For Each val As String In values
        Console.WriteLine("Added values is: {0}", val)
    Next

    dict.Remove("Key1", "Val2")
    values = dict.Values
    For Each val As String In values
        Console.WriteLine("After Remove: {0}", val)
    Next

    Dim removeVals As String() = {"Val1", "Val3"}
    dict.RemoveMany("Key1", removeVals)
    For Each val As String In values
        Console.WriteLine("After RemoveMany: {0}", val)
    Next

    dict.Remove("Key1", "Val4")
    Console.WriteLine("Items in dictionary: {0}", dict.Count)
End Sub
```

```csharp
[C# code]
public void LoadAndAccessDictionary() {
    MultiDictionary<string, string> dict;
    dict = new MultiDictionary<string, string>(false);

    dict.Add("Key1", "Val1");
    dict.Add("Key1", "Val1");
    dict.Add("Key1", "Val2");
    dict.Add("Key1", "Val3");
    dict.Add("Key1", "Val4");

    IEnumerable<string> values;
    values = dict.Values;
    foreach (string val in values)
        Console.WriteLine("Added values is: {0}", val);
```

```
        dict.Remove("Key1", "Val2");
        values = dict.Values;
        foreach (string val in values)
            Console.WriteLine("After Remove: {0}", val);

        string[] removeVals = {"Val1", "Val3"};
        dict.RemoveMany("Key1", removeVals);
        foreach (string val in values)
            Console.WriteLine("After RemoveMany: {0}", val);

        dict.Remove("Key1", "Val4");
        Console.WriteLine("Items in dictionary: {0}", dict.Count);
    }
```

This example starts out by filling its dictionary with a series of string values. You'll notice that the example attempts to add a series of different values using the same key value, Key1. Now, before MultiDictionary<TKey, TValue> came along, each one of these calls to the Add() method would have replaced the prior value with the new value. However, because this new dictionary allows you to associate multiple values with a key, each of they values is successfully added. Well, that's almost true. The MultiDictionary<TKey, TValue> class still requires values to be unique. So, when you attempt to add the values Val1 the second time, this value is not added.

Next, the example provides an example of how you can retrieve data from your dictionary. Now that the dictionary can have multiple values for a single key, the dictionary's interface must accommodate this new multiplicity. In the example, this is achieved by accessing the dictionary's Values property, which returns all the values for all the keys in the collection.

The example also highlights a difference with the Remove() method. For the MultiDictionary<TKey, TValue>, you must supply both a key and a value when you want to remove a specific, individual value. You also have the option of removing multiple values for a key by supplying a collection of values to be removed. This collection is passed with the key to the RemoveMany() method to remove the specified items.

One last call is made to remove at the end of the example. This last call ends up removing the last value associated with Key1 and, because no values remain associated with the key, it is removed from the collection. This is verified by checking the number of items that remain in the collection after the removal. The count returned here is 0, which is what you should be expecting.

## MultiDictionaryBase<TKey, TValue>

MultiDictionaryBase<TKey, TValue> provides you with a base class that can be easily extended to introduce your own customer MultiDictionary<TKey, TValue> implementation. This class, like the other base classes provided by the Power Collections library, includes much of the core functionality that will be immediately useful to classes that specialize in this type.

The following table is an alphabetical listing of all the methods and properties that are associated with the MultiDictionaryBase<TKey, TValue> class.

| Method or Property | Description |
|---|---|
| Add() | Adds a new key/value pair to the dictionary. If values already exist for the specified key, the value will be added to the values collection associated with this key. |
| AddMany() | Adds a key and a collection of one or more values that are associated with that key. |
| Clear() | Removes all items from the dictionary. This method must be overridden. |
| Contains() | Returns true if the specified key/value pair exists within the dictionary. |
| ContainsKey() | Returns true if the specified key exists within the dictionary. |
| GetEnumerator() | Returns the IEnumerator<T> with all the keys in this dictionary. |
| Item | Indexer returns the collections of values associated with the supplied key. |
| Keys | Returns a collection containing all the keys in the dictionary. |
| KeyValuePairs | Returns a collection of all the KeyValuePair objects in the dictionary. If multiple values exists for a key, each value will appear as part of a separate KeyValuePair entry in the returned collection. |
| Remove() | Removes the specified item (key or key/value pair) from the dictionary. This method must be overridden. |
| RemoveMany() | Removes the collection of values associated with the specified key. If a values collection is provided, those values (for the specified key) will be removed from the values collection associated with that key. |
| Replace() | Replaces all the values associated with the supplied key with a single value. |
| ReplaceMany() | Replaces all the values associated with the supplied collection of values. |
| ToString() | Creates a string that represents all the items in the dictionary. |
| Values | Returns a collection containing all the values in the dictionary. |

## OrderedBag<T>

An OrderedBag<T> class, as its name implies, is simply a sorted version of the Bag<T> class. With the addition of sorting functionality also come a handful of new methods to work with a sorted container. Overall, though, you should find the syntax, mechanics, and general behavior of OrderedBags closely mirrors characteristics of a Bag<T> class.

The following table is an alphabetical listing of all the methods and properties that are associated with the OrderedBag<T> class.

| Method or Property | Description |
|---|---|
| Add() | Adds the supplied item to the Bag and, if the item already exists, increments the instance count for that item. |
| AsList() | Returns a list representation of the items in the Bag. |
| Clear() | Empties the contents of the Bag. |
| Contains() | Determines if the Bag contains the specified item. If a match is found, the method returns true. |
| Count | Property that returns the number of items currently in the Bag. |
| GetEnumerator() | Gets an IEnumerator<T> representation of the items in the Bag. |
| GetFirst() | Gets the first item from the sorted Bag. |
| GetLast() | Gets the last item from the sorted Bag. |
| IndexOf() | Returns the index of the first item in the Bag that is equal to the supplied item. |
| LastIndexOf() | Returns the index of the last item in the Bag that is equal to the supplied item. |
| Remove() | Removes the first item that is found that is equal to the supplied item. |
| Reversed() | Retrieves OrderedBag<T>.View collection that contains all the items in the Bag sorted in reverse order. |

## Accessing and Removing Items

If you look at this class's interface closely, you'll discover that this class adds GetFirst() and GetLast() methods that allow you to easily access the first and last items of the Bag, respectively. The following code provides a brief example of how these methods are applied:

```
[VB code]
Dim strBag As New OrderedBag(Of String)(Comparer(Of String).Default)
strBag.Add("Item7")
strBag.Add("Item2")
strBag.Add("Item9")
strBag.Add("Item4")
strBag.Add("Item5")
DumpItems(Of String)(strBag)

Dim str As String = strBag.GetFirst()
Console.WriteLine("First Item : {0}", Str)

Str = strBag.GetLast()
Console.WriteLine("Last Item : {0}", Str)

strBag.RemoveLast()
strBag.RemoveFirst()
DumpItems(Of String)(strBag)
```

```
[C# code]
OrderedBag<String> strBag = new OrderedBag<String>(Comparer<String>.Default);
strBag.Add("Item7");
strBag.Add("Item2");
strBag.Add("Item9");
strBag.Add("Item4");
strBag.Add("Item5");
DumpItems(strBag);

String str = strBag.GetFirst();
Console.WriteLine("First Item : {0}", str);

str = strBag.GetLast();
Console.WriteLine("Last Item : {0}", str);

strBag.RemoveLast();
strBag.RemoveFirst();
DumpItems(strBag);
```

Now, for this example, you'll notice that the items are intentionally added in an unsorted order. Once the items are placed into the OrderedBag, you dump the contents of the collection and, as you would expect, the list is sorted. The GetFirst(), GetLast(), RemoveFirst() and RemoveLast() methods are also included here to make it clear that these methods will operate on the sorted position of items without regard for the order they were placed into the collection. The output of running this example is as follows:

```
1. Value : Item2
2. Value : Item4
3. Value : Item5
4. Value : Item7
5. Value : Item9

First Item : Item2
Last Item  : Item9

1. Value : Item4
2. Value : Item5
3. Value : Item7
```

## Range Operations

OrderedBag<T> also includes a series of additional methods for accessing ranges of items. Instead of using absolute indices, these range operations use the values of items to express the bounds for the sub-set of data that will be retrieved. The following code provides a few different examples of how these range methods operate:

```
[VB code]
Dim doubleBag As New OrderedBag(Of Double)()
doubleBag.Add(6419.84)
doubleBag.Add(2342.32)
doubleBag.Add(523.32)
doubleBag.Add(3211.08)
doubleBag.Add(43.65)
DumpItems(Of Double)(doubleBag)
```

```
Dim rangeView1 As OrderedBag(Of Double).View
rangeView1 = doubleBag.Range(500.0, true, 3500.0, true)
DumpItems(Of Double)(rangeView1)

Dim rangeView2 As OrderedBag(Of Double).View = doubleBag.RangeFrom(2000.0, True)
DumpItems(Of Double)(rangeView2)

Dim rangeView3 As OrderedBag(Of Double).View = doubleBag.RangeTo(550.0, True)
DumpItems(Of Double)(rangeView3)

Dim orderedBagView As OrderedBag(Of Double).View = doubleBag.Reversed()
DumpItems(Of Double)(orderedBagView)
```

```
[C# code]
OrderedBag<Double> doubleBag = new OrderedBag<Double>();
doubleBag.Add(6419.84);
doubleBag.Add(2342.32);
doubleBag.Add(523.32);
doubleBag.Add(3211.08);
doubleBag.Add(43.65);
DumpItems(doubleBag);

OrderedBag<Double>.View rangeView1;
rangeView1 = doubleBag.Range(500.00, true, 3500.00, true);
DumpItems(rangeView1);

OrderedBag<Double>.View rangeView2 = doubleBag.RangeFrom(2000.00, true);
DumpItems(rangeView2);

OrderedBag<Double>.View rangeView3 = doubleBag.RangeTo(550.00, true);
DumpItems(rangeView3);

OrderedBag<Double>.View orderedBagView = doubleBag.Reversed();
DumpItems(orderedBagView);
```

Each of the three different range methods appears in this example. The Range() method is used to find all items that fall between the values 500.00 and 3500.00. The results that are returned from this range call (and for all the range methods) are always represented as an OrderedBag<T>.View type.

The example also calls RangeFrom() and RangeTo() methods. RangeFrom() finds all items in the Bag that are greater than or equal to the specified value (in this case, 2000.00). And, as its counterpart, the RangeTo() method returns all items that are less than the supplied item (in this case, 550.00).

An example of a call to the Reversed() method is also included here. This method creates and returns a copy of the Bag that contains all of its items sorted in reverse order.

## OrderedBag<T>.View

The OrderedBag<T>.View class exists solely for the purpose of providing a mechanism for representing a synchronized view of a subset of items returned from an OrderedBag<T> collection. The Range(), RangeFrom(), RangeTo(), and Reversed() methods of the OrderedBag() class all return their results in OrderedBag<T>.View collections.

When working with OrderedBag<T>.View objects, you should keep in mind the fact that each view is synchronized with its associated OrderedBag<T> instance. So, if the OrderedBag changes, those changes will be reflected in the view. And, changes to the view will be reflected in the OrderedBag.

Items are typically accessed from an OrderedBag<T>.View using an enumerator interface. However, the class also supports methods for randomly accessing and modifying its contents.

## OrderedDictionary<TKey, TValue>

An OrderedDictionary<TKey, TValue> collection provides developers with the powerful combination of options, supporting both keyed random access along with all the characteristics of an ordered collection. The class is implemented as an extension DictionaryBase<TKey, TValue> abstract class.

The following table is an alphabetical listing of all the methods and properties that are associated with the OrderedDictionaryBase<TKey, TValue> class.

| Method or Property | Description |
|---|---|
| Add() | Adds a new key/value pair to the dictionary. |
| AddMany() | Adds the supplied list of KeyValuePair<TKey, TValue> objects to the dictionary. |
| Clear() | Removes all items from the dictionary. This method must be overridden. |
| Clone() | Creates and returns a shallow copy of all the items in the dictionary. |
| CloneContents() | Creates and returns a deep copy of all the items in the dictionary. |
| Contains() | Returns true if the collection contains an item that matches the key that is supplied as a key/value pair. This method uses Object.Equals to compare the key values. |
| ContainsKey() | Returns true if the collection contains an item that matches the supplied key. This method uses Object.Equals to compare the key values. |
| GetEnumerator() | Gets an IEnumerator<T> representation of the items in the dictionary. |
| GetValueElseAdd() | Retrieves the following key/value pair from the dictionary, inserting the item into the dictionary if it cannot be found. This method returns true if an existing item is found and returned. |
| Item | Indexer that is used to access or update individual items in the dictionary. This member must be overridden. |
| Range() | Accepts lower and upper bound items and retrieves all items that fall within the range specified by those two items. The results are returned in an OrderedDictionary<T>.View collection. |
| RangeFrom() | Finds all items that are greater than or equal to the supplied item. The results are returned in an OrderedDictionary<T>.View collection. |
| RangeTo() | Finds all items less than the supplied item. The results are returned in an OrderedDictionary<T>.View collection. |

| Method or Property | Description |
| --- | --- |
| Remove() | Removes the specified item (key or key/value pair) from the dictionary. This method must be overridden. |
| RemoveMany() | Accepts an IEnumerable<T> collection of items to be removed, searches for matching keys, and removes each item for which a match can be found. I |
| Replace() | Finds the item that matches the supplied key and replaces its value with the supplied value. |
| Reversed() | Retrieves an OrderedDictionary<T>.View collection that contains all the items in the dictionary sorted in reverse order. |
| TryGetValue() | Attempts to get the value associated with the supplied key. This method must be overridden. |

An OrderedDictionary<TKey, TValue> class holds a set of unique keys, each of which has an associated value. As such, all random access methods will use keys to find, update, and remove items from the dictionary. The following example performs some basic operations on this class so you can get a better feeling for what options you can use to maintain the contents of a dictionary:

```vb
[VB code]
Dim strDict As New OrderedDictionary(Of String, String)
strDict.Add("932", "Item7")
strDict.Add("111", "Item2")
strDict.Add("82", "Item9")
strDict.Add("32", "Item4")
strDict.Add("20", "Item5")
DumpItems(Of String, String)(strDict)

Dim aStr As String = strDict("82")
Console.WriteLine("First Item : {0}", aStr)

Dim tmpItem As String = "Item22"
Dim itemFound As Boolean = strDict.GetValueElseAdd("9329", tmpItem)
If (itemFound = False) Then
    Console.WriteLine("Key Not Found--item added")
End If
```

```csharp
[C# code]
OrderedDictionary<String, String> strDict = new OrderedDictionary<String,String>();
strDict.Add("932", "Item7");
strDict.Add("111", "Item2");
strDict.Add("82", "Item9");
strDict.Add("32", "Item4");
strDict.Add("20", "Item5");
DumpItems<String, String>(strDict);

String aStr = strDict["82"];
Console.WriteLine("First Item : {0}", aStr);
```

```
String tmpItem = "Item22";
bool itemFound = strDict.GetValueElseAdd("9329", ref tmpItem);
if (itemFound == false)
    Console.WriteLine("Key Not Found--item added");
```

This example uses the `Add()` method to populate its `OrderedDictionary` object. This method accepts a key as its first parameter and a value as its second parameter. If the key already exists in the dictionary when you call the `Add()` method, the value currently associated with that key will be replaced with the new value that was supplied in the call to the method. Once these values are added, the example writes out the list of values in the dictionary. The output appears as follows:

```
1. Key = 111  Value : Item2
2. Key = 20   Value : Item5
3. Key = 32   Value : Item4
4. Key = 82   Value : Item9
5. Key = 932  Value : Item7
```

The key point to recognize here is that `OrderedDictionary` has sorted all of its entries based on the string value assigned to each of its keys. The order in which items are added to the dictionary has no bearing on the ordering of the collection.

The next block of code makes use of the indexer property to acquire the item with a key of "82." The `OrderedDictionary<TKey, TValue>` class supports key-based access and updating via the indexer property.

The `GetValueElseAdd()` method provides an alternative approach to retrieving items from the dictionary that can be quite useful. It combines both lookup and adding of entries in a single call. Each time the method is called, it first determines if the supplied key already exists in the dictionary and, if the key is not found, the key/value pair is added to the dictionary. If the key is found, the existing value is returned. The `GetValueElseAdd` method also has a boolean return value that will be set to `true` if it finds a matching key in the dictionary.

`OrderedDictionary<TKey, TValue>` also includes a set of methods that allow you to retrieve and operate on subsets of the data. The `AddMany()`, `Range()`, `RangeFrom()`, and `RangeTo()` methods all fall into this category. The `AddMany()` method allows you to add all the items from one dictionary to another, whereas the range methods are used to retrieve a subset of items that fall within specific ranges of key values. The following example illustrates the usage of some of these methods:

```
[VB code]
Dim testDict As New OrderedDictionary(Of Double, Person)()
testDict.Add(9201.3232, New Person("Napolean", 111))
testDict.Add(129.9393, New Person("Kip", 321))
testDict.Add(3517.83, New Person("Jon", 423))
testDict.Add(789.12, New Person("Shondrella", 482))
testDict.Add(63729.0909, New Person("Tina", 131))
DumpItems(Of Double, Person)(testDict)

Dim rangeView As OrderedDictionary(Of Double, Person).View
rangeView = testDict.Range(3000.0, True, 10000.0, True)
DumpItems(Of Double, Person)(rangeView)

Dim mergeDict As New Dictionary(Of Double, Person)()
mergeDict.Add(1239.23, New Person("Effren", 9320))
```

```
    mergeDict.Add(32.32, New Person("Sandy", 1901))

    testDict.AddMany(mergeDict)
    DumpItems(Of Double, Person)(testDict)

    testDict.Replace(129.9393, New Person("Replaced", 555))
    DumpItems(Of Double, Person)(testDict)

    Dim reverseView As OrderedDictionary(Of Double, Person).View
    reverseView = testDict.Reversed()
    DumpItems(Of Double, Person)(reverseView)
```

```
    [C# code]
    OrderedDictionary<Double, Person> testDict;
    testDict = new OrderedDictionary<Double,Person>();
    testDict.Add(9201.3232, new Person("Napolean", 111));
    testDict.Add(129.9393, new Person("Kip", 321));
    testDict.Add(3517.83, new Person("Jon", 423));
    testDict.Add(789.12, new Person("Shondrella", 482));
    testDict.Add(63729.0909, new Person("Tina", 131));
    DumpItems<Double, Person>(testDict);

    OrderedDictionary<Double, Person>.View rangeView;
    rangeView = testDict.Range(3000.00, true, 10000.00, true);
    DumpItems<Double, Person>(rangeView);

    Dictionary<Double, Person> mergeDict = new Dictionary<Double, Person>();
    mergeDict.Add(1239.23, new Person("Effren", 9320));
    mergeDict.Add(32.32, new Person("Sandy", 1901));

    testDict.AddMany(mergeDict);
    DumpItems<Double, Person>(testDict);

    testDict.Replace(129.9393, new Person("Replaced", 555));
    DumpItems<Double, Person>(testDict);

    OrderedDictionary<Double, Person>.View reverseView;
    reverseView = testDict.Reversed();
    DumpItems<Double, Person>(reverseView);
```

Here, you fill the dictionary and invoke the Range() method to pull out a subset of the items that reside in your dictionary. In your call to Range(), you specify that you want to acquire just those items that had keys that fell within the range of 3000.00–10000.00. The found items are then placed in an instance of OrderedDictionary<TKey, TValue>.View object, leaving the source dictionary unchanged. When you dump out the contents of this view, you get the following output:

```
    1. Key = 3517.83    Value : Jon (423)
    2. Key = 9201.3232  Value : Napolean (111)
```

An example of the AddMany() method is also included here. For this example, you load up a new dictionary with values and call AddMany() in an attempt to add these new values into your existing dictionary. The merge succeeds. However, because one of items being merged in had the same key value as an existing item in the dictionary, the existing value associated with this key gets replaced with the new value that was passed into the AddMany() method. This may be the desired effect. Still, it's something you'll want to keep in mind each time you decide to use this method.

Finally, to mix things up, calls to the `Replace()` and `Reversed()` methods were added. `Replace()` is an alternate, more readable method that is used to update the value for an existing item. `Reversed()` creates a new `OrderedDictionary<TKey, TValue>.View` collection that contains the items from the dictionary in reversed order.

## OrderedDictionary<TKey, TValue>.View

The `OrderedDictionary<TKey, TValue>.View` class exists solely for the purpose of providing a mechanism for representing a synchronized view of a subset of items returned from an `OrderedDictionary<T>` collection. The `Range()`, `RangeFrom()`, `RangeTo()`, and `Reversed()` methods of `OrderedDictionary` all return `OrderedDictionary<TKey, TValue>.View` collections.

When working with `OrderedDictionary<TKey, TValue>.View` objects, you should keep in mind the fact that this view is synchronized with their associated `OrderedDictionary` instance. So, if the `OrderedDictionary` changes, those changes will be reflected in the view. And, changes to the view will be reflected in the `OrderedDictionary`.

Items are typically accessed from an `OrderedDictionary<TKey, TValue>.View` using an enumerator interface. However, the class also supports methods for randomly accessing and modifying its contents.

## OrderedMultiDictionary<TKey, TValue>

If you can have an ordered dictionary, it also makes sense to have an `OrderedMultiDictionary<TKey, TValue>` class. In reality, this class is very much the twin of the `OrderedDictionary<TKey, TValue>` class. Like its parent, this dictionary class allows you to associate multiple values with a given key. It's extra bonus is that it also retains the keys in a sorted order.

The following table is an alphabetical listing of all the methods and properties that are included in the `OrderedMultiDictionary<TKey, TValue>` class:

| Method or Property | Description |
|---|---|
| `Add()` | Adds a new item to the dictionary. |
| `Clear()` | Removes all entries from the dictionary. |
| `Clone()` | Returns a shallow copy of all the items in the dictionary. |
| `CloneContents()` | Returns a deep copy of all the items in the dictionary. |
| `Contains()` | Returns `true` if the dictionary contains an item that matches the supplied item. |
| `ContainsKey()` | Returns `true` if the dictionary contains an item that matches the supplied key. |
| `Count` | Gets the number of items in the dictionary. Each key/value combination (for a single key) is counted as a separate item. |
| `KeyComparer` | Returns the `IEqualityComparer<T>` that is used when comparing keys in this dictionary. |

| Method or Property | Description |
|---|---|
| KeyValuePairs | Returns a collection of `KeyValuePairs`, where each value for a key is returned as a separate item. |
| Range() | Returns an `OrderedMultiDictionary.View` that contains all the items that fall within the specified range of values. |
| RangeFrom() | Returns an `OrderedMultiDictionary.View` that contains all the items that are greater than or equal to the specified value. |
| RangeTo() | Returns an `OrderedMultiDictionary.View` that contains all the items that are less than or equal to the specified value. |
| Remove() | Removes the entry associated with the specified key. If a value is supplied with that key, the value associated with that key is removed from the values collection that corresponds to that key. |
| Reversed() | Returns an `OrderedMultiDictionary.View` that contains a copy of the dictionary's keys in reverse order. |
| ValueComparer | Returns the `IEqualityComparer<T>` that is used when comparing values in this dictionary. |

## OrderedMultiDictionary<TKey, TValue>.View

The `OrderedMultiDictionary<TKey, TValue>.View` class exists solely for the purpose of providing a mechanism for representing a synchronized view of a subset of items returned from an `OrderedMultiDictionary<TKey, TValue>` dictionary. The `Range()`, `RangeFrom()`, `RangeTo()`, and `Reversed()` methods of `OrderedMultiDictionary<TKey, TValue>` all return `OrderedMultiDictionary<TKey, TValue>.View` collections.

## OrderedSet<T>

An `OrderedSet<T>` class is simply a sorted version of the `Set<T>` class. With the introduction of sorting also comes a handful of additional methods. Overall, though, you should find the syntax, mechanics, and general behavior of `OrderedSets` closely mirrors the characteristics of a `Set<T>` class.

The following table is an alphabetical listing of all the methods and properties that are associated with the `OrderedSet<T>` class.

| Method or Property | Description |
|---|---|
| Add() | Adds the supplied item to the Set. |
| AddMany() | Adds all the items from the supplied `IEnumerable<T>` collection to the Set. If one of the items being added is equal to an item already in the Set, the current item is replaced with the new item. |
| AsList() | Returns a list representation of the items in the Set. |

*Table continued on following page*

| Method or Property | Description |
|---|---|
| Clear() | Empties the contents of the Set. |
| Clone() | Creates and returns a shallow copy of all the items in the Set. |
| CloneContents() | Creates and returns a deep copy of all the items in the Set. |
| Contains() | Determines if the Set contains the specified item. If a match is found, the method returns true. |
| Count | Property that returns the number of items currently in the Set. |
| Difference() | Computes the difference between the contents of this Set and the Set that is supplied. This difference is determined based on the difference in the number of instances of each item in this Set and the passed-in Set. A Set containing the computed difference is returned. |
| DifferenceWith() | Computes the difference between the contents of this Set and the Set that is supplied. The current Set is modified in place to represent the difference between the current Set and the supplied Set. |
| Exists() | Returns true if at least one item in the Set matches the criteria of the supplied predicate. |
| FindALL() | Finds and returns all the items in the Set that match the criteria of the specified predicate. |
| GetEnumerator() | Gets an IEnumerator<T> representation of the items in the Set. |
| GetFirst() | Gets the first item from the sorted Set. |
| GetLast() | Gets the last item from the sorted Set. |
| IndexOf() | Returns the index of first item in the list (in sorted order) that matches the supplied item. |
| Intersection() | Computes the intersection between this Set and another Set and returns a new Set that contains the items in this intersection. |
| IntersectionWith() | Computes the intersection between this Set and another Set and modifies this Set to contain the items that are in this intersection. |
| IsDisjointFrom() | Compares two Sets and returns true if no item from one Set is equal to any item from another Set. |
| IsEqualTo() | Returns true if this Set is equal to the supplied Set. |
| IsProperSubsetOf() | Returns true if this Set is a proper subset to the supplied Set. |
| IsProperSupersetOf() | Returns true if this Set is a proper superset of the supplied Set. |

| Method or Property | Description |
| --- | --- |
| IsSubsetOf() | Determines if all the items in this Set are valid members of the supplied Set. If every member in the current Set exists in the supplied Set, this method returns true. |
| IsSupersetOf() | Determines if this Set is the superset of the supplied Set. If all the items in the supplied Set are also in this Set, this method returns true. |
| Range() | Accepts lower and upper bound items and retrieves all items that fall within the range specified by those two items. The results are returned in an OrderedSet<T>.View collection. |
| RangeFrom() | Finds all items that are greater than or equal to the supplied item. The results are returned in an OrderedSet<T>.View collection. |
| RangeTo() | Finds all items less than the supplied item. The results are returned in an OrderedSet<T>.View collection. |
| Remove() | Removes the item that is equal to the supplied item. |
| RemoveFirst() | Removes the first item from the Set. |
| RemoveLast() | Removes the last item from the Set. |
| RemoveMany() | Removes any item from the Set that is equal to an item in the supplied collection. |
| Reversed() | Retrieves an OrderedSet<T>.View collection that contains all the items in the Set sorted in reverse order. |
| SymmetricDifference() | Compares the supplied Set and this Set, identifying those items that are unique to each Set. To qualify, an item must exist in one of these two Sets, but may not appear in both. The resulting difference will be placed in a new Set and returned from this method. The supplied Set and this Set remain unchanged. |
| SymmetricDifferenceWith() | Compares the supplied Set and this Set, identifying those items that are unique to each Set. To qualify, an item must exist in one of these two Sets, but may not appear in both. The resulting difference will be placed in this Set. |
| TryGetItem() | Attempts to find and return the item that is equal to the supplied item, returning true if the item is found. |
| Union() | Creates a new Set that represents the union of this Set and the supplied Set. Items that are duplicated in each of the two Sets are also duplicated the same number of times in the returned Set. This Set and the supplied Set remain unchanged. |
| UnionWith() | Modifies this Set replacing its contents with the union of this Set and the supplied Set. Items that are duplicated in each of the two Sets are also duplicated the same number of times in the returned Set. |

## OrderedSet<T>.View

The `OrderedSet<T>.View` class exists solely for the purpose of providing a mechanism for representing a synchronized view of a subset of items returned from an `OrderedSet<T>` collection. The `Range()`, `RangeFrom()`, `RangeTo()`, and `Reversed()` methods of `OrderedSet` all return `OrderedSet<T>.View` collections.

When working with `OrderedSet<T>.View` objects, you should keep in mind the fact that this view is synchronized with their associated `OrderedSet<T>` instance. So, if the `OrderedSet` changes, those changes will be reflected in the view. And, changes to the view will be reflected in the `OrderedSet`.

Items are typically accessed from an `OrderedSet<T>.View` using an enumerator interface. However, the class also supports methods for randomly accessing and modifying its contents.

## Pair<TFirst, TSecond >

The `Pair` class represents a very simple mechanism for packaging two data types into a single structure. This class is nothing more than a versatile data container that allows you to have a single, type-safe class that can be used to hold any number of permutations of paired data types. Without this class, you would be forced to create separate structures to represent each unique combination of types you want to hold in a common structure. The Power Collections library also includes a `Triple` class (described later in this chapter) that is used in situations where you want to use three type arguments.

The following table is an alphabetical listing of all the methods and properties that are associated with the `Pair` class.

| Method or Property | Description |
|---|---|
| CompareTo() | Compares the first and second values with the corresponding values from the supplied Pair object, returning `true` if all three values are considered equal. |
| Equals() | Compares two Pair objects and returns `true` if they share the same types and values for those types. |
| First | Gets the first item from the Pair. |
| GetHashCode() | Gets a hash code that represents the combined hash code for each of its values. |
| Second | Gets the second item from the Pair. |
| ToKeyValuePair() | Gets a `KeyValuePair` representation of this Pair. |
| ToString() | Creates and returns a string representation of the two items held by the Pair. |

## ReadOnlyCollectionBase<T>

`ReadOnlyCollectionBase<T>` is an abstract base class implementation of the `ICollection<T>` interface that provides you with a good basis for implementing your own read-only collections. At a minimum, all classes that extend this base class must implement the `GetEnumerator()` and `Count` members.

The following table is an alphabetical listing of all the members that are associated with the ReadOnlyCollectionBase <T> class.

| Method or Property | Description |
|---|---|
| Count | Returns the number of items in the collection. This member must be overridden. |
| Contains() | Returns true if the collection contains the specified item, using IComparable<T>.Equals or Object.Equals to identify matching items. |
| ConvertAll<TOutput>() | Converts all the items in the collection to TOouptut type, using the supplied Converter. |
| CopyTo() | Copies all the items in the collection into the provided array. |
| CountWhere() | Returns a count of the number of items that meet the criteria defined by the supplied predicate. |
| Exists() | Returns true if at least one item in the collection meets the criteria defined by the supplied predicate. |
| FindAll() | Returns a collection of all the items that meet the criteria defined by the supplied predicate. |
| ForEach() | Applies the supplied action to each item in the collection. |
| GetEnumerator() | Gets an IEnumerator<T> iterator that can be used to iterate over all the values from the collection. This member must be overridden. |
| ToArray() | Uses CopyTo() to create an array of all the items in the collection. |
| ToString() | Creates a string that represents all the items in the collection. |
| TrueForAll() | Returns true if all the items in the collection meet the criteria defined by the supplied predicate. |

## ReadOnlyDictionaryBase<TKey, TValue>

ReadOnlyDictionaryBase<TKey, TValues> is an abstract base class that extends the ReadOnlyCollectionBase class and implements the IDictionary<TKey, TValue> interface. It provides you with a good basis for implementing your own read-only dictionaries. At a minimum, all classes that extend this base class must implement the GetEnumerator(), TryGetValue(), Count, and Item members.

The following table is an alphabetical listing of all the members that are associated with the ReadOnlyDictionaryBase<TKey, TValues> class.

| Method or Property | Description |
|---|---|
| Count | Returns the number of items in the dictionary. This member must be overridden. |
| Contains() | Returns `true` if the dictionary contains an item that matches the key that is supplied as a key/value pair. This method uses `Object.Equals` to compare the key values. |
| ContainsKey() | Returns `true` if the dictionary contains an item that matches the supplied key. This method uses `Object.Equals` to compare the key values. |
| Item | Indexer that is used to access or update individual items in the dictionary. This member must be overridden. |
| Keys | Returns an `ICollection<T>` collection containing all the keys in the dictionary. |
| Remove() | Throws an unsupported exception if this method is called. |
| ToString() | Creates a string that represents all the items in the dictionary. |
| TryGetValue() | Attempts to get the value associated with the supplied key. This method must be overridden. |
| Values | Returns an `ICollection<T>` collection containing all the values in the dictionary. |

# ReadOnlyListBase<T>

`ReadOnlyListBase<T>` is an abstract base class that extends the `ReadOnlyCollectionBase<T>` class that is an implementation of the `IList<T>` interface. It provides you with a good basis for implementing your own read-only lists. At a minimum, all classes that extend this base class must implement the `Item` indexer and `Count` members.

The following table is an alphabetical listing of all the members that are associated with the `ReadOnlyListBase <T>` class.

| Method or Property | Description |
|---|---|
| Contains() | Returns `true` if the list contains an item that matches the supplied item. |
| Count | Gets the number of items in the list. This method must be overridden. |
| CopyTo() | Copies all the items in the list to an array, retaining the current order of the items. |
| Find() | Finds the first item in the list that meets the criteria defined by the supplied predicate. |
| FindIndex() | Finds the index of the first item in the list that meets the criteria defined by the supplied predicate. |
| FindLast() | Finds the last item in the list that meets the criteria defined by the supplied predicate. |

| Method or Property | Description |
|---|---|
| FindLastIndex() | Finds the index of the last item in the list that meets the criteria defined by the supplied predicate. |
| GetEnumerator() | Gets an IEnumerator<T> iterator that can be used to iterate over all the values from the list. |
| IndexOf() | Gets the index of the first item in the list that is equal to the specified item. |
| Item | Indexer that is used to access or update individual items in the list. This member must be overridden. |
| LastIndexOf() | Gets the index of the last item in the list that meets the criteria defined by the supplied predicate. |
| Range() | Gets a subset of items from the collection that fall within the specified range. |
| TryFind() | Attempts to find the first item that meets the criteria defined by the supplied predicate. |
| TryFindLast() | Attempts to find the last item that meets the criteria defined by the supplied predicate. |

## ReadOnlyMultiDictionary<TKey, TValue>

ReadOnlyMultiDictionary<TKey, TValues> provides a read-only version of the MultiDictionary<TKey, TValue>. The main goal with this class is to prevent users from modifying the state of the dictionary. The following table is an alphabetical listing of all the members that are associated with the ReadOnlyMultiDictionaryBase<TKey, TValues> class.

| Method or Property | Description |
|---|---|
| Count | Returns the number of items in the dictionary. |
| Contains() | Returns true if the dictionary contains an item that matches the key that is supplied as a key/value pair. |
| ContainsKey() | Returns true if the dictionary contains an item that matches the supplied key. |
| GetEnumerator() | Returns an enumerator that can be used to iterate over all the keys in the dictionary. |
| Item | Indexer that is used to access or update individual items in the dictionary. This member must be overridden. |
| Keys | Returns an ICollection<T> collection containing all the keys in the dictionary. |
| KeyValuePairs | Returns a collection of all the key/value pairs in the dictionary. |

*Table continued on following page*

| Method or Property | Description |
| --- | --- |
| ToString() | Creates a string that represents all the items in the dictionary. |
| TryGetValue() | Attempts to get the value associated with the supplied key. This method must be overridden. |
| Values | Returns an ICollection<T> collection containing all the values in the dictionary. |

# Set<T>

An earlier section looked at the Bag<T> class in great detail. The Set<T> class is actually very similar to this class. As you examine its signature, you'll discover that its interface is nearly identical to that of the Bag<T> class. The primary difference between the two is that the Set<T> class cannot contain duplicate items. Each item in a set is always guaranteed to be unique.

The following table is an alphabetical listing of all the methods and properties that are associated with the Set<T> class.

| Method or Property | Description |
| --- | --- |
| Add() | Adds the supplied item to the Set. |
| AddMany() | Adds all the items from the supplied IEnumerable<T> collection to the Set. If one of the items being added is equal to an item already in the set, the current item is replaced with the new item. |
| Clear() | Empties the contents of the Set. |
| Clone() | Creates and returns a shallow copy of all the items in the Set. |
| CloneContents() | Creates and returns a deep copy of all the items in the Set. |
| Comparer | Returns the IEqualityComparer<T> that is associated with this Set. |
| Contains() | Determines if the Set contains the specified item. If a match is found, the method returns true. |
| Count | Property that returns the number of items currently in the Set. |
| Difference() | Computes the difference between the contents of this Set and the Set that is supplied. This difference is determined based on the difference in the number of instances of each item in this Set and the passed-in Set. A Set containing the computed difference is returned. |
| DifferenceWith() | Computes the difference between the contents of this Set and the Set that is supplied. The current Set is modified in place to represent the difference between the current Set and the supplied Set. |
| GetEnumerator() | Gets an IEnumerator<T> representation of the items in the Set. |

| Method or Property | Description |
| --- | --- |
| Intersection() | Computes the intersection between this Set and another Set and returns a new Set that contains the items in this intersection. |
| IntersectionWith() | Computes the intersection between this Set and another Set and modifies this Set to contain the items that are in this intersection. |
| IsDisjointFrom() | Returns true if this Set does not contain a single item that is in another Set. |
| IsEqualTo() | Returns true if the contents of this set are equal to the supplied set. |
| IsProperSubsetOf() | Returns true if this Set is a proper subset of another Set. |
| IsProperSupersetOf() | Returns true if this Set is a proper superset of another Set. |
| IsSubsetOf() | Determines if all the items in this Set are valid members of the supplied Set. If every member in the current Set exists in the supplied Set, this method returns true. |
| IsSupersetOf() | Determines if this Set is the superset of the supplied Set. If all the items in the supplied Set are also in this Set, this method returns true. |
| Remove() | Removes the item that is equal to the supplied item. |
| RemoveMany() | Removes any item from the Set that is equal to an item in the supplied collection. |
| SymmetricDifference() | Compares the supplied Set and this Set, identifying those items that are unique to each Set. To qualify, an item must exist in one of these two Sets, but may not appear in both. The resulting difference will be placed in a new Set and returned from this method. The supplied Set and this Set remain unchanged. |
| SymmetricDifferenceWith() | Compares the supplied Set and this Set, identifying those items that are unique to each Set. To qualify, an item must exist in one of these two Sets, but may not appear in both. The resulting difference will be placed in this Set. |
| TryGetItem() | Attempts to find and return the item that is equal to the supplied item, returning true if the item is found. |
| Union() | reates a new Set that represents the union of this Set and the supplied Set. Items that are duplicated in each of the two Sets are also duplicated the same number of times in the returned Set. This Set and the supplied Set remain unchanged. |
| UnionWith() | Modifies this Set replacing its contents with the union of this Set and the supplied Set. Items that are duplicated in each of the two Sets are also duplicated the same number of times in the returned Set. |

Although this interface nearly mirrors that of the Bag<T> class, its set-based operations are much more straightforward with the elimination of support for duplicate items.

The creation, population, and updating of Sets match the patterns and behaviors that were illustrated as part of the Bag<T> discussion earlier. That said, the set-centric members of this class do produce some slightly different results. Here's an example that illustrates some of these differences:

```vb
[VB code]
Dim strSet1 As [Set](Of String)
Dim strVals As New List(Of String)(New String() {"Item2", "Item5", "Item6"})
strSet1 = New [Set](Of String)(strVals)
DumpItems(Of String)(strSet1)

Dim strSet2 As [Set](Of String)
strVals = New List(Of String)(New String() {"Item1", "Item2", "Item3", "Item4", _
                                            "Item5", "Item6"})

strSet2 = New [Set](Of String)(strVals)
DumpItems(Of String)(strSet2)

Dim isSubset As Boolean = strSet1.IsSubsetOf(strSet2)
Dim isSuperset As Boolean = strSet2.IsSupersetOf(strSet1)

Dim unionSet As [Set](Of String) = strSet1.Union(strSet2)
DumpItems(Of String)(unionSet)

strSet1.UnionWith(strSet2)
DumpItems(Of String)(strSet1)

Dim doubleSet1 As [Set](Of Double)
Dim doubleVals As New List(Of Double)(New Double() {232.23, 1.12, 99.21, 14.42})
doubleSet1 = New [Set](Of Double)(doubleVals)

Dim doubleSet2 As [Set](Of Double)
doubleVals = New List(Of Double)(New Double() {321.42, 14.42, 1.12, _
                                               74.32, 232.23, 9010.41})

doubleSet2 = New [Set](Of Double)(doubleVals)

Dim intersectionSet As [Set](Of Double) = doubleSet1.Intersection(doubleSet2)
DumpItems(Of Double)(intersectionSet)

Dim symmetricDiffSet As [Set](Of Double) =
doubleSet1.SymmetricDifference(doubleSet2)
DumpItems(Of Double)(symmetricDiffSet)
```

```csharp
[C# code]
Set<String> strSet1;
strSet1 = new Set<String>(new String[] { "Item2", "Item5", "Item6" });
DumpItems(strSet1);

Set<String> strSet2;
strSet2 = new Set<String>(new String[] { "Item1", "Item2", "Item3",
                                         "Item4", "Item5", "Item6" });
```

```
DumpItems(strSet2);

bool isSubset = strSet1.IsSubsetOf(strSet2);
bool isSuperset = strSet2.IsSupersetOf(strSet1);

Set<String> unionSet = strSet1.Union(strSet2);
DumpItems(unionSet);

strSet1.UnionWith(strSet2);
DumpItems(strSet1);

Set<Double> doubleSet1;
doubleSet1 = new Set<Double>(new Double[] { 232.23, 1.12, 99.21, 14.42 });

Set<Double> doubleSet2;
doubleSet2 = new Set<Double>(new Double[] { 321.42, 14.42, 1.12,
                                            74.32, 232.23, 9010.41 });

Set<Double> intersectionSet = doubleSet1.Intersection(doubleSet2);
DumpItems(intersectionSet);

Set<Double> symmetricDiffSet = doubleSet1.SymmetricDifference(doubleSet2);
DumpItems(symmetricDiffSet);
```

This example starts off by creating and populating two separate Sets. These Sets are then used as part of calls to the IsSubsetOf() and IsSupersetOf() methods. In this case, both of these methods will return true, because strSet1 is a valid subset of sterSet2 and strSet2 also represents a valid superset of strSet1.

Next, you invoke the Union() method, which merges the contents of both of your Sets. After calling this method, you get the following results:

```
1. Value : Item5
2. Value : Item1
3. Value : Item6
4. Value : Item2
5. Value : Item3
6. Value : Item4
```

With Sets, where duplicates are not supported, the Union() method yields a Set that contains one unique entry for each value that appears in either of the two Sets being merged.

> The Set(Of T) class creates a bit of a problem for Visual Basic developers. Because "Set" is already a VB keyword, all references to the Set(Of T) type need to be enclosed within square brackets to be successfully resolved by the compiler.

The last block of code in this example exercises the Intersection() and SymmetricDifference() methods. These two methods are exact opposites. Intersection() identifies only those items that are common to both Sets, whereas SymmetricDifference() identifies those items *not* common to the two Sets.

So, when you call `Intersection()` for the two `Set`s in this example, you get the following output:

```
1. Value : 232.32
2. Value : 14.42
3. Value : 1.12
```

And, to round this out, now look at what you'll get when you call `SymmetricDifferenc()` in the example:

```
1. Value : 321.42
2. Value : 74.32
3. Value : 9010.41
4. Value : 99.21
```

## Triple<TFirst, TSecond, TThird>

The `Triple` class represents a very simple mechanism for packaging three data types into a single structure. This class is nothing more than a versatile data container that allows you to have a single, type-safe class that can be used to hold any number of permutations of data types. Without this class, you would be forced to create separate structures to represent each unique combination of types you want to hold in your structure. The Power Collections library also includes a `Pair` class (described earlier) that is used in situations where you only have two data types to represent.

The following table is an alphabetical listing of all the methods and properties that are associated with the `Triple` class.

| Method or Property | Description |
| --- | --- |
| CompareTo() | Compares the first, second, and third values with the corresponding values from the supplied Triple object, returning true if all three values are considered equal. |
| Equals() | Compares two Triple objects and returns true if they share the same types and values for those types. |
| First | Gets the first item from the Triple. |
| GetHashCode() | Gets a hash code that represents the combined hash code for each of its three values. |
| Second | Gets the second item from the Triple. |
| Third | Gets the third item from the Triple. |
| ToString() | Creates and returns a string representation of all three items held by the Triple. |

# Additional Libraries

Although the Power Collections library has all the momentum and apparent backing of Microsoft, other grass roots teams are working on their own generic libraries. The C5, NCollection, and NGenLib libraries, for example, are all taking stabs at introducing generic libraries. Although these collections may not have the maturity or backing of Power Collections, they may include classes or concepts you may want to consider using.

# Summary

The goal of this chapter was to provide comprehensive coverage of all the elements of the Power Collections library. The chapter started out with a high-level, conceptual view of the framework's contents before digging into the specifics of each of the library's generic types. Along the way, the chapter supplied a number of examples to better illustrate the nuances of working with the library's algorithms class and containers. The generic types that are introduced as part of this library represent a valuable extension of those types that are part of the BCL.

# Index

# generic classes (continued)